Southeastern Whitewater

Southeastern Whitewater

Fifty of the Best River Trips
from Alabama to West Virginia

Monte Smith

Pahsimeroi Press
PO Box 190442
Boise, ID 83709

Cover photograph by Don Ellis. The paddler is Tim Ed Spangler, at Wonder Falls, on West Virginia's Big Sandy Creek.

Cover design by Melissa J. Osgood of Oliver, Russell & Associates, Inc., Boise, Idaho.

Interior design by Richard Norman of Pahsimeroi Press, Boise, Idaho.

ISBN 1-886694-00-1

Dedication

This book is dedicated to Don Ellis.

Without Don's steadfast support and encouragement -- manifest in at least a thousand different ways -- this work would have withered and died long ago.

Acknowledgements

It is not possible to recognize everybody who contributed to this book. But it is mandatory to express gratitude to the paddlers listed below, who graciously participated in the project that played a big part in making the book a reality. The ratings contributed by these people served as the cornerstone for development of the TRIP Rating Scale, the new river evaluation tool that is used throughout the text. Indeed, the importance of their contribution extends beyond the present work, and is especially relevant to river safety. The data they contributed provides the best insight to date of how experienced paddlers evaluate different classes of rapids. These paddlers have made a substantial contribution to river knowledge and safety by providing the first solid evidence of how rapids of different classifications are ordered along an underlying dimension of paddling difficulty.

Ben Becker
Don Bowman
Kathy Bragg
Mike Bragg
David Broemel
John Butcher
Bob Card
Dick Conner
Dick Creswell
Elise Creswell
Alan Davis
Don Ellis
Les Fry
M. Goddard
Bill Gordon
Maurice Greaver
Bill Griswold
Larry Gross
Lou Hannen
Bill Hay
Pat Hill

Doug and Sarah Howell
Stephen Hurst
Nat Johnson
Lance Krafft
Bert Lustig
Ed McAlister
Bill Marshall
Bill Micks
Bill Mitchum
Ronnie and Sandra Nichols
Richard Norman
John Pickett
Marc Raskin
Robert Reeder
Mike Sawyers
Dave Stout
Al Thompson
Mack Whitaker
Johnny Wingfield
Dick Wooten
Clay Wright

The Messenger

I lived in television land.

And from out of the wilderness
he came.
And said to me:
"Rise up.
Rise up from your tube.
For else you will rot . . .
In mind, spirit, and body . . .
You surely will rot."

And through the cloud
of my swirling ignorance
that I mistook for omniscience,
I sensed . . . ?
Something.
So I rose and followed,
And on faith did as bade.
And thenceforth all was different
in my life.
Different, but good.
Different, but right.

And after I knew this, I asked:
Who are you?
And he said:
"I am from the world within.
I am you."
And I said,
But I am a fool.
And he said:

"Now you are not alone."

About the Author

Monte Smith is a native of South Carolina. Educated at Berea College, Vanderbilt University, and the University of Georgia, he holds four college degrees, including a PhD and MBA.

He has worked in capacities as varied as research scientist, university professor, marketing executive, editor, fire fighter, bartender, truck driver, and heavy equipment operator. In addition to four books on whitewater sports, he is also author of one novel and over a score of articles in professional journals.

His first river trip was on the Chauga, in South Carolina, at age eleven, using a drift log as a makeshift conveyance. From drift logs and the Chauga he graduated to whitewater boats, the Chattooga, and myriad other streams up and down the eastern seaboard. He has been active in several paddling clubs, and is a past president of the Tennessee Scenic Rivers Association.

Within weeks of completing work on **Southeastern Whitewater,** he moved to Idaho with his wife (Bobbi) and daughter (Andrea), where he is active in whitewater paddling, backpacking, and both nordic and alpine skiing.

Other Books by Monte Smith

River Stories: Tales from Bo Rockerville

Smokescreen (a novel)

Rating Rapids and Rivers:
Development of the TRIP Scale

A Paddler's Guide
to the Obed/Emory Watershed

Table of Contents

Contents (Cont.)

Mike Hall on Big Splat. Big Sandy Creek. Mayo Gravatt photo.

Chapter One

Introduction

This book contains features that you won't find in any other whitewater guidebook. Of all the book's features, none is more important -- and certainly none is more innovative -- than the new river rating scale.

A New River Rating Scale

It's called the TRIP scale, which means:

> T : Trip
> R : Relational
> I : Information
> P : Profile

It's a Trip scale because it's used to evaluate entire river segments, not just individual rapids. It's a Relational scale because it compares and contrasts each river trip with all the others in the book. And it's an Information Profile because it yields a unique profile of each stream, a profile that provides a wealth of comparative information.

Because the name Trip Relational Information Profile is such a mouthful, it's referred to throughout the remainder of the book as simply the TRIP scale. And the information it yields is called the TRIP Profile.

What's a TRIP Profile?

A TRIP Profile consists of ten numbers. Nine of the numbers measure a stream on individual dimensions of difficulty (things like gradient, technicality, volume, and difficulty of rapids). The tenth number, a weighted composite of the other nine, represents overall difficulty.

The beauty of the scale is that each number measures a stream relative to all the other streams described in the book. By looking at one stream's TRIP scores, a reader can tell immediately how it compares with all the other trips. When all ten TRIP scores are examined together, they form a unique profile that shows each river's relative high and low points.

And the scale accomplishes even more. All ten TRIP scores are on the same metric, so that the average score on each dimension is 100. Scores above 100 indicate that a stream is more difficult than average on that dimension. Scores below 100 indicate that a stream is less difficult than average. Moreover, by examining score differences, readers can quickly gain an idea of how much more (or less) difficult one stream is than another.

At first, the TRIP scale sounds a little complicated, but the final result is simplicity itself: a set of tables that rates fifty streams on ten important dimensions of whitewater difficulty. Locate any stream that you're familiar with on one of these tables and you can quickly see how it compares with all the other trips in the book. (TRIP tables appear at the end of Chapter Two.)

**The TRIP Scale Lets Me Compare A
River I Know with Other Rivers
I've Never Been On?**

One of the best things about the TRIP rating system is that it encourages comparisons among different streams. Even if you've paddled only one or two of the fifty streams described in this volume, inspection of the TRIP rating tables at the end of Chapter Two will yield a good idea of how the trips you're familiar with stack up against all the other trips you've never run. By using the tables, you'll know not only how your favorite streams compare in overall difficulty with all the streams you've never run, but also how they compare on more specific dimensions such as average gradient, inaccessibility, difficulty of rapids, technicality, and potential entrapment hazards. By comparing streams that you've already run with those that you plan to run in the future, you'll have a much better idea of the magnitude of the challenge you're facing.

And when you get to the individual trip descriptions that appear later in the book, you'll discover that each one begins with a TRIP

Profile, ten scores that convey an immense amount of comparative information. These ten scores compare and contrast each selected stream with all forty-nine others described in the volume, on ten important dimensions.

What Happened to the Old Class I to Class VI Rating System?

Happily, the baby wasn't thrown out with the bath water. Although the new TRIP rating system is far more informative than traditional Class I to Class VI ratings, the old classification system is retained also. As you'll discover, the two systems are complementary. The TRIP scale excels in comparatively describing and rating river difficulty. That is, entire stretches of river can be rated with the TRIP scale. On the other hand, the traditional classification system is used to evaluate individual rapids. Together, the two rating systems provide the information that paddlers need in order to make more informed (and safer) decisions about paddling alternativoo.

How do I Learn More About the New TRIP Scale?

Start with Chapter Two, which is a non-technical explanation of the TRIP scale and how paddlers can benefit from using it. Although Chapter Two may seem somewhat forbidding at first (because of all the tables and strange new terms), you'll quiokly diocovcr that there's absolutely no need for a mathematical or scientific background In order to understand everything in it. There are no mathematical formulae waiting to ambush you. No convoluted statistical compilations that you have to memorize. No mind-bending leaps of faith that you have to endorse. Instead, you'll find a concise story of the underpinnings of the TRIP river rating system and a no-nonsense discussion of what it can mean to you as a whitewater paddler.

After reading Chapter Two, we think you'll agree that the TRIP scale is one of the most exciting developments in paddle sports in quite some time. You'll be pleased to discover, for example, that it's not just some ivory tower construction project. The TRIP scale is based on a research study that involved forty-two whitewater paddlers, with diverse but uniformly extensive paddling backgrounds.

(A list of participants can be found in the acknowledgements.)   As a group, these paddlers have logged about a bizillion river trips, on all kinds of water. With all this experience undergirding its development, the TRIP scale is anything but an idle academic exercise. The scale is solidly based on first-hand river experience.

If, after reading Chapter Two, you're still thirsting for details about how the TRIP scale was developed and how the group of paddlers above was involved in the project, then lay your hands on a companion volume available from Pahsimeroi Press: *Rating Rapids and Rivers: Development of the TRIP Scale,* by Monte Smith. This companion volume, in addition to providing insight into how experienced paddlers evaluate rapids, also lets you respond to some of the same questions that were used originally to construct the TRIP scale. That way, you can give the TRIP scale its ultimate test by deciding whether it reflects your personal whitewater viewpoint!

Okay, the TRIP Scale Seems Interesting, but is the Whole Book Just a Bunch of Technical Ratings?

Hardly. Trip descriptions, all written from the perspective of one paddler, are the heart and soul of the book.   And this volume contains a dandy collection of river trips. Every one -- and there're 50 of them -- is a premier whitewater run, one of the best in the Southeast, or it wouldn't be included. The collection of trips in this book is not exhaustive, but it nevertheless constitutes a broad cross-section of whitewater rivers, at all difficulty levels, within the seven-state region from Alabama to West Virginia.

Sounds Good So Far. But What About the Book's Other Innovative Features?

Here's a partial listing:

State maps that show each river's general location.

Computer-enhanced local maps that precisely locate every trip -- plus access points and shuttle routes -- without including a ton of useless clutter.

A "Top-to-Bottom Itinerary" for every trip that organizes and locates its key features (major rapids, landmarks, hazards, etc.).

For each described trip, a list of "Nearby Alternate Trips," an especially useful feature when exploring new territory and trying to optimally use limited time.

A list of "Other Information" at the end of each trip description, with details on campgrounds, hiking trails, points of interest, helpful maps, etc.

A separate "Water Levels" section for each trip, with gauge locations, phone numbers, suggested levels, and (when available) cfs conversion charts.

A concise "Miles From" table that locates each trip relative to major Southeastern cities. This feature helps in getting an overall geographic fix on a stream's location and in making decisions on realistic driving distances.

A "Similar To" feature, which identifies pairs of streams with common characteristics.

Plus fifty exciting new trip descriptions, each headed by a TRIP Profile that succinctly compares and contrasts each stream, relative to all others described in the book, on ten important dimensions of stream difficulty. And all of this is accomplished on a regional scale, covering the southern Appalachians from Alabama to West Virginia.

That's a Lot of New Stuff!

You bet it is. And admittedly, there's some danger of overload, especially at first. Because the book contains so many innovative features, the best approach is to proceed slowly. It's not the kind of book you want to read at one sitting. A better approach is to bite off one or two small pieces at a time, chew well, swallow with caution, and give each flavorful morsel some time to digest before coming back for more.

And don't get frustrated if the new river rating scale seems confusing at first. After all, the TRIP scale is new and different and loaded with numbers. At first glance, it can seem intimidating. If you have trouble at first, don't force it. Put it aside for a while and think about what it's saying. When you go back to it, odds are you'll see clearly the magic mosaic which it uniquely forms: a comparative road map to the most exciting whitewater in the Southeast!

And if you're a natural born doubting Thomas, reluctant to accept any argument without a thorough understanding of the issues, remember that a separate volume describes in detail how the TRIP scale was developed: *Rating Rapids and Rivers: Development of the TRIP Scale,* available from Pahsimeroi Press.

Is There a Suggested Plan for Moving Around in the Book?

Use Chapter Two as the fulcrum for exploring the book. Chapter Two is very important and every reader will benefit by spending some time with it and getting to know the TRIP rating scale before delving too far into the trip descriptions. The TRIP scale integrates and inter-links the trip descriptions, and enhances the verbal information contained in them.

Take an especially close look at the TRIP tables at the end of Chapter Two. Discuss the tables with your paddling buddies to see what they think of the comparative ratings. (Nobody will agree with all the ratings; that's not human nature.) But overall, do they reinforce the impressions you've formed since you've been paddling? We think they will. Are they sufficiently informative that you'll want to refer back to them before running that unknown stream you've been itching to get on? We think so.

Next, read some of the trip descriptions. Begin with one or two rivers that you know well. Are the descriptions accurate? Well-written? Is each write-up focused enough to be useful, yet not so cluttered with detail that it reads like a scientific treatise?

Now switch to the descriptions of a couple of rivers you've been wanting to run, but haven't yet tried. Are the descriptions informative? Can you gain a better understanding of the challenge you face by comparing their TRIP scores with TRIP scores from rivers you already know well? Do the maps quickly locate the new trips, regardless of whether they're hiding in some deep Alabama canyon, in an out-of-the-way corner of West Virginia, or any place in between? Does the local map show you clearly how to get to the putin and takeout? How to run the shuttle?

* * * * *

After checking out a few of the book's features, we think you'll agree that it's the most innovative whitewater guide on the market. Use it enough to get familiar with the new TRIP rating scale, and we think you'll find yourself referring back to its tables again and again. Read the trip descriptions carefully and we think you'll discover that they form a uniquely integrated reference work, an insider's guide to a magnificent collection of rivers, the best in the Southeast.

Chapter Two

The TRIP Rating Scale

Whitewater streams are not created equal. Some are far more difficult to paddle than others. A few are so difficult that they leave little margin for error, even for the best paddlers. Not surprisingly, relative difficulty is often the first information a paddler seeks before running a stream for the first time. To make matters more interesting, accurate information on relative difficulty is extremely hard to come by.

Everybody agrees that difficulty ratings are important. However, the method used to generate them leaves much to be desired. Most river runners use the International (sometimes called the "Eastern") classification scale, where difficulty varies from Class I (flatwater) to Class VI (extreme risk of life). Both individual rapids and entire river trips are rated using this system, where higher Roman numerals denote increasing levels of difficulty.

One of the first lessons a new whitewater paddler learns, however, is that not all people rate whitewater the same. One person's Class V whitewater literally can be another's Class III. A second fact that most paddlers confront at one time or another is that the next higher class of whitewater is not necessarily just "one step" more difficult, but often represents a quantum jump in difficulty, and hence in the skill and experience needed to run it safely.

With all this potential confusion, what's a poor paddler to do? After accumulating some experience, most paddlers recognize and accept the shortcomings and inherent subjectivity embedded in the six-point International scale and develop their own whitewater "benchmarks," whereby they communicate with other paddlers. In the Southeast, a common benchmark is the Ocoee River near Ducktown, Tennessee. Because so many paddlers have run the Ocoee at normal release (about 1,250 cfs), it's often used as a standard to

8

evaluate an unknown stream by asking, "How does it compare to the Ocoee?" If the response is that the unknown stream is harder than the Ocoee, the next question likely attempts to peg approximately how much harder, "Is it a lot harder than the Ocoee?" This process continues, touching upon rapids, gradient, length, accessibility, technicality and other characteristics, until the stream in question is understood relative to the Ocoee. Though imprecise, this process yields more and better information than sole reliance upon the International six point classification system.

Paddlers soon learn to take all river ratings with a grain of salt, due to the imprecision and inherent subjectivity that's invariably embedded in them. Nevertheless, they continue to use the International classification system. They use it because it's quick and simple and because it does communicate river conditions, albeit imperfectly.

What Does The TRIP Scale Add?

The Trip Relational Information Profile (TRIP) rating scale incorporates nine dimensions of stream difficulty. In developing the scale, each dimension was "weighted" to establish its contribution to overall difficulty. (See Figure 2-1.) Interested readers may refer to *Rating Rapids and Rivers: Development of the TRIP Scale* for details on how weights were determined.

Figure 2-1. Dimensions of River Difficulty and Their Weightings

Dimensions of River Difficulty	Weighting
Difficulty of Rapids	23%
Volume x Gradient Interaction	20%
Average Gradient	17%
Streambed Morphology	10%
Continuousness of Rapids	7%
Maximum Gradient In Any One Mile	7%
Total Gradient	6%
Inaccessibility	6%
Reputation	4%

Next, all fifty of the streams described in this volume were measured on the nine difficulty dimensions, producing a scale for each contributing dimension of difficulty, or nine separate scales. One additional scale (of overall difficulty) was created by combining the weighted contributions from each of the nine individual dimensions of difficulty. Thus, the overall difficulty scale is a weighted composite of the nine individual difficulty dimensions. This procedure controlled the relative contribution of each individual dimension. Finally, through a statistical procedure, the ten rating scales were all given the same average score, which is 100, and the same amount of score dispersion above and below the average.

Perhaps best of all, because of the statistical procedures that undergird the tables, distances between scale points are interpretable. For instance, a score of 120 is approximately the same distance above the average score of 100 as a score of 80 is below the average. Also, the difference in difficulty between 140 and 120 is approximately the same as the difference in difficulty between 60 and 80.

Although this may sound quite complicated, its result is gratifyingly simple: ten tables that show how the fifty trips in this volume stack up against each other not only on overall difficulty, but also on nine specific dimensions of difficulty. Paddlers will find that the wealth of information contained in the ten TRIP tables can be used in a number of ways. For example, after running one of the streams described in this book, paddlers can check the TRIP tables and easily evaluate that stream's relative difficulty versus all the others. By running only one stream and carefully comparing its TRIP Profile relative to other trips described in the book, a paddler can gain tremendous insight into what conditions are like on forty-nine other rivers! Also, by examining TRIP scores for the individual dimensions of stream difficulty, a paddler can establish *why* streams differ in difficulty. For instance, if a stream has an overall TRIP score of 120, (which is 20 points above the average for all the streams in the book), its score profile on the nine individual dimensions of difficulty will reveal the source (or sources) of its above average overall difficulty rating.

Understanding the Dimensions
of River Difficulty

An examination of Figure 2-1 will reveal that most of the dimensions of stream difficulty are self-explanatory. Two of the dimensions, however, deserve discussion. "Volume x Gradient Interaction" and "Streambed Morphology" are probably the two most mysterious terms in Figure 2-1. Although these two terms may be unfamiliar, they are critically important in evaluating the difficulty of whitewater streams. For that reason, the sections below will explain how these two concepts influence river difficulty ratings.

A third term from Figure 2-1 (Difficulty of Rapids), is familiar to virtually every paddler, yet it's nevertheless the source of never-ending discussion and disagreement. Therefore, the manner in which the TRIP scale measures difficulty of rapids is explained in a separate section below.

Volume x Gradient Interaction

Interactions occur when two dimensions combine to produce an effect that cannot be predicted from the effects of both dimensions operating independently. An interaction can occur, for instance, when a large volume of water combines with steep gradient to produce far more turbulence than might be expected from the effects of both dimensions operating independently. That is, steep gradient is usually found on small mountain creeks that carry limited volume. When steep gradient is combined with the volume of a large river, however, the turbulence can be surprising. The TRIP scale takes this volume x gradient interaction phenomenon into consideration.

Because volume is so important in forming accurate expectations of stream features, a stream size classification system was developed as part of the TRIP rating system. Stream size is listed in the Actual Stream Data box at the beginning of each stream description, immediately below the TRIP Profile data. Streams are characterized as micro, small, medium, and large.

Micro streams are ordinarily runnable only during peak runoff, following locally heavy rain. They're usually narrow, high gradient, low volume (typically less than 400 cfs) mountain creeks with Type 4 (scrambled) streambed morphologies. They have fast currents and require instantaneous decisions and fast reflexes. Examples in this book include Citico Creek, Island Creek, and Johns Creek.

Small streams typically channel 300 to 700 cfs at medium levels. A broad range of gradient is available in small streams, ranging from easy runs like the Lower Conasauga to high-gradient streams like the Tellico. The Watauga is a small stream in a medium-size riverbed.

Medium size streams range from technical runs like Goshen Pass to pool/drop rivers like the Obed downstream of its confluence with Daddys Creek. A medium size whitewater river may channel up to 1,200 cfs at medium flow, depending on streambed morphology.

Large streams channel more than a thousand cfs at medium flow, and range from the mild-mannered Hiwassee to more challenging runs like the New River Gorge, Tygart Gorge, and Gauley River.

Streambed Morphology

Streambed morphology is the structure of the streambed and the arrangement of obstacles in the streambed, including all the boulders that have tumbled from cliffs and landed in the streamflow, or rolled down tributaries during floods. Ledges that form waterfalls are also part of the streambed morphology. So are canyon walls when they constrict or redirect water flow. When paddlers say that a stream is "technical," they are referring to streambed morphology. Technical streams are ones with a high degree of morphological complexity.

Streambed morphology has five levels: 1) clear, 2) obstructed, 3) densely obstructed, 4) scrambled, and 5) complex. The types, however, rarely occur as pure cases. Most streambeds are mixtures of two or more types. Nevertheless, it is possible to classify most streams by the morphology that predominates.

Type 1: Clear. A river with a clear streambed morphology consists predominantly of an open concourse. There will be some obstacles, there always are, but they can be anticipated and avoided. Examples: Chattooga Section II, Hiwassee, Nantahala.

Type 2: Obstructed. An obstructed streambed contains a moderate number of obstructions that require maneuvering, but the best routes around them are usually recognizable from upstream. The streambed may contain ledges, forming small waterfalls. Occasional scouting may be prudent for less experienced paddlers.

Examples: Big South Fork Gorge, Chattooga Section III, French Broad, Nolichucky Gorge, Tygart Gorge.

Type 3: Densely Obstructed. A densely obstructed streambed requires frequent maneuvers. The best route often cannot be determined from upstream without scouting and/or creative eddy hopping. River-wide obstructions may occur. Precise boat control is a must. Examples: Daddys Creek Canyon, Little River Canyon in Alabama, Middle Fork of the Tygart.

Type 4: Scrambled. Scrambled morphology is typical of steep creeks, where the downstream view of a continuous jumble of rocks may horrify big volume aficionados, but will surely delight steep creek freaks. Examples: Doe River Gorge, Little River in the Smokies, Middle Prong of the Little Pigeon, Piney River, Wilson Creek Gorge.

Type 5: Complex. This streambed combines the extremes of Types 3 and 4, amounting to scrambled dense obstruction where blockages are continuous and unpredictable. This is the apotheosis of technical paddling, where paddlers are constantly faced with multiple chutes, none of which can be seen clearly from upstream, and some of which may end in cul-de-sacs. This kind of streambed is usually found on small streams with steep gradient. These streams are run from eddy to eddy, where one-boat and two-boat eddies are the order of the day. At high water, these runs become hallelujah experiences. Examples: Lower Big Sandy, Caney Fork Gorge, Watauga Gorge.

Streambed morphology is one of the most important determinants of stream characteristics and hence of stream difficulty. However, its influence is also largely manifest in gradient figures, in volume x gradient interaction, in continuousness of rapids, and especially in difficulty of rapids. (The structure of the streambed, after all, determines the nature of rapids.) Accordingly, much of the influence of streambed morphology is already captured when we measure these other dimensions of difficulty. Nevertheless, one element stands alone: undercut rocks and other entrapment hazards. Accordingly, each stream was separately evaluated for its undercut and entrapment hazard, and these ratings were factored into overall difficulty scores.

Difficulty of Rapids

The hardest part of constructing the TRIP scale was understanding how paddlers assign difficulty ratings to individual rapids. Getting to the bottom of the issue necessitated a research study that involved forty-two experienced whitewater paddlers. These paddlers rated individual rapids, assigned "difficulty points" to hypothetical rapids of various difficulty levels, nominated prototypical rapids of various difficulty classifications, and generally provided fundamental insight as to how paddlers approach the process of rating rapids.

One of the most fascinating outcomes of this research was the discovery of how much more difficult one class of rapids is than another. How much more difficult, for instance, is a Class IV than a Class III? Or how much more difficult is a Class V than a Class IV? These are questions that every paddler has considered, but no one had answered definitively until the aforementioned research study was performed.

Knowledge gleaned from the research study was incorporated into the tables at the end of this chapter. The detailed findings of the research, however, go well beyond the intended purposes of this book and hence are not presented here. Readers interested in further details may consult *Rating Rapids and Rivers: Development of the TRIP Scale* by Monte Smith, available from Pahsimeroi Press.

For purposes of understanding the tables at the end of this chapter, it is sufficient to know that paddlers in the study evaluated each stream described in this book at a specified water level: the stream's "midpoint" flow level, as defined by the paddlers themselves. These midpoint flows are listed in Table 1, at the end of this chapter, and in the Water Levels section of each stream description.

In interpreting TRIP profiles, readers should take into consideration the flow levels upon which the ratings were based. TRIP ratings are always pegged at the midpoint of the medium range of flows as specified by paddlers in the research study. When streams are running higher or lower than the specified midpoints at which the streams were evaluated, difficulty ratings should be adjusted accordingly. In doing so, paddlers should keep in mind that the relationship between changes in volume and changes in difficulty varies from stream to stream. On some streams the volume can increase 50% before difficulty increases appreciably. On others, an increase in volume of 25% can produce a significant increase in difficulty.

Putting It All Together

Tables 1 through 11 present the results of the TRIP rating scale. Table 1 contains overall TRIP difficulty scores, and it is followed by a separate table for each of the nine individual dimensions of difficulty. Streams are listed within Tables 1 through 10 according to their TRIP scores, from highest to lowest. The last table in the chapter, Table 11, summarizes scores on all dimensions. Streams within Table 11 are listed alphabetically.

How can TRIP scores be interpreted and used? Let's begin with TRIP Table 1 and see what information we can glean. (Remember that each table has the same average score [100] and the same amount of score dispersion both above and below the average.)

Comparing Different Rivers

First, it's easy to make comparisons between different streams. Based on data from the research study cited earlier, we know that streams that differ by only a few TRIP points are basically equal in difficulty. Generally, a discrepancy of five or more points is a noticeable difference, and about 10 TRIP points represent a meaningful difference (a change in difficulty of about 50%). A difference of 20 overall TRIP points represents an approximate doubling of difficulty. These difference relationships are summarized in Figure 2-2.

Figure 2-2. Interpreting TRIP Point Differences

Points	Interpretation
1-3	Not much difference (5 to 15%)
5	Noticeable difference (25%)
10	Meaningful difference (50%)
20	Significant difference (100%)

Using the TRIP Tables

How can we use this information? Let's say it's your first year in the sport and you've paddled the Nantahala (77 points according to

Table 1) several times with no problem. This past weekend you bit off Chattooga Section III for the first time (86 points). It was a lot tougher than the Nantahala (almost half again as difficult, according to the TRIP scale and Figure 2-2), but you did okay except for Bull Sluice, that big rapid near the end of the trip, which gnawed on you for a while before spitting out the remains. Even so, you weren't hurt. And you finally recovered your boat and most of your other gear. So . . . you're seriously thinking about challenging Chattooga Section IV next weekend. After all, it couldn't be any less hospitable than Bull Sluice, could it? Well, let's see. According to TRIP Table 1, Section IV has a score of 116, which is 30 points more than Section III. And a 20 point difference means double the difficulty? It's definitely time to reconsider. Perhaps something in the high 80's like Little River Canyon, or low 90's like Goshen Pass?

Or, let's say it's your second year in the sport, and you keep hearing about some big river in West Virginia. It's called the Gauley, and all your new paddling friends think it's the greatest thing since six-packs. Everybody you know is planning to attend the Gauley Festival during fall drawdown, and you can't imagine missing it. You decide to train during the summer on the Ocoee, and after numerous runs you're ready to make the plunge. After all, the Ocoee's a pretty tough river, right? Just to be sure, you check the TRIP tables at the end of this chapter. The Ocoee, at 104 overall TRIP points, is above average for all the rivers listed in the book (100 is average), but falls a whopping 34 points short of the Gauley's 138 points! By examining the TRIP tables, you realize that jumping from the Ocoee to the Gauley represents about the same magnitude of difficulty increase as moving from the Hiwassee to the Ocoee. Suddenly you know that you're facing the biggest challenge of your short career.

Table 1 is loaded with potential comparisons. For instance, the lower Chauga (79 points) is almost 50% more difficult than the Hiwassee (70 points), and Goshen Pass (92 points) is about twice as difficult as the Hiwassee. In turn, the Nolichucky Gorge (101 points) is almost 50% more difficult than Goshen Pass, and the upper Tellico (110 points) is almost twice as difficult as Goshen. Finally, the lower Big Sandy (133 points) is approximately double the difficulty of the upper Tellico and more than 50% tougher than the Middle Fork of the Tygart (118 points).

Remember the Water Level

Remember that the difficulty level of each stream is pegged to a specific water level. That water level is listed in Table 1, and in the Water Level section of each respective trip description. If you're paddling the streams at substantially higher or lower water levels than specified in Table 1, you'll want to adjust your expectations accordingly.

Comparing Rivers on
Individual Dimensions

The tables for individual dimensions of difficulty can be interpreted the same way as Table 1. For instance, in Table 3 (Average Gradient) the Ocoee's score of 105 is noticeably above average, but significantly lower than the lower Big Sandy's robust 127, and virtually flat compared with the nosebleed tilt of the upper Tellico, which clocks in with an average gradient TRIP score of 158.

The TRIP tables on individual dimensions of difficulty can also be used to quickly identify streams with especially attractive (or unattractive) characteristics. If you like continuous rapids, then the top entries in Table 7 should be on your priority list. Odds are, you won't be bored once you hit "The Rapids" on the upper Meadow. In fact, you can pretty much rest assured that none of the top entries in Table 7 will annoy you with a lot of long pools. (The Gauley, which has long pools, scores high on this dimension because of the length of its rapids.)

If you prefer a road alongside the run, look for low scores on the inaccessibility index in Table 9. Quite a few excellent whitewater runs are paralleled by roads, and the bottom of Table 9 is a good way to quickly identify them. Pick candidates from the bottom of Table 9 and match them against entries from the tops of Tables 3 and 7, and you'll have both high excitement and a nearby road. If undercut rocks give you the shakes, one glance at Table 8 flags the Piney River and Watauga Gorge as the worst offenders in this category, with the lower Big Sandy and Section IV of the Chattooga not far behind. If short bursts of extreme gradient turn you on, check out the top eleven entries in TRIP Table 4, which pinpoints streams with the highest maximum gradient in any one mile.

Interpreting TRIP Profiles

The Ocoee River

The ten TRIP scores for each stream form a unique profile which is loaded with information. Table 11 is a good way to study stream profiles. For instance, by looking at the Ocoee row in TRIP Table 11, we may discern that, relative to all other streams described in this book, the Ocoee scores high on volume x gradient interaction (123) and on continuousness of its rapids (123). We can tell that it has relatively few undercuts or entrapments (72) and that (due to its parallel road) it scores low on the inaccessibility index (65). Its reputation (117) somewhat exceeds its overall difficulty (104), but it contains above average rapids (110) nonetheless. The discrepancy between a below average total gradient score (91) and a relatively high average gradient score (105) tells us that it's a short run, and this information, coupled with the elevated volume x gradient interaction score, informs us that its volume is substantial.

New River Gorge TRIP Profile

Next, locate the row of TRIP scores in Table 11 for the New River Gorge. The first column tells us that it's about the same as the Ocoee in overall difficulty (106). By scanning across the rest of its scores, however, it's easy to see that average gradient (73) isn't the source of its above average overall rating. Nor is total gradient (69) or maximum gradient for any mile (65). But look at volume x gradient interaction (140). This tells us that volume must be enormous because we already know that gradient is nothing to write home about. The inaccessibility score (110) also adds to its overall difficulty -- although, due to a parallel railroad through the gorge, it's not nearly as high as might otherwise be expected. Its scores for undercut hazards (117), and reputation (128) also add to its overall difficulty. Moreover, it contains some pretty bodacious rapids (117).

Chauga Gorge TRIP Profile

Now scan up Table 11 to the row for the Chauga Gorge, a stream of about the same overall difficulty as the New River Gorge (109). The Chauga also has elevated scores on undercut hazards (117) and inaccessibility (119), but notice that its highest score is on maximum gradient for any one mile (145). Coupled with mediocre

Roll, roll, roll your boat. Monte Smith wrestles with a big drop on the Chattooga. Don Ellis photo.

overall gradient (98) and a middling score on the continuous rapids dimension (99), we can correctly conclude that the Chauga Gorge has some extremely tilted sections but that it also contains some flat water. (And a lot of strainers after the 1994 tornado.) Its elevated score on total gradient (113), combined with an only slightly above average score on volume x gradient interaction (107) suggests a rather long run of moderate volume.

Linking TRIP Scores
to Class I through VI Ratings

Every stream has a unique profile, and in interpreting them, it's important to recognize that the midpoint of the overall TRIP rating scale (100 points) is equivalent to Class III+ difficulty in the International classification system. Thus, the average difficulty of all fifty trips included in this book is about midway between Class III and Class IV.

Figure 2-3 is adapted from the aforementioned book, *Rating Rapids and Rivers: Development of the TRIP Scale*, available from Pahsimeroi Press. It shows how TRIP points in Table 1 correspond to "benchmark" rivers of different International classifications.

Figure 2-3. Benchmark Streams and Their
Corresponding Overall TRIP Points

Class	TRIP Points	Representative Rivers and (Actual Trip Points)
V+	140	Upper Gauley (138)
V	130	Lower Big Sandy (133)
IV+	120	Middle Fork Tygart (118)
IV	110	Upper Tellico (110)
III+	100	Obed, DBT to Nemo (101)
III	90	Goshen Pass (92)
II+	80	Nantahala (77)
II	70	Hiwassee (70)

Notice in Figure 2-3 how traditional classifications are spaced 20 TRIP points apart. (Twenty TRIP points represent a doubling of stream difficulty.) A benchmark Class II river like the Hiwassee scores about 70 overall TRIP points. A Class III river like Goshen Pass scores about 90 points. A Class IV stream like the upper Tellico ledges scores about 110 points. A Class V like the lower Big Sandy scores approximately 130 points.

Notice that the Nantahala River is more than Class II, but not quite Class III. Therefore, it's a Class II+ river and scores approximately 80 TRIP points (77 actually). Similarly, the Obed's DBT to Nemo is a Class III+ run, the Middle Fork of the Tygart is a Class IV+ run, and the upper Gauley clocks in as a Class V+ experience.

Figure 2-4 presents guidelines for what to expect on streams with various overall TRIP scores.

Figure 2-4. Expected Stream Conditions for Different
Ranges of Overall (Table 1) TRIP Points

Points	Stream Conditions
69-79	Predominantly Class II or II+, with Class III rapids appearing only rarely, and then primarily only in streams with TRIP scores in the high seventies.
80-89	Class II-III, with perhaps one Class IV somewhere in the run.
90-99	Class III, with perhaps some Class IV water.
100	TRIP scale midpoint, equivalent to Class III+.
100-109	Numerous Class III rapids and often one or more Class IVs. The Ocoee (104 Points) is representative of this level of difficulty.
110-119	Class IV to IV+. May contain some Class V conditions.
120-129	Class IV+ to borderline Class V. Probably contains some Class V conditions.
130+	Class V and up, containing continuous high difficulty rapids, waterfalls or other hazards.

TRIP Table 1
Overall Difficulty

142 Watauga Gorge at 350 cfs	101 Nolichucky at 1600 cfs
138 Upper Gauley at 2500 cfs	101 Obed (DBT to Nemo) at 2200
133 Lower Big Sandy at 6.5 ft	99 Big Laurel Creek at 300 cfs
131 Piney River at 2.5 ft	98 Big South Fk Gorge at 2000 cfs
118 Middle Fork Tygart at 370 cfs	98 Crab Orchard Creek at 9000 cfs
117 Doe River Gorge at 400 cfs	98 Mid Prong Little Pigeon at 300
116 Chattooga Section IV at 1.7	97 Clear Ck (J to Nemo) at 2400
116 Total Tellico at 500 cfs	96 Lower Tellico at 550 cfs
112 Cheat River Canyon at 2000 cfs	95 Upper Little River at 900 cfs
112 Johns Creek at 400 cfs	95 Obed (Goulds Bend) at 5000 cfs
112 Tygart Gorge at 1250 cfs	93 Middle Meadow at 1000 cfs
110 Upper Tellico at 500 cfs	92 Goshen Pass (Maury R) at 2.5 ft
109 Daddys Creek Canyon at 1.5 ft	89 Seneca Creek at 4.5 ft
109 Chauga Gorge at 2.8 ft	88 French Broad at 2250 cfs
109 Lower Gauley at 3250 cfs	88 Little River Canyon at 4.5 ft
108 Wilson Creek Gorge at 350 cfs	86 Chattooga Section III at 1.9
108 Island Creek at 325 cfs	79 Lower Chauga at 450 cfs
106 New River Gorge at 4000 cfs	77 Nantahala River at 400 cfs
104 Ocoee River at 1275 cfs	75 Catawba, North Fork at 400 cfs
104 Laurel Fk of the Cheat at 1.4 ft	74 Cartecay River at 400 cfs
104 Williams River at 425 cfs	73 James River at 3000 cfs
103 Cranberry River at 425 cfs	73 Hopeville Canyon at 4.2 ft
103 Lower Little River at 900 cfs	72 Conasauga River at 300 cfs
102 Upper Meadow at 1000 cfs	70 Hiwassee River at 2000 cfs
101 Citico Creek at 270 cfs	69 Clear Fork River at 325 cfs

Interpreting TRIP
Point Differences

Points	Interpretation
1-3	Not much difference (5% to 15%)
5	Noticeable difference (25%)
10	Meaningful difference (50%)
20	Profound difference (100%)

TRIP Table 2 Volume x Gradient Interaction	
176 Upper Gauley River	95 Williams River
150 Lower Gauley River	92 Chattooga Section III
144 Tygart Gorge	91 Clear Ck (Jett to Nemo)
143 Cheat River Canyon	91 Hiwassee River
140 New River Gorge	91 Lower Tellico
137 French Broad River	90 Johns Creek
133 Middle Fk (of the Tygart)	89 Crab Orchard Creek
132 Big South Fork Gorge	89 Lower Little River
129 Big Laurel Creek	88 Upper Tellico
126 Nolichucky Gorge	85 Obed (Goulds Bend)
123 Ocoee River	84 Citico Creek
114 Total Tellico	83 Upper Little River
113 Lower Big Sandy	82 James River
111 Upper Meadow River	82 Little River Canyon (AL)
111 Piney River	80 Middle Pr (Little Pigeon)
110 Obed (DBT to Nemo)	79 Seneca Creek
107 Chauga Gorge	73 Island Creek
104 Chattooga Section IV	72 Nantahala River
104 Daddys Creek Canyon	72 Wilson Creek Gorge
98 Goshen Pass (Maury R)	71 Cartecay River
97 Doe River Gorge	70 Lower Chauga
97 Laurel Fork (the Cheat)	68 Hopeville Canyon
97 Watauga Gorge	68 Catawba, North Fork
97 Middle Meadow	65 Clear Fork River
96 Cranberry River	60 Lower Conasauga

TRIP Point Differences	
Points	**Interpretation**
1-3	Not much difference (5% to 15%)
5	Noticeable difference (25%)
10	Meaningful difference (50%)
20	Profound difference (100%)

TRIP Table 3 Average Gradient	
158 Island Creek	94 Goshen Pass (Maury R)
158 Upper Tellico	93 Tygart Gorge
148 Watauga Gorge	90 Nantahala River
148 Citico Creek	89 Nolichucky Gorge
145 Wilson Creek Gorge	88 Big Laurel Creek
142 Doe River Gorge	87 Conasauga River
134 Middle Pr Little Pigeon	86 Hopeville Canyon
127 Lower Big Sandy	84 Upper Gauley
124 Lower Little River	83 Obed (Goulds Bend)
123 Middle Fk of the Tygart	82 Catawba, North Fork
123 Piney River	82 Little River Canyon (AL)
117 Seneca Creek	81 Upper Meadow
117 Total Tellico	80 Clear Ck (Jett to Nemo)
116 Upper Little River	80 Chattooga Section III
111 Johns Creek	79 Obed (DBT to Nemo)
106 Cranberry River	78 Cheat River Canyon
106 Williams River	77 French Broad River
105 Ocoee River	76 Lower Gauley River
104 Laurel Fork of the Cheat	73 Big South Fork Gorge
101 Lower Tellico	73 New River Gorge
98 Chauga Gorge	72 Lower Chauga River
98 Daddys Creek Canyon	71 Cartecay River
97 Middle Meadow	69 Hiwassee River
97 Chattooga Section IV	68 Clear Fork River
97 Crab Orchard Creek	65 James River

TRIP Point Differences	
Points	**Interpretation**
1-3	Not much difference (5% to 15%)
5	Noticeable difference (25%)
10	Meaningful difference (50%)
20	Profound difference (100%)

TRIP Table 4	
Maximum Gradient in Any One Mile	
159 Doe River Gorge	103 Crab Orchard Creek
152 Watauga Gorge	95 Goshen Pass (Maury R)
145 Upper Chauga	95 Tygart Gorge
138 Upper Tellico	93 Ocoee River
138 Total Tellico	88 Clear Ck (Jett to Nemo)
131 Lower Little River	88 Nolichucky Gorge
131 Citico Creek	85 Middle Meadow
131 Middle Pr Little Pigeon	81 Little River Canyon (AL)
131 Piney River	81 Catawba, North Fork
124 Island Creek	81 Nantahala River
124 Johns Creek	78 Upper Gauley
117 Cranberry River	78 Conasauga River
117 Lower Big Sandy	76 Lower Chauga
117 Middle Fk of the Tygart	76 Big South Fork Gorge
117 Chattooga Section IV	74 Clear Fork River
117 Wilson Creek Gorge	74 Obed (DBT to Nemo)
110 Upper Little River	74 Cartecay River
106 Big Laurel Creek	74 French Broad
106 Seneca Creek	74 Cheat River Canyon
105 Laurel Fork of the Cheat	74 Chattooga Section III
103 Daddys Creek Canyon	74 Hopeville Canyon
103 Upper Meadow	71 Lower Gauley
103 Obed (Goulds Bend)	65 New River Gorge
103 Lower Tellico	62 Hiwassee River
103 Williams River	59 James River

TRIP Point Differences	
Points	**Interpretation**
1-3	Not much difference (5% to 15%)
5	Noticeable difference (25%)
10	Meaningful difference (50%)
20	Profound difference (100%)

TRIP Table 5 Total Gradient			
174	Piney River	95	Daddys Creek Canyon
165	Laurel Fk of the Cheat	92	Cheat River Canyon
141	Citico Creek	92	Island Creek
139	Williams River	91	Clear Creek
135	Doe River Gorge	91	Ocoee River
135	Upper Little River	91	Chattooga Section IV
131	Upper Gauley	90	Big Laurel Creek
126	Watauga Gorge	88	Goshen Pass (Maury R)
125	Crab Orchard Creek	88	Lower Tellico
123	Total Tellico	86	Wilson Creek
118	Lower Little River	85	Upper Tellico
116	Seneca Creek	84	French Broad
115	Lower Big Sandy	83	Big South Fork Gorge
114	Upper Meadow	81	Conasauga River
113	Chauga Gorge	80	Middle Meadow
109	Tygart Gorge	79	Cartecay River
109	Cranberry River	78	Little River Canyon (AL)
107	Middle Fk of the Tygart	77	Lower Gauley
102	Middle Pr Little Pigeon	74	Catawba, North Fork
101	Nolichucky Gorge	71	Clear Fork River
99	Chattooga Section III	70	Lower Chauga
97	Obed (DBT to Nemo)	69	Hopeville Canyon
96	Nantahala River	69	New River Gorge
95	Obed (Goulds Bend)	63	Hiwassee River
95	Johns Creek	55	James River

TRIP Point Differences	
Points	**Interpretation**
1-3	Not much difference (5% to 15%)
5	Noticeable difference (25%)
10	Meaningful difference (50%)
20	Profound difference (100%)

TRIP Table 6
Difficulty of Rapids

178 Upper Gauley River	94 Big South Fork Gorge
178 Watauga Gorge	92 Nolichucky Gorge
166 Lower Big Sandy	91 Middle Meadow
134 Chattooga Section IV	90 Island Creek
133 Piney River	90 Lower Little River
129 Cheat River Canyon	89 Crab Orchard Creek
117 Johns Creek	89 Upper Little River
117 Mid Fork (of the Tygart)	88 Lower Tellico
117 New River Gorge	87 Citico Creek
117 Total Tellico	87 Goshen Pass (Maury R)
117 Wilson Creek Gorge	87 Little River Canyon (AL)
113 Daddys Creek Canyon	86 Big Laurel Creek
113 Lower Gauley River	86 Chattooga Section III
110 Ocoee River	82 Lower Chauga
108 Tygart Gorge	82 Middle Pr Little Pigeon
107 Upper Meadow	76 Cartecay River
106 Chauga Gorge	76 Seneca Creek
106 Doe River Gorge	76 French Broad River
105 Cranberry River	75 Catawba, North Fork
102 Williams River	72 James River
98 Laurel Fork of the Cheat	72 Hopeville Canyon
97 Upper Tellico	72 Nantahala River
96 Obed (DBT to Nemo)	69 Lower Conasauga
95 Clear Ck (Jett to Nemo)	69 Hiwassee River
95 Obed (Goulds Bend)	69 Clear Fork River

TRIP Point Differences	
Points	**Interpretation**
1-3	Not much difference (5% to 15%)
5	Noticeable difference (25%)
10	Meaningful difference (50%)
20	Profound difference (100%)

TRIP Table 7 Continuous Rapids and/or Length of Rapids	
135 Upper Meadow	111 Chattooga Section IV
135 Piney River	99 Chauga Gorge
135 Watauga Gorge	99 Middle Meadow
135 Wilson Creek Gorge	99 Nolichucky Gorge
123 Lower Big Sandy	99 Seneca Creek
123 Crab Orchard Creek	99 New River Gorge
123 Doe River Gorge	99 Obed (DBT to Nemo)
123 Upper Gauley	99 Goshen Pass (Maury R)
123 Island Creek	99 Tygart Gorge
123 Johns Creek	99 Clear Ck (Jett to Nemo)
123 Middle Fk of the Tygart	87 Nantahala River
123 Ocoee River	87 Big Laurel Creek
123 Upper Tellico	87 Big South Fork Gorge
123 Williams River	87 Obed (Goulds Bend)
111 Cranberry River	75 Little River Canyon (AL)
111 Daddys Creek Canyon	75 James River
111 Middle Pr Little Pigeon	75 Catawba, North Fork
111 Cheat River Canyon	75 Hiwassee River
111 Lower Gauley	63 Cartecay River
111 Lower Tellico	63 Chattooga Section III
111 Citico Creek	63 Lower Chauga
111 Total Tellico	63 Hopeville Canyon
111 Lower Little River	50 Clear Fork River
111 Laurel Fork of the Cheat	50 French Broad
111 Upper Little River	50 Conasauga River

TRIP Point Differences	
Points	**Interpretation**
1-3	Not much difference (5% to 15%)
5	Noticeable difference (25%)
10	Meaningful difference (50%)
20	Profound difference (100%)

TRIP Table 8
Undercuts and/or Entrapment Hazards

151	Piney River	94	Big Laurel Creek
151	Watauga Gorge	94	Cheat River Canyon
140	Lower Big Sandy	94	Doe River Gorge
140	Chattooga Section IV	94	Goshen Pass (Maury R)
128	Clear Ck (Jett to Nemo)	94	Laurel Fork of the Cheat
128	Daddys Creek Canyon	94	Middle Fk of the Tygart
128	Upper Gauley	94	Middle Meadow
128	Johns Creek	94	Nolichucky Gorge
128	Obed (DBT to Nemo)	83	Big South Fork Gorge
128	Total Tellico	83	Chattooga Section III
117	Chauga Gorge	83	Crab Orchard Creek
117	Island Creek	72	Catawba, North Fork
117	Lower Little River	72	Citico Creek
117	New River Gorge	72	Clear Fork River
117	Obed (Goulds Bend)	72	Conasauga River
117	Upper Tellico	72	French Broad
117	Lower Tellico	72	Hopeville Canyon
117	Williams River	72	James River
106	Lower Chauga	72	Upper Little River
106	Cranberry River	72	Upper Meadow
106	Lower Gauley	72	Ocoee River
106	Little River Canyon (AL)	72	Seneca Creek
106	Middle Pr Little Pigeon	72	Cartecay River
106	Tygart Gorge	60	Nantahala River
106	Wilson Creek Gorge	49	Hiwassee River

TRIP Point Differences

Points	Interpretation
1-3	Not much difference (5% to 15%)
5	Noticeable difference (25%)
10	Meaningful difference (50%)
20	Profound difference (100%)

TRIP Table 9 Inaccessibility	
137 Lower Big Sandy	110 Nolichucky Gorge
137 Big South Fork Gorge	110 Obed (Goulds Bend)
137 Cheat River Canyon	110 Tygart Gorge
137 Piney River	101 Clear Fork River
128 Daddys Creek Canyon	101 Conasauga River
128 Doe River Gorge	101 French Broad
128 Upper Gauley	92 Cartecay River
128 Little River Canyon	92 Lower Chauga
128 Obed (DBT to Nemo)	83 Catawba, North Fork
128 Watauga Gorge	74 Hopeville Canyon
119 Chattooga Section IV	74 Cranberry River
119 Chauga Gorge	74 Hiwassee River
119 Clear Ck (Jett to Nemo)	74 Middle Pr Little Pigeon
119 Lower Gauley	74 Seneca Creek
119 Island Creek	74 Wilson Creek Gorge
119 Upper Meadow	65 Goshen Pass (Maury R)
119 Middle Fk of the Tygart	65 Upper Little River
110 Big Laurel Creek	65 Lower Little River
110 Chattooga Section III	65 Nantahala River
110 Crab Orchard Creek	65 Ocoee River
110 James River	65 Upper Tellico
110 Johns Creek	65 Lower Tellico
110 Laurel Fork of the Cheat	65 Total Tellico
110 Middle Meadow	65 Williams River
110 New River Gorge	56 Citico Creek

TRIP Point Differences	
Points	Interpretation
1-3	Not much difference (5% to 15%)
5	Noticeable difference (25%)
10	Meaningful difference (50%)
20	Profound difference (100%)

TRIP Table 10 Reputation	
139 Chattooga Section IV	105 Doe River Gorge
139 Upper Gauley	105 Little River Canyon (AL)
139 Johns Creek	105 Upper Meadow
139 Watauga Gorge	105 Middle Fk of the Tygart
128 New River Gorge	105 Lower Tellico
127 Lower Gauley	94 Chattooga Section III
117 Lower Big Sandy	94 Lower Chauga
117 Big South Fork Gorge	94 Lower Little River
117 Cheat River Canyon	94 Upper Little River
117 Crab Orchard Creek	83 Big Laurel Creek
117 Cranberry River	83 Citico Creek
117 Daddys Creek Canyon	83 Laurel Fork of the Cheat
117 Goshen Pass (Maury R)	83 Williams River
117 Island Creek	72 Cartecay River
117 Nolichucky Gorge	72 French Broad
117 Obed (DBT to Nemo)	72 Middle Meadow
117 Obed (Goulds Bend)	72 Middle Pr Little Pigeon
117 Ocoee River	72 Nantahala River
117 Piney River	72 Seneca Creek
117 Upper Tellico	60 James River
117 Total Tellico	60 Catawba, North Fork
117 Tygart Gorge	60 Clear Fork River
117 Wilson Creek Gorge	60 Hopeville Canyon
105 Clear Ck (Jett to Nemo)	49 Conasauga River
105 Chauga Gorge	49 Hiwassee River

TRIP Point Differences	
Points	Interpretation
1-3	Not much difference (5% to 15%)
5	Noticeable difference (25%)
10	Meaningful difference (50%)
20	Profound difference (100%)

```
╔══════════════════════════════════════════════╗
║                 TRIP Table 11                  ║
║            Summary of TRIP Scores              ║
╠══════════════════════════════════════════════╣
║  1  Overall Difficulty      6  Rapids Difficulty  ║
║  2  Volume X Grad. Inter.   7  Continuous Rapids  ║
║  3  Average Gradient        8  Entrapments        ║
║  4  Maximum Gradient        9  Inaccessibility    ║
║  5  Total Gradient          0  Reputation         ║
╚══════════════════════════════════════════════╝
```

	1	2	3	4	5	6	7	8	9	0
Big Laurel Creek	99	129	88	106	90	86	87	94	110	83
Lower Big Sandy	133	113	127	117	115	166	123	140	137	117
Big South Fork	98	132	73	76	83	94	87	83	137	117
Cartecay River	74	71	71	74	79	76	63	72	92	72
Catawba (N Fork)	75	68	82	81	74	75	75	72	83	60
Chattooga Sec III	86	92	80	74	99	86	63	83	110	94
Chattooga Sec IV	116	104	97	117	91	134	111	140	119	139
Chauga Gorge	109	107	98	145	113	106	99	117	119	105
Chauga (Lower)	79	70	72	76	70	82	63	106	92	94
Cheat River	112	143	78	74	92	129	111	94	137	117
Citico Creek	101	84	148	131	141	87	111	72	56	83
Clear Creek	97	91	80	88	91	95	99	128	119	105
Clear Fork River	69	65	68	74	71	69	50	72	101	60
Conasauga (Lower)	72	60	87	78	81	69	50	72	101	49
Crab Orchard	98	89	97	103	126	89	123	83	110	117
Cranberry River	103	96	106	117	109	105	111	106	74	117
Daddys Creek	109	104	98	103	95	113	111	128	128	117
Doe River Gorge	117	97	142	159	135	106	123	94	128	105
French Broad	88	137	77	74	84	76	50	72	101	72
Gauley (Upper)	138	176	84	78	131	178	123	128	128	139
Gauley (Lower)	109	150	76	71	77	113	111	106	119	127
Goshen Pass	92	98	94	95	88	87	99	94	65	117
Hiwassee River	70	91	69	62	63	69	75	49	74	49
Hopeville Canyon	73	68	86	74	69	72	63	72	74	60
Island Creek	108	73	158	124	92	90	123	117	119	117
James River	73	82	65	58	55	72	75	72	110	60
Johns Creek	112	90	111	124	95	117	123	128	110	139

	TRIP Table 11 (Continued) Summary of TRIP Scores	
1 Overall Difficulty	6 Rapids Difficulty	
2 Volume X Grad. Inter.	7 Continuous Rapids	
3 Average Gradient	8 Entrapments	
4 Maximum Gradient	9 Inaccessibility	
5 Total Gradient	0 Reputation	

	1	2	3	4	5	6	7	8	9	0
Laurel Fork	104	97	104	105	165	98	111	94	110	83
Upper Little River	95	83	116	110	135	89	111	72	65	94
Lower Little River	103	89	124	131	118	90	111	117	65	94
Little River Canyon	88	82	82	81	78	87	75	106	128	105
Meadow (Upper)	102	111	81	103	114	107	135	72	119	105
Meadow (Middle)	93	97	97	85	80	91	99	94	110	72
Middle Fk Tygart	118	133	123	117	107	117	123	94	119	105
Mid Prong L Pigeon	98	80	134	131	102	82	111	106	74	72
Nantahala River	77	72	90	81	96	72	87	60	65	72
New River Gorge	106	140	73	65	69	117	99	117	110	128
Nolichucky Gorge	101	126	89	88	101	92	99	94	110	117
Obed DBT-Nemo	101	110	79	74	97	96	99	128	128	117
Obed Goulds Bend	95	85	83	103	95	95	87	117	110	117
Ocoee River	104	123	105	93	91	110	123	72	65	117
Piney River	131	111	123	131	174	133	135	151	137	117
Seneca Creek	89	79	117	106	116	76	99	72	74	72
Tellico (Upper)	110	88	158	138	85	97	123	117	65	117
Tellico (Lower)	96	91	101	103	88	88	111	117	65	105
Tellico (Total)	116	114	117	138	123	117	111	128	65	117
Tygart Gorge	112	144	93	95	109	108	99	106	110	117
Watauga Gorge	142	97	148	152	126	178	135	151	128	139
Williams River	104	95	106	103	139	102	123	117	65	83
Wilson Creek	108	72	145	117	86	117	135	106	74	117

Chapter Three

Background, Stream Selection Criteria, and River Safety

This book describes fifty of the best whitewater paddling trips in the southern Appalachians, ranging geographically from the Little River Canyon on Alabama's Lookout Mountain to northern West Virginia's Big Sandy Creek. Because all streams are described through the experience of one paddler, fifty diverse river trips are integrated within a common frame of reference. Trip descriptions also are interrelated through a new river rating system (the TRIP scale, discussed in Chapter Two) that profiles every trip on ten dimensions of paddling difficulty. Thus, trips as different as the gargantuan Gauley and the tiny Piney are evaluated on the same ten scales.

This Chapter begins by discussing the still small but increasingly substantial literary genre consisting of southeastern whitewater guidebooks. It continues by reviewing the criteria used for choosing the fifty river trips that were ultimately included in the volume. The chapter concludes with a frank discussion of river safety and the inevitable element of risk that is associated with paddle sports, and recognition that assumption of this risk logically falls on the shoulders of the individual paddler.

Background

Ancient History

As with any book, this one was influenced by the historical and literary context wherein it was conceived and into which it was born. A big chunk of that tradition is traceable to Randy Carter's landmark volume, *Canoeing Whitewater River Guide,* published early in the

Sixties. Carter's book was one of the first in the whitewater paddling guidebook genre and unquestionably one of the most influential.

As clearly implied in his title, Carter's interest was primarily in whitewater. He had little interest in writing about flatwater trips. Most of the streams he wrote about were in Virginia and West Virginia, although they ranged from South Carolina to Pennsylvania. (Interestingly, he apparently never ventured over the mountains into Tennessee.) Carter never pretended to offer comprehensive coverage of any particular geographic region, choosing instead to write about the streams he knew best, wherever he found them.

Carter and his contemporaries were river pioneers in many respects. Although his descriptions are dated, especially the difficulty ratings, his enthusiasm and spirit of adventure suffuse every page. Carter's book is a classic and still merits careful reading.

Another early work was Walter Burmeister's ambitious *Appalachian Water,* published in 1962. Whereas Carter seemingly was content to write about streams that he knew well, Burmeister tried to cover everything. Volume II, devoted to the mountain streams of the southeast, described approximately sixty rivers and creeks. Although an admirable feat, much of the detail in this leviathan volume is difficult to interpret and just about impossible to use. Payson Kennedy (writing in *First Descents*) has suggested that Burmeister didn't paddle all the streams described in his book, but relied on extensive map work and notes and recollections of other paddlers.

One State At A Time

Because of the inherent difficulty of describing every stream in a broad geographic region, most river guidebooks subsequent to Carter and Burmeister focused upon a delimited area, typically the boundaries of a single state, and attempted reasonably comprehensive coverage within that circumscribed area. Perhaps the exemplary work devoted to a single state has been Burrell and Davidson's *Wild Water West Virginia,* which appeared half a decade after Carter's first printing. Burrell and Davidson managed to create the prototypical statewide guidebook in large part because of virtually unlimited raw materials. West Virginia contains more "wild water" (that is, whitewater) per square mile than any other eastern state, permitting the authors to devote the entire volume to "wild water." The book's continuing success traces in no small part to the fact that an entire statewide paddling guide contains exclusively whitewater trip descriptions. (A revised edition of the venerable Burrell and Davidson volume was released recently under the able editorship of Charlie Walbridge.)

Following the success of Burrell and Davidson with their West Virginia book, guides for other southeastern states soon appeared. Some of these statewide guides have been quite good, perhaps exemplified by Ed Grove's recent guide to Virginia, *Classic Virginia Rivers.* But all statewide guides face a serious handicap: state boundaries rarely define meaningful groupings of whitewater streams. No other southeastern state is as uniformly mountainous as West Virginia, and hence statewide guidebooks often contain too many flatwater descriptions and too few good whitewater runs.

The impracticality of using a state boundary as an organizational format is nowhere better illustrated than with the state of Tennessee, which stretches from America's Mississippi River heartland to some of the highest peaks of the Appalachian Mountains. To get an idea of the immensely varied terrain that the Volunteer state incorporates within its boundaries, one need only commandeer a good map to observe that Johnson City, Tennessee, located in the Appalachians near the North Carolina and Virginia borders, is closer to Canada than it is to the city of Memphis! Moreover, Memphis is closer to the Gulf of Mexico than it is to Johnson City!

Sehlinger and Lantz, authors of a Tennessee paddling guidebook first published in 1979, were faced with the herculean task of describing streams from at least three distinct topologic regions. Small wonder they subsequently split the book, devoting one volume to the flat streams of western Tennessee and the other volume to rivers in the state's mountainous eastern third.

The Nealy Contribution

In the 1970's William Nealy began publishing creative and entertaining maps on individual rivers. They were maps uniquely his own, printed on a single long sheet of paper, depicting each stream as flowing from the top of the map into the reader's lap, with descriptive comments hand-scrawled in the margins. In the Carter tradition, he selected rivers from all over, from Alabama to West Virginia. These maps became immensely popular. They were intelligent, creative, informative and entertaining. Nealy illustrated not only rivers, but also in his accompanying cartoons the deeper flow of human psychology, laid bare to expose the throbbing frailty of ego.

Most of all, Nealy's works exuded legitimacy. Whitewater paddlers who had never met him could nevertheless tell at a glance that his maps, cartoons, and commentary were drawn from the reservoir of firsthand experience. Who but a paddler could coin the phrase ". . . guaranteed dynamic full-facial . . ." to describe the result of failing to complete a roll at the top of Wilson Creek's Class V Razorback? Or comment that the best thing about the Chattooga's notorious Bull Sluice rapid is that, due to its proximity to US 76, ambulances can practically drive up to it!

His maps, however, were not perfect. They were devilish to keep up with and cumbersome to use on road trips because they had to be folded and unfolded or, more commonly, unfurled like ancient scrolls. On road trips they invariably became tattered, beer-stained, bun crushed, and inadvertently kicked out the van door late at night during Bo Rocker's umpteenth emergency stop to "check the ropes." In the 1980's, Nealy published the maps in book form, with Volume 1 containing thirteen river descriptions and Volume 2 describing eight additional streams. Sad-to-say, something was lost in reducing the maps to 8.5 x 11 inch format. Even sadder, the long awaited third volume never materialized.

Limited Coverage Guidebooks

Guidebooks devoted to individual streams or to single watersheds appear from time to time. Most of these works focus on a single popular river, such as the Ocoee, Chattooga, or New River Gorge. These works have a way of suddenly going out of print due to production and distribution economics. An exception has been the author's *A Paddler's Guide to the Obed/Emory Watershed.* It first appeared in 1980 and was revised and updated in 1990. Although limited to a single watershed, the guidebook has proven resilient, due in no small part to the Obed's mystique, its status as a National Wild and Scenic River, and the fact that its labyrinthine canyon system contains eighteen different paddling trips, with something for paddlers of every skill level.

Committee Guidebooks

In 1986 Nealy and four other authors (Sehlinger, Otey, Benner, and Lantz) published an edited volume compiled from the best of previously published works. Entitled *Appalachian Whitewater Volume 1: The Southern Mountains*, the work described streams from Alabama to Kentucky. The volume described only premium whitewater trips, but from widely varying perspectives. In many ways it was like an album collection of greatest hits from several performing groups, and therein lay both its greatest strength and weakness. Due to multiple authorship, both writing style and coverage detail varied substantially from one trip description to the next. This is hardly surprising because distinctive writing styles made the contributing authors successful in the first place. A second volume, concentrating on the mountains of Virginia, West Virginia, Delaware, Maryland, and Pennsylvania was published subsequently by six other authors (Grove, Kirby, Walbridge, Eister, Davidson, and Davidson).

Approach of the Present Volume

With this background in place, we can now turn our attention to the current volume, and how it fits into the growing whitewater guidebook genre.

First, it adopts the Randy Carter/William Nealy practice of limiting streams to those the author knows personally. A stream was included only if the author had paddled it enough times to confidently and accurately describe it.

Second, it offers reasonably broad coverage. Its fifty trips represent a variety of stream conditions across a sizeable geographic area, and range in difficulty from easy Class II to challenging Class V. The book transcends state boundaries and selects the southern Appalachian Mountains as its organizing framework. Streams from the Appalachian regions of seven southeastern states are included in the volume.

Third, every word and every impression is written through the experience of one paddler, giving the work a stylistic and conceptual integration that is not possible when an editor attempts to integrate

Gwen Drescher leads the way at First Island on Big Sandy Creek.
Don Ellis photo.

the multiple perspectives and writing styles of several authors. To ensure that the work was not a mere compilation of one author's idiosyncratic way of looking at things, forty-two experienced paddlers provided structured input. (See Chapter Two for details.)

Fourth, and possibly most important, the book introduces the Trip Relational Information Profile (TRIP) rating scale, a new way of comparing rivers on both specific and global dimensions of difficulty. For the author, and hopefully also for the reader, the TRIP rating scale is the mechanism that integrates and interrelates the fifty trip descriptions in this book. The TRIP scales permit paddlers to quickly assess any stream on ten basic dimensions of paddling difficulty, and then to compare that stream with any other in the book. Because of the TRIP feature, a reader can often gain a "feel" for an unknown river by comparing and contrasting it with known streams along dimensions incorporated in the TRIP rating scales.

Stream Selection

Southeastern Whitewater contains descriptions of fifty whitewater trips on forty-two different streams. Although the book contains a lot of trip descriptions, it makes no claim to exhaustive coverage of the best paddling opportunities in the Southeast. Indeed, the region

Streams Were Selected From Seven Appalachian Mountain States
Alabama
Georgia
North Carolina
South Carolina
Tennessee
Virginia
West Virginia

contains many other fine whitewater streams. A stream was included in the book only if it met criteria associated with: geographical location, author familiarity, outstanding whitewater, and scenic beauty.

Location

Streams were selected from the southern Appalachian Mountains, which occupy parts of seven southeastern states. In the map at the right, each star locates one of the fifty trips described in this volume. As the pattern of stars illustrates, only West Virginia is predominantly mountainous. The other six states

are only partially occupied by the Appalachians. Approximately the eastern third of Tennessee, the western third of Virginia, the western 20% of North Carolina, the northern 20% of Georgia, and the northeastern and northwestern corners of Alabama and South Carolina, respectively, are mountainous. The pattern of stars on the map above defines the hypothetical state of southern Appalachia, a region that is about the size of Georgia, stretching from northern Alabama to the northern reaches of West Virginia. Not an official state, but well known, nevertheless, to paddlers from all over the eastern seaboard.

Author Familiarity

An important feature of this book is that all stream descriptions are from one paddler. The author made hundreds of paddling excursions to gather information for this volume. (It was a dirty job but somebody had to do it.) The author paddled some of the streams dozens of times over a period of years. Most streams were paddled several times before the first rudimentary description was penned.   Despite his best efforts, however, he couldn't paddle everything. (Though his wife will attest that he tried!) If your favorite stream is not included in the volume, don't feel slighted.   It was simply impossible to run all the good trips enough times to describe them meaningfully.   This book is not about *the fifty best trips,* but rather it's about *fifty of the best trips* in the Southeast.   An ironclad rule governed inclusion in the volume: a stream was included only if the author had paddled it enough times to write about it confidently and accurately.

Outstanding Whitewater

Only whitewater streams were included, although the amount of whitewater varies enormously from one stream to another. Some runs consist of continuous high difficulty rapids, others are pool-ledge with long quiet pools followed by thunderous drops through complex rock fields, while still others feature only occasional mild rapids but have exceptional scenery. The general criterion, however, in selecting some streams and excluding others was presence of whitewater.   This volume is, first and foremost, a compilation of whitewater paddling opportunities.   Streams without substantial whitewater action, notwithstanding scenic beauty, were excluded.

None of the streams in this book are appropriate for unaccompanied beginning paddlers.   Some prior experience is necessary to safely paddle even the milder streams described in the volume. The average difficulty is Class III(IV), about that of the Big South Fork Gorge in east Tennessee. Over a third (36%) of described trips are more difficult than the Ocoee, site of the 1996 Olympics and an oft-used benchmark of overall river difficulty. Most streams in this volume contain rapids of at least Class III difficulty, and hence are appropriate only for paddlers of intermediate and above skill levels. In fact, the more difficult runs in this volume are appropriate only for paddlers with a lot of Class IV river experience.

Don Ellis gets that sinking feeling. Wonder Falls. Big Sandy Creek.
Photo by Frank (the Flying Ace) Billue.

Scenic Beauty

And yes, some streams with only a modest number of rapids did sneak in primarily on the merits of their outstanding scenery (e.g., the lower Conasauga). Many others, however, have plenty of whitewater and scenic splendor.

River Safety

This book is based on hundreds of paddling excursions, incalculable hours of map work, bizillions of phone calls, and uncounted hikes and drives to check access points, geological features, scenic overlooks, etc. Every reasonable effort was made to describe streams and rapids accurately, including how their character and difficulty can change dramatically with variations in water level. The descriptions herein, however, cannot substitute for experience, training, common sense, or safety-consciousness. Although every reasonable precaution was taken in preparing and checking these descriptions, the reader is cautioned that no guidebook can be sufficiently detailed to pinpoint every potential hazard.

Changeable Stream Conditions

And then, there's the incontrovertible fact that rivers themselves change. This writer used to think that stream conditions changed very slowly, perhaps over the eons, or at the very fastest within a time frame that superseded human life expectancy. That line of thinking was, to say the least, a complacently naive conceptualization of how the forces of nature work.

The fact is, streams are changing all the time, often right before our very eyes. Sometimes the changes are so small they go unnoticed. But other times they're big enough to literally clamor for our attention. Changes in streambeds occur most often from the accumulation or shifting of debris, thereby blocking or altering previously navigable passageways. But changes also result from more cataclysmic forces. As the flood of 1985 persuasively demonstrated in parts of Virginia and West Virginia, entire streambeds of major rivers occasionally are radically reconfigured by the awesome forces of nature. Parts of Goshen Pass (Maury River in

Virginia) and the Cheat Canyon (West Virginia) bear little resemblance today to their pre-flood appearances.

Even local floods can transform otherwise placid streams into raging torrents. And floods can happen with little warning. This is possible with any river, but it's especially the case with many of the small-volume, high-gradient streams described in this volume.

During a flood that swept through Alabama's Little River Canyon in July, 1985, the river rose a foot every fifteen minutes for three and a half hours. On July 4, 1989 the Watauga River jumped from 154 cfs to 9,400 cfs in a matter of a few hours. On the same Independence Day weekend, campers alongside Wilson Creek were swept downstream in their tents as the water rose suddenly in pre-dawn darkness. *River Stories*, the author's collection of whitewater short stories, essays and personal reminiscences, contains an account of a flash flood on the upper Obed River (*Wild Bill Brownlee: Treetop Poet*). Although the story is humorous in retrospect, you can bet that nobody was laughing when it actually happened. Tornadoes that swept through upstate South Carolina and north Georgia in 1994 extensively rearranged timber alongside the Chattooga River and within the Chauga River corridor. Paddlers who were on the Chattooga that day saw the water rise from 2.2 to over 5.0 feet before they could get off the river!

As these examples vividly illustrate, river conditions (including streambed conformation itself) can and do change abruptly, and paddlers must keep this possibility in mind. Guidebooks and other written commentary are useful during pre-trip preparations, but no guidebook can completely forewarn paddlers of every potential hazard. Whitewater paddling, like any other water sport, is inherently risky. Once a paddler decides to assume the inevitable risk associated with running any particular stream, his or her responsibility is then to accumulate and assimilate as much knowledge of the impending trip as possible, and to overlay appropriate safety precautions. Guidebooks can materially assist in trip planning, but once on the river and face-to-face with swiftly changing circumstances that have potentially dire consequences, the most reliable running companions are always training, experience and vigilance.

A Last Word on River Safety

River running is an uplifting and fundamentally metaphoric enterprise, one of life's more interesting situational intelligence tests. But it's also an inherently risky endeavor, especially for the under-prepared. Proper training, pre-trip preparation, and on-river safety precautions can reduce the risk element of whitewater paddling to a level no higher than -- and probably lower than -- that involved in the transit to and from the river. But if there's enough water to float a boat, there's always a risk of drowning. Always. And if you're not willing to recognize that risk and shoulder the responsibility, you should stay off the river.

Chapter Four

Organization of Stream Descriptions

To facilitate locating information, all stream descriptions have the same organization. For each description, material appears in this sequence:

Trip Name
Trip Location
TRIP Profile Box
Actual Stream Data Box
Overview
Similar To
Top-To-Bottom Itinerary
Description
Summary
Water Levels
Access (Maps)
Miles From
Other Information
Nearby Alternate Trips

Trip Name

Trips are listed alphabetically, but there are a few special cases. If a stream has Big in front of its name (such as Big Sandy Creek or Big South Fork), it's listed under B, as if Big were part of its proper name. If a stream has Middle in front of its name (such as Middle Prong of the Little Pigeon or Middle Fork of the Tygart), it's listed under M, as if Middle were part of its proper name.

But just to keep you on your toes, North Fork of the Catawba is listed under C, North Fork of the South Branch of the Potomac is listed as Hopeville Canyon, and Virginia's Maury River is listed as

Goshen Pass, the name by which its popular whitewater section is most commonly known.

Location

Specifies the state where each stream is located. The specific area of the state is pinpointed later in the Access section.

TRIP Profile and Actual Stream Data Boxes

These boxes always appear immediately below the trip name and location, at the beginning of each trip description. TRIP Profile scores are explained in Chapter Two. The boxes always look something like the following, which are lifted from the Big Laurel Creek description:

TRIP Profile			
Scale Midpoint = 100			
Overall Difficulty	99	Rapids Difficulty	86
Volume x Gradient	129	Continuous Rapids	87
Average Gradient	88	Entrapments	94
Maximum Gradient	106	Inaccessibility	110
Total Gradient	90	Reputation	83

Actual Stream Data			
Max Rapids	III-IV	Stream Size	Micro & Large
Average Gradient	36	Length (in miles)	7.5
Maximum Gradient	85	Morphology Type(s)	3&2

The double entry (Micro & Large) for Stream Size in the Actual Stream Data box means that Big Laurel is a micro creek that flows into a big river (the French Broad). The Morphology Types (3&2) entry means that Big Laurel is Type 3 (Densely Obstructed) and the French Broad is Type 2 (Obstructed). Stream size categories and streambed morphology types are explained in Chapter Two.

Karen and Tracy Letterman on Bull Sluice. Chattooga River.
Julie Keller photo.

Andrea Smith paddles bow for Darth Vader (and still manages to smile!).
Chattooga River. Don Ellis photo.

Overview

The overview conveys the most salient information about the trip, and provides a context for all that follows. Overviews vary considerably in content, structure, and focus.

Similar To

Sometimes a great deal about a trip can be gained through comparing and/or contrasting it with other runs. All comparisons are strictly from the perspective of the author. If a stream does not readily suggest comparison with others, this section is omitted.

Top-To-Bottom Itinerary

Significant stream features, from the top to the bottom of each run, are conveniently listed. This list provides a quick preview of prominent stream features and landmarks. Paddlers will find it helpful to scan the itinerary prior to embarking on an unfamiliar stream. A review of this feature will also be useful when attempting to locate specific rapids on a trip.

Description, Summary, Water Levels, Access, Miles From

These sections convey exactly what their titles imply. The trip Description is a blow-by-blow account of the major features of each stream, elaborating upon each entry in the Top-to-Bottom Itinerary. The Summary reiterates key features of the trip. The Access section attempts to provide enough detail to enable a person to find putins and takeouts, including a detailed local map. Miles From provides a global idea of where the trip is located by referencing at least four population centers selected from the four points of the compass. (Mileages are approximate, to the putin, and do not include shuttle distances.)

The section on Water Levels specifies the location of gauges and suggests high, medium, and low flow levels. Water levels reflect both the author's experience and input from forty-two other paddlers. (For details, refer to *Rating Rapids and Rivers: Development of the TRIP Scale,* available from Pahsimeroi Press.) The "Low" level is the minimum water required to support an enjoyable trip. Basically, it is Randy Carter's idea of a "canoeing zero." The "Medium" level is the midpoint of the range of medium flows. "High" indicates the beginning of high flows. This usage differs from the common practice of specifying the maximum level at which a stream can be run.

Specifying maximum runnable levels ignores the indisputable fact that interpretation of maximum water levels changes over time. The general trend over the years has been toward running streams at higher and higher levels. Many levels that are common today were unthinkable only a few years back. If this trend continues, the levels specified as Low, Medium, and High in this book will require periodic upward adjustment.

The data in the table below are hypothetical. They are used to illustrate the following relationships between low, medium and high flow levels, as they would be reported in this book.

Water Levels	Gauge Reading	Interpretation
High	9	Real High
High	8	Medium High
High	7	Where "High" Begins
Medium	6	High Medium
Medium	5	Midpoint of "Medium"
Medium	4	Low Medium
Low	3	High Low
Low	2	Medium Low
Low	1	"Low" or Canoeing Zero

1. Canoeing zero starts at 1 in the accompanying table, and anchors the low end of a range of low flows. The low flow range extends upward (from 1 to 3), and then medium flows begin (at 4 in this example).

2. The midpoint of the medium range of flows is 5 in this example, but medium flows extend both above and below the midpoint (from 4 to 6 in this example).

3. High is the beginning point for high water. In this
example, high begins at 7 and extends upward.
Water that is "too high" is a personal, highly subjective, and constantly changing criterion.

The reader should keep in mind that gauge data are tenuous.
Not only do "acceptable" flow levels change over the years, but the
gauges themselves change. Many of the gauges cited in this
volume are affixed to bridge abutments. As these gauges wear faint
and are repainted, the new numbers may or may not exactly replace
the old ones. This problem is compounded, moreover, when bridges
themselves are replaced. Bridge replacement happens more
frequently than might be expected. During the preparation of this
manuscript (which admittedly spanned several years) new or
replacement bridges were erected across the Big South Fork of the
Cumberland, the Cheat River Canyon, the Piney River, the Tellico
River, and Wilson Creek. Additionally, replacement gauges were
erected on several other streams. Especially if the old gauge was
hand-painted by paddlers, there's virtually no way to guarantee
isomorphism with a new gauge.

Finally, streambeds themselves can shift around significantly,
changing the cross section at the gauging location and thereby
altering all former correlations between this reading and stream
conditions elsewhere along the run. At the distinct risk of preaching
to the choir, be especially wary when running a stream for the first
time (or for the first time in a long time) based on past readings
obtained from a bridge gauge, especially if that bridge or its gauge
has been replaced recently. In short, gauge readings should be
reconfirmed periodically and recalibrated as necessary. Major
unpleasantness and even outright risk of life can result from
misinterpretation of water levels. As always, the preferred policy is
a trip leader who has run the stream recently.

Other Information

This section is customized for each stream description. It
contains information on such things as camping, hiking trails, area

Lynn Aycock-Spangler in the Narrows. Chattooga River. Don Ellis photo.

attractions, suitability of the stream for rafting, and useful auxiliary maps.

Nearby Alternate Trips

This unique feature of *Southeastern Whitewater* identifies nearby whitewater streams, and can be especially helpful when paddlers are exploring unfamiliar territory and attempting to optimally use their limited time.

Conventions Classy and Otherwise

When using the Eastern classification scale to describe rapids in a river section, several conventions have been used.

Convention 1. Use of a single class, such as saying that a certain stretch of river is Class III, denotes that Class III rapids are both prevalent and the most difficult that will be encountered on that run.

Oftentimes, however, trips contain an admixture of rapids of various difficulty levels. In these cases, the following conventions hold.

Convention 2. Two classes separated by a dash, such as saying that a stretch of river is Class II-III or Class III-IV, indicate that multiple rapids of both difficulty levels appear on the run. Thus, Class III-IV indicates that the run consists of both Class III and Class IV rapids, and more than one of each difficulty level can be expected. The Top-To-Bottom Itinerary and Description sections of each stream description will reveal where on the trip major rapids of each difficulty level can be anticipated.

Convention 3. One difficulty class followed by another in parentheses, such as saying that a stretch of river is Class II(III) or Class III(IV), indicates that the stream consists predominantly of rapids of the first difficulty level, but that it has one noteworthy rapid of the level indicated within the parentheses. Thus, Class III(IV) identifies a stream with several Class III rapids and one Class IV rapid. Take note that the two difficulty classes need not be adjacent on the difficulty scale. Goulds Bend on the Obed River, for example, is a Class III(V) trip.

Convention 4. A combination of the two conventions above, such as Class II-III(IV), indicates a trip with multiple Class II and Class III rapids plus a single, noteworthy, Class IV rapid. Chattooga Section

III is an example of a Class II-III(IV) river. The Top-To-Bottom Itinerary and Description sections will identify and locate the parenthetical rapid (Class IV Bull Sluice in the case of Chattooga Section III).

Rapids Plus and Minus

Another interesting outcome of the research study cited in Chapter Two was the finding that one rapid can be almost twice as difficult as another, even though both properly have the same difficulty classification. (An explanation of this finding can be found in *Rating Rapids and Rivers: Development of the TRIP Scale*, by Monte Smith, available from Pahsimeroi Press.)

In recognition of the finding that not all rapids of the same classification are equally difficult, and in fact can differ by almost 100%, a plus (+) and minus (-) convention is utilized throughout this book. To signify that a rapid is on the upper end of its class difficulty range, a plus (+) is entered after its rating, such as Class III+. If a rapid is considered on the lower end of its class, a minus (-) is entered after its rating, such as in Class III-.

Is It Putin, Put in, or Put-in?
Takeout, Take out, or Take-out?

When used as nouns, putin and takeout are spelled as single, un-hyphenated words. (Example: The creek's putin is isolated; its takeout, however, is across from City Hall in downtown Maynard-ville.)

When used as verbs, put in and take out are spelled as two words, un-hyphenated. (Example: Put in at the bridge, and be sure to take out before the ninety foot waterfall, lest you inadvertently mimic Harlan Gamble and plunge to your miserable death on the jagged rocks at the base of the falls.)

Big Laurel Creek

(North Carolina)

TRIP Profile			
Scale Midpoint = 100			
Overall Difficulty	99	Rapids Difficulty	86
Volume x Gradient	129	Continuous Rapids	87
Average Gradient	88	Entrapments	94
Maximum Gradient	106	Inaccessibility	110
Total Gradient	90	Reputation	83

Actual Stream Data			
Max Rapids	III-IV	Stream Size	Micro/Large
Average Gradient	36	Length (in miles)	7.5
Maximum Gradient	85	Morphology Types	3&2

Overview

Big Laurel Creek flows into the French Broad River near Hot Springs, North Carolina, about twenty-five miles due north of Asheville. It's a small creek, but the last three and a half miles of the trip are on the French Broad, which is a sizeable river.

At the putin, Big Laurel looks inconsequential. Downstream, it twists and turns uneventfully for half a mile before serving up its first ledge. It's not much of a ledge, either, but the first one is soon followed by another, and then another. Then bigger drops occur as the tempo builds steadily. Before long the Narrows appear, a high velocity Class IV rapid, even at low water. Once through this fast-moving, steep-walled "Narrows" section, the creek barely slows, spitting and kicking all the way to the French Broad, as if determined to compensate for its diminutive stature and short four mile length with an endless array of technical rapids.

When the creek finally reaches the massive French Broad, the contrast is astonishing, something on the order of a river running into an ocean. In the blink of an eye the environs transition from an intimate cascading creek to one of the largest rivers in the southern mountains, from the stony corridors of Staircase and the Narrows to the big water swells and boils of Frank Bells Rapid. The size contrast between the two streams is extreme, providing a dynamic paddling combination of technical micro creek and big river flush in the same trip.

Similar To. Big Laurel is a blend of Crooked Fork Creek (without the waterfalls) in the Obed/Emory watershed and Little River in the Smokies above the "Sinks." The juxtaposition of a small technical creek with a large river is reminiscent of West Virginia's Middle Fork and Tygart Gorge combo, although the difficulty level of the Carolina duo is substantially less than that of their northern counterparts.

Mile(s)	Big Laurel Creek Top-To-Bottom Itinerary
0.0	Put in at the US 25/70 bridge between Walnut and Hot Springs.
0.5	Four foot ledge (Class II+).
1.0	Staircase (Class III).
1.7	Seven or eight foot ledge with Suddy Hole (Class III) on river right.
2.5	The Narrows (Class IV).
3.0 to 3.5	Several rocky Class II+ and Class III rapids, and one Class III+ boulder jam with pinning potential at low water.
4.0	Confluence with the French Broad.
5.6	Kayak Ledge (Class III).
6.2	Frank Bells Rapid (Class IV).
7.5	Take out upstream of US 25/70 bridge in Hot Springs, at the commercial outfitter on river right.

Description

At first the little creek doesn't seem like much, rocky and winding. Then about half a mile below the putin, it introduces its first ledge, a four foot jumbled drop. After several bumpy Class II or II+ rapids, Staircase is the first real Class III, with three drops spaced so close together that water accelerates in velocity as it plunges through the narrow chutes. The course through Staircase is obvious, but it's a good idea to scout the triple drop for obstructions because it's so constricted. Only at high flows does the rapid become wide enough to permit much variation in how it's run. With high flows a strong hole develops on river right near the final drop and the preferred route eventually shifts from right to left of center. Scout from river right.

The next major ledge contains Suddy Hole (Class III). Situated on river right of the highest ledge on the run, Suddy Hole is formed by a fracture in the face of the rock that produces a highly aerated potential cul-de-sac. Those who drop into Suddy should do so by choice. Scout it first. Otherwise, run left of center over the sloping main drop.

Several other ledges and rapids are exciting but they pale in comparison to the Narrows (Class IV), where Big Laurel necks down between sheer stone walls and flushes at high velocity through a rocky corridor. It's something like a down-sized Worser Wesser (on the Nantahala, below the Outdoor Center). The water through here really moves. The most turbulent part is the last drop, a real bell-ringer. At 2.0 feet on the bridge gauge, this quarter mile section moves like the Ocoee stood on its ear. At lower levels most of the holes disappear but the overall difficulty barely attenuates because of increased technicality and (as paradoxical as this sounds) seemingly faster-moving water. (Perhaps it only seems to move faster at lower water because more of the consequences lurking just beneath the surface are visible.) Paddlers can obtain a "birds eye" view of the last section of the Narrows by scouting from river left. From an old narrow gauge railbed, one can look straight down into the rock-infested concourse. It's quite a sight, and site, but this vantage point literally overhangs the rapid. One misstep will produce an unwanted "splatdown" somewhere in the Narrows.

From the bottom of the Narrows it's only a mile to the French Broad, but in this short distance Big Laurel tries hard to make up for its introductory doldrums. True, there's nothing to match the Class IV intensity of the Narrows, but several smaller rapids appear, one with a particularly nasty undercut alongside the river right cliff (reminiscent of Pat Hills Locker on Crab Orchard Creek), and there's another that's the most obstructed drop on the run, a place that looks like it was imported from the Doe River Gorge.

The French Broad

Big Laurel seems Lilliputian when it reaches the French Broad. From the constricted mayhem of a small, steep creek, paddlers confront the wide open spaces of the French Broad. Although the big river is predominantly flat, Kayak Ledge (Class III) and Frank Bell (Class IV) rapids are noteworthy. When the French Broad carries 10,000+ cfs these two rapids epitomize heavy water, but paddlers able to run Big Laurel Creek at flush should be able to bob through the big stuff if care is exercised to miss the big hydraulics, especially at Kayak Ledge. The French Broad is described separately in this volume. Refer to that description for more information on this part of the trip.

Summary

The Big Laurel and French Broad combination provides not only a lot of whitewater but also a dynamic juxtaposition of radically different rapids and streambed morphologies, from tight and technical steep creek obstructions to big waves and holes in a river with thousands of cfs. Notice that both The Narrows and Frank Bells are commonly rated Class IV in difficulty, although it is hard to imagine two more dissimilar rapids.

Water Levels

Big Laurel is runnable only when the French Broad is fairly high. Generally, about 4,000 cfs are needed on the French Broad (Newport gauge) in order to run Big Laurel Creek, although this will vary according to local rainfall patterns. Another gauge is at the putin. A good range on this gauge is between 0.5 and 1.0 feet. At 1.5 and above, the small stream becomes a grungy flush and loses much of its picturesque charm, but none of its excitement. When Big Laurel is running in excess of 1.5 feet, the French Broad may have 10,000+ cfs and Kayak Ledge and Frank Bell take on conspicuous big water characteristics. Call TVA at (800) 238-2264 for French Broad at Newport gauge readings. (Press code "3" after the recorded message.) Unfortunately, French Broad and Big Laurel flows don't correlate highly.

| Big Laurel Creek Gauge Locations ||
Putin Bridge	French Broad at Newport
Low: 0.0 Medium: 0.6 High: 1.4	Low: 4,000 cfs Medium: 6,000 cfs High: 7,500 cfs

Access

Big Laurel is in western North Carolina almost due north of Asheville, with a putin where US 25/70 crosses the creek between Walnut and Hot Springs. Park on river left downstream of the putin bridge. Take out upstream of the US 25/70 bridge in Hot Springs on river right at the commercial outfitters (obtain permission).

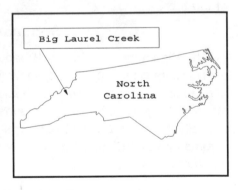

To run the shuttle from the putin, drive north on US 25/70 to the French Broad bridge. Turn right before crossing the French Broad and loop back under the bridge (staying on river right), then continue upstream to the commercial outfitter.

Miles From Big Laurel Creek	
Asheville, NC 27	Johnson City, TN 50
Knoxville, TN 78	Winston-Salem, NC 180

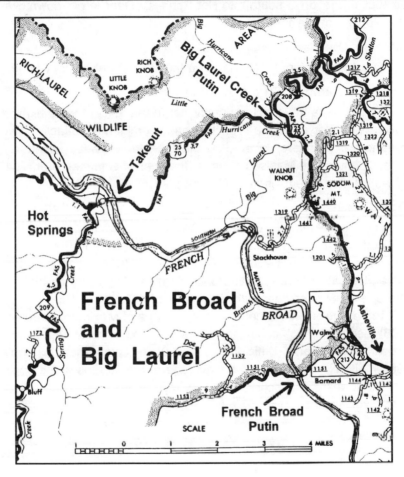

Other Information

Camping

Rocky Bluff National Forest Campground is located three miles south of Hot Springs on NC 209. Directions: From the US 25/70 takeout bridge drive south into Hot Springs. Bear left in downtown Hot Springs at the fork onto NC 209.

Hiking

The Appalachian Trail runs down the main street of Hot Springs.

Rafting Suitability (On a 1 to 7 Scale): 1

Big Laurel is too small and technical to raft, except at its highest flow levels. However, the French Broad is eminently suitable. Two commercial outfitters, located at the takeout, provide guided raft trips. (Contact the Madison County Chamber of Commerce at (704) 689-9351 for current phone numbers.)

TRIP Profile

The most elevated TRIP score (Volume x Gradient Interaction = 129) reflects the large volume of the French Broad and the fact that this large volume drops substantially in the mile that contains both Kayak Ledge and Frank Bells Rapid. (The reader will recall that the average TRIP score on each dimension of difficulty is 100.)

The above average Inaccessibility (110) and Maximum Gradient (106) scores reflect conditions on steep and narrow Big Laurel Creek. The Overall Difficulty score (99) indicates that this trip's overall difficulty is just about the average of the 50 runs in the book.

The lowest TRIP score (83) is for reputation. Big Laurel Creek is not well known.

Nearby Alternate Trips		
Alternate Trip	Rapids Difficulty	TRIP Points
French Broad	III(IV)	88
Nolichucky Gorge	III(IV)	101

Big Sandy Creek

Lower Section: Rockville to Jenkinsburg
(West Virginia)

TRIP Profile			
Scale Midpoint = 100			
Overall Difficulty	133	Rapids Difficulty	166
Volume x Gradient	113	Continuous Rapids	123
Average Gradient	127	Entrapments	140
Maximum Gradient	117	Inaccessibility	137
Total Gradient	115	Reputation	117

Actual Stream Data			
Max Rapids	IV-V(VI)	Stream Size	Small
Average Gradient	77	Length (in miles)	5.5
Maximum Gradient	100	Morphology Type	5

Overview

Big Sandy Creek is steep and continuous, with technical rapids, eye-popping undercut rock formations, and dramatic waterfalls. Photographs of paddlers running its two biggest waterfalls have appeared on posters, guidebook covers, and in paddling magazines. What those dramatic photos fail to convey, however, is that the big drops are only a small part of the total package on this whitewater tour de force. This trip concentrates a lot of heavy-duty whitewater in a few miles. The run includes one Class VI waterfall (Big Splat), a seventeen foot Class IV waterfall (Wonder Falls), a Class V rapid (First Island), impressive rapids like Zoom Flume (Class IV) and Little Splat (Class IV+), a two-mile stretch of continuous Class III-IV

63

water, a Class III rapid with a Class VI hazard (Undercut Rock Rapid), and an astronomical undercuts-per-mile ratio.

Located in Preston County in the northern part of West Virginia, Big Sandy Creek is a tributary of the Cheat River, entering about one hundred yards below Jenkinsburg bridge, the takeout for the Cheat Canyon trip.

Mile(s)	Big Sandy Creek Top-To-Bottom Itinerary
0.0	Rockville Bridge putin. Gauge is on river right.
0.8	Seventeen foot Wonder Falls (Class IV).
1.3	Undercut Rock Rapid (Class III with a Class VI hazard on river right).
2.2	Zoom Flume (Class IV). Visually impressive.
2.7	Little Splat (Class IV+).
2.9	Approach to Big Splat (Class IV).
3.0	Big Splat (Class VI).
3.0 to 5.5	Unremitting Class III-IV water.
5.0	First Island (Class V).
5.4	Second Island (Class IV+).
5.5	Takeout at Jenkinsburg bridge (same takeout as for the Cheat River Canyon trip).

Description

Be sure you're ready to ride this train before the conductor punches your ticket at Rockville. Once on board, you'll discover that the Big Sandy is an express that heads downhill fast and makes no local stops. After two or three forward strokes at the putin, the rest of the day will be an exercise in back paddling and desperately diving for eddies. The Big Sandy is one of the more pushy streams around. Two miles clock in around 100 feet/mile and short distances drop far in excess of that rate.

Class III rapids begin soon after the putin. The first Class III+ sequence occurs at 0.8 miles below the putin and is not overly difficult except that it forms the approach to Wonder Falls (Class IV), a seventeen foot sheer drop. Scout or portage on river right.

Liz Garland at Zoom Flume. Big Sandy Creek. Don Ellis photo.

Undercut Rock Rapid is located a half mile below Wonder Falls and has a Class VI undercut hazard. It's a river-wide ledge with a large rock poised on the brink of the drop on river right. Most of the stream heads toward river right and it also looks like the best place for the paddler. At lower flows, it isn't. The ledge forms a curler/hole which, at lower water levels, surfs objects into the undercut rock. A safer route is to run left of the large rock anywhere there's sufficient water, then eddy out on river right and walk back up to view the undercut situation from downstream. As with many undercuts, this one is more dangerous at low water.

Several other spirited rapids bring the paddler to Zoom Flume, a visually spectacular Class IV that is easier than it appears. The biggest problem is bridging the strange envelope hole in the approach. The flume itself can be run just about anywhere. With higher water the hole on the bottom left is rambunctious.

Big Sandy Gradient	
Mile	**Gradient**
1	50
2	90
3	100
4	70
5	80
0.5	35
Total	425

Big Sandy's real action begins in its third mile with a phenomenon called Little Splat (Class IV+), a multi-drop proposition consisting of ledges, boiling holes, waves, cluttered drops, and slides. Bottom left can be nasty, and that is where most of the water goes. This rapid is best run with an entry on river left, skirting the edge of a boiling hole at the top, working consistently right between obstructions to catch a slide and eddy, before choosing the best approach to the final drop.

Fast water continues into Big Splat, only 150 yards downstream, where the fast current slingshots boats into the Big Splat approach (Class IV), which features an undercut monolith that filters water into a U-shaped drop and then into Big Splat proper, a fifteen foot sheer drop onto a slanting rock. Big Splat is Class VI, West Virginia's answer to State Line Falls on the Watauga Gorge. Photographs of Big Splat hardly do it justice. The approach is bad enough. And then the water lands on a slanted rock!

By this point the river has served up three miles of continuous whitewater, with one Class IV waterfall, one Class VI undercut rock hazard, one Class IV+ (Little Splat), visually dramatic Zoom Flume, and Class VI Big Splat with its intimidating approach. By now the first-time paddler is thinking the remaining miles must be anticlimactic. But in fact, the fun has just begun. The next two and a half miles contain some of the best, most continuous, technical Class III-IV whitewater described in this book. Not a single pool can be found anywhere, but eddies abound. This is technical paddling at its very best, some of the finest play water in the East.

And then, First Island (Class V) appears, looking like something delivered COD from outer space. It embodies immense turbulence. Survive a swim from near the top of First Island and you might win the coveted Annual Eighth Wonder of West Virginia Award! At levels above 6.0 feet, a rocky cheat opens on river left.

Not far downstream, Second Island (Class IV+) appears, and the river right course is preferable. Second Island is like the two miles upstream of First Island, except tighter and steeper.

Finally, the Big Sandy joins forces with the Cheat only a few yards downstream of Jenkinsburg bridge. Take out on river left, just upstream of the confluence, and carry through the rhododendron up to the parking area near the bridge.

Summary

When it ends, paddlers are often in a daze. The stream is outstanding, outrageous, and has few peers when it comes to continuous technical Class III-IV water. Glenn Miller, who shuttles hundreds of paddlers every year from the Cheat Canyon and a few from this stream, has yet to meet anyone who didn't rave about Big Sandy. He recounts the story of one man who finished the run so excited he wanted to show the stream to his fiancee the same day. It was two o'clock in the afternoon. "When's your next shuttle run?" the paddler asked.

"A group's due down the Cheat at six o'clock sharp," replied Glenn.

"We'll be here," the man replied confidently.

Mike Hall on Wonder Falls. Big Sandy Creek. Mayo Gravatt photo.

"Sure enough," recounts Glenn. "He rode out on my two o'clock shuttle, found his fiancee, drove with her back to Rockville, ran the Big Sandy again, and the two of them were already waiting for me when I returned to Jenkinsburg at six o'clock!"

Water Levels

The generally accepted minimum is 5.8 feet (445 cfs) on the Rockville gauge. It has been paddled considerably lower, but the run is unduly risky at sub-minimal levels because its undercut entrapments are so difficult to avoid. Six feet on the Rockville gauge is adequate but still low, and 6.4 (720 cfs) is just about right. High begins about three drops above ideal, and seven feet (1,120 cfs) is generally considered the cutting point between highness and madness. With its ample gradient, it's always pushy. With its inhospitable streambed morphology, it's always risky. Rockville gauge readings can be obtained from (703) 260-0305.

Big Sandy Gauge Location
Rockville Putin
Low: 5.8
Medium: 6.4
High: 6.8

Rockville Gauge Conversion			
Feet	**Cfs**	**Feet**	**Cfs**
5.8	445	7.2	1,280
6.0	530	7.4	1,440
6.2	620	7.6	1,600
6.4	720	7.8	1,770
6.6	830	8.0	1,950
6.8	960	9.0	3,000
7.0	1,120	10.0	4,250

Access

The Big Sandy is located near Albright, West Virginia, a hundred miles south of Pittsburgh and 35 miles from Morgantown.

Put in at the Rockville bridge. To get to Rockville, starting from the commercial campgrounds on Route 26 on the north side of Albright, drive six miles north on WV 26 to Valley Point. Turn left onto Route 15 (Hudson Road). Continue 4.8 miles to Mt. Nebo. Turn right and continue to Rockville.

(At the bottom of the detailed map on the next page, ignore the Albright putin pointer. That putin is for the Cheat River Canyon.)

To shuttle to the takeout, backtrack to Mt. Nebo, bear right at the intersection, and go 2.3 miles to the edge of Cheat Canyon. The takeout is at Jenkinsburg Bridge, 1.2 miles downhill. Glenn Miller, a local resident, runs shuttles for a nominal consideration. He's the definition of dependability and if he's still in business when you read this, his services are highly recommended. The road from Mt. Nebo to Jenkinsburg is rough in good weather. In bad weather, it's a white knuckle special.

A longer route with better roads is available, but it makes for a long shuttle from Rockville. It entails driving south on WV 26 to Albright, across the river to Kingwood, right on WV 7 to Masontown and cross country to arrive at Jenkinsburg from river left. (For details on this alternate shuttle, see the Cheat Canyon description.)

As of this writing, Jenkinsburg Bridge still spanned the Cheat River, but the bridge was closed to vehicular traffic.

Miles From the Big Sandy	
Morgantown, WV 35	Roanoke, VA 242
Pittsburgh, PA 107	Washington, DC 254

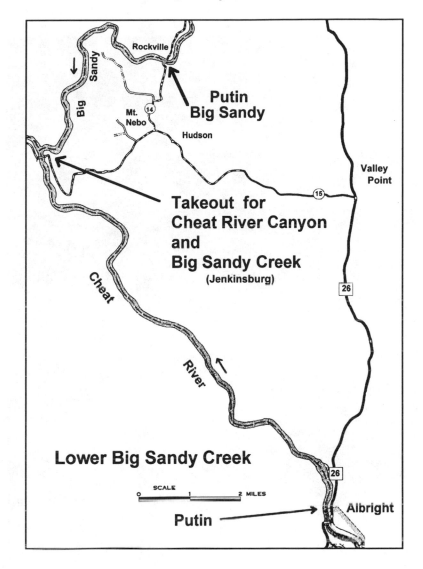

Other Information

Camping

For camping recommendations, see the description of the Cheat River Canyon in this volume.

Rafting Suitability (On a 1 to 7 Scale): Forget it.

Fritz Drescher at Little Splat. Big Sandy Creek in West Virginia.
Don Ellis photo.

TRIP Profile

The TRIP profile for Lower Big Sandy consists of triple digits, top to bottom. The Rapids Difficulty score of 166 makes it the third highest in the book. Entrapments (140) is also sky high, and Inaccessibility (137) and Overall Difficulty (133) are not far behind. Obviously, the lower Big Sandy is not the preferred location for a laid-back Sunday afternoon float trip.

The lowest score in the profile, Volume x Gradient Interaction (113), can be interpreted to mean that nobody gets on this stream when it's carrying a whole lot of water.

Nearby Alternate Trips

When water on the Big Sandy is too low, check out the Cheat River Canyon, Class IV of another kind with the same takeout at Jenkinsburg Bridge.

Big South Fork Gorge
of the Cumberland River
Burnt Mill Bridge to Leatherwood Ford
(Tennessee)

TRIP Profile			
Scale Midpoint = 100			
Overall Difficulty	98	Rapids Difficulty	94
Volume x Gradient	132	Continuous Rapids	87
Average Gradient	73	Entrapments	83
Maximum Gradient	76	Inaccessibility	137
Total Gradient	83	Reputation	117

Actual Stream Data			
Max Rapids	III(IV)	Stream Size	Large
Average Gradient	20	Length (in miles)	11
Maximum Gradient	40	Morphology Type	2

Overview

High on the Cumberland Plateau in Tennessee, the Big South Fork of the Cumberland creates one of the most remarkable and least heralded river gorges in the eastern United States. The sheer sandstone walls of the Big South Fork provide riparian splendor on a scale difficult to believe until experienced first-hand, and impossible to fully appreciate until viewed from river level. This awesome gorge is noteworthy for its magnitude, scenic splendor, rugged inaccessibility, and enjoyable whitewater. It is part of the Big South Fork National River and Recreation Area (BSFNRRA).

74

Although it's one of the most imposing gorges in the Southeast, it's relatively unknown to river runners. Its shuttle is long, it's distant from population centers, and the Obed watershed to the south has more paddling options. Nevertheless, those paddling this relatively unknown chasm for the first time typically arrive at the Leatherwood Ford takeout babbling about its size and majesty. It simply dwarfs most other southeastern gorges. And of the few that it doesn't dwarf in scale, it outdoes entirely in how close it lets paddlers come to its vertical walls as they flush downstream. In the section known as Jakes Hole, the paddler bobs between riparian cliffs which have to be seen to be believed.

The run begins small (Clear Fork River) and becomes large when the New River (*not* the New River of North Carolina, Virginia and West Virginia fame) joins Clear Fork to form the Big South Fork of the Cumberland River. The memorable rapids (and cliffs) occur after confluence of these streams.

Mile(s)	Big South Fork Top-To-Bottom Itinerary
0.0	Put in at Burnt Mill Bridge on Clear Fork River.
4.0	Confluence of Clear Fork and New River, forming the Big South Fork of the Cumberland River.
5.0	Double Falls (Class III+).
5.1	Washing Machine (Class II+).
5.3	The El (Class IV).
5.5	Long pool. Honey Creek Overlook on river left.
5.6 to 6.0	Class III rapids.
6.0	Rions Eddy (Class III+).
7.0 to 8.0	Jakes Hole, with sheer cliffs of 300 to 400 feet and continuous Class II-III rapids. Steepest gradient of the run.
8.5	O & W Railroad trestle. Last (Class III-) rapid.
9.5	North White Oak Creek confluence on river left.
11.0	Takeout at Leatherwood Ford Bridge.

Similar To. Similar to the Cheat Canyon in West Virginia. In common with the Cheat, the Big South Fork has an awesome gorge, horrendous shuttle and rugged inaccessibility, but it has less volume than the Cheat, a less obstructed streambed, fewer big rapids and several stretches of flat water. With 3,000 cfs the Big South Fork looks a lot like the New River Gorge.

Description

Clear Fork River

Average gradient in the four miles from Burnt Mill Bridge to the New River confluence is 23 feet/mile. Watch for three Class II-III rapids near the confluence. The first rapid in the series is a succession of steep ledges with fast-moving water. At the second rapid in the series, the flow is constricted to a width of about twenty feet and dropped four feet into a riverwide hole. The third of these "warmup" rapids is another ledge-garden.

Big South Fork Gorge

From its origin at the confluence of the New and Clear Fork Rivers, the Big South Fork of the Cumberland River flows north -- and deep into Kentucky -- before turning around and heading back south through Nashville, Tennessee. Its first seven miles are unquestionably its most majestic, as its waters plunge through one of America's scenic treasures, the Big South Fork Gorge, now a National River and Recreation Area.

After the confluence, the Big South Fork sweeps commandingly to the right and into a series of waves and holes which appear inconsequential, but one or two strokes in this water and it's obvious that the hydraulic gears have shifted. The stream character has changed from a small, technical stream to a full-grown river. The power of the first few rapids contrast dramatically with the smaller ones upstream on Clear Fork.

The overall gradient of the Big South Fork in its first seven miles to Leatherwood is 18 feet/mile, but this modest figure belies the power of its major rapids. The Big South Fork in these miles has a pool/ledge conformation, with long pools accounting for little gradient followed by sudden, forceful drops. The force is nowhere better demonstrated than about a mile below the Big South Fork origin where three of the most powerful rapids in the Gorge appear in close succession. The first of the triumvirate, Double Falls, occurs with no

Awesome backdrop courtesy of the Big South Fork (of the Cumberland) Gorge. Water courtesy of the El. Flawless tandem paddling courtesy of Dick and Elise Creswell. Photo courtesy of Don Ellis.

Ed Caudill at Double Falls in the Big South Fork (of the Cumberland) Gorge. Don Ellis photo.

warning other than a complex boulder field into which the stream disappears and through which the paddler cannot see. Scout this double declivity (Class III+) from river right. Both drops are formidable, and the large rock at river left near the end may be undercut. Unlike most rapids, Double Falls does not become much easier at lower flows. Portage is easier along river left, and a left "cheat" chute opens at high flows.

Washing Machine (Class II+), consisting of a turbulent drop between two boulders, is only a few yards below Double Falls. Around the next bend is the El (Class IV). Although not as impressive visually as Double Falls, it's at least as difficult, with a 50 yard approach through funny water that culminates with a swirling plunge over a low ledge. The drop over the ledge is complicated by a diagonal curler (a tube, almost), holes, rocks, evil spirits, etc., but the real nemesis is a hole upstream of the ledge. This hole looks innocuous but it grabs boats, paddles, floating bodies, etc, with a vengeance. Throw ropes and safety boats are often needed at the bottom of the El.

Below the El is a long pool. It ends at the base of Honey Creek overlook (mile 5.5) in the Honey Creek Pocket Wilderness. On river left an emergency access trail can be located. A strenuous climb leads to the Honey Creek overlook and then via secondary roads to either Burnt Mill Bridge (the putin) or Armaithwaite. After the Honey Creek pool comes half a mile of Class III rapids. These rapids are both technical and powerful. As the intensity of the water builds, the height and majesty of the sheer gorge walls increase commensurately. In this section, the Big South Fork resembles the Cheat Canyon, both in scenery and whitewater.

Seven miles downstream of the putin, sheer bluffs attain heights of 300 to 400 feet. Pine Creek enters on river right and marks the beginning of a broad 180 degree turn as the river sweeps into a place called Jakes Hole. Jakes Hole features the most impressive cliffs in the gorge, a mile of continuous Class II-III whitewater, and the trip's steepest overall gradient (40 feet/mile).

The old O & W railroad trestle, at mile 8.5, marks the last good rapid. Downstream of O&W, a long pool leads to confluence with North White Oak Creek (river left), below which the current speeds up considerably. About a half mile above the Leatherwood Ford takeout, the Big South Fork swings suddenly right and into several large boulders, producing the last good play spot on the river.

Summary

The Big South Fork Gorge is a Tennessee Cumberland Plateau classic, as notable for its setting as for its whitewater. The river runs through a gorge with towering vertical cliffs, many of which rise straight up from river level for hundreds of feet, having few parallels in eastern America.

Water Levels

Gauge readings (at Stearns, several miles downstream of the takeout) are available from the Army Corps of Engineers at (615) 736-5635.

Big South Fork Gauge Location Stearns
Low: 1,000 cfs Medium: 2,000 cfs High: 3,000 cfs

Access

The Big South Fork Gorge is in northeast Tennessee between Jamestown and Oneida.

The main access routes include I-75, US 27, and US 127, which run north-south, and I-40, TN 52, TN 53, and KY 92, which run east-west.

From I-75 take either KY 92 or TN 63, both of which connect with US 27, a north-south route that parallels the eastern BSFNRRA boundary. From I-40, west-bounders should take US 27 north, and east-bounders should take US 127 north to TN 52, which skirts the southern boundary of the BSFNRRA.

Put in at Burnt Mill Bridge on Clear Fork River. To reach Burnt Mill from US 27, look for a turn to the east about half a mile south of the New River crossing. Continue through Mountain View and

Black Creek to Crossroads.
Turn right and drive about a
mile to Burnt Mill Bridge.

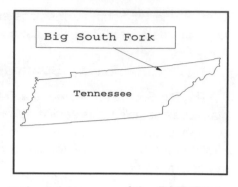

Take out at Leatherwood
Ford Bridge, near Oneida.
To reach Leatherwood Ford
from Oneida, take Route 297
(also called Coopertown
Road) east for about five
miles, then continue on Lea-
therwood Ford Road, the only east-west traverse of the BSFNRRA.
Anticipate at least an hour and a half for the round-trip shuttle.

Miles From the Big South Fork Gorge	
Knoxville, TN 70	Chattanooga, TN 125
Nashville, TN 155	Asheville, NC 190
Cincinnati, OH 225	Atlanta, GA 240

Other Information

Camping

The principal campground facility in the area is Bandy Creek,
located on Leatherwood Ford Road in the heart of the BSFNRRA,
about three miles west of the Leatherwood Ford takeout. This
campground is about midway between Oneida and Jamestown.

Pickett State Park, located on TN 154 north of Jamestown, also
has a campground.

Hiking

No established trails parallel the river through the gorge. Walking
within the main gorge is exceedingly difficult because of the many
huge boulders. A better approach is to walk along the gorge rim.
Honey Creek Pocket Wilderness provides an excellent view of the
upper gorge, and some strenuous hiking for those wishing to
descend into the chasm.

According to park rangers, it's possible to cross the river on the
old O&W railroad trestle, about three miles upstream of Leatherwood

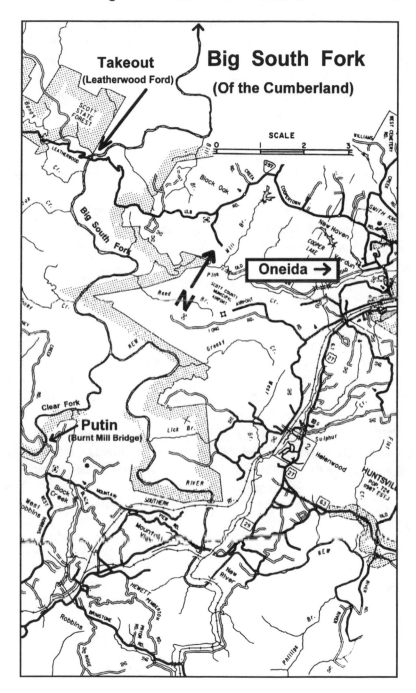

Big South Fork
(Of the Cumberland)

Takeout
(Leatherwood Ford)

Oneida →

Putin
(Burnt Mill Bridge)

Ford, and continue up North White Oak Creek to the vicinity of Zenith Mines. For other hiking suggestions, contact the BSFNRRA administrators: National Park Service; Route 3, Box 401; Oneida, TN 37841. Phone: (615) 879-3625.

Also, nearby Pickett State Park (on TN 154 north of Jamestown) has several hiking trails.

Lodging

Cabins are available at Pickett State Park.

Charit Creek Lodge, located at the confluence of Charit Creek and Station Camp Creek, is open year-round and operates similar to LeConte Lodge in the Smokies. (It's managed by the same group.) It has no electricity and is accessible only by horseback or foot trail. Open year-round. Call (615) 429-5704 for more information.

(For other information on Mt LeConte Lodge, see the section on Hiking for the upper Little River in the Smokies.

Maps

A color map which clearly marks river access points is available from the Park Service for a nominal charge. A trail map is also available for part of the BSFNRRA. (Contact: National Park Service; Route 3, Box 401; Oneida, Tennessee 37841; Phone (615) 879-3625). **Suitability for Rafting (On a 1 to 7 Scale):** 7

The Big South Fork is premier rafting water. Raft rentals and commercial guided raft trips are available in Oneida, Jamestown, Whitley City (KY), and Knoxville. The Park Service issues an annual Fact Sheet on commercial licensees. (Contact: National Park Service; Route 3, Box 401; Oneida, Tennessee 37841; Phone (615) 879-3625)

TRIP Profile

The two most elevated scores, Inaccessibility (137) and Volume x Gradient Interaction (132), tell the story. It's isolated, and when the water rises the rapids get big. Notice the puny gradient figures.

Nearby Alternate Trips

Clear Fork River from Brewster Bridge to Burnt Mill Bridge is described elsewhere in this volume. This is the section of Clear Fork River that lies upstream of the putin for the Big South Fork Gorge.

North White Oak Creek, a Class II-III Big South Fork tributary, is runnable after locally heavy rainfall. Unfortunately, the North White Oak Creek shuttle is even longer than the one for the Big South Fork Gorge. Nevertheless, when the water is up and the shuttle can be arranged, it's a worthy wilderness excursion.

The twenty-five miles of the Big South Fork downstream of Leatherwood Ford are used for overnight camping trips, with a takeout in the vicinity of Blue Heron. Predominantly flat water, the trip has one Class III+ (Angel Falls, about two miles downstream of the putin) and two spirited Class II+ rapids near the takeout. This overnighter makes a fine fall colors trip.

All the above alternate trips can be located on maps available from the National Park Service. See above for the address and phone number.

Another paddling alternative is the Obed/Emory watershed, approximately an hour's drive south of the Big South Fork Gorge, with its 142 miles of whitewater trips. Several Obed trips are described in this volume, and the entire watershed is treated in detail in *A Paddler's Guide to the Obed/Emory Watershed* by Monte Smith.

Cartecay River

(Georgia)

TRIP Profile			
Scale Midpoint = 100			
Overall Difficulty	74	Rapids Difficulty	76
Volume x Gradient	71	Continuous Rapids	63
Average Gradient	71	Entrapments	72
Maximum Gradient	74	Inaccessibility	92
Total Gradient	79	Reputation	72

Actual Stream Data			
Max Rapids	II(III)	Stream Size	Small
Average Gradient	18	Length (in miles)	9
Maximum Gradient	40	Morphology Type	2

Overview

Novice and intermediate paddlers looking for moderately difficult technical rapids will enjoy the Cartecay, located near Ellijay, Georgia. Several of its miles contain sufficient gradient to produce continuous Class II water conditions, along with three easy Class III rapids. One mile drops 40 feet and four others exceed 20 feet/mile. Its rapids provide a good training course for novices and junior intermediates interested in honing their whitewater maneuvering skills. Rapids in the middle miles are small-scale versions of steep creek conditions found on more difficult runs, providing opportunities for practicing eddy turns, ferrying techniques, and eddy hopping.

Mile(s)	Cartecay River Top-To-Bottom Itinerary
0.0	Putin.
0.0 to 0.9	Mostly flat with small riffles.
0.9	Cabins and summer homes appear on river right.
1.0	Two foot ledge, after which stream picks up tempo.
1.0 to 1.7	Fast-moving mild whitewater.
1.8	Signal Island.
1.9 to 5.0	Class II(III).
1.9	First Class III- rapid.
2.0	Swerving Right Turn (Class II+).
2.5	First Falls (Class III-).
2.6	Class II+ rapid.
2.7	Covered bridge across stream.
3.0	Long pool.
3.2 to 3.6	Moving flatwater with intermittent shoals.
3.7 to 4.0	Class II rapids.
4.0	Clear Creek Falls (Class III-).
4.0 to 5.0	Rock gardens, some to Class II+.
5.0 to 6.0	Fast-moving, mild whitewater.
6.0	Alternate takeout. Not open year-round.
6.0 to 9.0	Flat water with current.
9.0	Take out beside GA 52

Description

For a mile downstream of the putin, the Cartecay meanders through north Georgia hill country and a mixed forest of hardwoods, white pine, and rhododendron. For most of the first mile the stream is completely covered by a canopy of overarching branches.

When cabins first appear on river right, stream tempo increases noticeably. Then, for almost a mile the stream moves along at a pleasantly rapid pace and features one or two spots that may be Class II. The first Class III- rapid appears after a small island, and is a U-shaped configuration with a double drop through a small rock garden. This rapid is followed immediately by Swerving Right Turn, a Class II+ rapid.

The first of two sizeable "slides" is called First Falls (Class III-). It's more like one of the lower Chauga's slides than a waterfall, with a total drop of about eight feet. Upon first inspection it's rather intimidating, but it looks worse than it is. As good a route as any is down the middle, full speed ahead through all the waves and holes. Outlet from a small pool at the bottom is into a stretch of fast-moving technical Class II rapids upstream of a covered bridge spanning the stream. The next major drop is Clear Creek Falls (Class III-), which is preceded and followed by a stretch of technical Class II rapids. More like a waterfall than the upstream slide, Clear Creek Falls is also potentially more hazardous. The best route depends on water flow, although at most flows the only route is far left. Scout from river left and beware the river left ledge of rock. A casualty reportedly occurred here several years ago, a head injury. It probably occurred at low water following a capsize into the river left rock ledge. At high flows a hydraulic develops along the base of the drop.

Very pleasant Class II technical rapids follow Clear Creek Falls for some distance, followed by a mile or so of fast-moving mild whitewater. Then the tilt of the streambed progressively moderates, producing conditions of moving flatwater. The last three miles are flat, but current continues to the takeout. A final small ledge appears just upstream of the usual takeout.

Summary

The middle miles offer about a dozen substantial rapids that range in difficulty from Class II to Class III-, including two "slides" similar to those found on the lower Chauga in South Carolina. The stream moves along in a lively fashion most of the time, even when rapids are absent.

Once a showcase of north Georgia rolling hill country, aesthetic qualities of the stream have deteriorated due to progressive encroachment of cabins, cottages, and summer homes. Fortunately, most of the structures blend reasonably well with their surroundings.

Hopefully, owners of the structures will take an active interest in preserving stream quality.

Water Levels

The stream is small and ordinarily runnable only in winter and spring. About 1.8 feet on the Ellijay gauge is paddling zero. Two and a half to three feet is about right for experienced paddlers. Mountaintown Expeditions, located nearby, may be able to provide a gauge reading: (706) 635-2524 or 635-2726.

Cartecay Gauge Location River right at the takeout
Low: 2.0 = 210 cfs Medium: 2.6 = 470 cfs High: 3.0 = 720 cfs

Cartecay Takeout Gauge Conversion			
Feet	**Cfs**	**Feet**	**Cfs**
1.8	160	3.2	880
2.0	210	3.4	1,020
2.4	360	3.6	1,210
2.6	470	3.8	1,390
2.8	590	4.0	1,570
3.0	720	5.0	2,550

Access

The Cartecay is located due north of Atlanta, near Ellijay, on GA Route 52 between Dahlonega and Chatsworth.

Put in at the 101 Lower Cartecay Road bridge. To reach the putin from Ellijay, take GA 52 east about five miles and look for the right turn beside an apple packing house. Parking is limited at the putin.

The usual takeout is alongside GA 52 near the gauge about a mile east of Ellijay. The shuttle is easy, a straight shot along GA Route 52 and 101 Lower Cartecay Road.

An alternate takeout avoids the last three miles of flatwater, but is not open year-round. To reach the alternate takeout from Ellijay, travel east on Highway 52 and turn right at the garbage dumpsters (first road after the Gilmer County jail).

Miles From the Cartecay River	
Chattanooga, TN 65	Greenville, SC 148
Atlanta, GA 89	Birmingham, AL 185

Other Information

Camping

Amicolola State Park is 16 miles east of the takeout (on GA 52) and Fort Mountain State Park is 20 miles west on the same serpentine roadway. Lake Conasauga Campground is north of Fort Mountain on the edge of the Cohutta Wilderness.

Hiking

The southern terminus of the Appalachian Trail is nearby (Springer Mountain), and the Cohutta Wilderness is a few miles northwest.

Miscellaneous

Mountaintown Outdoor Expeditions (MOE) is located on the river (just off 101 Lower Cartecay Road). MOE operates a hostel, rents boats, and runs shuttles: (706) 635-2524 or 635-2726.

Suitability for Rafting (On a 1 to 7 Scale): 5

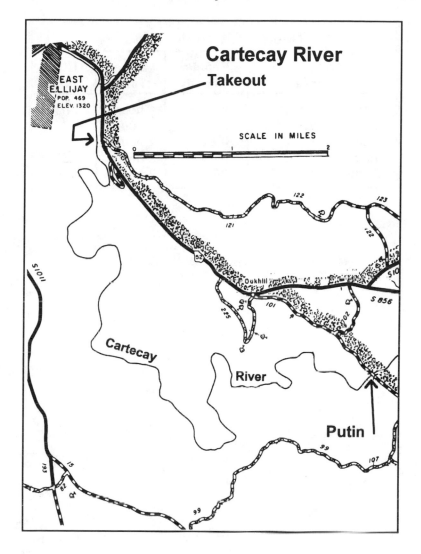

Cartecay River

Takeout

SCALE IN MILES

Putin

Nearby Alternate Trips			
Alternate Trip	Rapids Difficulty	Drive Time	TRIP Points
Upper Conasauga	IV	1 hour	na
Lower Conasauga	II	1 hour	72
Ocoee River	III(IV)	1 hour	104
Chattooga Section III	III(IV)	2 hours	86
Chattooga Section IV	IV(V)	2 hours	116

North Fork of the Catawba

(North Carolina)

TRIP Profile			
Scale Midpoint = 100			
Overall Difficulty	75	Rapids Difficulty	75
Volume x Gradient	68	Continuous Rapids	75
Average Gradient	82	Entrapments	72
Maximum Gradient	81	Inaccessibility	83
Total Gradient	74	Reputation	60

Actual Stream Data			
Max Rapids	II(III)	Stream Size	Small
Average Gradient	29	Length (in miles)	5.5
Maximum Gradient	50	Morphology Type	2

Overview

The North Fork of the Catawba, located near Marion, North Carolina, has an abundance of Class II rapids and a few easy Class IIIs. It's located in the vicinity of Wilson Creek, and when that little firecracker is too high to run, the Catawba is probably about right. Neither its rapids nor its scenery are on a par with Wilson Creek, but the Catawba is nevertheless a pleasant run. At least until the last two miles, where flatwater predominates, forests have been over-timbered, and mining activities infringe. Water quality varies from crystal clear to sediment-laden, depending on rainfall patterns.

The overall gradient of 29 feet/mile is not uniformly distributed. The first three miles contain most of the gradient, with the first two miles dropping at nearly 50 feet/mile through technical, rocky Class II and Class II+ rapids, some of which become Class III- at higher

91

flows. The action doesn't abate substantially until near the end of mile three. The next two miles are considerably flatter, although not without a surprising rapid here and there. Tempo revives considerably during the last half mile, and the trip ends with a nice one-two combination of good Class II(II+) rapids.

Mile(s)	N. Fork Catawba Top-To-Bottom Itinerary
0.0	Put in at the railroad trestle one mile outside Woodlawn.
0.0 to 2.0	Steepest gradient of the run, at 40 to 50 feet/mile. Numerous technical Class II rapids.
0.3	First technical Class II+.
2.7	Railroad trestle. Class II+ rapid underneath.
3.0	Class III ledge.
3.5	Another Class III ledge.
3.6 to 5.3	Relative inaction. Scenery degrades.
5.3 to 5.6	Class II rapids again.
5.6	Takeout.

Description

The first rapid appears about 600 yards downstream of the putin, just as farmer Brown's barn recedes from view. It's a long, technical rock garden, indicative of other rapids in the first three miles.

A railroad crosses the stream 2.7 miles below the putin. Beneath the trestle sits a small island, forming Class II+ rapids on both sides. The left side drops gradually; the right side is steeper.

The trestle signals that two sizeable ledges are imminent. The first ledge appears only a few yards downstream of the trestle. The sloping drop of about five feet can be run most anywhere. Scout from river right. The second ledge, with about six feet in total drop, appears about a half mile downstream. This one requires some maneuvering during the drop if run on the right side. Scout it from river right. Both ledges are big enough to get the adrenalin pumping, but they're basically easy, sloping descents.

Unfortunately, the second ledge introduces about two miles of relative inaction. These miles are not entirely flat but the quality and frequency of rapids diminish relative to the miles above the two big ledges. Just upstream of the bend revealing the takeout bridge is an enjoyable Class II+ rapid and then, only 100 yards from the takeout, is another Class II. These last two rapids are strategically located, leaving the paddler with a pleasant taste of whitewater after the dose of flatwater in the previous two miles.

Summary

Known mostly to local paddlers because of its small drainage and fast runoff, this one is well worth checking out if you're in the area and enjoy paddling Class II-III technical creek water. The big question about the Catawba is always water availability. The drainage area is tiny, and hence runoff occurs quickly.

Water Levels

A gauge is on the railroad trestle abutment at the putin. From afar, the Nolichucky is a crude index of water availability in this stream. Generally, the Nolichucky must be over 3,000 cfs. High readings on the Doe and Watauga (in the vicinity of 700+ cfs) are positive indicators also.

North Fork Catawba Gauge Location Putin
Low: 0.0
Medium: 0.5
High: 1.0

Access

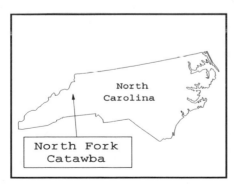

The North Fork of the Catawba is in western North Carolina between Asheville and Morganton, a few miles north of Marion. Marion is 35 miles east of Asheville, near I-40.

From the interstate, take the US 221 exit north through Marion and another eight miles to the small community of Woodlawn. Turn right and drive a short distance past the thread plant to the river. Turn right and follow the stream 150 yards to the putin at the railroad trestle. The gauge, what's left of it, is painted on this trestle.

To reach the takeout, backtrack to Woodlawn and drive south on US 221 about 5.7 miles to Hankins Road (#1501). Turn left and drive about 3.5 miles to Burnetts Landing on Lake James. Turn left and drive one mile to the takeout.

Miles From the North Fork of the Catawba	
Asheville, NC 50	Charlotte, NC 95
Johnson City, TN 70	Winston-Salem, NC . . 120

Nearby Alternate Trips		
Alternate Trip	Rapids Difficulty	TRIP Points
Doe River Gorge	III-IV	117
French Broad	III(IV)	88
Nolichucky Gorge	III(IV)	101
Watauga Gorge	IV(V)	142
Wilson Creek	IV(V)	108

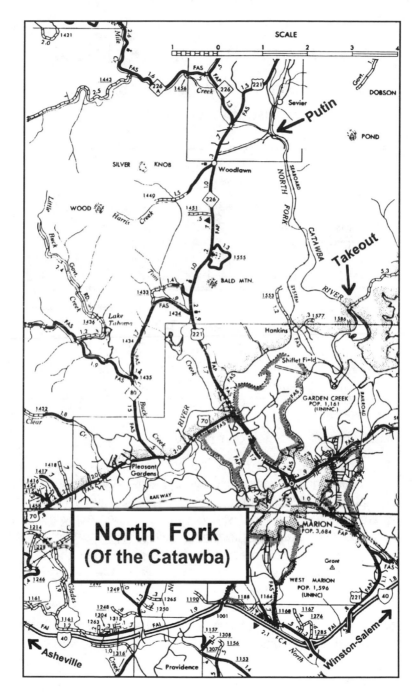

North Fork
(Of the Catawba)

Chattooga River: Section III

Earls Ford to US 76

(South Carolina)

TRIP Profile			
Scale Midpoint = 100			
Overall Difficulty	86	Rapids Difficulty	86
Volume x Gradient	92	Continuous Rapids	63
Average Gradient	80	Entrapments	83
Maximum Gradient	74	Inaccessibility	110
Total Gradient	99	Reputation	94

Actual Stream Data			
Max Rapids	III(IV)	Stream Size	Medium
Average Gradient	27	Length (in miles)	12
Maximum Gradient	40	Morphology Type	2

Overview

The Chattooga, which forms the border between Georgia and South Carolina, is unquestionably one of the most attractive streams in the Southeast. It's also one of the most popular, justly famous for its gnarly rapids, stands of towering white pine, and eerily beautiful rock formations. Much of the movie *Deliverance* was shot on the Chattooga, and that widespread cinematic exposure brought the river an enormous amount of attention. Its popularity has never waned. It's one of the most floated rivers in the country.

Three sections of the Chattooga are boatable. (Section I is closed to boaters.) Section II is predominantly flat and therefore not described in this volume. Sections III and IV are the popular

96

whitewater runs. Whatever you do, don't get them confused. Section III, starting at Earls Ford and ending at US 76, is moderate whitewater that's suitable for intermediate paddlers. Section IV, beginning at US 76 and ending on Lake Tugaloo, is suitable only for advanced paddlers.

On Section III (the focus of this description) rapids are Class II-III, with the exception of Class IV Bull Sluice near the end of the run. But what this magnificent section lacks in continuous or high difficulty rapids, it more than compensates for in scenery.

Mile(s)	Chattooga Section III Top-To-Bottom Itinerary
0.0	Earls Ford putin.
0.4	Warwoman Rapid (Class II).
1.7	Rockgarden. Look for slanting rocks in the stream.
2.5	Dicks Creek Ledge (Class III).
3.0	Sandy Ford (Alternate putin).
3.5	The Narrows (Class III).
4.1	Second Ledge (Class III).
5.7	Eye-of-the-Needle (Class III).
8.5	Fall Creek Falls (River left).
8.6 to 9.5	Class II+ water, including Rollercoaster.
9.5	Painted Rock (Class III+).
9.6 to 10.5	Pools, slow current.
11.7	Bull Sluice (Class IV).
11.8	Take out on river left.
12.0	US 76 bridge.

Description

The first two miles are filled with pleasant Class I-II rapids, with one Class II+ that requires an "S" turn on river left. Some of the rock formations, especially about two miles downstream of the putin, are easily recognizable from the movie *Deliverance*.

Dicks Creek Ledge (Class III) is the first rapid of significance. Recognizable from upstream by water cascading down a rock face on river right, Dicks Creek Ledge (aka First Ledge) requires good boat control through two 90 degree turns. Except at high water, it's scoutable from a rock ledge in mid river. Above 2.0 feet on the US 76 bridge gauge, alternate routes consisting of four-to-five foot drops are possible to the right of the scouting rock.

A mile downstream of Dicks Creek (just past Sandy Ford) look for the Narrows (Class III). This is a long, two-stage rapid, with funky, boiling cross currents. The first stage is a staircase that funnels the river to about 40 feet in width, with the biggest drop/hole/wave at the bottom. In the second stage, the stream twists through a stony corridor of eerie rock formations. Stay river right toward the end of stage two. River left can be blocked with logs.

Second Ledge is a half mile below the Narrows (about four miles downstream of the putin). The stream fans out to a hundred yards or wider and pitches over a five to six foot ledge. A few feet off the river left bank is the best place to run over the drop. Once the initial intimidation factor is overcome, this waterfall is a great play spot, an excellent place to practice waterfall "jumping." The drop has a "soft" landing and decent recovery opportunity. Scoutable left or right. Easily portaged at lower flows over the exposed rocks to the right of the preferred drop, but at higher flows, trying to portage is more effort than it's worth.

Eye-of-the-Needle is next, a Class III chute produced by a river right outcropping. The chute directs the paddler toward river left rocks, but a pillow and cross current kicks boats back right and through the chute.

The best route through the next major rapid, Painted Rock (Class III+), depends on water level. The old way of running this rapid was pretty stupid, entailing an entrance on the left that required paddling like hell toward river right in order to avoid ramming the rock at the bottom. (The rock was allegedly "painted" by all the boats it had crunched.) Except at very low water, a preferred route is to enter right of center angled sharply toward river right paddling briskly to make a dynamic turn into the big eddy at the bottom.

The Notorious Bull Sluice

After Painted Rock, relative slackwater ensues for about 2.5 miles. These miles are slow at low water, consisting predominantly of long pools. With more than 3.0 feet on the US 76 gauge, however, they pass in a flash.

And regardless of water level, the grand finale of the trip is yet to come, located just above the takeout. It's called Bull Sluice, and it's unquestionably the piece de resistance of the whole run, a benchmark Class IV of the same general caliber as the best and biggest rapids on Section IV. Formidable at all flow levels, the Bull is best treated with circumspection. (If not circumambulation!) This bull has killed. It embodies immense power, and like numerous other Chattooga rapids, it harbors "honeycomb" rock formations. From upstream the rapid can be recognized by a gargantuan outcropping of rock from river right (Georgia side). In summer months a gargantuan gaggle of would-be paddlers will be perched on the rock, agonizing over whether to go for the juice or to portage the intimidating drop. Unless you've run it many times, Bull Sluice is not the rapid to run blind. Stop well above on river right and walk down to the large rock to scout.

This rapid has been run successfully using every conceivable route. However, a mistake at Bull Sluice can result in a drubbing. Many people are fooled by the angle of the ledge, and run over the drop with their boats pointed parallel with the flow of the current. Invariably, this approach results in a thrashing. Study the ledge angles carefully and consider, at low to moderate water, taking the drop perpendicular to the angled ledge into the big hole (with your boat pointed toward Georgia), turning hard left after the first drop and exiting river right of Decapitation Rock.

As with all big, powerful rapids, this one pushes you into it faster than you think it will. When you start into the Bull, the approach will be moving much faster than it seemed to be moving five minutes earlier, when you were safely perched on the big Georgia rock, condescendingly watching other hapless turkeys as they made their pathetically inadequate moves. The velocity of its approach is one reason why the Bull is so hard to run. The current blows boats over the ledge before most paddlers have time to set their desired angle. To slow things down, some paddlers elect to visit the big river left eddy before taking the drop into the hole. But peel outs from this eddy are dynamic affairs, and always deliver the paddler to the brink of the drop sooner than anticipated.

Monte Smith rides the river bull. Bull Sluice, that is. Chattooga River. Don Ellis photo.

Locals know this rapid well (they body surf it and play in its honeycombs at low water), and they didn't name it the Bull without good reason. (William Nealy once wrote that the best thing about the Bull is that ambulances can practically drive up to it!)

The huge rock on Georgia's side (river right) provides a splendid viewing stand. Linger awhile on a high traffic summer weekend and enjoy the procession. The takeout is only 200 yards downstream of the Bull.

(A story about Bull Sluice, entitled: On The Cover of Drift Indicator, appears in *River Stories: Tales From Bo Rockerville,* by Monte Smith, available from Pahsimeroi Press.)

Summary

With 2.0 to 3.0 feet on the US 76 gauge, Section III is an ideal tandem canoe run. There's enough action to challenge most tandem teams, yet the rapids are generally forgiving in case of mishap. Portages around the more difficult rapids are easy. Photographic opportunities abound.

Tandem runs can be appropriate in another way. A partner can be helpful in getting equipment to the putin. A quarter-mile haul lurks between the Earls Ford parking lot and the putin. And it's a long quarter mile.

The biggest hazard on this section of the river -- aside from raft tourists yelling inane questions like, "Hey, are you Mel Gibson?" -- is Bull Sluice. Those unfamiliar with this rapid definitely should scout it before running it for the first time.

Water Levels

Low runs on Chattooga Section III are pretty miserable affairs because in many places the river fans out across shallow shoals and gravel bars. And the pools seem endless at low water. Technically skilled solo paddlers can navigate Section III as low as 1.4 feet (350 cfs) on the US 76 gauge. The 1.4 level, however, will produce a lot of discord for tandem crews, as well as frustration for solo paddlers averse to low water runs. For most paddlers, paddling zero falls somewhere around 1.7 feet (570 cfs). Many tandem crews have found the range between 1.8 feet (650 cfs) and 2.4 feet (1,280 cfs) to be ideal. A moderately healthy level (for any boat) is 3.0 feet (2,000 cfs), and Bull Sluice at this level is the devil.

The Chattooga holds its water pretty well because of its watershed size. It's runnable during the spring and through most of the summer. Various outfitters around the Chattooga will report the water level by phone.

Chattooga Whitewater Shop	803 647 9083
Nantahala Outdoor Center	704 488 2175
Southeastern Expeditions	706 782 4331
Wildwater, Ltd.	803 647 5336

Chattooga Gauge Location
US 76 Bridge - River Left

Low:	1.7 =	570 cfs
Medium:	2.4 =	1,280 cfs
High:	3.0 =	2,000 cfs

Chattooga Gauge Conversion

Feet	Cfs	Feet	Cfs
1.0	155	2.0	840
1.1	195	2.2	1,040
1.2	240	2.4	1,280
1.3	290	2.6	1,510
1.4	355	2.8	1,750
1.5	420	3.0	2,000
1.6	490	3.4	2,550
1.7	570	3.6	2,840
1.8	650	4.0	3,450
1.9	740	5.0	5,200

Access

The Chattooga River forms the state boundary between South Carolina and Georgia. (Downstream, its name changes to the

Savannah.) All official putins and takeouts are located on the South Carolina side.

US 76 is the usual vehicular conduit to this part of up-state north-western South Carolina. The US 76 bridge over the Chattooga River is about midway between West-minster, South Carolina and Clayton, Georgia. This bridge is the focal point in most Chattooga excursions, serving as the takeout for Section III and the putin for Section IV, as well as the location for the visitor center. The gauge (river left) is located here also.

The putin for Section III is at Earls Ford and takeout is at or above the US 76 bridge. To run the shuttle from the US 76 bridge, drive 2.5 miles into South Carolina toward Long Creek. Turn left onto SC 196 and head toward Oconee State Park, passing the Nantahala Outdoor Center Chattooga Outpost along the way. In about six or seven miles, intersect with Whetstone Road (SC 193). Turn left at the 4-way stop intersection and drive about four miles to the parking lot, where the road ends.

All river user groups must fill out a registration form (one form per group), available at the Earls Ford and US 76 parking areas. The carbon copy of this form is your permit to run the river, and someone in each group must keep it in their possession at all times while on the river. Registration requirements change from time-to-time. Check the posting boards at the US 76 visitor center to make sure you're complying with the latest requirements.

Miles From the Chattooga River	
Greenville, SC 70	Asheville, NC 135
Atlanta, GA 135	Knoxville, TN 144

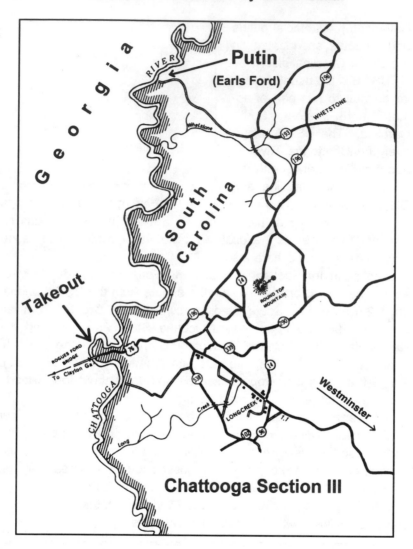

Other Information

Camping

    A primitive campground is located alongside US 76. Look for the unmarked turnoff on the left, about half a mile into South Carolina. It's free, and not an unpleasant site, located in thick piney woods. If you rise early and slip through the woods to the river (well upstream of the US 76 bridge), you can often spot (or at least hear) wild turkeys. Commercial campgrounds come and go. Look for signs, or ask a local outfitter.

Oconee State Park, on SC 107, is about 20 miles from the US 76 bridge crossing.

Maps

The Sumter National Forest map provides a useful overview of this region. Contact the District Ranger, Andrew Pickens Ranger District, (USFS, 112 Andrew Pickens Circle, Mountain Rest, SC 29664, or phone (803) 638-9568. The Chattooga National Wild and Scenic River map is also published by the US Forest Service, and depicts the river corridor in detail.

Suitability for Rafting (On a 1 to 7 Scale): 7

Beware Bull Sluice if you're guiding your own raft.

Several commercial outfitters are located nearby. 1) Wildwater Ltd. is located in the old Longcreek Academy building. 2) A Nantahala Outdoor Center outpost is situated alongside the Section III shuttle route. 3) The Chattooga Whitewater Shop is on US 76 near the turnoff to the Section IV takeout. Others are in the vicinity. Look around or ask locally. The Clayton (Georgia) or Westminster (South Carolina) Chambers of Commerce may be of some help.

TRIP Profile

The Chattooga's relative isolation is reflected in its elevated Inaccessibility score (110). Notice that all other TRIP scores are in double digits. The next highest score (Total Gradient = 99) reflects the offsetting influence of stream's relatively long length (12 miles) and modest average gradient (TRIP score = 80). The river's lowest TRIP score (Continuous Rapids = 63) reflects the presence of a substantial amount of flatwater between its major rapids.

Nearby Alternate Trips

Section II of the Chattooga is located upstream of Section III. It's a mild mannered Class I-II float.

Section IV, anything but a mild mannered float, is located downstream of Section III. It's discussed in the trip description following this one.

The Chauga River, located only a few miles away, is a high water alternate. The Chauga has two sections, both described in this volume. The upper Chauga, a Class III-IV gorge run with several falls and cascades, is a micro stream with stretches of intense technical rapids. It's more difficult than Section III of the Chattooga, but less demanding than Section IV. It's overall TRIP score is 109. The lower Chauga is a ledge-pool Class II-III run with one Class IV rapid. It has an overall TRIP score of 79, making it less difficult overall than Section III.

Chattooga River: Section IV

US 76 to Lake Tugaloo

(South Carolina)

TRIP Profile			
Scale Midpoint = 100			
Overall Difficulty	116	Rapids Difficulty	134
Volume x Gradient	104	Continuous Rapids	111
Average Gradient	97	Entrapments	140
Maximum Gradient	117	Inaccessibility	119
Total Gradient	91	Reputation	139

Actual Stream Data			
Max Rapids	IV(V)	Stream Size	Medium
Average Gradient	45	Length (in miles)	6
Maximum Gradient	100	Morphology Types	2&3

Overview

When James Dickey published *Deliverance,* a tale about four good ol' boys from Atlanta who ventured into the north Georgia hills for a long weekend canoeing trip, it didn't take Hollywood long to recognize a prize-winning story. A movie soon followed. But unlike the fate that awaits most good stories when they fall into the grimy clutches of the movie moguls, Dickey shrewdly negotiated creative control over the cinematic version of his novel. He wrote the screen-play himself, and as shooting progressed, he was continually on the scene, stubbornly insisting on strict adherence to the original story line.

The film makers signed the most popular actors of the era for the lead roles, and John Boorman (who also directed *The Emerald Forest)* masterfully staged the whole production against the spectacular backdrop of the Chattooga, Chauga, and Tallulah Rivers in South Carolina and Georgia. The result was a stunningly successful film, both artistically and at the box office. Rendered to cinema, Dickey's chronicle galvanized interest in river running and lionized both stars: Burt Reynolds and the Chattooga River.

After the film's immense commercial success, a cast of thousands decided to join Burt and the boys on the Chattooga. Aware that *Deliverance* was partly filmed there, suspecting that the cinematic montage of river footage contained lots of special effects (it did), and convinced that if the movie character "Fat Bobby" could do it then anybody could, too many ill-equipped and untrained floaters found their way to the Chattooga. Not a few of them never found their way back home.

They usually put in where the main access road crosses the river, at the US 76 bridge, at the top of Section IV, on inner tubes, trailing six-packs behind. After an hour or two of pleasantly titillating water they encountered stark terror. No, not a hillbilly pervert like in the story, but the terror of everlasting spin-cycle at a place called Woodall, an innocuous-looking Class II ledge that local rescue squad members called a "suck-hole" and paddlers soon knew as a deadly recirculating hydraulic, probably the worst on any river in the South. The river quickly took a ghastly toll. A lot of tubers drowned at Woodall Shoals, more than anybody cares to admit. The fatalities gained a killer reputation for Section IV, and bolstered the view of whitewater sports as suitable only for the lunatic fringe.

When the Chattooga was named a National Wild and Scenic River, minimum safety standards were imposed and enforced, including an outright ban on tubing the river. These measures, together with the growing skill and sophistication of hard boat paddlers and the availability of commercially outfitted raft trips for less skilled adventurers, dramatically reduced fatalities.

Keep in mind, however, that it's still a hazardous river. Although Chattooga Section IV no longer enjoys top spot on the spectrum of whitewater bravado, it's still formidable. With a good head of water, Five Falls will make you give back things you never stole.

Tim Ed Spangler's version of a mystery move. Seven Foot Falls on the Chattooga. Julie Keller photo.

(An essay on the Chattooga's special mystique appears in *River Stories: Tales From Bo Rockerville,* by Monte Smith, available from Pahsimeroi Press.)

Mile(s)	Chattooga Section IV Top-To-Bottom Itinerary
0.0	US 76 bridge putin.
0.7	Screaming Left Turn (Class III).
1.6	Rock Jumble (Class III).
2.0	Woodall Shoals (Class VI).
2.5	Seven Foot Falls (Class IV).
3.4	Raven Rock (Class III+).
4.2 to 4.5	Calm-Before-the-Storm.
4.6 to 4.9	Five Falls.
	#1: Entrance (Class III+).
	#2: Corkscrew (Class IV).
	#3: Crack-in-the-Rock (Class VI).
	#4: Jawbone (Class IV).
	#5: Sock-em-Dog (Class III to Class V)
5.0	Shoulder Bone (Class III+).
6.0	Tugaloo Lake.
8.0	Takeout. Lake left.

Description

From the Section IV putin at the US 76 bridge, it's hard to picture the fury that awaits downstream.   The river at the putin is soft-spoken, inviting. To make matters even more deceptive, there are only two Class II-III rapids in the first two miles below the putin bridge. Then, at the end of a pool, a rock snakes out from river left. An introductory drop that appears to be of Class II difficulty is followed by a long Class III+ rapid. That innocuous looking introductory drop, however, forms a recirculating hydraulic known as Woodall Shoals (Class VI), a spot that once claimed more tubers than anybody bothered to accurately record. It's not nearly the threat to hard boat paddlers that it was to tubers. Nevertheless, if you come out of your boat in this hole, you'd better have a friend nearby with a throw rope. Otherwise, you could end up as fish food. River left provides a grand spot for scouting, and a short and easy portage. At levels above 2.0 feet on the bridge gauge, the drop on far river right is runnable. Once around the introductory drop and its hydraulic, the rest of the long shoals is a romp, with at least a hundred different routes to the bottom.

Seven Foot Falls (Class IV) is not far downstream, a powerful drop that slams the full force of the Chattooga into a river left abutment. "Cheatable" down a river right chute at higher flows, Seven Foot also deserves a scout. The drop itself is a powerful, twisting descent that has to be finessed. Even more troublesome, however, is the approach, some of the funkiest water on the Chattooga.

Almost a mile below Seven Foot Falls, Long Creek enters on river left in the middle of a lengthy Class II(III) stretch of water called Deliverance Rock Rapid. (A lot of *Deliverance* footage was shot on this rapid.) Long Creek enters the Chattooga with a final waterfall in a beautiful grotto-like setting. Time permitting, stop and walk to the base of the falls. Breathe in the serenity and keep it with you as you head toward the tempest that lies downstream.

Raven Rock, a robust Class III+ is next (scout from river left), followed by a mile of inconsequential water until . . . Five Falls.

Five Falls

Five Falls is something else. Few other one-third mile stretches exceed it for sheer excitement. At 2.0 feet and above on the bridge gauge, the Five Falls have to be seen to be appreciated. As the water rises above 2.0 feet, the falls progressively lose their individuality as they blend into an uninterrupted maelstrom of frothing, crashing, churning, exhilarating whiteness. First trips on Section IV should include ample scouting time with a trip leader willing to point out hazards and suggest routes for running the rapids. Even with ample time to scout, the drops in Five Falls harbor unpleasant surprises that are next to impossible to discern merely from scouting. The first falls, Entrance Rapid, is a good example. Ninety percent of the river washes over a drop that looks okay. It isn't. This rapid should be run where the remaining 10% of water flows, far right. Although it's not real difficult itself (Class III+), if you bungle it here

Julie Keller and Francis Cheung at Entrance Rapid on the Chattooga River.
Don Ellis photo.

you're in for a quick succession of rude surprises because the other four drops are closely spaced. If you do screw up at Entrance Rapid, swim for shore with determined alacrity. Do not flush boatless into the next rapid, Corkscrew. If Corkscrew doesn't chew you to a frazzle, it's downstream brethren surely will. Scout Entrance Rapid from river right.

The next rapid in Five Falls, Corkscrew, is a turbulent Class IV if you run it cleanly, a Class V if you swim it, and a Class VI if your swim continues into the next rapid below it. Corkscrew's name is remarkably appropriate. Cork is short, but violent. Ride it once sans boat and you'll never forget the experience. River right provides the best scouting vantage as well as a much easier portage, but don't try to run it down the right side. Corkscrew is one of those rare rapids that's actually more difficult than it looks. Its holes are a whole heck of a lot stickier than they look, too. Ask anybody who's ever plopped into one of them.

Trying to describe Corkscrew verbally is a waste of time. To visualize the rapid, think of a scene of wild hydraulic action, sprinkled liberally with come-hither holes. Close the western-hemisphere, linear-trained side of your brain and think non-linear. Think twisting, churning. Think how one of Carl Jung's nightmares must have looked. Think of how your stomach felt that Saturday night as a teenager when you drank too much for the first time and puked all over the seat covers of your old man's new car. Now you're getting the picture. Corkscrew!

Even more unpleasant than a swim through Corkscrew would be a swim through its washout, Crack-in-the-Rock (Class VI). Left crack has claimed lives, and middle crack has traumatized numerous paddlers with near-terminal swims. Run the right crack (if clear) or portage river right. To underestimate this place is a mistake. At levels over 2.0 feet on the US 76 gauge, currents at the base of this drop approach a state of malevolence.

Jawbone (Class IV) is next, and at low to moderate flows it may be the best rapid on the river. Catch the big eddy at the top on the left. (At levels above 2.0 feet, it's hard to punch the eddy line.) From the eddy, get out and look. Take a good look at Hydroelectric Rock, hunkered in the middle of the washout. Hydro is undercut, and people have washed into and under it, surfacing downstream in various states of thankful glossolalia, only to look straight into the jaws of Sock-em-Dog, which is the next stop on this thrilling itinerary.

Actually, Sock-em-Dog is highly variable in temperament, ranging from not-so-bad Class III at low water to irascible Class V at higher flows. At levels above 2.0 feet, this rapid grows almost unbelievably quick and powerful. At any level, moreover, Sock-em-Dog is not the rapid to practice swimming. Scout it carefully before running, from both sides of the river. Set throw ropes on river right; they're virtually useless on river left. The approach is blind, fast, and screaming. The bottom hydraulic is surprisingly sticky. Portage on river left. And remember: most rapids are easier to run than to portage; Sock-em-Dog isn't.

The one remaining rapid of substance, Shoulder Bone (Class III+), is spiteful in nature. Positioned elsewhere it would be a significant rapid. Here it's just a nuisance, grabbing and clutching, vainly imitative of upstream rapids.

Below Shoulder Bone, riffles soon peter out as the proud Chattooga succumbs to the Tugaloo impoundment. The two mile slackwater paddle to the takeout access always seems like ten. But the slackwater paddle isn't what you'll remember about Section IV. The memories you'll keep are of the gnarly drops in Five Falls.

The River in Review

Even if you've never paddled Section IV, odds are you've nevertheless heard a lot about it. The stories abound. Its reputation is awesome. If you've never run it, here are seven soothing thoughts to keep in mind during your first descent:

1. Relax in the first two miles.
2. Consider giving Woodall a wide berth. More and more paddlers are surfing it, but keep in mind that although you can surf it or skirt it, you cannot bluff it. Get careless, and Woodall will test your mammalian diving reflex.
3. Stop and scout all of the Five Falls.
4. At Corkscrew, at levels approaching 2.0 feet, consider posting at least two throw ropes on river left. If anybody swims here, get them out of the water quickly, before they wash into Crack-in-the-Rock. The higher the flow, the faster swimmers must be retrieved.

*What a ride. Liz Garland at Seven Foot Falls. Chattooga River.
Don Ellis photo.*

5. Crack-in-the-Rock is dangerous. Don't believe anybody who tells you otherwise. A lot of good paddlers make a point of always portaging this drop. If you run it, watch out for the weird recirculating currents at the base of the drop, especially at higher flows. They're deceptively strong and at high water there's absolutely no way to swim out of them without outside assistance.

6. Sock-em-Dog. This may be hard to believe, but people (and boats) have literally disappeared here. At healthy flows this ledge forms a hydraulic that's as unpredictable as it is powerful. The ledge-face of the drop may be undercut, forming a double-hydraulic with the second one pulling objects back under the ledge. Who knows? With the force blowing over this drop, anything's possible.

7. In the pool below Sock, stop. Look around, breathe easy. You made it! And you're at the bottom of an enormous gorge which in all probability you'd not even noticed until now.

Summary

Much of *Deliverance* was filmed here, forging an immediate link in the public's mind between whitewater adventure and the Chattooga River. For a few years after release of the movie, this stream was the sine qua non of whitewater paddling. It *was* the east coast qualifying cruise for expert paddler status. At one time Corkscrew and Sock-em-Dog were the working definitions of Class V rapids. Then word spread about the Gauley. Intrepid paddlers who ventured thereupon witnessed a new definition of Class V. Chattooga rapids became Class IVs (although many paddlers still rate Sock-em-Dog as Class V). For a time the upper Gauley became the east coast expert qualifying cruise. More recently, that distinction has bounced around among a collection of rivers that includes the Watauga, Green, lower Meadow, Russell Fork, Caney Fork, upper Yough, or in the Chattooga's own headwaters, Overflow Creek. Nonetheless, Section IV remains a formidable stretch of whitewater. The run is unique in many ways, and it's always a treat.

Few rivers live up to their reputation. Section IV does.

Water Levels

Minimum is about 1.3 on the US 76 bridge gauge (South Carolina side, river left), which equates to about 290 cfs. Read the gauge closely, however, because a tenth of a foot increase (from 1.3 to 1.4, for example) translates into a 22% increase in volume! A one inch increase at US 76 will mean many additional inches in the Five Falls.

Except for Sock-em-Dog, the run is pretty reasonable until about 1.7, where Five Falls starts getting pushy. At 2.0 feet and above, the Five Falls area becomes a serious challenge, even for advanced paddlers. For gauge readings, check with one of the cooperative outfitters located near the Chattooga:

Chattooga Whitewater Shop	803 647 9083
Nantahala Outdoor Center	704 488 2175
Southeastern Expeditions	706 782-4331
Wildwater, Ltd.	803 647 5336

Chattooga Gauge Location
US 76 Bridge - River Left

Low:	1.3 =	290 cfs
Medium:	1.7 =	570 cfs
High:	2.2 =	1,040 cfs

Chattooga Gauge Conversion

Feet	Cfs	Feet	Cfs
1.0	155	2.0	840
1.1	195	2.2	1,040
1.2	240	2.4	1,280
1.3	290	2.6	1,510
1.4	355	2.8	1,750
1.5	420	3.0	2,000
1.6	490	3.4	2,550
1.7	570	3.6	2,840
1.8	650	4.0	3,450
1.9	740	5.0	5,200

Access

The Chattooga River forms the state boundary between South Carolina and Georgia. All official putins and takeouts are located on the South Carolina side.

US 76 is the usual vehicular conduit to this part of upstate South Carolina. The US 76 bridge over the Chattooga River is about midway between Westminster, South Carolina and Clayton, Georgia. This bridge is the focal point in most Chattooga excursions, serving as takeout for Section III and putin for Section IV, as well as location for the visitor center. The gauge (river left) is located here also.

Put in at the US 76 bridge, or thereabouts. Take out at Lake Tugaloo, on the left side as you're paddling toward the dam. To run the shuttle from the US 76 bridge putin, drive three miles into South Carolina, past the turnoff to Earls Ford, to the first paved road on the right. Take this road through apple orchards to a sometimes apple packing house/sometimes small manufacturing plant. Bear right and continue several miles to the next juncture. Bear right here also and look for Damascus Church on the left. Just past the church, turn right and in about two or three miles the road pitches into the Chattooga Gorge. It's partly paved and narrow. (This shuttle invites wrong turns, but it's a cinch if you just remember to keep turning right.)

All river user groups must fill out a registration form (one form per group), available at the Earls Ford and US 76 parking areas. The carbon copy of this form is your permit to run the river, and someone in each group must keep it in their possession at all times while on the river. Registration requirements change from time-to-time. Check the posting boards at the US 76 visitor center to make sure you're complying with the latest requirements.

Miles From the Chattooga River	
Greenville, SC 70	Asheville, NC 135
Atlanta, GA 135	Knoxville, TN 144

Other Information

For information on Camping, Outfitters, Maps, and Nearby Alternate Trips, see the Chattooga Section III description.

Hiking

A trail leads into the Five Falls region of Section IV. Medium in difficulty and only about three miles round trip, it provides splendid grandstand views of the Five Falls. Look for the trailhead on the right as you drive toward Damascus Church on the Section IV shuttle run. This trail parallels Shoulder Bone Branch and reaches the gorge bottom just downstream of Shoulder Bone rapid. Once to the river, it's only a short scramble upstream to the surreal world of Five Falls. (Don't get confused and hike in much farther upstream at Long Creek Falls or Fish Trap Branch.)

Woodall Shoals is also accessible by foot. A gravel road leads to within a quarter mile of the river, and a graded trail leads down to the water. Look for the Woodall sign on the right hand side of the shuttle road, soon after turning off US 76.

Suitability for Rafting (On a 1 to 7 Scale): 3

Consider guiding your own raft only if you're thoroughly familiar with the river's hazards. A mistake at Woodall Shoals or Crack-in-the-Rock could be fatal. Passengers can be thrown from rafts at Seven-Foot Falls. Sock-em-Dog, especially, is not raft friendly.

Raft trips down Section IV are best enjoyed by paying the going tariff and joining one of the local commercial outfitters. Their safety records are excellent.

TRIP Profile

Section IV generates a TRIP profile worthy of comment. Its Average Gradient score is only 97, about average for other trips in the book. And Total Gradient (91) is even more wimpy. (At six

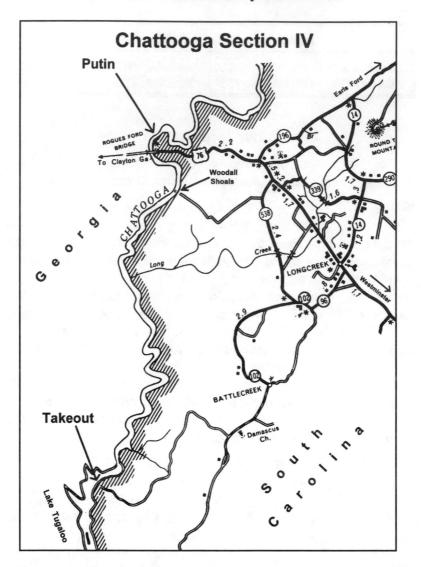

Chattooga Section IV

Putin

Takeout

miles it's a relatively short run.) But check out the Rapids Difficulty (134) and Entrapments (140) scores. Its elevated Reputation score (139) is well deserved, too. TRIP Profile and Actual Stream Data at the beginning of the Chattooga Section IV trip description do not include the two miles of required paddling on Lake Tugaloo.

Don Ellis showcases his letter-perfect technique on the Chattooga's gnarliest rapid, Sock-em-Dog. Photo by Dick Creswell.

The bottom of Slanted Crack on the lower Chauga. Monte Smith photo.

Chauga River Gorge

Cassidy Bridge to Budd Cobb Bridge
(South Carolina)

TRIP Profile			
Scale Midpoint = 100			
Overall Difficulty	109	Rapids Difficulty	106
Volume x Gradient	107	Continuous Rapids	99
Average Gradient	98	Entrapments	117
Maximum Gradient	145	Inaccessibility	119
Total Gradient	113	Reputation	105

Actual Stream Data			
Max Rapids	III-IV(VI)	Stream Size	Small
Average Gradient	46	Length (in miles)	9
Maximum Gradient	140	Morphology Types	3&4

Overview

The Chauga and Chattooga watersheds are separated by only one ridge. Strangely enough, this close proximity has a lot to do with why recognition has been so slow in coming to the Chauga. Any stream with the unmitigated temerity to aspire to whitewater notoriety in the same neck of the woods as the Chattooga had best anticipate its comeuppance. And such has been the legacy of the Chauga, although its gorge section is noteworthy for aesthetics, short bursts of gradient, and memorable cascades.

The Chauga's other drawback is water availability. Its watershed is diminutive compared to the Chattooga, and it's ordinarily runnable only at selected times during rainy spring seasons. Catch its gorge

122

with enough water, however, and it offers miles of high-gradient excitement through a pristine hardwood and hemlock-shrouded gorgeway. Unlike most mountain streams that tumble more or less continuously, the Chauga Gorge alternates surprisingly flat sections with some of the steepest gradient in the southern mountains.

Mile(s)	Chauga Gorge Top-To-Bottom Itinerary
0.0	Put in at Cassidy Bridge on Stumphouse Road near Long Creek.
0.0 to 0.7	Mostly flat, until . . .
0.7	A 12 ft cascade (Class IV), the first of . . .
0.7 to 2.0	Several large cascades.
1.0 to 5.0	Four miles of technical, twisting drops, up to Class IV.
2.0	Spider Valley Creek enters on river right.
2.5 to 3.5	Maximum gradient: 140 feet/mile.
5.0 to 6.0	Mostly flatwater, mixed with light rapids.
6.0 to 6.8	Class II-III, with 40 feet/mile gradient.
7.0	Alternate takeout. Use it to avoid flatwater.
7.5	Riley Moore Falls (Class VI).
7.5 to 9.0	Flatwater timewarp.
9.0	Budd Cobb Bridge takeout.

Description

From the putin bridge to the first cascade, the story is mostly flatwater and the paddler on a first trip begins to wonder, "Did I put in at the wrong bridge?" But when the action begins, it's continuous for several miles.

The signal that the fun is about to begin is the first cascade, about 0.7 mile into the run. This is the first of several potentially runnable (Class IV) falls and cascades. Scout or portage from river left, the side with a diagonal chute veering across the face of the 12 foot drop. The main drop is more of a cascade than a sheer waterfall. Nevertheless, the cascade ends in a vertical plummet into a foamy rock-infested bed. Because the landing is obstructed, this cascade (and the others on the run) merit Class IV ratings. (The river left portage is easy.) If the first big drop is more than you expected, consider poling or paddling back to the takeout because several similar drops occur in the next two miles. (All of which are most easily scouted from river left.)

Chauga Gorge Gradient	
Mile	**Gradient**
1	34
2	55
3	121
4	76
5	40
6	20
7	35
8	25
9	12

Once the bigger drops are past, the little stream switches gears and serves its gradient in the form of twisting, technical hairball rapids. High flows will push some of these drops into Class IV territory.

After about four miles of this nonstop frolic, the gradient eases up and the rapids moderate to Class I-II for a mile, then pick up intensity again for almost another mile before slowing to a flatwater pace. Near the start of this flat section, approximately seven miles after putin, the alternate takeout can be located on river right. If road conditions allow access, this alternate takeout will avoid a lot of flatwater and one "entrapment hotel." Otherwise, it's more flatwater until, just as it seems the whole world has been sucked into an interminable flatwater timewarp, the stream picks up velocity and slingshots toward Riley Moore Falls (Class VI). Considered a mandatory portage by most people, it's runnable at precisely selected spots at high water. Scout or portage on river left.

Below Riley Moore Falls, a welcome current returns to offer a brief respite. Then the flatwater returns. When the rusty old Budd Cobb Bridge appears, it is a welcome sight indeed.

Summary

The Chauga Gorge is almost as difficult as Section IV of the Chattooga, but different in character, consisting of steep, technical rapids and cascades in an intimate causeway of outrageous beauty. Small, tempestuous, a steep creek freak's delight. Underskilled paddlers will flush over waterfalls, pin against or under undercuts, and experience terror. Not recommended for anyone without previous steep creek experience.

Water Levels

Two gauges are available, one at the Cassidy Bridge putin, and the other on the Chattooga at US 76. The Chattooga gauge gives only a rough approximation of Chauga flow levels, but the reading often can be obtained with a phone call to a local outfitter. Obtaining a reading from the Cassidy gauge, on the other hand, usually requires a trip to the putin bridge. Using the US 76 Chattooga bridge gauge, a zero level for the Chauga Gorge is about 2.2 feet. A better level is in the vicinity of 3.0 feet. As with all high gradient runs, however, the dividing line between "fun" and "flush" on the Chauga Gorge is thin. A flush run through the Chauga Gorge is serious business. The gauge painted on Cassidy Bridge seems to be a Randy Carter indicator, with zero representing the lowest possible run. Half a foot above zero is a pretty good level on this gauge and corresponds (approximately) to 2.6 feet on the US 76 Chattooga marker.

Access

The Chauga runs its full length in northwestern South Carolina, beginning in the mountains and running into the Piedmont. As with its close neighbor the Chattooga, the key to locating the Chauga is US 76, running between Westminster, South Carolina and Clayton, Georgia. To find the putin at Cassidy Bridge on Stumphouse Road, locate the apple-growing mecca of Long Creek, which is about

midway between Westminster
and Clayton, on the South
Carolina side of the Chattooga. In Long Creek, take the
turnoff at the Post Office and
go to the intersection just
past the old Long Creek Academy building (which now
houses an outfitter). Hang a
sharp right turn on Stumphouse Road. Cassidy

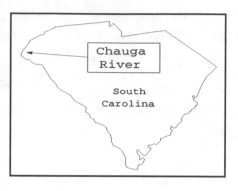

Bridge, the putin, is about 2.25 miles east. A gravel parking lot is
beside the bridge.

Miles From the Chauga River Gorge	
Greenville, SC 65	Charlotte, NC 157
Atlanta, GA 137	Chattanooga, TN 165

(Warning: Don't make the mistake of putting in at the wrong
bridge. The right putin is at Cassidy Bridge on Stumphouse Road.
The wrong putin is at Blackwell Bridge, the next upstream crossing
of the Chauga, on Whetstone Road, which leads to a Class VI sluice
known locally as the Chauga Narrows.)

Take out at Budd Cobb Bridge on Budd Cobb Road. This
location was the scene of friction between paddlers and a local
hothead resident in past years. Things seem to have improved with
the demise of that particular resident and the increased visibility of
the paddling community via establishment of a bed-and-breakfast
location by Wildwater Ltd on river right (the "River House") beside
the bridge (Phone: 803 647-5336). Limited parking. Budd's road
forms a loop off US 76. The inconspicuous northern terminus of the
loop is five miles south of Long Creek. The southern terminus of the
loop is another 4.5 miles toward Westminster, at Calvary Church.

An alternate takeout is located about 2.25 miles upstream of
Budd's bridge. To locate it from Budd's Bridge, drive toward the US
76 northern terminus of Budd's loop (which will be river right of the
Chauga) for about .75 mile. Turn right onto Spy Rock Trail. Go two

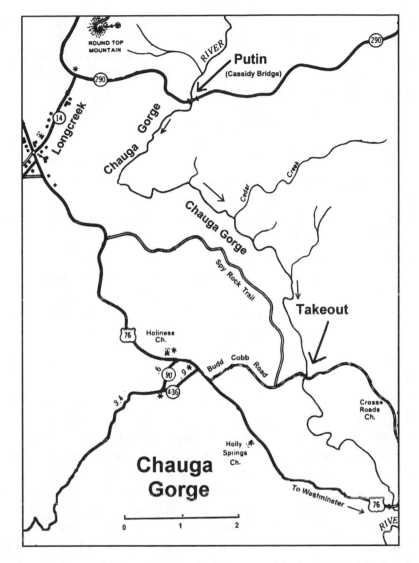

miles and turn right on 748B, which is passable by 2WD vehicles in good weather (which is not when you'll be running this section). It's about a mile down to the river.

The shuttle from the Cassidy Bridge putin to the Budd Cobb Bridge takeout is all paved, about 50 minutes round trip. From Cassidy Bridge, drive to Long Creek, turn left on US 76 and drive south five miles to the northern terminus of Budd's loop road. If you miss it, turn left after another 4.5 miles at Calvary Church (just after crossing the Chauga), and bear left at the only major fork.

(A story about Budd Cobb, the bridge's namesake, appears in *River Stories: Tales From Bo Rockerville,* by Monte Smith, available from Pahsimeroi Press.)

Other Information

Camping

Oconee State Park is about an hour away. (Refer to the Chattooga Section III Access section for directions.) Primitive camping is available near the US 76 crossing of the Chattooga River, on the South Carolina side. Commercial campgrounds also are located in the Chattooga vicinity.

Maps

A map of the Sumter National Forest is helpful in running shuttles. It can be obtained from the District Ranger, Andrew Pickens Ranger District (USFS, 112 Andrew Pickens Circle, Mountain Rest, SC 29664, or phone (803) 638-9568.

Suitability for Rafting (On a 1 to 7 Scale): 0

Too small; too precipitous.

Tornado Damage

Both the Chauga and Chattooga corridors were hit by tornadoes in 1994. Damage to the Chattooga was largely confined to the hills surrounding Lake Tugaloo. The Chauga Gorge, however, wasn't so fortunate. The storm deposited numerous deadfalls in its narrow streambed. As this book went to press, it was not possible to determine the extent of the damage. Until the next big flood clears out the debris, however, paddlers should exercise extreme caution. Before putting on the gorge, check with local paddlers and outfitters for an update.

TRIP Profile

The Chauga Gorge TRIP profile is a study in contrasts. Its gradient is average (TRIP score = 98), yet it contains long stretches of flatwater, leavened by bursts of extreme gradient, as reflected by its elevated Maximum Gradient score (145), the third highest in the book.   It's laced with Entrapments (117) and runs through an isolated gorge, as shown in its Inaccessibilty score (119).

Nearby Alternate Trips		
Alternate Trip	Rapids Difficulty	TRIP Points
Chattooga Section II	II	na
Chattooga Section III	III(IV)	86
Chattooga Section IV	IV(V)	116
Lower Chauga	II-III(IV)	79

Lower Chauga River
Budd Cobb Bridge to Horseshoe Bridge
(South Carolina)

TRIP Profile			
Scale Midpoint = 100			
Overall Difficulty	79	Rapids Difficulty	82
Volume x Gradient	70	Continuous Rapids	63
Average Gradient	72	Entrapments	106
Maximum Gradient	76	Inaccessibility	92
Total Gradient	70	Reputation	94

Actual Stream Data			
Max Rapids	II-III(IV)	Stream Size	Small
Average Gradient	19	Length (in miles)	7
Maximum Gradient	40	Morphology Type	2

Overview

The lower Chauga, located near Westminster, South Carolina, offers six Class II-III rapids and a seventh that is an easy Class II-III on one side of the river and a Class IV on the other side. The average gradient on this run is a modest 19 feet/mile. However, one spirited mile drops 40 feet, producing several memorable rapids. Overall, the lower Chauga is not as aesthetically pleasing as its upstream gorge, except for the one mile stretch beginning shortly below its US 76 bridge crossing, in the vicinity of Chau Ram Park.

Similar To. Whereas the upper Chauga is a small mountain trout stream with alternating flatwater and bursts of intense gradient, the lower stream is ledge/pool in nature with several runnable "slides." The slides are reminiscent of those on Georgia's Cartecay River.

Mile(s)	Lower Chauga Top-To-Bottom Itinerary
0.0	Putin Slide (Class III), a long, sloping slide of a rapid about 100 yards long.
0.5	Dennys Plunge (Class II+), a river-wide slide about 8 feet high.
3.5	Powerline, a river-wide ledge. Class III-.
4.4	US 76 double bridges.
4.6	Beginning of steepest gradient (40 feet/mile), best scenery, and best rapids.
4.6	Park Entrance (Class III-).
4.7	Slanted Crack, aka Pumphouse (Class IV), on river right, and Jennifer (II+ or III-) on river left.
4.8	Municipal pump intake.
4.9	Chau Ram Park and Ramsey Creek confluence.
5.2	Suicide Slide (Class III), aka Can Opener, aka Boat Buster.
5.4	Glass Rapid (Class III), a "U" shaped ledge, grabby at high flows.
7.0	Take out at Horseshoe Bridge.

Description

The putin is underneath Budd Cobb Bridge at the top of a long, swerving slide of a Class III rapid. The surface of this slide is solid stone, which means that water attains substantial velocity as it rushes over it. Generally the stone surface tilts to river right, concentrating water on that side. With enough water this slide is a real hoot. It's the first of seven memorable rapids.

The second rapid is Dennys Plunge (Class II+), a river-wide "slide" about eight feet high. Rapid #3 (Powerline) is also a river-wide ledge (Class III-), with most water channeled through a cluttered sluice on river left that occasionally is clogged with logs. An overhead power cable forewarns this rapid.

Double bridges over the river (US 76) signal entrance into the part of the Chauga with the best scenery, steepest gradient and most exciting whitewater. Locals once referred to this section of the river as the Town Park. Years before a river conservation ethic became politically correct, residents of nearby Westminster created a park along the banks of this scenic stretch of the Chauga, complete with swinging bridges and bath houses -- a prime example of how river assets can be valued and protected instead of desecrated. In recent years care of the park has reverted to Oconee County and it has been renamed Chau Ram, in recognition of the confluence of the Chauga River and Ramsey Creek, which occurs at the park site.

Shortly past the double bridges is Park Entrance, a Class III-rapid that heralds the approach to Slanted Crack, recognizable from upstream by a rounded midstream hump of rock and beyond that, at the base of the river left cliff, by a mechanical monstrosity that is actually scaffolding for a pump which draws water from the Chauga for the nearby municipality of Westminster. Slanted Crack, sometimes called Pumphouse by paddlers or the Shoals by locals, is actually a double rapids formed by a rather unique midstream upthrust of rock. To river left of the upthrust is mild-mannered "Jennifer" (Class II or III-, depending on water), a series of small drops scattered along a narrow, fast-moving chute. Slanted Crack is on river right of the midstream upthrust, a single-drop Class IV that is undercut on the left side. Not only is the left side undercut, but there's a huge cavern back under there. (During summertime low water, local kids play hide-and-seek by crawling back underneath the falls.)

Below Slanted Crack is Town Park (or Chau-Ram Park), marked by a sandy beach on river left. Shortly downstream, where the Chauga bends sharply right, Ramsey Creek enters on river left. A hundred yards up Ramsey Creek are some high cascades. The base of these cascades was the site of a gun factory that was destroyed by Confederate defenders in the waning days of the Civil War, as Sherman's troops drew near. The historic site can be reached most easily by stopping at the sandy beach upstream of Ramsey Creek.

At the Ramsey Creek confluence, the lower Chauga makes a sharp right jag and then, within a quarter mile, reaches its scenic peak in the vicinity of Suicide Slide (aka Can Opener, aka Boat Buster), the sixth rapid of consequence on this trip. It's a short Class III "slide" with an obstructive rock at its base. This rock will open anything that crashes into it, but is easily avoided on river right.

Next is Glass Rapid (Class II+ or III), where the stream drops over a crescent-shaped ledge into a grabby, boiling cauldron. Eddy out downstream of Glass and look around. This is the lower Chauga at its scenic best, a terrific spot for a picnic, a swim, or other afternoon delight.

Unfortunately, downstream of Glass Rapid the whitewater soon disappears, the banks change to mud, and the gorgeous white pine melds into undistinguished fourth growth heterogeneity. The next highway crossing (Horseshoe Bridge) is the takeout. This road was named after a Revolutionary War hero, Horseshoe Robinson, whose home was nearby.

Summary

The lower Chauga, although lacking the whitewater punch of its upstream gorge section, is a worthwhile alternative to Section III of the Chattooga, especially by paddlers who have run the latter several times and are looking for variety. The lower Chauga is a river of contrasts. The one mile section in the vicinity of Chau Ram Park resembles Section III, but other stretches of the river are mud-bank Piedmont in character. The lower Chauga is often run when the Chattooga is considered too high. Unfortunately, the Chauga tends to run "muddy" at high flows.

Water Levels

Levels are rough approximations. At least 2.2 is required on the US 76 Chattooga gauge. A reading of 3.0 feet provides ample water but often is accompanied by muddied stream conditions. Thus, a trade-off may be necessary between clear water and lots of water.

Access

The Chauga River is located in western upstate South Carolina near the communities of Westminster and Long Creek, on the fringe of the Blue Ridge Mountains.

The key to locating both putin and takeout is US 76, which runs north from Westminster, South Carolina to Clayton, Georgia. Put in at Budd Cobb Bridge (limited parking), which is also the takeout for the more demanding Chauga Gorge run. Budd Cobb Road forms a loop off US 76. If driving from Westminster, proceed about three miles north (toward Clayton Georgia) and turn right at Calvary Church. (If you cross the Chauga you've missed the turn.) After turning at Calvary, bear left at the fork in about three miles.

Takeout at Horseshoe Bridge on Horseshoe Bridge Road. Limited parking. This road intersects US 76 about 1.25 miles south (toward Westminster) of Calvary Church.

Miles From the Lower Chauga	
Greenville, SC 65	Charlotte, NC 157
Atlanta, GA 137	Chattanooga, TN 165

Other Information

For information on Camping, Maps, and Nearby Alternate Trips, refer to the upper Chauga description.

Miscellaneous

With all the impoundments in the southern mountains, its hard to comprehend how the rivers in this region once flowed, before the dams were constructed. For the record, the original streamflow pattern is outlined in the following paragraphs. Be forewarned, however: only river trivia buffs will want to read the following paragraphs.

The Chattooga River begins in the North Carolina mountains, near Cashiers. Flowing south, it leaves its native state at the point where North Carolina, Georgia, and South Carolina meet. From this point, the Chattooga defines the border between South Carolina and Georgia, flowing through rugged mountainous terrain. Paddlers know most of these border miles as Sections II, III and IV.

Section IV of the Chattooga ends when it encounters an impoundment named Lake Tugaloo, which was one of the first major lakes constructed in the southern mountains. Beneath the surface of this impoundment lies the former confluence of the Chattooga with a stalwart from north Georgia called the Tallulah River. When these two southern mountain titans joined forces, their combined flow was named the Tugaloo River, hence the name of the impoundment that now drowns their confluence.

The Tugaloo River, which today is almost completely obliterated by yet another impoundment, formerly flowed southeast for twenty-five miles, continuing to define the border between Georgia and South Carolina. Its first major tributary, which flowed out of South Carolina and entered the Tugaloo on river left, was the Chauga River. The Tugaloo-Chauga confluence is now inundated by Lake Hartwell, which also covers a point about fifteen miles downstream, near what is now Clemson University, where the Tugaloo confluenced with the Seneca River. The combined flows of the Tugaloo and the Seneca gave birth to the Savannah River, which defined the border between Georgia and South Carolina from its inception to its terminus in the Atlantic Ocean near Savannah, Georgia.

This entire region, particularly the Tugaloo bottomlands, was once a stronghold of the Cherokee Nation. Chauga, Chattooga, Tallulah, and Tugaloo are Cherokee names. Actually, they're Anglicized variants of the original Cherokee names. Sock-em-Dog, for example, is probably the English and Scotch-Irish settlers' translation of whatever term it was that the Cherokee called this powerful rapid. Odds are, they weren't calling the place Sock-em-Dog, but rather something that sounded like that to the early settlers. But then, who knows? The rapid is certainly capable of socking any dog dumb enough to get near it.

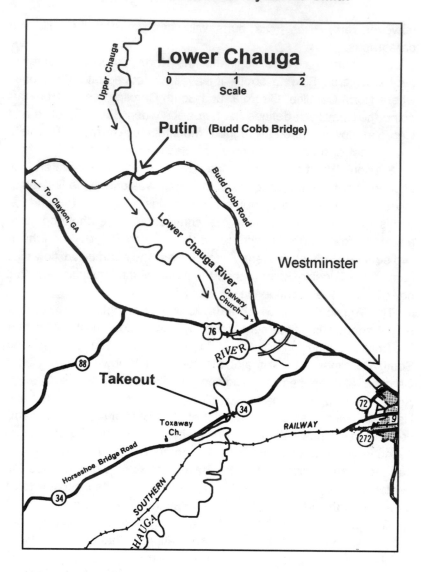

Lower Chauga

Upper Chauga

Scale
0 — 1 — 2

Putin (Budd Cobb Bridge)

Budd Cobb Road

← To Clayton, GA

Lower Chauga River

Calvary Church→ x

Westminster

76

88

Takeout

RIVER

34

72

9

272

Toxaway Ch.

RAILWAY

Horseshoe Bridge Road

34

SOUTHERN

CHAUGA

Suitability for Rafting (On a 1 to 7 Scale): 4

Raftable at higher flows.

Nearby Alternate Trips		
Alternate Trip	Rapids Difficulty	TRIP Points
Chattooga Section II	II	na
Chattooga Section III	III(IV)	86
Chattooga Section IV	IV(V)	116
Upper Chauga	III-IV	109

Cheat River Canyon

Albright to Jenkinsburg
(West Virginia)

TRIP Profile			
Scale Midpoint = 100			
Overall Difficulty	112	Rapids Difficulty	129
Volume x Gradient	143	Continuous Rapids	111
Average Gradient	78	Entrapments	94
Maximum Gradient	74	Inaccessibility	137
Total Gradient	92	Reputation	117

Actual Stream Data			
Max Rapids	IV+	Stream Size	Large
Average Gradient	25	Length (in miles)	11
Maximum Gradient	40	Morphology Types	2&3

Overview

The Cheat River drains the largest undammed watershed in the East, a huge chunk of rugged northern West Virginia. The canyon section of the Cheat, containing its finest whitewater, lies about ninety miles south of Pittsburgh, with a putin at Albright and a takeout eleven miles downstream at Jenkinsburg Bridge. The canyon is remote, inaccessible, and chock full of powerful Class III and IV rapids. At low flows the rapids are Class III, separated by short pools. With higher flows, the pools disappear and the run becomes continuous Class III-IV with two possible Class Vs. The canyon resembles that of the Gauley and some of the rapids are

138

reminiscent of its southern cousin as well. Both powerful and technical, the stream is large and strewn with boulders.

Someone once counted 38 "significant" rapids in the canyon. The count stuck, and was cited in both Burrell and Davidson and Nealy. However, since the last big flood, in 1985, individual rapids are less distinct, and the predominant characteristic of whitewater in the gorge is its continuous nature. Regardless of the exact number of rapids, however, you can rest assured they are both multitudinous and bodacious. The streambed alternates from moderately to densely obstructed. Most rapids have multiple drops and several holes. William Nealy aptly characterized the pre-flood Cheat Canyon as a cross between the lower Gauley and New River Gorge. It combines the big water technical intensity of the New with the wide-open, hundreds-of-yards-long wave/hole bodaciousness of the lower Gauley. After the flood it is this and more. The "more" consists of about a million boulders scattered randomly throughout the streamb-ed. With all these obstructions to negotiate, when the water rises on the Cheat, it is a formidable whitewater challenge.

Similar To. The Cheat Canyon is a blend of the lower Gauley, the New River Gorge, and a couple of Goshen Passes.

Mile(s)	Cheat River Canyon Top-To-Bottom Itinerary
0.0 to 1.0	Put in at the bridge in Albright or at one of the private campgrounds on WV 26 on the edge of town.
1.5	Class III rapids begin with Decision (Class III).
2.5	Beech Run (Class III+).
3.5	Big Nasty (Class IV). Dodge the hole.
4.0	Even Nastier (Class IV).
7.2	Teardrop (Class III+), harbinger of High Falls.
7.5	High Falls (Class IV+).
8.0	Colosseum (Class IV+).
8.2	Lower Colosseum (Class IV).
11.0	Takeout at Jenkinsburg bridge.

Description

This big, rumbling West Virginia mountain river has few equals for sheer number, complexity, and size of rapids.   It is full of powerful Class III and IV rapids from top to bottom, few of which are individually described herein. If you require detailed descriptions or diagrams of powerful and complex Class III and IV rapids, then the Cheat Canyon is probably not right for you. Although several rapids should be scouted (notably Big Nasty, High Falls, and Coliseum), most others have to be "read and run" from the boat. Because of their numbers, length, complexity, and the size of the streambed, it is not practical to scout all major rapids. The gorge is full of Class IIIs at all levels, and as the water rises, from four to twelve Class IVs appear, with two of the latter (High Falls and Coliseum) creeping up toward Class V at 4.0 feet or higher on the Albright gauge. The best way to run the river is tight behind somebody who knows it pretty well.   Lacking that, most of the trip can be accomplished by the "read-and-run" technique, saving scouting excursions for the largest rapids, especially Coliseum.

Cheat Canyon rapids are both large scale and technical, producing a most enjoyable admixture that requires water reading and maneuvering skills as well as the ability to negotiate fairly heavy whitewater.   Even the most congested rapids, however, invariably offer alternate routes. And although there are undercuts and pinning opportunities, most rapids are relatively forgiving in nature,

Big Nasty (Class IV) is the first rapid to require special attention. All the flow is focused river right where it drops over a ledge forming its namesake hole. Dodge the hole is the theme when running Big Nasty, and tight left is the route. If in doubt, scout -- from river left.

High Falls (Class IV+), the next biggie, is an imposing rapid. It's recognizable from far upstream by the towering sandstone cliff and waterfall on river left, but don't forget that Teardrop (Class III+) has to be negotiated first. Scout High Falls from river right. The stream sweeps broadly to the left and over a series of wide ledges, forming waves and holes galore. There are many routes through High Falls, and the best line changes with flow. Regardless of the flow level and chosen route, this rapid has a way of knocking you around more than you might anticipate.

A couple of rapids later the most imposing spot in the Cheat Canyon appears, Coliseum Rapid (Class IV+). A huge stubblefield appears on river left, channeling the flow toward the cliff on river right and into a wide sluiceway containing a hole called Cyclotron and a ragged ledge. Scout from river right to see if you can spot a path that bypasses the Cyclotron and weaves through the mess at the bottom. Several routes are possible, two of which entail skirting Cyclotron on the left and flirting with Mind Bender rock on river left of the bottom drop. Another route is to skirt Cyclotron on river right, catch the eddy, and then run the bottom drop from right to left, paddling hard to miss the holes and waves produced by the irregular face of the ledge. Safety ropes are more helpful on river right. Swims here can be lengthy because Lower Coliseum continues for a long, long way. At levels above 3.5 feet on the Albright gauge, a "cheat" opens through the stubblefield on river left. (Could this be inspiration for a country song? How about, Is it fair to cheat on the Cheat? Or, I lost my darling when I started cheating on the Cheat? Or, That sorry ol' river caused me to cheat? Or, Your cheatin' chute will tell on you?)

Anyway, once through Lower Coliseum, rapids continue unabated but with diminished intensity. Then the real adventure begins. The takeout!

Summary

The Cheat Canyon is one of the finest runs in the East. At levels of 3.5 feet and higher on the Albright gauge, it becomes one of the toughest. It has something for all tastes: complex rapids, big rapids, bigger holes, scenery, magnificent canyon. Try it before Donald Trump builds that cantilevered hamburger palace at Cyclotron.

Water Levels

Readings on both the Parsons and Albright gauges are normally available from the National Weather Service at (412) 644-2890. When available, the Albright reading is preferable because the gauge is at the head of the canyon.

Cheat Canyon Gauge Locations	
Albright	Parsons
Low: 1.5 Medium: 2.5 High: 4.0	Low: 2.7 Medium: 3.7 High: 4.7

Access

The Cheat flows through spectacularly rugged northern West Virginia.

Put in at, or below, Albright. The most common putin is at one of the commercial campgrounds on WV 26, downstream of Albright, where there may be an access fee. Take out at Jenkinsburg Bridge. The shuttle into Jenkinsburg is almost as exciting as the canyon run. A small, rough road sneaks down the canyon wall. Rutted, rocky, washed out in spots, it's truly an adventure. In good weather, the road is passable by a high-clearance 2WD, but the vehicle and its passengers will take a beating. During inclement weather, it's unwise to head into the canyon with 2WD. Most paddlers arrange to have

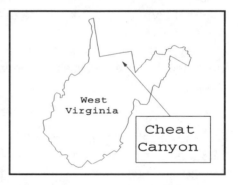

Glenn Miller meet them at the takeout with his truck. For a nominal fee he meets groups at Jenkinsburg and hauls boats and bodies back to the putin. Unless you get off on driving rough roads, his fee is money well spent.

If you decide to run your own shuttle, Jenkinsburg can be approached from either river left or right. The shorter way, naturally, is rougher. Starting from the northern outskirts of Albright, take WV 26 north six miles to the community of Valley Point. Turn left onto Route 15 (Hudson Road). Continue 4.8 miles to Mt. Nebo. Go straight through the intersection for 2.3 miles to the edge of the

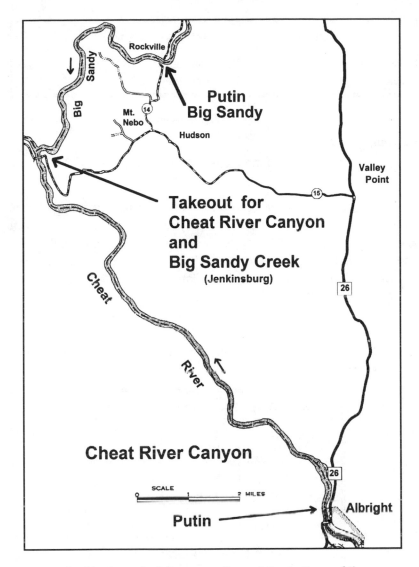

canyon. Jenkinsburg is 1.2 more miles, at the bottom of the canyon.
A one way trip takes about 45 minutes. For the longer (river left)
shuttle route, head south on WV 26, cross the Cheat and drive into
Kingwood.   Turn right onto WV 7 and drive to Masontown.   In
downtown Masontown, at the corner of Main and Depot, turn right
and continue north toward Bull Run. A small stream will be on your
left when the road forks. Bear right and head down into the canyon.

Miles From the Cheat River Canyon	
Morgantown, WV 32	Pittsburgh, PA 107
Washington, DC 237	Roanoke, VA 242

Other Information

Camping

Commercial campgrounds are near Albright, on WV 26.

TRIP Profile

The volume x gradient interaction effect is alive and well in the Cheat Canyon. With puny average (78) and maximum (74) gradient scores, the big river still generates rapids (129) that will make anybody sit up and take notice. It accomplishes this feat with volume (Volume x Gradient Interaction = 143) and an obstructed streambed (Morphology Types 2 & 3).

Nearby Alternate Trips

When the water is high, several Cheat tributaries and headwater streams are runnable:

Cheat River Headwater Streams		
Alternate Trip	Rapids Difficulty	TRIP Points
Dry Fork	II-III	na
Glady Fork	II-III	na
Laurel Fork	III+	104
Shavers Fork	IV	na
Cheat River Tributaries		
Alternate Trip	Rapids Difficulty	TRIP Points
Big Sandy	IV-V(VI)	133
Blackwater	IV-V(VI)	na

Citico Creek

(Tennessee)

TRIP Profile			
Scale Midpoint = 100			
Overall Difficulty	101	Rapids Difficulty	87
Volume x Gradient	84	Continuous Rapids	111
Average Gradient	148	Entrapments	72
Maximum Gradient	131	Inaccessibility	56
Total Gradient	141	Reputation	83

Actual Stream Data			
Max Rapids	III(IV)	Stream Size	Micro
Average Gradient	99	Length (in miles)	6
Maximum Gradient	120	Morphology Types	2&3

Overview

Citico Creek, cousin of the Tellico River, drains the Jeffreys Hell section of the rugged western slopes of the Joyce Kilmer-Slickrock Wilderness, a few miles southwest of the Great Smoky Mountains National Park in Tennessee. This small watershed forms part of the Tellico High Country, a region that's definitely off the beaten track; not exactly easy to locate the first time you go looking for it. Visit one time, however, and you're guaranteed to come back time and again.

Citico Creek is a premier trout stream, and so are the nearby Tellico, North, and Bald Rivers. The surrounding mountains are laced with hiking trails. This rugged terrain is a favorite of backpackers, day hikers, mountain bikers, and horse riders.

Similar To. Little River in the Smokies, or a miniature Cranberry.

Mile(s)	Citico Creek Top-To-Bottom Itinerary
0.0	Put in where Indian Boundary Road first approaches the creek.
0.3	Sharp, twisting right-hand turn followed by Class III water. Recognizable by boulders obstructing the streamflow.
0.5	Constricting rocks produce a five foot drop followed by a narrow sluiceway (Class III+).
0.7 to 1.6	Continuous highly technical Class III rapids. Busy, fast, continuously eventful.
1.7	Pigs in Space rapid (Class IV). Drops 15 feet over several jumbled, diagonal ledges as the creek twists around large boulders through several right angle turns. Scout from the road on river left.
2.0	Doublecamp Creek Campground. Alternate putin or takeout.
2.0 to 2.9	Series of Class II and III ledges.
2.5	Dam.
3.0	Steel bridge.
4.0	Another steel bridge, followed by a five foot broken, irregular ledge (Class III), at junction of Farr Gap Road (Forest Service 26).
4.6	Eight foot sloping ledge (Class III).
4.8	Ten foot cascade (Class III).
5.0	Another steel bridge and beginning of the loop.
5.5	Creek returns to road.
6.0	Tavern Branch takeout.
6.9	Twisting Class III chute.
7.4	Small island. Run on either side.
7.5	Small ledges.
7.8	Alternate takeout.

Description

The first two miles are definitely the most intense, with an average gradient of 120 feet/mile and a big chunk of the total difficulty. The stream is tiny in these first two miles and because of the healthy gradient whizzes along at a torrid pace. Fortunately, a parallel Forest Service road permits convenient scouting and determination of the best place to put in. If the section above Pigs in Space is too intense, consider a putin at Doublecamp Creek. In any event, Pigs in Space deserves careful consideration. (Because of its name if for no other reason!) In a fast succession of twists, drops, and turns this rapid sheds about 15 feet of elevation in a short distance. Pigs is tight, steep, and screaming. It's a real squealer. There is one way in at the top, a couple of ways over the big drop, and one twisting, careening way out the bottom. After Pigs in Space the gradient relents for a few yards but quickly resumes below Doublecamp Creek Campground to a lively 90 feet/mile for the next two miles.

A half mile below Doublecamp, a series of ledges lead to a dam. Class II+ rapids continue for the next mile and a half until a Class III ledge is encountered where Farr Gap Road intersects with Citico Creek Road. In the next mile two memorable ledges occur. The first is about eight feet high, but it's not a sheer drop. The second, only a few hundred feet downstream, is a ten foot cascade. Both are more fun with lots of water. Neither is particularly difficult. After these drops, the creek loops away from the road for about half a mile, beginning at a steel bridge 400 yards downstream of the ten foot cascade. The loop is jam-packed with technical Class II-III rapids. When the creek returns to the road, gradient once again moderates.

The first take out opportunity is at Tavern Branch, half a mile downstream of the loop. There are other rapids, including a twisting Class III chute a mile downstream, but basically the stream is Class II in the remaining distance to the alternate takeout.

Summary

This stream is noteworthy for its absolutely delightful setting as much as for its whitewater. It's next door to the Smokies and only a few miles (as the crow flies) from the Tellico River. This region is arguably the prettiest mountain country in eastern America.

The stream is small, especially upstream of Doublecamp Creek, anchoring the "micro" end of the scale of navigability. As with most streams this size, the drawback is water availability. It's runnable only after locally heavy rains, and the runoff is fast. When it pumps up, it usually lasts only a day or so. Catch it if you can. It's worth the effort.

Water Levels

The Citico is runnable only after locally heavy rains. When the Tellico is flooding, the Citico *may* have enough water. To obtain Tellico flow levels, refer to instructions in the upper Tellico trip description.

Access

From Tellico Plains, take TN 165 a quarter mile to the Tellico River. Turn right (which is still TN 165) and head up the river. In four miles the road forks. Take the left fork (the Tellico-Robbinsville trans-mountain highway), which immediately heads up the mountain. About 13 miles up the mountain, watch for the left turn to Indian Boundary. At the entrance to Indian Boundary, bear right on Forest Service 36. In about a mile, the Forest Service road drops down the back side of Miller Ridge and lands in the lap of Citico Creek. Put in at the base of Miller Ridge, 2.5 miles "behind" Indian Boundary Campground. Take out at any of several convenient spots downstream. A parallel National Forest Service road provides access.

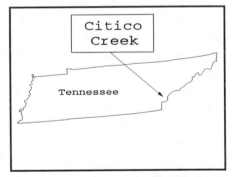

Miles From Citico Creek			
Knoxville, TN	65	Asheville, NC	125
Chattanooga, TN	85	Nashville, TN	207

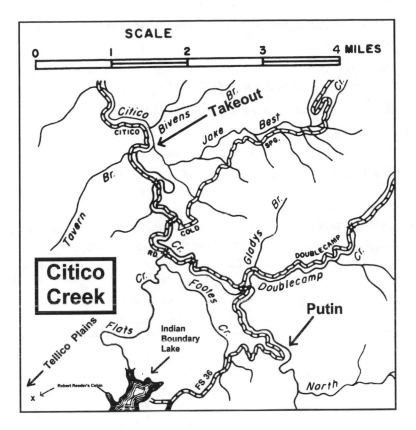

Other Information

Camping

The Citico is in the middle of the car camping mecca of eastern America. Indian Boundary Campground is 2.5 miles from the putin. Double Camp Creek is part way through the run. Numerous sites are available alongside Citico Creek, as well as on the nearby Tellico, North, and Bald Rivers. Generally, campsites are in short supply only on July 4th and Labor Day weekends. For more details, refer to the upper Tellico trip description

Hiking

Slickrock and Joyce Kilmer wildernesses are nearby. The hills surrounding the Citico are honeycombed with hiking trails. Maps are available at the Ranger Station on Tellico River Road near the lower Tellico takeout.

Fishing

This region is a trout fishing mecca.

Suitability for Rafting (On a 1 to 7 Scale): Forget it.

TRIP Profile

The Citico Creek trip Profile is another study in contrasts. The gradient scores are all triple digit (148, 131, and 141), producing constant rapids (111). However, the volume is modest (Volume x Gradient Interaction = 84), there's a parallel road (Inaccessibility = 56), the entrapments aren't particularly invidious (72), and the rapids, although continuous, aren't inordinately rambunctious (87). These elements combine to produce an overall average level of stream difficulty (101).

Nearby Alternate Trips		
Alternate Trip	**Rapids Difficulty**	**TRIP Points**
Hiwassee River	II	70
Ocoee River	III-IV	104
Upper Tellico	III-IV	110
Lower Tellico	III	96

Clear Creek

Jett to Nemo
(Tennessee)

TRIP Profile			
Scale Midpoint = 100			
Overall Difficulty	97	Rapids Difficulty	95
Volume x Gradient	91	Continuous Rapids	99
Average Gradient	80	Entrapments	128
Maximum Gradient	88	Inaccessibility	119
Total Gradient	91	Reputation	105

Actual Stream Data			
Max Rapids	III+	Stream Size	Small-Med
Average Gradient	27	Length (in miles)	10
Maximum Gradient	60	Morphology Types	2&3

Overview

Clear Creek is a major tributary of the Obed River and possibly the most popular trip in the Obed/Emory watershed. This section of Clear Creek offers sparkling water, mildly technical rapids, and one of the most spectacular small canyons in eastern America. In fact, Clear Creek downstream of Lilly Bridge is one of the standout attractions of a watershed justly famous for its canyon scenery.

The Jett to Nemo run begins on Clear Creek, then continues on the Obed and Emory Rivers. It provides two and a half miles of delightful Class II(III) warmup rapids between Jett and Lilly bridges, followed by a mile and a half of Class III+ water in a sheer-walled canyon between Lilly Bridge and confluence with the Obed River,

151

and then six miles of less technical but more powerful Class II-III rapids on the Obed and Emory Rivers. Its rapids include the Grunch, Lilly, Jacks Rock, Camel Rock, Wootens Folly, Rockjumble, Focus Falls, Keep Right, and Widowmaker.

The first four miles of the trip, between Jett Bridge and the Obed River confluence, have something for paddlers of every skill level. Beginning paddlers can rock scramble below Lilly Bridge and marvel at the water conditions they'll navigate someday. Novice paddlers can challenge the 2.5 miles from Jett to Lilly. Intermediates can venture cautiously below Lilly Bridge. And advanced paddlers confident of their skills can try lower Clear Creek at higher flows.

Mile(s)	Jett to Nemo Top-To-Bottom Itinerary
0.0	Put in at Jett Bridge on Genesis Road. Limited parking and danger of vandalism.
0.0 to 1.5	Continuous Class II creek water.
1.5	The Grunch (Class II+)
1.7	Spinner (Class II+).
1.9	Pour Over (Class II+).
2.5	Lilly Bridge and Lilly Rapid (Class III-).
2.8	Jacks Rock (Class III).
3.0	Camel Rock (Class III+).
3.3	Wootens Folly (Class III+).
3.5	Rock Jumble (Class III).
3.8	Focus Falls (Class III).
4.0	Obed River confluence.
4.8	Canoe Hole.
5.1	Unnamed Class III.
5.3	Unnamed Class III.
5.6	Keep Right! (Class III).
6.0	Widowmaker (Class III).
8.5	Emory River confluence.
10.0	Nemo Bridge (Takeout).

Ray Brown paddling Clear Creek's Camel Rock Rapid. Part of the Obed National Wild and Scenic River system. Don Ellis photo.

Description

Jett to Lilly

The 2.5 miles between Jett and Lilly Bridges are delightful Class II(III) in character, with a moderate 24 feet/mile gradient. In this section Clear Creek is a miniature Obed, with large boulders in the streambed and thick streamside vegetation. Aptly named, Clear Creek's water is sparkling clear.

Ask anyone who has ever paddled from Jett to Lilly and they'll tell you it has some of the best Class II rapids anywhere. There are several named rapids, but also a scad of others without names. The first one with a name is the Grunch, about a mile above Lilly Bridge, a tricky Class II+ consisting of a converging drop into a hole with substantial turbulence, followed by a small rock garden. At higher water the rock garden forms a second drop. As much as any rapid on any river, the Grunch changes character with fluctuations in water. At levels above 3,500 cfs two powerful holes appear, and the rapid edges into Class III difficulty.

At Spinner (Class II+), a hundred yards downstream of the Grunch, the stream flows around a large boulder and into an auto eddy. Spinner is the site of an old water-powered grist mill (so is Lilly Rapid downstream). The rock and tree stubble on river right downstream of the large boulder in Spinner is part of the old diversion dam. Look closely at the upstream end of the row of stubble and the old mill wheel can still be located (about two feet under water when the Jett Bridge gauge reads 3.3).

Pourover (Class II+) is only a few yards downstream of Spinner. At 6.0 feet and above on the Jett Bridge gauge, the rock in the middle of the stream forms a pourover. At lower levels the rapid can be recognized from upstream by a large rock overhang on river left, directly across from the pourover site.

The next rapid of consequence is Lilly, with its runout beneath the bridge of the same name. A Class II+ at lower flows, Lilly becomes Class III somewhere around 3,000 cfs. Ranging in length from 50 to 150 yards (depending on flow) Lilly features a drop into a narrow chute with a rock ledge along the right side. After this drop the paddler is treated to a splashy, bouncy ride to the bottom. At high water, Lilly runs well past the bridge and has two holes at the very bottom.

Lilly Bridge to the Obed River (Clear Creek Canyon)

Only a mile and a half in length, this is nevertheless a premier stretch of whitewater, where Clear Creek drops through its canyon at the rate of 53 feet/mile. This gradient figure is somewhat deceptive, however, for the canyon is a ledge/pool run.

There are four Class III-III+ rapids in Clear Creek Canyon. Jacks Rock, the first major declivity, is encountered 500 yards below Lilly Bridge. This visually impressive Class III is often called Jacks Rock Falls, and deserves the "falls" designation because the stream drops about 12 feet in a distance of 15 yards. Most of the decline is accomplished via an angled slide that dumps into a small pool. But the slide ends short of the pool and the final descent is a vertical drop. The difficulty of the rapid is not so much the slide or the drop as it is the approach. The initial approach is through a rockgarden situated on the brink of the slide that culminates in the drop. The trick is to enter the slide at precisely the desired angle, because corrections are difficult on the way down. To scout Jacks Rock before attempting it, catch the small eddy on river right at the top of the falls. (Note: A splendid spot for photographers is the large rock at the base of Jacks Rock. It can be reached by walking and rock scrambling downstream from Lilly Bridge on river left.)

Two hundred yards downstream is Camel Rock, a boat eater rapid named for the large rock that splits the current, forcing a third left, a third right, and pulling the rest underneath. To run Camel Rock, get right and stay right. The stream is constricted to a turbulent course through a narrow zigzag crevice. A miscalculation or delay in execution in this channel can spell trouble. It has put many a paddler down for a rough swim. But whatever the peril of the preferred river right course, it pales into insignificance when compared to the left side. Avoid river left around Camel Rock. It is undercut and the current pulls boats and bodies under the Camel's Hump.

From Camel Rock to the Obed there's no let up. The gradient is constant, the water is technical, and constrictive boulders are everywhere.

The next rapid is Wootens Folly, which is usually Class III+. It becomes Class IV, however, somewhere around 3,500 cfs. This is a tricky rapid (ask Mr. Wooten!), and a mistake at the top can result in a hundred yard swim over multiple drops. A rock at the entrance to the rapid divides the water. The preferred route is to the right of the entrance rock followed by a quick swerve back left to avoid Barnetts Rock which sits dead center downstream. There is a sizeable drop on either side of Barnetts Rock, followed by several smaller drops and holes. The boulder on river right near the bottom of the rapid is undercut, radically.

The pool at the end of Wootens Folly offers an excellent opportunity to stop and observe the vertical 300 foot cliffs on both sides, especially river left.

Rock Jumble Rapid (Class III) is next, 120 yards long and densely congested. A large flat rock at the bottom provides a good lunchstop site.

The last named rapid on Clear Creek is Focus Falls (Class III). At higher flows, the water action exhibits a corkscrew action. Run it from right to left, catching the left-side eddy between drops. A small rock overhang on river left provides a convenient lunch shelter in bad weather.

For an inspiring view of two canyons of the Obed, stop on river right of Clear Creek at the Obed confluence and hike up the short trail to the overlook. On one side is the canyon of Clear Creek. On the other side is the Obed's most majestic canyon. The deep rumble emanating from the Obed canyon is a rapid known as Rockgarden (Class IV).

Obed Confluence to Nemo

Union with the Obed triples the volume and transforms stream character from a technical creek to a medium volume river with holes, standing waves and mostly straightforward Class II-III rapids. About 0.75 miles below the confluence, a long pool known as Canoe Hole locates a river left 4WD road that provides emergency egress from the canyon, the first since Lilly Bridge. Canoe Hole can also serve as a low water putin. Technically adept paddlers can run the Obed below this access at levels as low as 300 cfs on the Oakdale gauge.

The Obed below Canoe Hole contains from two to four (depending on water level) Class III rapids and a spate of Class II and Class II+ spots. In the first half mile below Canoe Hole, two mild Class III rapids appear (these are Class II+ below 2,500 cfs). The two named Class IIIs, Keep Right and Widowmaker, appear about three-quarters of a mile below Canoe Hole, in quick succession. These rapids, and the one mile of the Emory below the Obed confluence, are described in more detail in the Obed River description (Devils Breakfast Table to Nemo) in this volume.

Summary

The Jett to Nemo section of Clear Creek has three distinct sections. From Jett Bridge to Lilly Bridge, it's easy Class II. From Lilly to the Obed confluence, it's semi-serious Class III+ technical paddling. Below the confluence, it's a medium volume Class II-III run.

Clear Creek below Jett Bridge is a National Wild and Scenic River. It deserves that designation. It has resplendent scenery with sheer canyon walls, pristine water quality, and technical whitewater.

(Keep your eyes open as you float under Lilly Bridge. It's been the site of reported revelrous dancing. See the story entitled Early Daze in the Obed; The Bridge Dancers, in *River Stories: Tales From Bo Rockerville,* by Monte Smith, available from Pahsimeroi Press.)

Water Levels

Clear Creek flows into the Obed River and the Obed flows into the Emory River. The only telemetric gauge in the system is located at Oakdale on the Emory River, near the bottom of the Obed/Emory watershed. Thus, the Emory at Oakdale gauge provides, at best, an approximate indication of streamflow conditions on tributaries like Clear Creek, which carry only part of the Oakdale volume. The proportion of volume that Clear Creek carries at any given time varies widely, depending on local rainfall patterns. If rainfall is uniform across the watershed, Clear Creek will carry approximately 25% of Oakdale volume. Thus, "high" levels on Clear Creek begin as the Oakdale gauge rises above 3,500 cfs, producing an actual Clear Creek volume of 875 cfs. However, the proportion of Oakdale volume actually carried by Clear Creek following any specific rainfall can vary from 5% to 70%! Thus, when the Oakdale gauge reads 6,000 cfs, Clear Creek may carry as little as 300 cfs or as much as 4,200 cfs. The good news among all his indeterminacy is that when the gauge at Oakdale has a high reading, the water has to be coming from somewhere, so something in the Obed/Emory system is running at optimal level.

Emory at Oakdale readings are available from the Tennessee Valley Authority (TVA): (800) 238-2264. (Press code "3" after the recorded message.)

Clear Creek Gauge Locations	
TVA Emory at Oakdale	Jett Bridge
Low: 1,200 cfs Medium: 2,500 cfs High: 3,500 cfs	Low : 3.0 Medium: 4.0 High: 5.0

Access

Clear Creek is part of the Obed/Emory watershed, located on the Cumberland Plateau in Tennessee near Crossville. The main access to this part of the world is I-40. The putin is at Jett Bridge on Genesis Road and the takeout is at Nemo Bridge near Wartburg.

To reach Jett Bridge, take the Genesis Road exit off I-40 near Crossville and drive northeast about 20 miles.

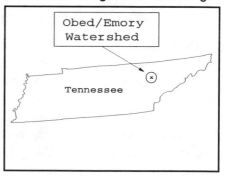

To reach the takeout from Jett, drive east on Genesis Road a short distance to the TN 62 intersection. Turn right toward Lancing. Continue through the metropolis of Lancing, across the rail tracks, and up the hill. At the top of the hill (about 0.25 mile past the rail crossing) a road forks to the right. Take this right fork. It crosses the Emory River and continues one mile to an intersection with old US 27. Turn right on old US 27 and drive up the mountain to the edge of Wartburg. Look carefully on road right for a faded sign that points the way to Catoosa. Turn right on this road. Bear right after one block and then persevere. With a little luck and considerable perseverance the paved road will turn to a gravel surface and thereafter to dirt and/or mud.

Miles From Clear Creek	
Knoxville, TN 70	Atlanta, GA 240
Nashville, TN 135	Cincinnati, OH 310

Eventually the road plunges downward. At the bottom, the Emory River is spanned by ancient Nemo Bridge. Round trip shuttle from Jett Bridge is 70 to 90 minutes, depending on driving style. Limited parking is available beside the river at the takeout (on river left).

A suggestion. If access at Canoe Hole were improved, Clear Creek Canyon could be run three or four times in the same day. Moreover, Canoe Hole could be used as takeout for trips originating from Antioch Bridge on Daddys Creek. A 14 mile run from Antioch Bridge to Canoe Hole would combine two of the top trips in the Obed/Emory system (Daddys Creek Canyon and Devils Breakfast Table to Nemo on the Obed), producing a run that would lodge near the top of every advanced paddler's list of favorites. Improvement of the Canoe Hole access also would permit running this stretch of whitewater while the Catoosa Wildlife Management Area is closed to vehicular traffic during much of the prime springtime paddling season.

Other Information

Camping

Camping is available at Frozen Head State Park off TN 62, five miles east of Wartburg. The large building on the way into Frozen Head is a minimum security prison. Sweet dreams!

Campsites are also available at Cumberland Mountain State Park, off US 127 about six miles south of Crossville.

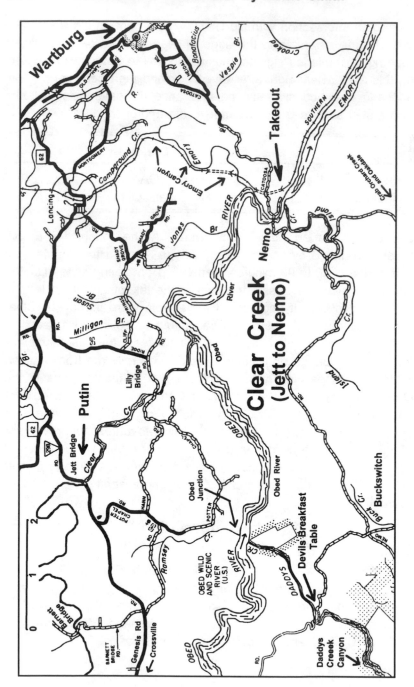

Hiking

At Lilly Bridge on river right, a short trail leads to the cliff top, providing a bird's eye glimpse into the top of Clear Creek Canyon.

At the confluence of Clear Creek and the Obed River a short trail leads upward to a narrow razorback ridge which provides a breath-taking view into two impressive canyons, those of Clear Creek and the Obed River.

Longer hiking trails are available in Frozen Head State Park near Wartburg.

Maps

Excellent maps of the Obed watershed exist. The trick is to find one of them. Here's how it's done. Send $4 to: TVA, 1101 Market Street, 101 Honey Bldg, Chattanooga, TN 37402, or phone (615) 632-6082.

Suitability for Rafting (On a 1 to 7 Scale): 3

Raftable at higher flows, but beware Camel Rock, which could be a serious bottleneck.

TRIP Profile

Notice that the two most elevated scores are for entrapments (128) and Inaccessibility (119). This pattern characterizes many Obed/Emory streams, which flow through deep, spectacularly scenic canyons that are, unfortunately, laced with undercut rock formations.

Nearby Alternate Trips

The Obed/Emory watershed contains 18 different trips with at least Class II whitewater, all in a remarkably circumscribed geographic area. Some of the Obed/Emory runs are through sheer-walled canyons that are among the most scenic in the Southeast. The complete system is described in *A Paddler's Guide to the Obed/Emory Watershed*, by Monte Smith.

Other Obed/Emory runs described in the present volume are listed in the following table:

First Island on Big Sandy Creek. Ray Brown is the paddler. Mayo Gravatt photo.

Bill Hay at the top of Wootens Folly. Clear Creek in the Obed/Emory Watershed. Mayo Gravatt photo.

Alternate Trip	Rapids Difficulty	TRIP Points
Crab Orchard Creek	III+	98
Daddys Creek Canyon	III-IV	109
Island Creek	III-IV	108
Obed River: Goulds Bend	III(V)	95
Obed River: DBT to Nemo	III(IV)	101

Clear Fork River

Brewster to Burnt Mill
(Tennessee)

TRIP Profile			
Scale Midpoint = 100			
Overall Difficulty	69	Rapids Difficulty	69
Volume x Gradient	65	Continuous Rapids	50
Average Gradient	68	Entrapments	72
Maximum Gradient	74	Inaccessibility	101
Total Gradient	71	Reputation	60

Actual Stream Data			
Max Rapids	II	Stream Size	Small
Average Gradient	14	Length (in miles)	10
Maximum Gradient	40	Morphology Types	1&2

Overview

Clear Fork is part of the Big South Fork National River and Recreation Area (BSFNRRA), in north-central Tennessee. It joins the New River to create the Big South Fork of the Cumberland which flows north into Kentucky. This section of Clear Fork, between Brewster Bridge and Burnt Mill Bridge, has a ledge/pool streambed morphology, an isolated setting, and many streamside sheer cliffs. The average gradient is modest (14 feet/mile), but it's not uniform, fluctuating from 5 to 40 feet/mile. Because of variable stream conditions caused by fluctuating gradient, the trip is inappropriate for novices unless accompanied by more experienced paddlers.

The scenery is almost as variable as the gradient, ranging from unimpressive in the first mile below the putin to exceptional at several places, including two mini-gorges that contain many scenic bluffs. Approximately half way through the trip, at a place called "Meeting of the Waters" near the historic community of Rugby, Whiteoak Creek enters and changes Clear Fork from a creek with technical rapids to a small river with bouncy and open whitewater.

Similar To. Upper Clear Creek in the Obed/Emory watershed, with alternating ledges, pools, and sheer cliffs.

Mile(s)	Clear Fork River Top-To-Bottom Itinerary
0.0	Put in at Brewster Bridge on TN 52 between Rugby Historic Community and Armathwaite.
0.0 to 1.5	Parallel 4WD road on river left.
0.1 to 0.3	Mild riffles and shoals.
2.0 to 2.5	River right bluff, increased gradient, mild rapids and shoals.
3.2	Class II(II+) rapid with undercut rock hazards.
3.2 to 4.2	Beginning of Clear Fork Gorge, with continuous small rapids (some to Class II+) and the maximum gradient of the trip (40 feet/mile).
4.3	Historic "Meeting of the Waters," confluence with Whiteoak Creek.
4.4 to 6.7	Gorge deepens, with sheer bluffs on river left and great scenery.
6.8 to 7.7	Gorge ends; flatwater begins.
7.8 to 8.5	Another gorge, this time with a series of Class II rapids.
8.6 to 9.9	More flatwater.
10.0	Burnt Mill Bridge takeout.

Description

Below Brewster Bridge, Clear Fork River narrows noticeably between vertical cliffs and produces fast current and small waves. After a short distance the cliffs recede and long pools commence, broken occasionally by mild riffles. Human intrusion is evident, especially along river left where a four-wheel-drive road parallels Clear Fork River until Goad Spring Branch at mile 1.5, where the road appears to end. Below here the streamsides appear undisturbed.

At mile 2.0 a bluff appears on river right and runs about half a mile. This stretch is marked by an increase in gradient and a series of easy shoals and rapids. The first Class II rapid appears at approximately mile 3.2, just after Clear Fork River completes a sweeping 180 degree north-to-south turn around Little Bend. This rapid poses a problem because of undercut rocks on both sides. The left-side course is probably safer but it demands careful maneuvering and entails dropping into a surprisingly strong hole. Fortunately, this rapid can be recognized from upstream by its roar (it comes after a stretch of quiet water) and by the obviously undercut rock snaking out from river right. It's scoutable from either side. Immediately downstream a small rock garden creates another rapid.

Next, Clear Fork enters a small gorge with continuous Class I(II) rapids. Some of the small rapids require good boat control and novices may have problems. The gradient in this stretch is a relatively robust 40 feet/mile. Large boulders line both banks, along with stands of white pine and hemlock.

The confluence with Whiteoak Creek (Meeting of the Waters) is at mile 4.2. Here, the river broadens markedly and volume increases substantially. With the added volume from Whiteoak Creek, rapids also change character, becoming less technical but more powerful, with many standing waves. The gorge grows deeper and more scenic, with vertical bluffs on river left sometimes threatening to overhang the river. The scenery is now Class A+.

In the vicinity of mile 6.7 the bluffs recede from the river, the gorge ends abruptly and so do the Class II rapids. Long pools become the norm, broken only occasionally by a mild riffle. At mile 7.2 the river executes a right angle turn to the south and presents a series of Class I(II) shoals which relieve the tedium of flat water paddling. Just about when the paddler concludes that all whitewater is past, the river sweeps left and then powerfully back right into the first of several exhilarating Class II rapids, and in the process enters yet another strikingly beautiful gorge. When this series of rapids ends, however, long pools again predominate in the last 1.5 miles to the Burnt Mill Bridge takeout.

Summary

Clear Fork River is an excellent setting for a leisurely-paced family float trip. Because of the long pools that separate its rapids, allow about five to six hours for this float. Although there are no really significant rapids, there are many easy Class IIs. One of the special charms of Clear Fork is that its rapids change character dramatically when Whiteoak Creek adds its volume near the midpoint of the trip.

Water Levels

The Army Corps of Engineers (615) 736-5635 maintains a gauge on the Big South Fork at Stearns. Approximately 2,000 cfs is the minimum for a Clear Fork trip, and at this level the first 4.5 miles to Whiteoak confluence will be rocky. (Only a fraction of the gauge reading will be in Clear Fork at the Brewster Bridge putin. The Stearns gauge also reflects volume from the New River, North Whiteoak Creek, Whiteoak Creek, and numerous smaller tributaries.) Clear Fork is runnable at all but flood levels, but given the likelihood that novices will predominantly constitute the traffic on this headwaters stream of the Big South Fork of the Cumberland, a prudent maximum is somewhere around 5,000 cfs.

Access

The principal access route into this area is US 27, which runs north-south along the eastern boundary of the BSF-NRRA. US 27 can be reached from I-75 by taking either KY 92 or TN 63. From I-40, westbounders should take US 27 north, and east-bounders should take US 127

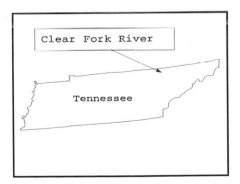

Clear Fork River

Tennessee

north to TN 52, which skirts the southern boundary of the BSF-NRRA.

The Brewster Bridge putin is on TN 52, which connects US 27 and US 127. This bridge is between Allardt and Rugby. Take out at Burnt Mill Bridge, which is also the putin for the Big South Fork (of the Cumberland) Gorge. To run the shuttle from the putin, drive east toward Elgin on TN 52. Approximately one mile before the junction with US 27 at Elgin, turn left (north) on a county back road and (with luck) follow it about five miles to the river.

Miles From Clear Fork River			
Knoxville, TN	70	Chattanooga, TN	125
Nashville, TN	155	Asheville, NC	190
Cincinnati, OH	225	Atlanta, GA	240

Other Information

Camping

The principal campground facility in the area is Bandy Creek, located on Leatherwood Ford Road in the heart of the BSFNRRA, about three miles west of the Big South Fork Gorge takeout at Leatherwood Ford. This campground is about midway between Oneida and Jamestown.

Pickett State Park, located on TN 154 north of Jamestown, also has a campground.

Lodging

Cabins are available at Pickett State Park.

Charit Creek Lodge, located at the confluence of Charit Creek and Station Camp Creek, is open year-round and operates similar to LeConte Lodge in the Smokies. (It's managed by the same group.) It has no electricity and is accessible only by horseback or foot trail. Call (615) 429-5704 for more information.

(For other information on Mt LeConte Lodge, see the section on Hiking in the upper Little River in the Smokies trip description.)

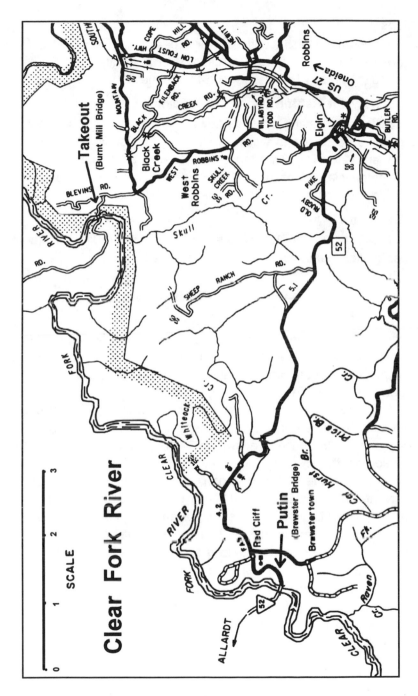

Maps

A color map which identifies river access points is available from the Park Service for a nominal charge. (Big South Fork; Route 3, Box 401; Oneida, Tennessee 37841; Phone (615) 879-3625)

Suitability for Rafting (On a 1 to 7 Scale): 5

Suitable for rafting at higher flows. Raft rentals and commercial guided raft trips are available in Oneida, Jamestown, Whitley City (KY), and Knoxville. The Park Service issues an annual Fact Sheet on commercial licensees. (Big South Fork; Route 3, Box 401; Oneida, Tennessee 37841; Phone 615\879-3625)

TRIP Profile

The distinguishing TRIP score is Inaccessibility (101). Its remoteness makes Clear Fork River a scenic standout.

Nearby Alternate Trips

Clear Fork joins with the New River (*not* the New River of West Virginia notoriety) to form the Big South Fork of the Cumberland. The gorge run on the Big South Fork, with a putin at Burnt Mill Bridge, is one of the most scenic in the Southeast and is described elsewhere in this volume (see Big South Fork).

A tributary of Clear Fork, Whiteoak Creek, is occasionally runnable. It has an enjoyable gorge section of Class II rapids in its last half mile, but price of admission to the gorge is a long flatwater paddle from the TN 52 bridge, unless a better access can be located somewhere in the Rugby Historic District.

North Whiteoak Creek (a tributary of the Big South Fork) with a putin at the old Zenith Mine site, is a splendid early spring Class II(III) trip. However, access to the putin is a real challenge and the round-trip shuttle can take as long as four hours.

The Obed/Emory watershed is less than an hour south. (Take US 27 to Wartburg.) The Obed system, which includes 18 whitewater trips, is described in *A Paddler's Guide to the Obed/Emory Watershed,* by Monte Smith.

Conasauga River

Below Jacks River Confluence
(Georgia/Tennessee)

TRIP Profile			
Scale Midpoint = 100			
Overall Difficulty	72	Rapids Difficulty	69
Volume x Gradient	60	Continuous Rapids	50
Average Gradient	87	Entrapments	72
Maximum Gradient	78	Inaccessibility	101
Total Gradient	81	Reputation	49

Actual Stream Data			
Max Rapids	II+	Stream Size	Small
Average Gradient	34	Length (in miles)	6
Maximum Gradient	45	Morphology Types	1&2

Overview

Georgia or Tennessee, that's the question. Although most of the lower Conasauga trip is through Tennessee territory, its headwaters lie entirely within Georgia. Moreover, the stream plays tag with the Georgia/Tennessee state boundary, twice darting back across the line into its home state. And shortly downstream of the alternate takeout, it breaks off its flirtation with the Volunteer State altogether and returns permanently to Georgia, heading due south to join the Coosawattee to form the Oostanoula which in turn confluences with the Etowah to form the Coosa River.

In its upper stretches, the Conasauga is as pristine as any boatable water in the southeast. With its headwaters in North

171

Georgia's Cohutta Wilderness, threats of contamination are reduced. The water is sparkling, brilliantly clear and the stream's banks are profuse with hemlocks. When the landscape is snow-covered, the contrasts between snow, green hemlocks and sparkling clear water are dazzling, especially on a sunny day. From the alternate putin where the access road veers away from the stream until the road re-encroaches five miles downstream, there is no more lovelier small mountain stream. Although the gradient is a respectable 35 feet/mile, there are no really difficult rapids, with only a couple at Class II+ (or easy III-) difficulty.

Now the bad news. The stream is small, the runoff is fast, and it's usually runnable only in winter and early spring. Obtaining a water reading can be a problem also. Generally, the Conasauga is runnable only after local rains. The optimal time for a planned trip is from mid-February to mid-April. On the positive side, the Conasauga is near a number of other popular runs including the Ocoee, Hiwassee, Tellico, Cartecay, and Amicolola. If you happen to be paddling one of these other streams after heavy rains, the Conasauga is probably also running.

Mile(s)	Conasauga River Top-To-Bottom Itinerary
0.0	Put in at Jacks River confluence.
0.6	Alternate putin.
0.7	Taylor Branch Rapid (Class II+).
2.2	The "Falls" (Class II+).
6.7	Preferred takeout.
6.7 to 10.0	Pastoral stream.
10.0	Alternate takeout at US 411 bridge.

Description

The first five miles of the lower Conasauga are as pretty as any creek in the Southeast. The rapids are moderate in difficulty and relatively few in number, but the gradient is healthy and hence a swift current prevails even in the absence of whitewater. Jacks River confluence provides a convenient putin. Half a mile downstream, a large pool marks the alternate putin, just upstream of Taylor Branch Rapid (Class II+), a rocky ledge which requires some maneuvering and is most easily run far left.

Swift current, mild shoals, and easy rapids convey the paddler to the "Falls" at mile 2.2. Novice paddlers will want to scout this Class II+ drop from river right. It's not really a waterfall, per se, but it certainly is the biggest rapid on the run. It's also difficult to clearly see the drop from either bank.

Below the Falls there are no other named rapids, but numerous small, easy drops appear before civilization encroaches. Unless the preferred takeout is selected, the trip ends in a three mile flatwater paddle to US 411.

Summary

Aesthetically outstanding. Mild rapids. Southern Appalachia at its best.

Water Levels

Runnable only after sustained rains.

Access

The Conasauga is located in northern Georgia and southeastern Tennessee. The key to finding the stream is US 411, a main north-south highway through northern Georgia and eastern Tennessee. US 411 crosses the Conasauga River a few miles north of the Tennessee-Georgia state line.

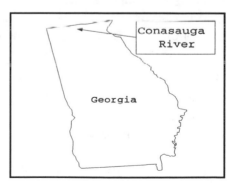

Head north from the US 411 bridge and make a right turn (east) on the first road. Cross the railroad tracks and turn right at the first intersection. The paved surface ends in a few miles, in the vicinity of the takeout (refer to the accompanying map). The road continues past the takeout and eventually pitches off a precipitous ridge into the Alaculsy Valley, providing an exciting glimpse of the river far below.

Put in at Jacks River confluence or a half mile downstream at Taylor Branch. Take out on river right, where houses first begin to appear along the river.

The Conasauga also is accessible from Cisco (located on US 411 thirteen miles south of the state line) via GA 2, and from Thunder Rock campground on the Ocoee River via a network of Forest Service backroads.

Miles From the Conasauga River	
Chattanooga, TN 52	Knoxville, TN 125
Atlanta, GA 112	Asheville, NC 172

Other Information

Camping

Primitive camping is possible at the alternate putin. Sylco Campground is nearby on Forest Service backroads. Thunder Rock Campground on the Ocoee River is only a dozen or so miles distant (as the crow flies), or about thirty miles via US 411 and US 64. Gee Creek Campground (hot showers!) is off US 411 near the Hiwassee River, approximately 20 miles north of the alternate Conasauga takeout, and Quinn Springs Campground is only a few miles from Gee Creek, on TN 30. Lake Conasauga Campground is 10 miles east of Cisco on GA 2. Fort Mountain Campground is 10 miles east of Chatsworth on GA 52.

Hiking

Hiking trails abound in this region. One trail begins at the Conasauga-Jacks River confluence, on the fringe of the 34,000 acre Cohutta Wilderness, and winds up Jacks River to Jacks River Falls. This trail requires several crossings of Jacks River and hence may be impassable when the Conasauga is runnable.

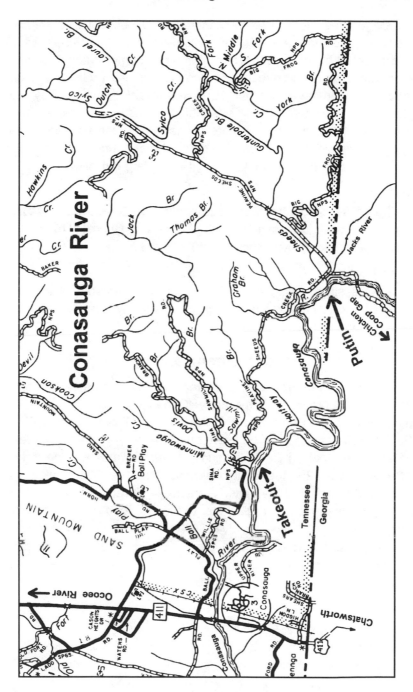

Other trails are located throughout the Ocoee Wildlife Management Area to the north. These woods, however, are inhabited by wild boar. Although these animals can attain some pretty frightening proportions and can be menacing because of their protruding tusks, they aren't ordinarily dangerous unless startled, when they can stampede. Because of poor eyesight, their size, and the fact they live in groups of a dozen or more animals, they can unintentionally run you over. If you walk up on a gang of them, make a lot of noise and chances are they'll make a point of getting out of your way.

Maps

Maps of the Cohutta Wilderness and the Chattahoochee National Forest are available from the Cohutta Ranger District, USFS, 401 Old Ellijay Road, Chatsworth, GA 30705, or phone (706) 695-6736.

TRIP Profile

Inaccessibility is the story. The stream is unremarkable in every other category, but it winds through an absolutely spectacular north Georgia and Tennessee wonderland.

Nearby Alternate Trips

Other than the trips listed in the table below, one other possibility (for the hardcore only) is the upper Conasauga (Class IV), with a putin at Chicken Coop Gap on GA Route 2. From Chicken Coop Gap, the river can't even be seen, and it takes something of a leap of faith to go looking for it. To find it, head downhill for one-eighth mile (and about 260 feet of vertical descent). The little creek at the bottom of the bluff is the upper Conasauga River. From this point it's eight miles and 421 vertical feet to the first road access, for a 53 feet/mile gradient. However, over 80% of the drop occurs in the first four miles, so the action is spirited while it lasts. Once or twice each spring, the river's high enough to make the famous Chicken Coop Gap run. One thing about it: it's never crowded.

Alternate Trip	Rapids Difficulty	TRIP Points
Amicalola	II-III	na
Cartecay	II(III)	74
Hiwassee	II	70
Ocoee	III-IV	104
Upper Tellico	III- IV	110
Lower Tellico	III	96

Crab Orchard Creek
Flat Rock Ford to Oakdale
(Tennessee)

TRIP Profile			
Scale Midpoint = 100			
Overall Difficulty	98	Rapids Difficulty	89
Volume x Gradient	89	Continuous Rapids	123
Average Gradient	97	Entrapments	83
Maximum Gradient	103	Inaccessibility	110
Total Gradient	126	Reputation	117

Actual Stream Data			
Max Rapids	III+	Stream Size	Micro
Average Gradient	45	Length (in miles)	13.5
Maximum Gradient	80	Morphology Type	2

Overview

Crab Orchard Creek is part of the Obed/Emory watershed in Tennessee. It flows into the Emory River a few miles downstream of the Obed/Emory confluence. Crab Orchard is micro-to-small in size with robust gradient and continuous Class II-III rapids. In the early miles its rapids are moderately technical. Toward the bottom of the run, the streambed widens considerably, producing lively wave fields with surprisingly hungry holes.

Crab Orchard Creek came of age in the 1980's, becoming one of the most popular trips in the Obed watershed, probably the favorite intermediate high water run. Its popularity is well founded. With the right flow level this can be the most fun trip in the Obed/-

178

Emory watershed, if not in the entire Southeast. Of the 10.5 miles from the putin to its confluence with the Emory River, Crab Orchard is 80% whitewater. Mile after mile of Class II and Class III rapids, with only one or two spots that surge toward Class IV difficulty at higher flows.

Does it sound too good to be true? Admittedly there's one small fly in the ointment: water availability. Unfortunately, the minimum required flow of about 7,000 cfs on the Emory at Oakdale gauge is a relatively rare occurrence.

Similar To. Crab Orchard Creek is a smaller-scale, slightly more technical southern version of West Virginia's Laurel Fork of the Cheat. Crab Orchard has more rapids in its upper miles than Laurel Fork and its rapids are more technical, but in the bottom miles both streams open out into wave fields.

Mile(s)	Crab Orchard Top-To-Bottom Itinerary
0	Put in at Flat Rock Ford.
0-2	Mild riffles, small rapids.
3	Better rapids.
4	Even better rapids.
5	Outstanding rapids.
6	More rapids.
7	Even more rapids.
8	Bridge. Rapids change character.
9	Wave train rapids.
10	More wave train rapids.
10.5	Emory River confluence.
10.5 to 13.5	Big river, some waves, fast current.
13.5	Takeout at Oakdale.

Description

The first half mile is discouragingly flat, but after the current picks up, easy Class II rapids begin to appear, and soon the Class IIs and

IIIs are continuous. The rapids in the upper part of the trip are technical, often requiring considerable maneuvering. About four miles into the run care is necessary to avoid Pat Hills Locker where the stream tucks into a river right undercut ledge.

Because Crab Orchard is so small, downed trees may block its streamflow following heavy rains. Other than this problem, and Pat Hills Locker, the other hazard to watch for is a rapid so congested with rocks that it may not be runnable. Recognizable from upstream by a small tree on river right growing at the edge of the water, it can usually be run down a "cheat" chute on the extreme right side.

About three miles above confluence with the Emory River a bridge crosses. This point can be reached from the shuttle road near Oakdale. The bridge provides a convenient alternate access for emergencies or abbreviated trips. The three miles of Crab Orchard below this bridge gradually change in character due to added volume from several tributaries and a change in streambed morphology. The rapids are larger, less technical but more powerful, consisting predominantly of extended wave fields, and the holes grow tenacious.

Old strip mines encroach in the last three miles before confluence with the Emory, but aren't overly noticeable from the stream itself. Crab Orchard joins the Emory about one-third mile downstream of Camp Austin. The three miles from this confluence to Oakdale, the takeout, are flat, but with 10,000+ cfs they pass in 40 minutes or less.

Summary

Crab Orchard is a joyful run. Although most rapids are Class II-III, it deserves an overall rating somewhat higher than this because the action is unremitting. This stream literally has nine miles of whitewater. The major drawback is that the required minimum of 7,000 cfs on the Emory at Oakdale gauge is a relatively rare occurrence. If you're in the Obed/Emory system and discover that Crab Orchard is running, forget everything else and jump on it. Although it lacks the high difficulty tingle of Daddys Creek Canyon (in the same watershed), it's at least as continuous, every bit as much fun, and can be enjoyed by a lot more people, water permitting.

Water Levels

Crab Orchard is runnable only after locally heavy rainfall. If water at the putin is at least six inches deep across the stone surface of Flat Rock Ford, a decent run is at hand. The only convenient telemetric gauge is located at Oakdale on the Emory River, where a minimum reading is about 7,000 cfs. (Call TVA at (800) 238-2264 and press code "3" after the recorded message.) However, because the Oakdale gauge registers drainage from the entire Obed/Emory watershed, it may or may not reflect accurately on Crab Orchard Creek stream conditions. For instance, Crab Orchard may be runnable on one occasion with a 5,000 cfs Oakdale reading, and not runnable on another occasion when the gauge reads 10,000 cfs. A lot depends on whether rainfall was uniformly distributed across the watershed. With uniform rainfall, ideal levels for Crab Orchard are in the 10,000 to 12,000 cfs range. At higher levels, upstream rapids tend to wash out and the run isn't as much fun.

Access

Crab Orchard Creek is near Crossville, Tennessee, between Knoxville and Nashville. From I-40, take the Westel Road exit (between Crossville and Harriman) and drive north on Route 299 for 2.2 miles. Turn left and drive 4.5 more miles to the Catoosa Wildlife Management sign. Turn left and go one mile.

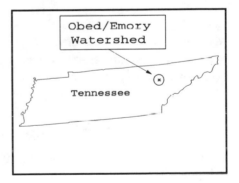

Putin at Flat Rock Ford, 200 yards downstream of the bridge. When the Catoosa Wildlife Management Area (CWMA) is open, the putin also can be reached from Wartburg by taking the Catoosa Road across Nemo Bridge and into the CWMA.

The takeout is at Oakdale. From the putin, drive one mile back to the Catoosa WMA sign. Turn left. Oakdale is seven miles downhill. In downtown Oakdale, turn right and follow the Emory

River three-quarters of a mile to a public access area. Round trip shuttle is about an hour.

Miles From Crab Orchard Creek	
Knoxville, TN 57	Atlanta, GA 240
Nashville, TN 135	Cincinnati, OH 292

Other Information

Camping

Camping is available at Frozen Head State Park, off TN 62, five miles east of Wartburg, and at Cumberland Mountain State Park, off US 127, about six miles south of Crossville.

Maps

Excellent maps of the Obed watershed exist. The trick is to find one of them. Check with TVA at 1101 Market Street, 101 Haney Bldg, Chattanooga, TN 37402, or phone (615) 632-6082.

Suitability for Rafting (On a 1 to 7 Scale): 1

TRIP Profile

Crab Orchard is a roller coaster, of the aquatic variety, as revealed by robust total gradient (126) and continuous rapids (123) scores. The rapids aren't particularly difficult (89), but the stream courses through a remote area (Inaccessibility = 110), and it's part of the mysterious Obed/Emory system (Reputation = 117).

Nearby Alternate Trips

Crab Orchard Creek is one of 18 whitewater trips in the Obed-/Emory watershed. Other trips described in this volume are are listed in the next table:

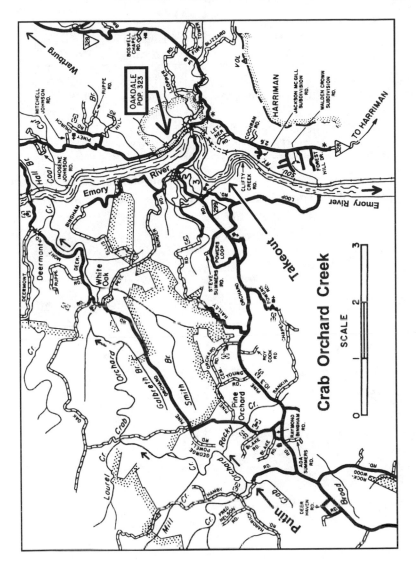

Alternate Trip	Rapids Difficulty	TRIP Points
Clear Creek	III+	97
Daddys Creek Canyon	III-IV	109
Island Creek	III-IV	108
Obed River: Goulds Bend	III(V)	95
Obed River: DBT to Nemo	III(IV)	101

Generally, whenever Crab Orchard is runnable, so too is Island Creek (another small Emory tributary). The Obed/Emory system is described in detail in *A Paddler's Guide to the Obed/Emory Watershed* by Monte Smith.

Cranberry River

Cranberry Campground to Big Rock
(West Virginia)

TRIP Profile			
Scale Midpoint = 100			
Overall Difficulty	103	Rapids Difficulty	105
Volume x Gradient	86	Continuous Rapids	111
Average Gradient	106	Entrapments	106
Maximum Gradient	117	Inaccessibility	74
Total Gradient	109	Reputation	117

Actual Stream Data			
Max Rapids	III-IV	Stream Size	Small
Average Gradient	55	Length (in miles)	7
Maximum Gradient	100	Morphology Type	4

Overview

Located in southern West Virginia in the Monongahela National Forest near Richwood, the Cranberry is a tributary of the Gauley. Virtually its entire drainage is a protected area (the Cranberry Backcountry), producing pristine water quality in this mountain trout stream.

Shortly after it emerges from the protected backcountry, the Cranberry pitches into a technical Class III-IV whitewater frenzy. The stream is steep, with constant ledges and boulders and a scrambled streambed morphology, producing technical rapids that require intense maneuvering. It's a steep creek freak's delight.

A parallel National Forest Service road provides easy access. Camping is permitted at designated spots along the Forest Service road and is also available at large campgrounds located at the putin (Cranberry Campground) and near the takeout (Big Rock Campground). Although the Forest Service road parallels the river, it's never very close. The perception from the river is that of wilderness.

Similar To. The Cranberry is a cross between the Tellico River and the Little River in the Smokies (below the Sinks), with a dash of Goshen Pass (Maury) thrown in to increase the width of the streambed.

Mile(s)	Cranberry River Top-To-Bottom Itinerary
0.0	Put in at Cranberry Campground.
0.0 to 2.0	Fast current and 35 feet/mile gradient.
1.9	Alternate putin at picnic area beside a small tributary.
2.0 to 3.0	100 feet/mile gradient.
3.1 to 4.0	Continuous Class III-III+.
4.1	S-Turn or Cranberry Twist (Class IV).
4.2 to 6.9	Continuous Class II-III water.
7.0	Take out at bridge.
7.0	Gauge on river left 25 yards downstream of bridge.

Description

From the putin at Cranberry Campground, the first two miles are flat. However, the gradient through this relatively quiet section is 35 feet/mile, producing fast current. The real action begins just below a picnic area 1.9 miles downstream of the campground. This picnic area provides a dandy alternate putin.

Below the picnic area the gradient jumps immediately to 100 feet/mile, starting with a long, rambunctious, technical Class IV rapid with ledges, boulders, and a twisting courseway. This is the biggest rapid for some time, but what follows are two miles of absolutely continuous Class III water through some of the most intricate boulder arrangements in the Southeast. For those seeking Class III technical paddling at its very best, these two miles of the Cranberry are hard to beat. The section features numerous convoluted blind turns where precise maneuvering is mandatory.

Then it gets serious. About two miles below the alternate putin, where the river is especially obstructed, the streamflow pours through a left-side channel and then veers right . . . into the Cranberry Twist (Class IV) a rapid with substantial pinning/entrapment potential. The washout is ragged. A swim through any part of this rapid would be rough. Although runnable, the Twist should be anticipated and scouted. From upstream it looks just like a dozen other jumbles, but its blind approach conceals its potential consequences.

From Cranberry Twist to the takeout, both gradient and difficulty moderate but the action is continuous nevertheless. Take out at the bridge. The gauge is 25 yards downstream on river left.

Summary

One of the best technical runs in the Southeast, it's impossible for a creek paddler to see the Cranberry with a good head of water and not smile. At high water it'll blow you downstream so fast your eyeballs will sting from windburn.

Water Levels

The Cranberry is runnable only after substantial local rainfall. Run off is swift. For daily cfs readings, call (304) 529-5127.

Cranberry Gauge Location
Takeout
Low: 3.5 or 300 cfs
Medium: 4.2 or 550 cfs
High: 4.7 or 790 cfs

If the Cranberry reading is not available, the Gauley at Craigsville gauge can be used as a crude indicator. (Craigsville 11.5 = Cranberry paddling zero.)

Access

The Cranberry is in southeastern West Virginia near Richwood. The best routes into the vicinity are US 219 running north and south and WV Route 39 running east and west (although its road signs insist it runs north and south). From Richwood, drive east (or south according to the road signs) on Route 39 toward Marlinton about a mile and look for a Cranberry Recreation Area sign. Turn left and go straight up the mountainside. At the crest the road pitches down the other side toward the Cranberry. The bridge across the Cranberry River near Big Rock Campground is the takeout for the run.

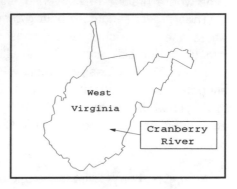

Access to the putin is simple, thanks to a parallel Forest Service road. Put in at Cranberry Campground or the picnic area two miles downstream.

Miles From the Cranberry River	
Charleston, WV 110	Richmond, VA 240
Roanoke, VA 155	Washington, DC 285

Other Information

Area Attractions

Snowshoe, the premier southern ski resort, is only a few miles away. So is the Cass Scenic Railway.

Camping

At the putin. Near the takeout. In-between along the river. Over the ridge at the Williams River. If all else is full, a large campground

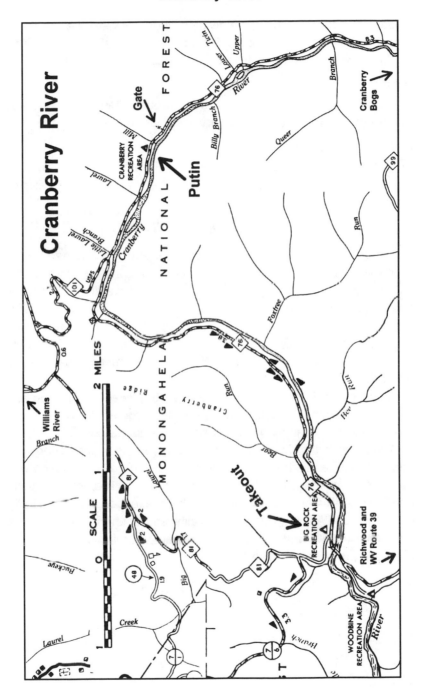

is located at the very top of the dividing ridge between the Cranberry and the Williams. Locals claim it's infested with rattlesnakes. That could be why there're always so many vacant campsites.

Hiking

Although gated at Cranberry Campground, the road continues upstream into the backcountry, providing an interesting walk.

Maps

A map of the Monongahela National Forest, available from the USFS, is an invaluable asset in locating the Cranberry and Williams Rivers.

Nearby Alternate Trips

If the Cranberry is too high to run, the nearby Williams River is probably just right. Whereas the steepest two mile section of the Cranberry turns into a raging cataract at high water, the Williams more gracefully accommodates big volume. The Williams River is only three miles from the Cranberry putin, as the crow flies. Although considerably farther by road, it's still possible to run both streams in the same day. The Williams is described elsewhere in this volume.

The Cherry River runs alongside WV 39 between Richwood and Cranberry Glades, and most of it can be scouted from the road. Both it and the Cranberry can be run in the same day.

When both the Cranberry and Cherry are too high, check out Laurel Creek, a tributary of the Cherry River (not to be confused with Laurel Fork of the Cheat River, also in West Virginia, or Big Laurel Creek in North Carolina). Laurel Creek confluences with the Cherry in Richwood. Although its water quality and scenery are degraded by extensive headwaters mining, the gradient is healthy and some paddlers (not this one) are fond of it.

Daddys Creek Canyon

Antioch to Devils Breakfast Table
(Tennessee)

TRIP Profile			
Scale Midpoint = 100			
Overall Difficulty	109	Rapids Difficulty	113
Volume x Gradient	104	Continuous Rapids	111
Average Gradient	98	Entrapments	128
Maximum Gradient	103	Inaccessibility	128
Total Gradient	95	Reputation	117

Actual Stream Data			
Max Rapids	III-IV	Stream Size	Small
Average Gradient	46	Length (in miles)	6.5
Maximum Gradient	80	Morphology Type	3

Overview

Daddys Creek Canyon is the most difficult of the frequently paddled sections of the Obed/Emory watershed in Tennessee, and with copious water it's probably the toughest run in the system. It flows through an absolutely spectacular canyon, features a two mile stretch of intense whitewater, and harbors nightmare undercut rock formations.

At low water, it's not much. But pour some water down its throat and its reputation will be fully appreciated. Run Daddys Creek Canyon at 2.0 feet on the Antioch Bridge gauge (about 5,000 cfs on TVA's Emory at Oakdale gauge) and the source of its reputation will be obvious. As the water rises above 2.0 feet on Antioch Bridge, the

191

canyon metamorphoses into something approaching a religious experience. Class II+ rapids change into Class IVs, holes begin to chant in unison, "Feed me, feed me!" and the whole canyon section becomes a benchmark for the term "pushy." Difficulty of the canyon section increases exponentially as more water is added. Modest changes in volume produce big changes in how pushy it feels. Even with modest flows, moreover, Daddys Creek Canyon deserves a smidgen more respect than a standard Class III-IV run because of its numerous undercuts.

Memories of Daddys Creek are prominently adorned with rocks. Rocks are everywhere in this staggeringly beautiful canyon of the Obed. And not just regular-sized rocks, either. But big, house-sized boulders. Everywhere. In the stream. Along the streambanks. Ahead of you. Behind you. Everywhere.

Similar To. The closest parallel to Daddys Creek Canyon is probably Johns Creek in Virginia, but in many ways the canyon part of the run also mimics (on a miniature scale) the upper Gauley, particularly Lost Paddle. Daddys Creek Canyon is like many other Cumberland Plateau canyon runs in that it is extraordinarily scenic, pool/ledge in morphology, and hazardous due to streamwide obstructions and radically undercut rocks.

Mile(s)	Daddys Creek Top-To-Bottom Itinerary
0.0	Put in at Antioch Bridge.
0.0 to 1.0	20 feet/mile gradient.
1.0 to 2.0	60 feet/mile gradient.
2.0 to 4.0	20 feet/mile gradient.
3.5	Yellow Creek enters on river right.
3.6 to 5.5	Yellow Creek Canyon.
4.1	Spike (Class III+). River right is undercut.
4.2	Fang of the Rattlesnake (Class III+ to IV+).
4.5	Rocking Chair, aka Tree Rapid (III+ to V). Undercut rock on river left.
4.5 to 6.0	Continuous rapids.
6.5	Takeout at Devils Breakfast Table (DBT).

Description

The first mile below Antioch Bridge drops at 20 feet/mile. The next mile has a 60 feet/mile gradient with several technical Class II rock jumbles that become Class III rapids at about 1.8 on the putin gauge. The next two miles have moderate gradient (20 feet/mile) and permit the paddler to leisurely ponder the significance of the 200 foot vertical sandstone cliffs looming downstream. After paddling 3.5 miles Yellow Creek enters from river right. Downstream, the paddler can see into the top of the canyon.

The canyon section, about two miles in length, begins a half mile below Yellow Creek with a rapid called Spike (Class III+), which is an abrupt drop through a narrow corridor. A rock (the "spike") sits in the main flow on the left side of a constricted chute. The right side of the corridor is undercut. Spike is the only rapid in the canyon that actually gets easier at higher water, when both the spike and river right undercut are covered. Higher water, however, produces a foul-tempered hole between Spike and the next rapid, along with some weird cross currents.

The next rapid is known as Rattlesnake, one of the most visually impressive rapids in the canyon. It begins where the stream flows into a row of boulders and seems to dead end, the river is so congested with room-sized boulders. But there is a winding course on river left leading to the infamous "fang" of the rattlesnake, where the stream drops five feet through three cracks. The rapid is less formidable than it looks, but because of the congestion at the base of the drop, it's difficult to run below 2.0 feet without landing on a rock. Somewhere around 2.0 feet on the Antioch gauge the water rides up and covers the large rock that separates the middle and right chutes. When this occurs the Rattlesnake loses much of its venom and the best route is straight over the top of the rock. Aim for the highest point on the horizon and use the large rock like a launching pad. Hit the launch pad paddling hard and you'll catch air before making a dramatic splatdown.

Rocking Chair (aka Tree Rapid), a succession of drops with the biggest near its bottom, is next. It's a rollicking Class III+ bouncy ride at lower levels. With more water, it quickly jumps to Class IV difficulty and, at about 2.0 feet, it becomes Class V. It nestles an undercut rock formation on river left, near its bottom. This undercut is more hazardous at low water, but at higher levels, although not visible, it's still menacing. Also, the large rock that all the water slams into down at the bottom of the rapid may be undercut. The best tactic is to run down the right side of the Chair at moderate levels and carry on the right bank when the water gets too high.

The section of Daddys Creek Canyon downstream of Rocking Chair manifests a Dr. Jekyll and Mr. Hyde character, depending on water level. At low to moderate levels the rapids in this section are not especially hazardous or difficult, although they continue in quick succession for the next mile and a half producing an exhilarating stretch of technical whitewater. Beginning somewhere around 1.8, however, this section changes into a veritable tempest. Rapids double or triple in difficulty and the "pushiness" increases commensurately. At 2.0 feet, paddlers should expect 10 to 12 strong Class IIIs below Rocking Chair and three or four powerful Class IVs. Regardless of water level, stop occasionally and look around, especially at the views upstream. The canyon is remarkable, one of the finest in the Obed watershed.

The canyon walls recede from the river and diminish in height as the stream approaches Devils Breakfast Table. (This impressive landmark, a capstoned monolith, is often referred to as simply DBT.) The last mile before DBT features a moderate gradient of about 35 feet/mile.

Summary

Daddys Creek Canyon is one of the top ten technical whitewater runs in the Southeast. It's a demanding run at any level and at high water it blasts into hydro hyper space. It's sometimes called Yellow Creek Canyon, possibly because Yellow Creek enters just above commencement of the canyon section. Whatever its proper name, this canyon is outrageously wild, remote, beautiful, and (at higher water) difficult. The canyon proper is only two miles in length but it's a furious two miles because of the 70 feet/mile gradient and the fact that the streambed is continuously chock-full of boulders, some of them radically undercut. In places, very large boulders tower above the paddler's head, sometimes on every side, conveying the relative insignificance of the human element in this pristine riverine setting.

The immense boulders on every side lend a sense of "closed-in-ness" quite unlike any other stream.

Water Levels

Daddys Creek is a tributary of the Obed River, which is a tributary of the Emory River. The only telemetric gauge is 20 miles and many tributaries downstream near the bottom of the watershed on the Emory River, at Oakdale. Because of the indirect measurement, recommended levels are approximate. Emory at Oakdale readings are available from TVA at (800) 238-2264. (Press code "3" after the recorded message.)

Ideal flow is about 1,800 to 4,000 cfs, but above 3,000 cfs Daddys Creek gets a bit pushy. Above 5,000 cfs, it gets real pushy.

Another gauge is painted on a pylon at the Antioch Bridge putin. This gauge can be interpreted about like the one for Section IV of the Chattooga on the US 76 bridge in South Carolina.

Daddys Creek Gauge Locations	
Antioch Bridge	Emory at Oakdale
Low: 1.2 Medium: 1.6 High: 2.0	Low: 1,200 cfs Medium: 3,000 cfs High: 5,000 cfs

Access

Daddys Creek is located in the Obed/Emory watershed, atop the Cumberland Plateau between Nashville and Knoxville. To reach the putin at Antioch Bridge, take the Peavine Road Exit off I-40 near Crossville. Antioch Bridge is 10 miles north of the Interstate, over secondary paved roads, past all the

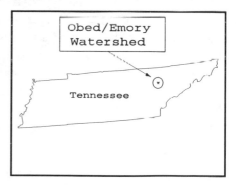

Obed/Emory Watershed

Tennessee

retirement communities. It's accessible year-round, and can also be reached from Crab Orchard, off I-40.

Takeout is at the Devils Breakfast Table (DBT) in the Catoosa Wildlife Management Area (CWMA). The CWMA is closed to vehicular traffic from January to April and on other weekends during managed hunts.

If the CWMA is closed, the alternate takeout is at Obed Junction (OBJ), which marks the confluence of Daddys Creek with the Obed River. This alternate takeout adds two miles of Class II paddling to the run. However, the OBJ access road is a narrow, rocky 4WD only, overhung with tree limbs. The alternatives to driving a 4WD vehicle into OBJ are to walk out with one's equipment (a distance of one-half mile) or stash boats and return the next day to paddle the 11 remaining miles to Nemo Bridge. Another disadvantage to the OBJ alternate takeout is the shuttle. If the CWMA is closed, one must drive back to I-40 west, exit at Genesis Road, and follow Genesis Road until the last right turn before Jett Bridge. Round trip shuttle from Antioch Bridge to Obed Junction is 65 miles and about two hours.

Miles From Daddys Creek Canyon	
Knoxville, TN 60	Atlanta, GA 230
Nashville, TN 125	Cincinnati, OH 290

The ideal takeout for a Daddys Creek Canyon trip would be at Canoe Hole on the Obed River, about a mile downstream of the Clear Creek confluence. This takeout would provide a 14 mile trip through both Daddys Creek Canyon and the main canyon section of the Obed River. However, the road into Canoe Hole is even rougher than the one into Obed Junction, and the shuttle is longer.

It's also possible to put in at Antioch Bridge and paddle to Nemo Bridge on the Emory River, 18 miles downstream. However, the shuttle run is like something out of Idaho.

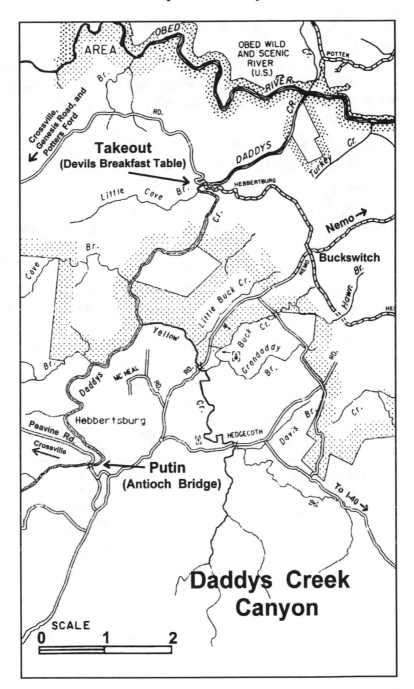

Daddys Creek Canyon

Other Information

Camping

Camping is available at Frozen Head State Park, off TN 62, five miles east of Wartburg, and at Cumberland Mountain State Park, off US 127, about six miles south of Crossville.

Maps

Check with TVA at 1101 Market Street, 101 Haney Bldg, Chattanooga, TN 37402, or phone (615) 632-6082.

Suitability for Rafting (On a 1 to 7 Scale): 1

It could be done, but it'd be a chore due to many narrow, cluttered, blind chutes. Rattlesnake might be a particular problem.

Nearby Alternate Trips

The Obed/Emory watershed contains 18 trips with at least Class II whitewater, all in a remarkably circumscribed geographic area. Some of the Obed/Emory runs are through sheer-walled canyons that are among the most scenic in the Southeast. The system is described in detail in A *Paddler's Guide to the Obed/Emory Watershed*, by Monte Smith. Other Obed/Emory runs described in the present volume are in the table below:

Alternate Trip	Rapids Difficulty	TRIP Points
Clear Creek	III+	97
Crab Orchard Creek	III+	98
Island Creek	III-IV	108
Obed River: Goulds Bend	III(V)	95
Obed River: DBT to Nemo	III(IV)	101

Doe River Gorge

Blevins to Hampton
(Tennessee)

TRIP Profile			
Scale Midpoint = 100			
Overall Difficulty	117	Rapids Difficulty	106
Volume x Gradient	97	Continuous Rapids	123
Average Gradient	142	Entrapments	94
Maximum Gradient	159	Inaccessibility	128
Total Gradient	135	Reputation	105

Actual Stream Data			
Max Rapids	III-IV(V)	Stream Size	Small
Average Gradient	93	Length (in miles)	6
Maximum Gradient	160	Morphology Types	3&4

Overview

Doe River drains the high country around Roan Mountain, center-piece of a massive natural "bald" area in the Unakas near Elizabeth-ton, Tennessee. Straddling the North Carolina and Tennessee state line, Roan Mountain lifts its rocky promontories to over 6,000 feet elevation, providing stunning vistas. Interspersed with the natural balds are stands of balsam fir, red spruce, and acres of rhododen-dron that burst into brilliant profusion every June. In summers before the advent of air conditioning these high altitude and naturally cool environs were a favorite haunt of well-to-do flatlanders. In 1870 the Cloudland Hotel opened, eventually expanding to a 150 room, three-story operation attracting many luminaries of the era, including

199

Mark Twain. Foundations of the old hotel can be located where the Appalachian Trail crosses the top of the mountain.

Precipitation on Roan's western slopes collects in the nascent Doe River and trickles through Roan Mountain State Park and the small community of Roan Mountain. The stream collects additional tributaries until it reaches Blevins, where it jumps into its remote, deep, and scenic gorge, replete with Tennessee technical whitewater at its very best, full of twisting, churning, rock-jammed rapids, most of which have no clear routes, and require successive 90 degree turns amidst a plethora of pinning opportunities. Intense maneuvering is the norm and frequent scouting may be necessary on a first run.

Don't be disappointed if junk litters the banks in the first half mile. A few miles downstream, where human feet have seldom trod, you'll be gawking up at black rock overhangs a thousand feet overhead, mystified by this eerily remote east Tennessee river canyon.

Mile(s)	Doe River Gorge Top-To-Bottom Itinerary
0.0	Put in at Bear Cage Road Bridge in Blevins.
0.0 to 0.6	Easy Class II water.
0.7	Bear Cage Rapid (Class III).
0.8	Buckeroo (Class III).
1.3	The Davis Dash (Class III).
1.3 to 2.2	Technical rock jumbles.
2.6	Body Snatcher (Class IV+).
2.8	First Diagonal (Class III).
3.1	Second Diagonal (Class IV).
3.2 to 3.7	Deepest part of the gorge.
3.4 to 5.0	Rapids open up.
5.0 to 6.0	Anticlimactic (but watch for barbed wire).
6.0	Take out at the US 19E bridge.

Description

The tiny stream is subdued at the putin, almost pastoral. But it changes quickly. Within a half mile it bends sharply, flows under a bridge that once served as a trestle, and soon enters the first of many technical Class IIIs, the putin road namesake, Bear Cage Rapid, where a boulder jam forces all water into a narrow, turbulent sluice that drops out of sight as it flushes into the cliff on river right. It's a tight, technical, twisting "elbow" of a turn. Next is Buckeroo (Class III), a high velocity drop with a hump situated strategically in the turn. This rapid, benign in appearance, has doused some good paddlers. For a successful run, hang left all the way.

Slightly over a mile into the run comes the longest and best rapid yet, as the stream sweeps left around a bend, threads through 100 yards of technical Class II-III rocks and ledges and culminates with a bodacious drop into a narrow slot requiring a left turn of about 140 degrees (Davis Dash, Class III). Half a mile downstream a wide bend directs Doe River underneath yet another erstwhile trestle through technical water. By this point gradient has increased to 80 feet/mile, about half of what it will attain two miles farther downstream.

Better than words, gradient figures tell a graphic story of what to expect on the Doe River Gorge. In the table below, notice that after the first mile even the flatter sections have a gradient of 80 feet/mile.

Doe River Gradient	
Mile	Feet/Mile
1	40
2	80
3	120
4	160
5	80
6	80

Soon the gradient is well over 100 feet/mile and the stream is trucking downhill through densely obstructed, scrambled, and complex rock formations. Virtually all these rapids are "dirty." That is, there's no clear route through them. Each one is a technical slalom course. Sometimes the chutes are barely wide enough for a boat. Precise eddy turns are a must. In this section of the Doe every vertical foot of drop is a technical contest with the incredibly contorted streambed. No major waterfalls account for big chunks of descent (the highest sheer drop is the final six foot plunge in Body Snatcher). The predominant characteristic of this steepest section is that water rushes pell mell through successive scrabble fields of dark rock.

Body Snatcher (Class IV+) lurks in the heart of the gorge, helping to define maximum streambed tilt. The Snatcher commences with a river-wide rock sieve like something off the Watauga. Getting through the introductory rock sieve is a challenge. What follows is 30 yards with several drops, angled holes, and a final six foot sheer plunge. Watch the final plummet. The shape of the underlying rocks gave the rapid its name. Scout along the left (poison oak-enshrouded) bank to check for logjams before running.

Passing the Snatcher is a landmark accomplishment in more ways than one. Not only is the Snatcher the most difficult rapid in the gorge, but it's also about midway through the run. Moreover, the stream undergoes a noticeable morphological change after Body Snatcher, with rapids opening up more and shedding some of their dense obstructions.

Two rapids a short distance downstream of Snatcher are especially memorable because they feature diagonal hydraulics quite unlike anything else on the river and hence their names, First Diagonal and Second Diagonal. Both rapids have cliffs for background on river left, along with stone walls at river level to buttress a defunct railbed. First Diagonal (Class III) is a mere warmup for Second Diagonal (Class IV), which consists of successive, angled ledges, with the added attraction of a railroad rail lodged near the bottom, pointing (naturally!) upstream. The two diagonal hydraulics at the top of this rapid are deceptively powerful.

Although the intensity moderates in the last two miles, the whitewater action never stops, with the final couple of miles consisting of two and three foot ledges with shoals and turns. In the last mile most all the upstream congestion disappears and the rapids open up to reveal clear routes, a delightful end to one of the most scenic and challenging gorges in the Southeast. Near the end of the run, watch for barbed wire across the stream. Spring floods often wash it into oblivion, but when low-water summer months return so too does some rancher to string more strands across the river.

Summary

As steep, technical, and difficult as the Doe River Gorge is, it is often used as a "warmup" run for the nearby Watauga Gorge. It is theoretically possible to run both the Doe and Watauga in the same day, producing a total drop of over 1,000 technical feet.

Water Levels

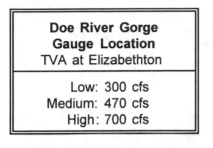

Doe River Gorge Gauge Location TVA at Elizabethton
Low: 300 cfs Medium: 470 cfs High: 700 cfs

TVA maintains a telemetric gauge at Elizabethton, several miles downstream of the gorge. (Call TVA at (800) 238-2264 and press code "3" after the recorded message.) Because the stream channel in the gorge is so focused, surprisingly little water is required to make this run. Also, it quickly goes from ideal to high. A hundred cfs make a considerable difference.

Access

The Doe Gorge is in far east Tennessee near the small town of Hampton. US 19E runs past Hampton and also serves as the shuttle route. Put in on Bear Cage Road in Blevins, about 100 yards off US 19E. Take out at the US 19E bridge on the outskirts of Hampton. A parking area is located on river right about 100 yards downstream of the takeout bridge. The shuttle is along US 19E, a four-lane divided highway, with only a short jag on Bear Cage Road to reach the putin.

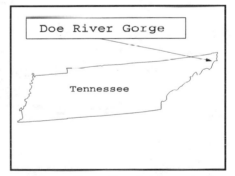

Miles From Doe River Gorge	
Johnson City, TN 25	Charleston, WV 245
Asheville, NC 90	Atlanta, GA 315

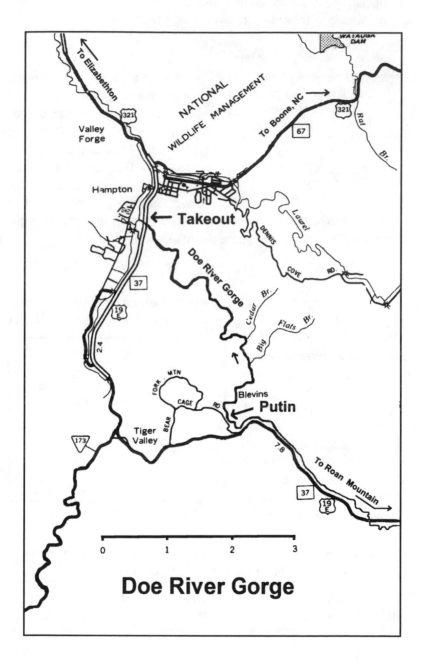

Doe River Gorge

Other Information

Camping

Roan Mountain State Park is about ten miles from the putin. Take US 19E to the community of Roan Mountain. Turn south on TN 143 and follow the signs.

Hiking

The Appalachian Trail crosses Roan Mountain on its north-south traverse of eastern America. The miles from the summit of Roan and south across Carvers Gap to the vicinity of Grassy Knob are extremely scenic.

Nearby Alternate Trips		
Alternate Trip	Rapids Difficulty	TRIP Points
Elk River	V(VI)	na
Nolichucky Gorge	III(IV)	101
Watauga Gorge	V(VI)	142

French Broad

Barnard to Hot Springs
(North Carolina)

TRIP Profile			
Scale Midpoint = 100			
Overall Difficulty	88	Rapids Difficulty	76
Volume x Gradient	137	Continuous Rapids	50
Average Gradient	77	Entrapments	72
Maximum Gradient	74	Inaccessibility	101
Total Gradient	84	Reputation	72

Actual Stream Data			
Max Rapids	III(IV)	Stream Size	Large
Average Gradient	24	Length (in miles)	8.5
Maximum Gradient	40	Morphology Type	2

Overview

Ask every paddler in the Southeast to list their three favorite rivers and odds are the French Broad won't appear on a single list. Why?

The answer in a moment. But first, let's consider its good points.

It has some enjoyable whitewater. The rapids above Stackhouse are of the boulder-studded variety and Frank Bell, near the end of the run, is noteworthy due to its Gauleyesque size, complex structure, and wave and hole action at the bottom.

The river threads through impressive Unaka Mountain scenery. Not quite on a par with the Nolichucky Gorge thirty miles northeast, but scenic nonetheless. Moreover, because of its large watershed, it's runnable for much of the summer. Hence, when the Nolichucky is too low and all else in the region is dry, the French Broad still affords Class II-III(IV) rapids. And for added interest, it has a tributary called Big Laurel (described elsewhere in this volume), a steep and technical creek that enters the French Broad a half mile below Stackhouse.

So, with all that going for it, why isn't it anybody's favorite? Truth is, its water quality leaves something to be desired. Were it not for the turbidity of its water the French Broad would be a premier moderate-difficulty whitewater stream. Part of its turbidity is industrial pollution contributed by cities to the south. Other parts are natural, however, as even unpolluted streams in this vicinity tend to carry heavy natural sediment. And, like other big wide rivers, it can be windy.

Similar To. The upper miles are similar to the Nolichucky in scenery, though not quite as majestic.

Mile(s)	French Broad Top-To-Bottom Itinerary
0.0	Put in at Barnard.
1.0 to 3.0	Several Class III rapids; all with boulder obstructions that form several chutes.
2.0 to 3.0	Steepest gradient: 40 feet/mile.
2.1	The bawdiest Class III in the upper section, Big Pillow.
3.0	Sandy Bottom, followed by the rapid of the same name.
4.3	Stackhouse, with a river-wide row of rebar.
5.1	Confluence with Big Laurel Creek (river right).
6.7	Kayak Ledge/Needle Rock (Class III).
7.3	Frank Bells Rapid (Class IV).
8.5	Take out river right at commercial outfitters.

Description

The first three miles below Barnard contain several Class III rapids, all cluttered with boulders. Intermediate paddlers will find this water challenging above 3,000 cfs, when powerful holes develop. The biggest and best rapid in this stretch is called Big Pillow, about two miles below the putin. The main chute on Big Pillow is on river left.

Sandy Bottom, at mile three, can be recognized by streamside development on river right. Sandy Bottom Rapid (Class III) is just downstream. After Sandy Bottom the stream flattens out considerably, but still has good current at medium flow levels.

Stackhouse, on river right, is recognizable by the river-wide row of rebar protruding from the stream (visible below 4,000 cfs) and generally pointing upstream. River left is relatively free of this hazard.

The real nemesis of the French Broad (aside from pollution) often appears in this section: wind. Always from downstream. Occasionally powerful enough to nullify the combined effects of both current and vigorous paddling. Fortunately, the wind usually abates in the vicinity of Kayak Ledge, where the island at Needle Rock forms a diversion.

From upstream, Needle Rock appears as a glimmering rock outcropping far above a large island (Mountain Island). It's possible to run left of the island through a series of standing waves, but the real fun is on river right over Kayak Ledge where the river drops over a five foot ledge producing a hydraulic on its left side with submerged rocks in the middle. Scout from river right. Kayak is a two-part rapid. The second drop is milder than the first. Swimmers and equipment usually can be retrieved between drops. As volume increases, the best route migrates toward river right (although the vertical drop increases). At 10,000 cfs it's wise to avoid the hydraulic altogether and run the seven foot waterfall which forms on far river right.

After Kayak Ledge, the French Broad gathers its remaining gradient into a single rapid. And what a rapid! Frank Bell will be recognized from upstream by its stentorian roar. For whatever reason -- perhaps its sheer size or perhaps because of the large rocky island that splits the current and forms a natural acoustic tunnel -- Frank Bell screams out warning to the unwary. And well it should. Avoidable entirely by veering far left of the island, otherwise there's no uneventful path through this rapid, which is formed by a huge semi-circle shelf of rock and river detritus. Once over (or through) this sieve, the stream is channeled left into a wave train that culminates in two big holes. (The legendary "deep swim" holes.) The rapid can be run in a variety of ways. The hero's route is straight down the left side through the biggest waves and holes. A route down the far right side is feasible at high water. Other paddlers enter the top of the rapid and doggedly work right around the upstream perimeter of the semi-circle to locate a breach in the barrier where they make a ninety degree turn and drop through the boulders before playing the biggest holes near the bottom. Frank Bells can be scouted from the railroad on river right or from the island. It's hard to get a good view from either side, however, because of the large scale.

For several years this place was alternately known as Railroad Rapid because a derailment on the parallel railroad pitched a boxcar into the river. The boxcar washed to the bottom of the rapid and promptly disappeared, never to be seen again.

The name that seems to have stuck, however, is Frank Bell, after the late paddling pioneer. An account of Bells inaugural run, and his infamous "deep swim" through the hole at the bottom, appears in Randy Carter's landmark *Canoeing Whitewater River Guide*.

One last ledge remains in the mile paddle to the takeout. Keep to river right in order to enjoy the steepest drop.

Summary

To conjure up an image of the French Broad and its environs, think of quaint mountain communities at the putin and takeout nestled among ancient rolling Appalachian Mountains, with a broad shiny river coursing through them. The access communities are among the most picturesque in the southern highlands, with Hot Springs having enjoyed fame as a resort since 1790.

Water Levels

Due to the size of its watershed, the French Broad is runnable most of the year. Because of its large streambed, the French Broad can channel a lot of water and it's hard to say how much is high. It

French Broad Gauge Location TVA French Broad at Newport
Low: 1,750 cfs Medium: 2,500 cfs High: 4,000 cfs

depends on previous paddling experience. Four thousand cfs will seem high to intermediates, but many paddlers will see the lower half of this run at over 5,000 cfs when they run Big Laurel Creek, a tributary, and continue downstream to a takeout at Hot Springs. In fact, a bare minimum run on Big Laurel Creek will correspond to at least 4,000 cfs on the French Broad, and a high run will translate to about 10,000 cfs, a level that produces a potentially terminal hydraulic at Kayak Ledge. To check the level, call TVA at (800) 238-2264 and press code "3" after the recorded message.

Access

Located in western North Carolina almost due north of Asheville, the French Broad region is most easily accessible via US 19/23 and US 25/70.

Put in at Barnard, North Carolina, near the mountain community of Walnut. To reach the putin from Asheville, take US 19/23 north to the US 25/70 cutoff toward Marshall. Take the Marshall bypass to Walnut, a total of 27 miles from Asheville. At Walnut, turn left (southeast) and wind down the side of the mountain to Barnard.

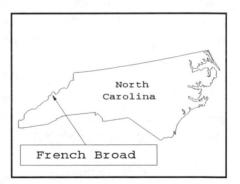

Take out across the river from Hot Springs, North Carolina. From Walnut proceed eleven serpentine miles to the US 25/70 bridge over the French Broad, on the outskirts of Hot Springs. The takeout is on river right just upstream of the bridge.

Miles From the French Broad River	
Asheville, NC 31	Roanoke, VA 230
Knoxville, TN 100	Atlanta, GA 240

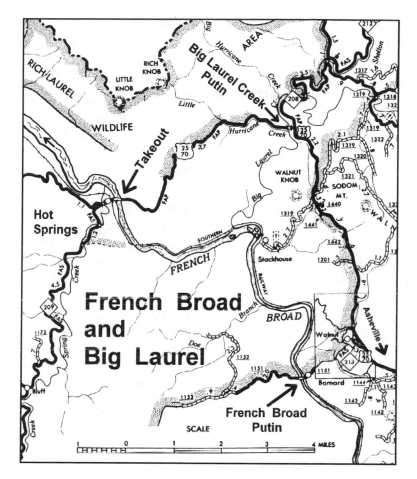

French Broad and Big Laurel

Other Information

Camping

Stony Bluff National Forest Campground is three miles south of Hot Springs on NC 209. From the US 25/70 takeout bridge drive south into Hot Springs. Bear left at the fork onto NC 209.

Hiking

The Appalachian Trail runs down main street in Hot Springs.

Suitability for Rafting (On a 1 to 7 Scale): 7

Two commercial outfitters are headquartered at the takeout. They provide guided raft trips and canoe rentals. Check with the Hot Springs Chamber of Commerce for current phone numbers.

Nearby Alternate Trips

Whenever the French Broad is above 4000 cfs, Big Laurel Creek, a tributary, is potentially runnable. Big Laurel is described elsewhere in this volume.

Other sections of the French Broad, both upstream and down, are runnable. Although most of its other sections are numbingly flat, two stretches between Asheville and Barnard contain Class II(III) water. This is also the case for the stretch below Hot Springs. These alternate runs are described in some detail in Benner's *Carolina Whitewater*. Without question, however, the stretch described here, from Barnard to Hot Springs, contains the best whitewater on the river.

The alternate big mountain river is the Nolichucky Gorge, only some thirty miles northeast. The Nolichucky Gorge has a shorter season, but when water permits, it and the French Broad can be run in the same weekend. The Nolichucky, almost half again as difficult as the French Broad (97 overall TRIP points versus 88 for the French Broad), is described elsewhere in this volume.

Upper Gauley River

Summersville Dam to Peters Creek
(West Virginia)

TRIP Profile			
Scale Midpoint = 100			
Overall Difficulty	138	Rapids Difficulty	178
Volume x Gradient	176	Continuous Rapids	123
Average Gradient	84	Entrapments	128
Maximum Gradient	78	Inaccessibility	128
Total Gradient	131	Reputation	139

Actual Stream Data			
Max Rapids	V+	Stream Size	Large
Average Gradient	31	Length (in miles)	17
Maximum Gradient	45	Morphology Type	2&3

Overview

Few streams live up to their reputation. The Gauley does, in spades.

There are bigger rivers. There are badder runs. But nothing in the East quite equals the Big G in sheer unadulterated mayhem. This river literally alters the phenomenological perspective of every paddler venturesome enough to challenge it. After one trip down the Big G, everything else is filtered through a different perceptual lens. It's really that impactful. It's big, bad, alluring, intoxicating, exhilarating, intimidating, addictive, outrageously wild and beautiful, and a dominatrix non-pareil. There's little neutral territory when it comes to Gauley attitudes. Paddlers either love it and come back year after

213

year or they try it once and that was enough, thank you! Make a mistake and it will administer a drubbing. A bad day on the Gauley ranks right up there with the time your mother-in-law decided to take up residence in your spare bedroom.

At one time the Gauley was considered the East coast qualifying cruise for "expert" status. It's no longer considered the toughest thing around, but in many ways it's still in a class by itself. For one thing, it's a long trip, twenty-five miles in total. It's so long that few paddlers attempt the entire run in one day, yet there's no convenient public access to the canyon. Many paddlers cover the first fourteen to seventeen miles in one day, stash their boats, walk out for the night and traipse back the following day to complete the remaining eight to eleven miles. Others paddle the first eleven miles and carry their boats out at Panther Creek. Also, several outfitters have access between Sweets Falls and Peters Creek, but prior permission to use their access roads must be obtained.

Flow volume is dictated by Summersville Dam releases. Annual drawdown of the Summersville reservoir occurs in September and October, when hundreds of paddlers show up to enjoy releases that generally range from 2,200 to 3,600 cfs. In other seasons the reservoir is maintained at a constant level to facilitate lake recreation. Most of the time, this translates as sporadic and negligible streamflow. However, whenever heavy rains in the upstream tributaries raise the reservoir level, unscheduled releases (usually 300 to 1,500 cfs) occur. At these lower levels the Gauley is surprisingly different than at standard release levels. At 1,100 cfs it's a technical run with many of its radical undercuts exposed and an astonishing number and variety of sizeable drops that are smoothed out by higher flows. The Gauley at 1,100 cfs and at 2,700 cfs are almost different rivers, with only the major Class Vs looking essentially the same.

Stream morphology is drop/pool with rapids ranging from obstructed to densely obstructed. The most densely obstructed and complex rapids are located in the first nine miles where the gradient is steepest. These rapids frequently require precise maneuvering in heavy water. The sheer number of difficult rapids boggles the mind. In the upper run alone, five Class V rapids are sandwiched among a dozen Class IV+ and uncounted Class III+ rapids. Several of the

Johnny Wingfield (canoe) and Ed Caudill (C1) run Pillow Rock Rapid on the upper Gauley River. Don Ellis photo.

most outstanding rapids in the Southeast are on the Big G. Lost Paddle (at any level) and Pillow (at standard release) are in a class by themselves, and Iron Ring, Sweets Falls, and Insignificant are not far behind. Many rapids harbor radically undercut obstructions. The river runs through an isolated canyon. To make matters even more interesting, the Gauley seems to have its own rating scale. A Gauley Class III would qualify as a Class IV on most other south-eastern streams. Major rapids from most other streams could be dropped amidst the fever and tumult of Pillow or Lost Paddle and an observer would never notice the difference. Alternatively, Lost Paddle could be necked-down, rechanneled and redistributed over a two-mile slalom course of continuous Class II-III rapids, were such riparian legerdemain possible.

The Gauley gradient figure that's most often cited is 28 feet/mile, and that number is accurate if calculated over the entire 25 miles from Summersville Dam to Swiss, the takeout for the lower run. However, 25 miles is a long distance for calculating whitewater gradient. A careful inspection of these 25 miles reveals two distinct slopes. The first nine miles from Summersville Dam to Panther Creek (just downstream of Sweets Falls) tilt at 38 feet/mile, with three of the nine miles clocking in at 40 or above. Thereafter, the 16 miles to Swiss drop at the rate of 22.5 feet/mile. The upper nine miles of the Big G are 69% steeper than the lower sixteen miles!

If 38 feet/mile gradient doesn't sound like much, think again. Remember the Chapter Two discussion of the volume x gradient interaction effect? The Gauley, you see, is pool/drop in conforma-tion. Much of the stream is flat. But when it drops, it drops big time. When 2,500 cfs drop twenty-five feet over a distance of 60 yards through a boulder field (as at Pillow Rapid) the display of energy is awesome.   When this much water crashes down a 600 yard sluiceway filled with every conceivable boulder obstruction and both vertical and horizontal sieves (as at Lost Paddle), the result can be intimidating.   If there's a saving grace for the poor paddler who bobbles in over his or her head, it's the pools. Every big rapid has a pool after it except Lost Paddle, which melds into Tumble Home. These pools permit rescue of swimmers and equipment, as well as affording the opportunity to hold long, earnest talks with oneself.

Mile(s)	Upper Gauley Top-To-Bottom Itinerary
0.0	Put in at Summersville Dam.
0.0 to 9.0	Steepest gradient: 38 feet/mile.
0.5	Initiation (Class III+).
1.1	Buds Boner (Class IV).
2.2	Insignificant (Class V).
3.7	Iron Curtain (Class IV).
4.6	Pillow (Class V). Trail on river right.
5.4	Carnifax Ferry. Trail on river right
5.5	Meadow River confluence, river left.
5.7 to 6.1	Lost Paddle and Tumblehome (Class V+).
7.0	Table Rock (Class IV). Aka Shipwreck Rock.
7.7	Iron Ring (Class V+).
8.5	Sweets Falls (Class V).
9.2	Panther Creek, river right. Alternate access.
9.2 to 17.0	Gradient moderates, from 38 feet/mile to 24 feet/mile.
11.0	Woods Ferry (Class III+). Emergency access, river left. Commercial outfitter access nearby, which is the first good access.
11.8	Ender Waves (Class III).
13.8	Koontz Bend Tunnel Entrance, river left. Alternate (walkout) exit.
14.2	Five Boat Hole (Class IV), aka Boatender.
14.5	Commercial outfitter access, river right. Prior permission needed.
15.0	Koontz Flume (Class IV+).
15.8	Canyon Doors (Class III+).
16.5	Junkyard (Class III+).
17.3	Peters Creek, river right. Traditional upper Gauley walkout along the railroad tracks with a next day return for the lower run.

A wise move when making your first descent on the Big G is to follow behind someone who has run the stream several times, and who is patient enough to explain its special hazards. This strategy is a good idea on most streams but on the Gauley it's practically mandatory. Gauley rapids are so big, complex, powerful, and laced with boat-gobbling hydraulics and undercut rock entrapments that an unguided first descent can turn quickly into a nightmare.

Those on the Gauley for the first time invariably underestimate its power. If it looks like three strokes will propel you to the safety of an eddy, think again. It'll probably take four strokes, or five! Repeat this little underestimation exercise a thousand times and the utter exhaustion that first time paddlers feel at the takeout is better understood.

Similar To.   Nothing is quite like the Big G, but the closest contender is probably New River Gorge with three feet or more of water on the Fayette Station gauge. If you've run the New River Gorge at over 3.0 feet and can remember the crazy agitation of Double-Z and Undercut Rock, you have a good idea of what to expect on most of the rapids in the first nine miles of the upper Gauley.

Description

Post-Freudian Vibrations

Before embarking, walk over to the base of Summersville Dam and treat yourself to a view of the release tubes. When these colossal phallic symbols are belching out two or three thousand cfs, it's enough to make good ol' Sigmund twitch in his casket. It's also enough to make the very earth tremble. These tubes blow water downstream a hundred thunderous feet with terrifying force. Reportedly, some kayaker once shoved off from on top of one of the tubes, expecting a grand ride. Days later, the county coroner was still picking up pieces.

In the descriptions that follow, please keep in mind that it is not possible to describe in detail every significant rapid. Aerial photographs of the Gauley reveal approximately 100 patches of extended aeration between the Summersville Dam release tubes and the Swiss takeout for the lower run. This account describes all the Class Vs and mentions most of the Class IVs. There are numerous Class IIIs, however, that are not mentioned. Some of these would be Class IVs on other streams and some harbor undercuts and other novel traps, all the more reason to accompany experienced paddlers on Big G trips until most of these nuances are decoded.

Sluicing Down the Big G

The upper Gauley run begins with two miles of relatively easy warmup paddling. On the upper Gauley relatively easy simply indicates an absence of Class V rapids. A good example is Initiation rapid, a Class III+ about half a mile below Summersville Dam. Avoid the right side of the ledge because of pinning possibilities. Run the ledge left of center and get ready in the waves and holes below for an introduction to the power of this river. Buds Boner is next and is another good reason why first time Gauley runners should follow an experienced paddler. In Buds Boner the river begins to demonstrate how it can conceal hazards among seemingly innocuous wave trains.

The pace picks up substantially at Insignificant (a misnomer if ever there was one!), the Gauley's first Class V. This Gauleyesque-sized declivity is a wide-open assemblage of rocks, holes, waves, drops, and several more holes. It's so big that only the top third or so can be seen from the eddies at the top. It can be scouted, but it takes a long time. This is another excellent place to ask advice from someone who has run it more than once, preferably always in their boat! From the top, try to spot a large, sloping rock near the bottom right of the rapid and use that as a landmark. The object is to head toward the sloping rock, generally staying right of center to avoid several monstrous holes, until just upstream of the landmark, then veering sharply left with the main flow to avoid the undercut rocks on bottom right. (Insignificant also can be run down the left side.) Some of the holes in this rapid are downright vicious. A much better name for it would be Initiation because it really is a good indicator of what to expect for the next 23 miles.

Riparian Pillow Party

For those who thought they'd seen it all at Insignificant, about two and a half miles farther downstream the Big G throws a pillow party that will just about peg out anybody's entertainment meter. It's called Pillow Rapid, or Pillow Rock Rapid, and it's a most excellent place to scout. Paddlers on the river for the first time will benefit by scouting from both sides of the river! Short by Gauley standards, about 60 yards, the stream nevertheless drops some twenty-five vertical feet in this short distance through a boulder-choked quasi box canyon where it explodes with insane intensity as it feverishly searches for outlets near the bottom. Over its relatively short course Pillow is a veritable maelstrom of unrepentant energy with exploding waves, voracious holes, roostertails, standing waves, whirlpools, partially submerged obstructions and a "Room of Doom."

This big Class V is some of the wildest water in the Southeast and upon first inspection appears absolutely unrunnable. (And so it has remained for many!) Much of the current blows into a large rock at bottom left, thus forming the namesake "pillow" and creating the place you never want to go lest you wind up in the dreaded Room of Doom, a recirculating eddy on river left adjacent to the pillow. River right harbors a humongous hole about midway down the rapid and many paddlers, understandably eager to avoid this monster, skirt too far left. This mistake is compounded by the fact that the water in pillow runs right to left (toward the pillow) with disarming force.

A successful run through Pillow entails skirting just left of the big river right hole. A few feet to river left of the hole is a tongue. Hitting this tongue is the key to a successful run but the tongue is not easy to reach. Enter center or right of center and work to the tongue, avoiding successive nuisances like exploding waves. More effort is required to maneuver in this heavy and crazy water than is apparent. Also remember, the natural tendency of the currents is to push left toward the pillow with far more force than apparent until one is caught up in the vortex. Avoid an initial approach from too far left as it is virtually impossible to work back right through the crazy cross currents of the main rapid. An entrance from the left inevitably leads to a wet tango with the pillow monster, an encounter that has terrified more than a few paddlers. Toward the bottom, the best bet is to veer back to the right as far as possible before taking the last drop. At far right near the bottom, a big eddy provides safe haven from which to watch the next turkey descend into the bowels of this craziness. For the 90% who miss the river right eddy near the bottom, watch for the megachunk of sandstone (affectionately dubbed Volkswagen Rock) which sits in the center of the last drop.

Either side of VW Rock is okay, but don't get too far back toward the pillow on river left and drop into a whirlpool.

The Mother of All Rapids

Pillow is brief but intense. With the possible exception of Iron Ring nothing else on the river has this much concentrated energy. But now we come to a rapid that is anything but short, Lost Paddle, and nothing if not energized. The confluence of the Meadow on river left signals that Lost Paddle is just around the bend. It's 600 yards long and some paddlers insist it's half a mile. Once you're in it, it can seem interminable. Most veteran Gauley paddlers rate it as the most difficult rapid on the river and when you consider that it's so integral with Tumblehome that they in reality form a single rapid, there can be little doubt. Lost Paddle is *the* spot on the upper Gauley where it's absolutely mandatory to stay in your boat.

For all of Pillow's furious display, it's relatively benign with respect to traps (with the exception of the notorious room of doom). Not so Lost Paddle, which is a lair of sieves and entrapments of macabre configuration. Swimming Lost Paddle is about as good an idea as spitting on your IRS auditor. Scouting is an onerous expedition, and a day hike to Pluto is easier than portaging. So what's left? Running it, of course!

Here's what to expect. The first two hundred yards of Lost Paddle form the entrance (known as Part One), and consist of successive drops through fast-moving water laced with holes and concealed obstructions. (The lower the flow, the tougher the approach.) Although somewhat like running a minefield, the approach's significance lies less in its objective difficulty rating of Class III-IV than in the realization that it's merely the entrance to more hazardous water downstream.

Part Two of Lost Paddle (often called Second Drop) is identifiable from upstream by a dramatic narrowing of the river and by an ominous horizon line. Eddies are available on either side at the top of the drop. Catch one of them and boat scout the drop as much as possible. Although little is visible downstream, from an eddy one can at least identify key features on the lip of the drop and perhaps observe veteran paddlers line up for it. The key feature to locate is a curler wave extending out from the river left bank. Most paddlers elect to take the drop just to river right of the edge of this curler, thus avoiding the worst hole below, but it also can be run way over on river right over a pourover into the edge of a diagonal hole if you're prepared for the rough landing and the possibility of being surfed halfway across the river and flushed into Six Pack Rock. At the bottom of the explosive big drop an eddy awaits on river left. Grab it.

Second Drop is a notorious boat flipper. If you flip at the base of the drop and come out of your boat, try to stay away from Six Pack Rock, in the main current. It's undercut, as are most of the rocks along river left. If Second Drop does a number on you and you find yourself swimming Part Three of Lost Paddle, it's imperative that you get out of the water before Tumblehome, which is two hundred yards or more downstream. Go with the current for a ways until an eddy appears, and then swim aggressively into it. Keep stroking until you're completely out of the water. If you miss your eddy turn, attempting to hug up onto one of the undercut rocks is a poor tactic. The current through Part Three of Lost Paddle is deceptively strong and will pull you into the undercut. If you're trying to assist a swimmer, escort them into an eddy and stay with them until they're completely out of the water on the bank. Needless to say, this is no place to fret over lost equipment. Let the stuff flush.

Part Four of Lost Paddle (and what a grand finale!) is Tumblehome. Those running it for the first time should not only scout (to whatever extent that's possible), but also obtain explicit directions from an experienced paddler and watch several others execute runs. Look for a trapezoid-shaped rock which marks the midstream entrance. Although it's possible to run just left (or right) of Trapezoid Rock and then weave in and out of the huge boulders that jumble the bottom drop, many paddlers choose the far left approach, through a shallow hole and left eddy. From the harbor of this eddy the required path is fairly obvious. One must execute an upstream ferry between Washing Rock and its slightly offset Downstream Breathern, catch the tongue of water, spin 180 degrees and drop to the right of a pinning spot beside Downstream Breathern, then work like crazy either toward river left to avoid a strainer that sits dead ahead and line up for the final drop through an opening between two boulders, or work over to an eddy on river right.

Tumblehome in isolation would be a Class IV+ rapid with a Class V danger rating. But it's not in isolation. It's situated as the capstone of Lost Paddle, which itself would be another Class IV+ rapid if it appeared in isolation. With the two rapids so closely juxtaposed, however, they meld into a single Class V+ rapid with a Class VI danger rating because of Tumblehome's many undercuts and rock strainers. The bottom of Tumblehome is literally a sieve, with both vertical and horizontal crevices. (The jumble of rocks on river left contains several potential entrapments.)

Moving Right Along . . .

Table Rock (or Ship Rock) is visible from far upstream. An enormous wave train leads into, around, and under this gigantic rock. The most prudent path is to stay far right all the way. Rafts generally run far left, and a left approach is necessary at lower flows. Don't drift up against this behemoth, as it is undercut and boatless paddlers have literally been pulled under it.

Iron Ring (Class V+) is the next biggie on the agenda, located about half a mile below Tumblehome. It's possibly the most infamous rapid on the Big G, named for the large iron ring that was anchored (until some miscreant swiped it!) in the river left rock, a vestige of a scheme by loggers to widen the river at this bottleneck to alleviate logjams, back in the days when the river was used to float logs downstream to sawmill sites. Their blasting work left a swiss cheese hazard on river left (mostly submerged at standard release levels) at the base of one of the strongest holes on the Big G.

At this spot, the river necks down to a narrow channel and drops about eight feet into double holes. Most of the stream circulates through the left hole and exits over, around, and through Swiss Cheese Alley. A fraction of the current, however, divides the holes and shoots down a tongue on far river right, smashes into the river right rocks and blows out a narrow chute into the right side of yet another hole, forming the most turbulent single spot on the entire river.

Iron Ringers must avoid at all cost getting caught in the left hole after the first drop and flushing out through Swiss Cheese Alley. A successful run entails an approach from left of center, skirting to the right of two holes, then working hard right to line up for the all-important tongue of fast water. Inches on the approach are critical. There is virtually no margin for error. At the bottom of the drop, holes await on both sides. Stay out of the left hole. Kiss the edge of the river-right hole and squirt through the last drop, prepared for a crash landing.

The famous formula for a successful run on Iron Ring is to get right, stay upright, and keep the sphincter tight. Curiously, canoes have as good or better a success rate through here as decked boats, perhaps because they tend to bridge holes a little better. (Or maybe because anybody trying this place in a canoe had better be a pretty good paddler in the first place.)

With more and more people running Iron Ring, it may seem like the thing to do. And perhaps it is. But if you don't like its looks, the river left portage is short, safe, and easy.

The Biggest Drop

A short distance below Iron Ring comes Sweets Falls, the most visually impressive rapid on the river. Named for the gentleman who ran it in his raft on the first known descent in 1961, the river at Sweets Falls drops over a ten foot ledge into a rock jumble. To see this place with no water in the streambed is sobering. Yet with 1,100 cfs or more of padding it's relatively innocuous *if* you hit the lip of the drop at exactly the right spot. As with Iron Ring, the margin for error is thin. Look for a "crease," or "seam" at the left edge of the curling wave that runs along the right side of the drop. This crease is not obvious but it's the place to hit the drop because it marks a tongue of relatively unimpeded water that blasts straight through the hole at the bottom. Too far right on the main drop can result in a drubbing in the hole at the base of the falls. Too far left (toward Snaggle-Tooth, or Launch, Rock) can produce dire results, especially at partial release levels.

As with many other Big G rapids, those running the river for the first time will benefit greatly from advice of veteran paddlers because the best line at Sweet Falls is not obvious. Even better, climb to the grandstands on river right and watch a passel of others run first. Follow a good paddler in your kind of craft and mimic his or her every maneuver during the approach.

On one of the first club-sponsored paddling trips on the upper Gauley, a canoeist dropped over the falls too far left and his boat was pinned vertically. The paddler was trapped inside his boat, shoved forward (and partly under the center thwart) by the impact. Although totally submerged for two hours and twenty minutes, the paddler survived by breathing from an air pocket formed by the water as it crashed around his helmet.

If the main drop at Sweets Falls isn't your cauldron of tea, consider the Class III+ cheat chute down far river left. Of course, some people claim the cheat's harder than the main drop, and that's probably true as long as the approach to the main drop is executed perfectly.

Denouement

Downstream of Sweets, things ease up considerably. At Panther Creek, about a mile below Sweets, the gradient eases up also. Panther is a bear of a takeout because of the steep trail, but it serves as a fair downhill putin.

About two and a half miles below Sweets, look for Woods Ferry (Class III+), chock full of holes, rocks, and ledges. An access is on river left, leading up to a rudimentary road which leads out to Leander and, eventually, US 19. A commercial outfitter access is also located on river left in this vicinity, and is the first good point of egress. The next notable rapid is a popular play spot, Ender Waves (Class III).

The Access Dilemma

After Ender Waves, paddlers face a hard choice concerning egress from the river. Basically, there are three options. The first option is to paddle the remaining five miles to the first standard access, Peters Creek. These miles include Koontz Bend, where the river forms a huge loop before swinging back to less than a mile from where the loop begins. There are several rapids in these miles, including Class IV+ Koontz Flume, but most of the distance consists of flatwater. After reaching Peters Creek by river, paddlers are faced with carrying boats over a mile up railroad tracks to the nearest road access, or stashing boats by the river and returning next day to paddle them downriver to Swiss.

The second option makes use of a railroad tunnel which penetrates the ridge that forces the river into Koontz Bend. Some paddlers prefer to stash their boats near the upstream entrance to the tunnel, walk through the tunnel -- which emerges on the other side of the barrier ridge at the mouth of Peters Creek -- and continue up the railroad tracks to the nearest road access.

Options 1 and 2 both entail stashing boats and walking up the railroad tracks to the Peters Creek road access. They both entail walking back to the river the next day and paddling out. The only real difference between the options is which day the five river miles that include Koontz Bend will be paddled, and whether or not to walk through a tunnel. Many paddlers opt for the tunnel stroll because this option more nearly equalizes the number of river miles in a two-day trip from Summersville Dam to Swiss. In choosing between options 1 and 2, however, consider that the railroad is active, and dodging fast trains in narrow tunnels is no lark, this author can attest.

The third option -- which is vastly preferable to either option 1 or 2 -- is to arrange with one of the local outfitters to use their takeout. That way, instead of spending day two on the lower Gauley, you can go back up to Summersville Dam and run the upper section again. A particularly convenient access is located a short distance upstream of Koontz Flume Rapid. Access terms, however, must be negotiated with the outfitters.

Koontz Bend

The upstream entrance to the railroad tunnel is on river left approximately a mile and a half downstream of Ender Waves.

Five Boat Hole (Class IV) signals approach to the commercial access upstream of Koontz Flume. Just around the bend from this river right access, Koontz Flume (Class IV+) begins with a humongous hole at top left. This hole is the last thing that many paddlers remember of Koontz Flume. That hole is grabby and sticky. Avoid it by entering right of center and working back left to enjoy the immense waves and avoid the undercut garbage toward bottom right. At some levels an alternate route opens tight left all the way down. Regardless of how you run Koontz Flume, you'll discover that it's the biggest rapid on the river since Sweets Falls.

Two named rapids remain between Koontz Flume and Peters Creek. They can be enjoyable if you've just put in at one of the alternate access points, or rather anticlimactic if you're on the last leg of a seventeen mile journey from Summersville Dam. In any event, Canyon Doors (Class III) is a spectacular sight as the Gauley River curves left beneath sheer 300 foot cliffs. Junkyard (Class III+), the last notable rapid above Peters Creek, was named, ostensibly, for a junkyard that once was operated on the edge of the cliff.

The access at Peters Creek is recognizable by the trestle protruding from the tunnel. Take out on river right and stash your boat, or carry it with you a mile up the tracks.

Summary

Several pages have been devoted to describing the upper Gauley and even so only the biggest, most memorable rapids were mentioned, some cursorily. That's because there's an enormous amount of whitewater in the upper miles. The stretch was first rafted in 1961, first paddled in whitewater boats in 1968, and first paddled by canoe in 1977. In 1986 it was paddled for the first time by a tandem canoe team.

Without doubt, this trip is a whitewater classic, but with tandem canoes making runs down the upper Gauley, it could no longer serve as the qualifying cruise for expert status, so that distinction migrated up to Sang Run, or over to Breaks Interstate Park, or down to the apple orchards around Overflow, or the ski slopes around Watauga Gorge, or some other equally outrageous, unknown, and inaccessible drainage ditch. The upper Merced Canyon it ain't, but the upper Gauley is one heck of a fine run, probably the best big water paddling trip in the East.

Water Levels

The Gauley is ordinarily runnable only when Summersville Dam is releasing water. (The exception occurs when the Meadow, a major tributary at mile 5.5, is dumping in a large volume and access is possible at or below this confluence.) Each fall during late September and early October the Summersville reservoir is "drawn down" to anticipate winter and spring rains. Typical releases during drawdown are 2,200 cfs to 3,000 cfs.

Unscheduled releases occur throughout the year to stabilize reservoir level or provide water downstream for lock operation on the Kanawha or Ohio Rivers. These unscheduled releases are typically 300 cfs to 1,500 cfs, but they can be at any rate. Many paddlers consider 700 cfs to be paddling zero, although everything but Tumblehome and Sweets Falls can be run at half this volume by technically skilled paddlers. Overall difficulty is significantly reduced at 700 cfs, but the undercut/entrapment hazard is exacerbated. At 1,100 cfs the Gauley is a pushy technical run with surprisingly big drops. In the range from 700 to 3,000 cfs, some veteran paddlers think the Gauley is toughest and most dangerous around 1,100 cfs.

Above 3,500 cfs, it's "Katie bar the door," but as always high is relative. One of the paddlers who responded to the survey cited in Chapter Three reported that his most difficult trip ever was a run down the upper Gauley at 17,500 cfs. Although it was the most taxing run he had ever made, he said it took less than half a day to cover the entire 25 miles from Summersville Dam to Swiss!

A recorded message at (304) 529-5127 provides reservoir release in cfs at Summersville Dam, as well as gauge and cfs readings for the Belva gauge (located on the Gauley downstream of the Meadow River confluence). Most of the discrepancy between Summersville Dam release numbers and cfs at the Belva gauge is accounted for by the Meadow River (q.v.).

Access

Southern West Virginia is the site and the two main arteries into it are I-64 from the east and I-77 (the West Virginia Turnpike) from the north and south. Both interstates lead to Beckley. From there, it's only some forty miles on US 19 to the marked turnoff (onto WV 129) that leads to the putin at Summersville Dam. Look for the sign to the dam about a mile south of Summersville. WV 129 runs across the top of the dam. Put in at the base of the dam, just downstream of the release tubes. The takeout is wherever you can find one that suits you. The Gauley Access table below lists several possible takeouts, in the order they appear on the river.

All river right access points are reached via WV 129, the spur that runs west off US 19, across Summersville Dam, and into WV 39. The turn to Carnifax Ferry is clearly marked about three miles west of the dam. Panther Creek is reached via Panther Mountain Road (Route 22), a backwoods boulevard which meanders all over the north rim of the canyon. Route 22 is a left turn off WV 129 when headed west from the dam toward Drennen. To reach Peters Creek and the river right access near Koontz Flume, take WV 129 west until it dead ends into WV 39 at Drennen. Turn left (south) onto WV 39 and take a left in about

Upper Gauley Access Points	
Mile	**Description**
4.6	Pillow Rapid. River right. Emergencies only. Steep, rough (but short) trail, leading to Carnifax Ferry Overlook.
5.4	Carnifax Ferry. River right, across from the mouth of the Meadow River. Good trail. About a mile hike to Carnifax Ferry Overlook.
9.2	Panther Creek. River right. Steep trail, about 0.75 mile, leading to Panther Mountain Road which loops off WV 129.
11.0	Commercial outfitter access on river left. Road may be gated.
13.8	Koontz Bend Tunnel entrance. Almost a mile through a railroad tunnel, then another mile up the tracks to Peters Creek parking area.
14.5	Commercial outfitter access on river right. May be gated.
17.3	Peters Creek on river right. Then a mile hike up the railroad tracks to the parking area.

Pillow Rock Rapid on the upper Gauley River.   Mayo Gravatt photo.

Mayo Gravatt in the Kitchen. Goshen Pass (Maury River).
Sarah Gravatt photo.

three miles at Otter School. Follow Peters Creek, cross the railroad tracks and take the first right turn to reach the Peters Creek access or the third right turn to reach the access near Koontz Flume. The latter access may be impassible in wet weather. In fact, it may be impassible in good weather.

Miles From Summersville Dam	
Pittsburgh, PA 198	Washington, DC 300
Cincinnati, OH 245	Cleveland, OH 300
Greensboro, NC 265	Atlanta, GA 560

Other Information

Area Attractions

The New River Gorge Bridge is twelve miles south of Summersville on US 19. Longest single-arch steel bridge in the world, it's also the second highest bridge in the United States, surpassed only by the Royal Gorge Bridge in Colorado. In October, the local community of Fayetteville sponsors "Bridge Day," when one side of the structure is blocked to traffic, and fun and frivolity ensues, including BASE jumpers who parachute from the bridge into the chasm 876 feet below. (BASE jumpers take their acronym from the first letters of the objects they jump from: Buildings, Antennae, Structures, Earth.)

Camping

Limited camping is available on the downstream end of the parking lot at the base of the dam. It's a zoo, with lots of strutting, preening, and turkey gobble. A Corps of Engineers facility (Battle Run) with hot showers is located half a mile west of the dam, on the lake shore. Some paddlers prefer the Garvey Hilton near Lookout on US 60. A slew of commercial campgrounds are located along US 19 in the vicinity of the New River Gorge Bridge.

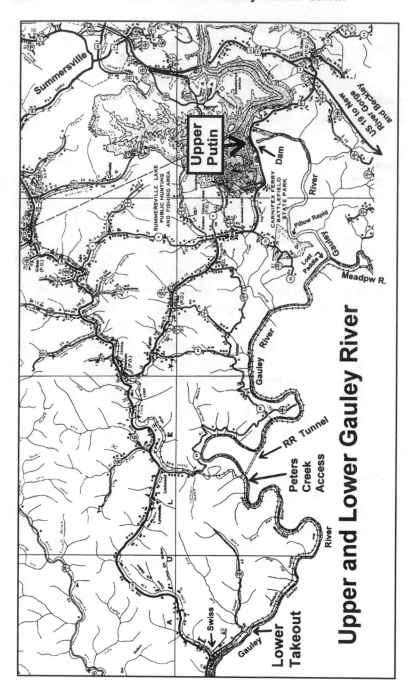

Upper and Lower Gauley River

Hiking

If you're not quite ready to challenge the upper Gauley in a boat, but would like to get an up-close and personal look at what everybody talks about when they return from a trip on it, try the short, steep trail that leads downward from the Carnifax Ferry Overlook to Pillow Rapid. This is a nice spot to spend a few hours during fall release. The large rocks by the river provide an exceptional view of paddlers running Pillow Rapid. The entertainment is Class V exciting and admission is free. The turnoff to Carnifax Ferry Overlook is clearly marked on WV 129, which is the shuttle route for the upper Gauley trip. From the Carnifax Overlook parking area, look to the left for a non-obvious trail.

If you like what you see at Pillow and would like to get a look at another well-known rapid, return to the Overlook and take the obvious trail behind the picnic area. It leads downstream to historic Carnifax Ferry. From here it's only a short distance downstream to Lost Paddle. A bit of bushwhacking is involved, as there is no established trail beyond the ferry site. The going will be slow due to house-sized boulders and thick vegetation but the reward will be a bird's-eye view of a 600 yard rapid of epic proportions. As with the hike into Pillow, the best tactic is to count on spending at least half a day. Take a picnic lunch, liquid refreshments and binoculars. (Yes, you'll need binoculars; the rapid really is that long.)

Suitability for Rafting (On a 1 to 7 Scale): 6

Only expert rafters should consider piloting their own boat down the upper Gauley. A preferred tactic is to use one of the commercial outfitters located near Fayetteville, on US 19. Most require previous whitewater experience before they'll allow you on the upper Gauley, but they're often willing to provide it the prior day on either the lower Gauley or the New River Gorge. And they're right to require previous experience. This river is not the place for a first raft trip. Even ten or twelve passenger rafts can get crunched in the tremendous power of the larger rapids. Raft the New Gorge a time or two before tackling the Big G. (Hint: Make commercial reservations months in advance to secure desired dates. Call the Fayetteville Chamber of Commerce for outfitter names and numbers.)

Nearby Alternate Trips		
Alternate Trip	Rapids Difficulty	TRIP Points
Cranberry	III-IV	103
Lower Gauley	IV+	109
New River Gorge	IV+	106
Upper Meadow	III+	102
Middle Meadow	III	93

Lower Gauley River

Peters Creek to Swiss
(West Virginia)

TRIP Profile			
Scale Midpoint = 100			
Overall Difficulty	109	Rapids Difficulty	113
Volume x Gradient	150	Continuous Rapids	111
Average Gradient	76	Entrapments	106
Maximum Gradient	71	Inaccessibility	119
Total Gradient	77	Reputation	128

Actual Stream Data			
Max Rapids	IV+	Stream Size	Large
Average Gradient	23	Length (in miles)	8
Maximum Gradient	30	Morphology Type	2

Overview

The lower Gauley is a fine, fun, big river with some bodacious West Virginia-sized rapids. Its only problem is limited access. The unequivocal recommendation is to paddle the lower Gauley by putting in at Summersville Dam and running the upper section first. That's certainly the easiest putin. Admittedly, however, nothing else about that strategy is easy, and for the person wanting to run the lower section without first trying the big drops upstream, the alternatives aren't real attractive unless one can gain access via one of the commercial outfitter sites between Sweets Falls and Peters Creek. These accesses are often open during spring and summer (when unscheduled releases occur), but may be closed during

235

scheduled fall releases, when outfitters can't risk having their access roads clogged with private boaters.

Other points of ingress include Panther Creek, just downstream of Sweets Falls. This entails hauling boats down to the river and results in a sixteen mile river trip, much of it consisting of pools. At partial release levels, it's a long trip. A shorter trip (eight miles) is available by using the Peters Creek putin, but that entails carrying boats a mile down a railroad track in order to reach the river.

The stream description below assumes a putin at Peters Creek -- not because that access is recommended -- but because the preceding description of the upper Gauley covers the river down to that point. **Similar To.** The lower Gauley displays much of the power of the upstream section but little of the technical craziness and big-drop intensity. From Peters Creek downstream, rapids on the lower Gauley are somewhat like an oversized Ocoee.

Mile(s)	Lower Gauley Top-To-Bottom Itinerary
0.0	Peters Creek.
0.9	Mash (Class IV).
1.3	Diagonal Ledges (Class III+).
1.9	Gateway to Heaven (Class III+).
2.8	Stairsteps (Class III+).
3.5	Riverwide Hole (Class III+).
4.3	Rollercoaster (Class III).
4.6	Cliffside (Class III).
4.9	Rattlesnake (Class III).
5.2	Roostertail (Class III).
5.8	Pure Screaming Hell (Class IV+).
6.4	Kevins Folly (Class III), the last rapid.
7.8	Take-out at Swiss railroad siding.

Description

The good news is that the lower Gauley contains the Gateway to Heaven. The bad news is that you can successfully pass through the Pearly Gates and still get lost in Pure Screaming Hell!

Once upon a time this river must have scared the pure scream-ing sanctimonies out of some religious fundamentalist. How else could we have arrived at such graphic appellations? (Consider also the "Room of Doom" on the upper run.)

Just because all the big Class Vs are upstream, don't think the lower section won't make you sit up and take notice. At standard release levels of 2,200 to 3,600 cfs the lower Gauley is big and powerful and it wastes no time establishing that fact. First time paddlers will be surprised at the power of even the minor rapids that begin shortly downstream of Peters Creek. When Mash (Class IV) arrives, there can be no remaining doubt that this really is the Gauley River, not just some distant relative of the famous upstream section. Mash is a two-part rapid with a huge eddy in between. Upper Mash angles right through a minor boulder garden. Catch the humongous eddy and scope out lower Mash because it definitely is the more difficult half. It consists of a river wide ledge in the shape of a U, with the prongs pointing downstream. The waves and holes and ensuing wave train are wild and crazy.

The next big rapid is Gateway to Heaven, where the river constricts to fifteen feet, or thereabouts, and threads through two sentinel rocks called, naturally, the Pearly Gates. Whenever this much volume is constricted this radically, strange patterns of energy erupt in the water. The best route through the Gates varies with water level, but the righteous path is always some variation on the basic theme of dodge the biggest holes. A big one covers the right side of the river about half way to the gates and another swirlpool of temptation is located in the gates themselves.

Nine or ten Class III to Class III+ rapids follow Gateway in regular succession. Some of these will edge into the Class IV category with higher flows. And then comes one of the most aptly named rapids on any river: Pure Screaming Hell (Class IV+). This rapid is decidedly more difficult than anything else below Peters Creek. The only other rapid that even comes close is Mash. If you've never paddled the upper Gauley and crave to know what its big rapids are like, the bottom part of Pure Screaming Hell is a pretty good imitation. The main wave train through the approach delivers the paddler into a gigantic hole at the bottom and some of the most intense turbulence on the Gauley. Unless you particularly enjoy getting knocked around, it's best to avoid the right side of this bruiser as you approach the bottom. In addition to the hole, a strainer rock formation on river right could be terminal. The easiest route is to enter center or left of center and bear left all the way down, dodging the bigger holes as you go. Marginal paddlers will benefit from scouting (river right) and safety ropes here are a commendable precaution.

Below Pure Screaming everything is anti-climactic, although several smaller rapids like Kevins Folly clamor for attention.

Summary

It's less intense than the section upstairs but it has some adrenalin pumpers nonetheless, and one juicy taste of the upper Gauley called Pure Screaming Hell.

Water Levels

The Belva gauge is the relevant one (rather than Summersville Dam releases). It measures dam release plus Meadow River contribution. Call (304) 529-5127.

Lower Gauley **Gauge Location** Belva
Low: 1,000 cfs Medium: 2,500 cfs High: 4,000 cfs

Access

Four points of ingress are possible:

1. Paddle in from Summersville Dam.
2. Panther Creek.
3. Commercial outfitter sites in the vicinity of Koontz Flume.
4. Peters Creek.

The problem with #1 is that it entails paddling through eight miles of Class V water. The second alternative, Panther Creek, is a questionable choice at partial release levels because of all the miles of downstream flatwater. Access via a commercial outfitter's site is the preferred option, but often

their access roads are not open when needed, that is, during the annual fall draw down. Using the Peters Creek access means a long carry on foot, down a set of railroad tracks, to reach the river. None of the putins are particularly easy to find. For information on highway access, consult the upper Gauley description.

Takeout is upstream of Swiss (as far upstream as you can get, because the river is flat by the time it approaches the community).

Miles From Summersville Dam	
Roanoke, VA 134	Cincinnati, OH 245
Pittsburgh, PA 198	Washington, DC 300
Cleveland, OH 300	Atlanta, GA 560

Other Information

For information on Area Attractions, Camping, Hiking, and Nearby Alternate Trips, see the upper Gauley description.

Rafting Suitability (On a 1 to 7 Scale): 7

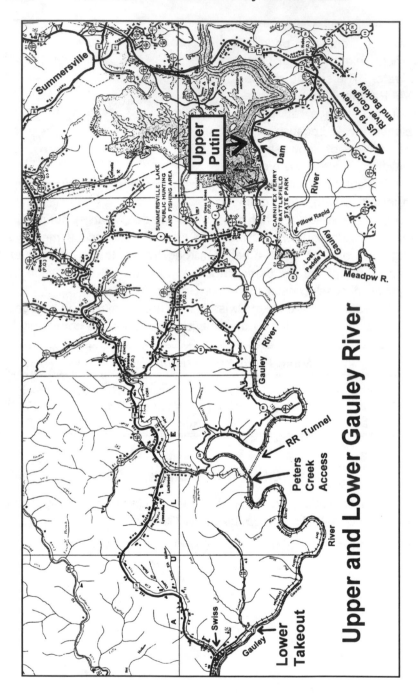

Upper and Lower Gauley River

Goshen Pass

of the Maury River
(Virginia)

TRIP Profile			
Scale Midpoint = 100			
Overall Difficulty	92	Rapids Difficulty	87
Volume x Gradient	98	Continuous Rapids	99
Average Gradient	94	Entrapments	94
Maximum Gradient	95	Inaccessibility	65
Total Gradient	88	Reputation	117

Actual Stream Data			
Max Rapids	III(IV)	Stream Size	Medium
Average Gradient	42	Length (in miles)	6
Maximum Gradient	70	Morphology Types	3&4

Overview

The Maury is an interesting study in how a flood can dramatically change a river. In 1985, large sections of Virginia and West Virginia experienced flooding so powerful that many streambeds were radically altered. With the possible exception of West Virginia's Cheat Canyon downstream of Albright, no river was more altered than the Goshen Pass section of the Maury, near Rockbridge Baths, Virginia, where raging waters scoured the gorge walls, ripping loose entire cliffsides and flushing them into the streambed. In the process, immense boulders were swept up like grains of sand and deposited far downstream. Before the flood, Goshen Pass had a ledge-pool conformation, with distinct routes through a moderately

241

obstructed streambed. (Except for the Kitchen, of course, which has been an impossibly scrambled mess for as long as anybody can remember.)

After the flood, much of Goshen Pass was cluttered with rock and boulder detritus, which had been swept along in the flood like pollen in the wind and eventually deposited haphazardly in huge rubble fields of debris.   A stream that once revealed its main avenues at a glance now hides them in maze-like rock jumbles. Parts of the stream today bear little resemblance to the old river. It's far more congested and requires substantially more maneuvering, and a trip leader who knows the river is now a definite asset in the more complex rock gardens.

Mile(s)	Goshen Pass Top-To-Bottom Itinerary
0.0	Put in alongside VA 39 at the crest of Goshen Pass or at a parking area 100 yards off the paved road.
0.6	Undercut Rock (Class II+), far river right.
0.7	Roadside (Class III), a congested rockgarden.
0.7 to 1.3	Technical congested rock gardens (Class III+).
1.3	Devils Kitchen (Class IV).
1.8	Class III rock garden, ending at picnic area.
1.9	Picnic area (alternate putin or takeout).
2.1	Class II+ ledge.
2.3	Corner Rapid (Class III+).
2.5	Wall Rapid (Class III).
2.8	Indian Pool (cabins begin to appear).
3.1	Alternate access.
4.0	Strong hole (river left).
5.5	Brillo Falls (Class II+).
6.0	VA 39 Bridge.
6.5	Take out at the old mercantile in Rockbridge Baths.

Description

The Maury River is born at the confluence of the Calfpasture and Little Calfpasture, and almost immediately begins its descent through Goshen Pass and down the mountain toward Rockbridge Baths. Its first three miles feature continuous action that includes one Class IV rapid (Kitchen), another rapid that occasionally edges into Class IV difficulty (Corner), and, depending on flow level, eight to twelve other Class III rapids.

The first significant rapid is Undercut Rock, a Class II+ with an undercut on river right. Although clearly visible from upstream, the rock is a potential hazard at some flow levels because a deceptively strong current sweeps from left to right toward the undercut. Run the rapid either from right-of-center angled back left paddling hard, or give the ugly mess on the right side a wide berth by dropping over a three foot ledge on river left into an uppity hydraulic. Roadside (Class III) is next. The main channel, to the extent there is one anymore, is funneled to the right, against the road embankment.

A half mile of technical (Class III+) rock garden boulder-dodging leads to Class IV Kitchen. Although only a hundred yards long, or less, it seems longer once you're in it, probably because it's chock full of traps, trolls, and devilishly positioned rocks. There's no way to describe Kitchen adequately, and there's no clear path through it. River right tends to snag drift logs, so it's generally best to concentrate on running left or at least left of center. The preferred route can vary considerably, however, depending on water level. The best procedure at Kitchen is always to scout it (from river left) and plan your route according to available water. At medium to high flow levels, consider catching the eddy behind the large river left boulder at the top of the rapid. At all water levels, it's an excellent rapid not to swim.

The picnic area is conveniently located near the Kitchen, about half a mile downstream. Corner Rapid, about 0.4 mile below the picnic area, is a bony, congested Class III+ that may be toughest at lower flow levels because of its exposed rocks. Run far right over a five foot drop for the sensation of plunging into a washing machine, far left over a jumble of rocks for the ultimate rock dodging experience (using care to avoid the garbage pile at the very bottom), or thread the needle around the center rocks and through funky waves, holes and turbulence for that coveted rock and roll effect. Paddlers unfamiliar with Corner will benefit by taking the time to scout it, from river left. Wall Rapid (Class III+), next on the agenda downstream of Corner, is similar to some of the longer ledge sections of Wilson Creek Gorge.

Due to gradually diminishing gradient, the excitement slackens somewhat in the last half of the run and cabins begin to appear at streamside. Still, a decent gradient continues until near the takeout, and several congested Class III rock gardens will be encountered from below Wall Rapid all the way to Brillo Falls. At approximately Mile Four, a slide on river left produces a strong hole which can be skirted through a technical rock garden on river right.

As the Maury makes a sharp left turn at about mile 5, the VA 39 bridge is momentarily visible almost a mile downstream, over a rubble of flood debris. Such an extended stretch of boulder rubble is seldom seen in the Appalachians except toward the mouths of small tributaries where they confluence with larger streams, and this one offers mute but convincing testimony to the power of the 1985 flood.

Shortly after the VA 39 bridge is glimpsed, the stream drops into the aforementioned boulder rubble. (Actually, a succession of boulder fields.) It's almost a mile farther downstream before the bridge can again be sighted. Brillo Falls (Class II+), near the end of the run, is a four foot riverwide sloping ledge. Downstream of Brillo, in the final mile to the takeout, the gradient eases to 20 feet/mile.

Summary

This run on the Maury is named for the pass, or gap, which it traverses. The river is an impressive sight as it literally pours from the highlands through this narrow mountain defile into the valley below. The parallel shuttle road high on the side of the pass provides eye-popping panoramic views of several of the rapids, including Kitchen and Corner. Although degraded by the flood, it's still a beautiful river, especially where the stream first begins its descent in the vicinity of the Kitchen.

The top half of Goshen Pass is hard to beat for technical Class III+ whitewater. Considering that it's runnable most of the year, Goshen Pass is arguably the best all around whitewater in Virginia.

Water Levels

Readings from the gauge located behind the old mercantile in Rockbridge Baths are often available from the James River Basin Canoe Livery in Buena Vista. Phone: (703) 261-7334. (Do not call between 8 pm and 9 pm.)

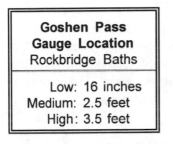

**Goshen Pass
Gauge Location**
Rockbridge Baths

Low: 16 inches
Medium: 2.5 feet
High: 3.5 feet

Goshen Pass can be run down to about 12 or 14 inches, but one must be exceedingly fond of technical water to tackle it below 16 inches on the Rockbridge Baths gauge. It starts getting pushy above three feet. Somewhere around 3.5 it transitions to high gear.

Access

The Goshen Pass section of the Maury River flows alongside VA 39 between Rockbridge Baths and Goshen, about fifty miles west of Charlottesville. Route 39 can be accessed near Buena Vista/Lexington near the junction of I-81 and/or I-64.

Put on at the top of Goshen Pass, just off VA 39, about five road miles northwest of Rockbridge Baths, Virginia. Take out behind the old mercantile in downtown Rockbridge Baths.

Route 39 is the shuttle

Goshen
Pass

Virginia

road. It parallels the river. Round trip shuttle is only twenty minutes. Stop at the pullovers near Corner and Kitchen rapids and drink in the beauty of this outstanding mountain gap.

Miles From Goshen Pass on the Maury River	
Lynchburg, VA 60	Roanoke, VA 245
Charlottesville, VA 85	Greensboro, NC 180
Charleston, WV 200	Washington, DC 205

Other Information

Area Attractions

VA Route 39 continues through Goshen Pass and into the mountains, past the famous resort at Warm Springs, across the West Virginia state line and into the southern Monongahela National Forest high country around Snow Shoe ski resort, the Cranberry River, and the Williams River. It's a beautiful drive.

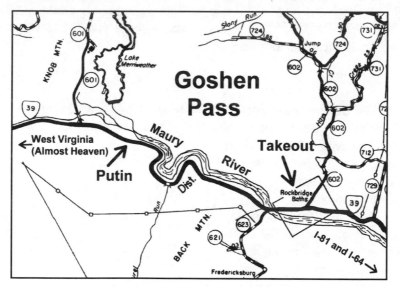

Camping

Not a lot to choose from. An urban campground is available on the outskirts of Buena Vista (take US 501 south toward Glasgow and watch for the campground signs on road right). Primitive (but scenic) camping is available at the putin clearing at the top of Goshen Pass. Because it's at the putin it's a very convenient place to wake up. However, it's not a designated campground and locals do occasionally roll in late at night ready to party.

Nearby Alternate Trips

When Goshen is too low, the Balcony Falls section of the James River is usually runnable, near Glasgow. It's a short and often windy Class II+ run. The Cranberry and Williams Rivers are approximately 90 miles (or 2.5 hours) north on VA and WV Route 39. Johns Creek (Class IV) is about 85 miles (or 2.5 hours) south, at New Castle, Virginia, which is near Roanoke. Johns Creek has a small drainage and it's often too low to run. When it has water, it's even more spirited than the first three miles of Goshen Pass. Balcony Falls, Johns Creek, the Cranberry, and the Williams are described elsewhere in this volume.

Hiwassee River

Appalachian Powerhouse to Reliance
(Tennessee)

TRIP Profile			
Scale Midpoint = 100			
Overall Difficulty	70	Rapids Difficulty	69
Volume x Gradient	91	Continuous Rapids	75
Average Gradient	69	Entrapments	49
Maximum Gradient	62	Inaccessibility	74
Total Gradient	63	Reputation	49

Actual Stream Data			
Max Rapids	II+	Stream Size	Large
Average Gradient	15	Length (in miles)	6
Maximum Gradient	22	Morphology Type	1

Overview

This section of the Hiwassee River has provided thousands of paddlers with their first exciting splash of whitewater. A lot of that first exposure came about because several local paddling clubs hold beginning whitewater canoe and decked boat clinics here. The largest of these efforts are the instructional programs sponsored by the Tennessee Scenic Rivers Association (TSRA). These renowned weekends of camaraderie, dating back to the late 1960's, are known for both quality and sheer size. Importantly, this school and others like it provide new paddlers with a no-nonsense introduction to the philosophy of safety first in all paddling activities. Considering that all instruction is by volunteers (between 60 and 70 are involved each

248

year), the clinics are exemplars of how volunteer organizations can provide valuable public service. The TSRA canoe school is so popular that its 200 to 250 spaces fill up fast every year. The school has such a reputation that one year the US Coast Guard sent representatives to learn to canoe, as well as to observe -- we suspect -- how the folks at TSRA manage to teach so effectively and still have a great time in the process!

Undoubtedly, part of the popularity of the clinics held on this stream -- by TSRA and a number of other paddling organizations -- is the Hiwassee River itself, with its broad, sweeping expanses of gentle Class II ledges, shoals, and waves nestled in the remarkably scenic terrain that the big river forms as it cuts through the last barrier ridges of the Unaka Mountains into the Tennessee Valley.

Similar To. The Hiwassee has a lot in common with the Balcony Falls section of the James in Virginia. Both are big, broad streams with moderate gradient and numerous small ledges.

Description

Hiwassee water comes out of the bottom of Appalachia Lake and it's always cold, which is a strong incentive to limit the number and duration of immersions. Nonetheless, some hardy souls float this stream on inner tubes!

The run is characterized by sweeping riparian vistas, and by many small ledges, commonly aggregated in wide "stairsteps." One ledge (Oblique Falls) is about three or four feet high (on far river left), but most are in the range of six inches to a foot in height.

Needles (Class II) is a favorite spot for instruction on eddy turns. At Bigneys Rock (Class II) beginning paddlers struggle valiantly to maintain boat control in unpredictable cross-currents. The last rapid is the best, Devils Shoals (Class II+), culminating in a series of standing waves.

No rapid on the Hiwassee exceeds Class II difficulty, and hence the river is appropriate for all but totally inexperienced paddlers. Despite its immense popularity, it rarely seems overly crowded, perhaps due to its width.

Summary

    It's a favorite for laid-back mid-summer float trips and for instruction. Because of its mild whitewater, forgiving nature, and the fact that releases for power generation continue during summer months, it's very popular.

Water Levels

    Water is controlled by TVA via power generation releases from Appalachia Lake in North Carolina. Weekend releases during the summer are standard fare, but if in doubt call one of the local outfitters or TVA at: (800) 238-2264. One generator means the river will be low but runnable. Two generators mean plenty of water.

Access

    Located in the extreme southeastern corner of Tennessee in Polk County near Reliance, the Hiwassee is a Tennessee State Scenic River. The main access roads into this region are US 64 running east-to-west and US 411 running north-to-south. The picturesque hamlet of Reliance, the takeout, is reached via TN Route 30, a road that forms a loop between US 64 and US 411. The takeout is a parking lot on river left a few hundred yards upstream of Reliance.   To reach the putin, cross the river at Reliance (to river right) and take the first right. Drive about five miles, making right turns at two forks, until the road ends at a parking lot by the river. About midway to the putin, at the top of the ridge, stop to enjoy a spell-binding view of the river.

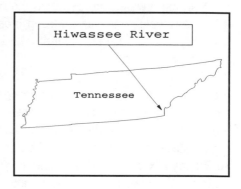

Hiwassee River

Tennessee

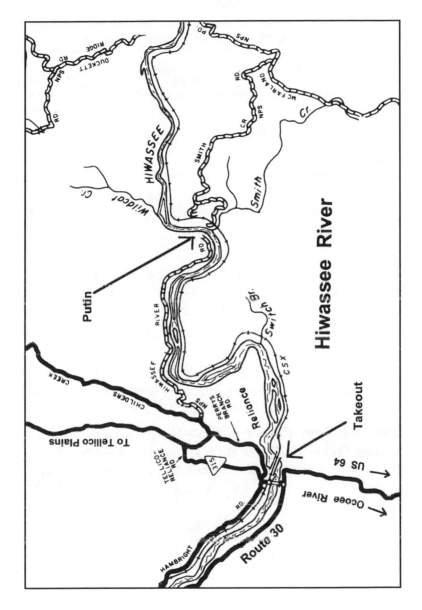

Miles From the Hiwassee River	
Chattanooga, TN 60	Nashville, TN 195
Knoxville, TN 85	Atlanta, GA 175

Other Information

Camping

Quinn Springs (on TN 30 between US 411 and Reliance) and Gee Creek (off US 411 a few yards north of the Hiwassee) are convenient. Gee Creek has hot showers. Camping is also available at the outfitter located near the takeout.

History

The beautiful countryside surrounding the Hiwassee was the very heartland of the Cherokee Nation. Little wonder that when they were forcibly driven from it, their pathetic pilgrimage formed a veritable "Trail of Tears," in America's darkest embrace of domestic Apartheid.

Maps

Pick up a copy of the Cherokee National Forest map. The nearest ranger stations are at the Ocoee River on US 64 and at the Tellico River, about five miles upstream of Tellico Plains.

Rafting Suitability (On a 1 to 7 Scale): 7

Several commercial outfitters are located near the river, including River Sports (headquartered in Knoxville), which has an outpost at the intersection of US 411 and TN 30. Phone (615) 338-1580.

Nearby Alternate Trips

The Ocoee River (Class III-IV) is thirty minutes south via TN 30 and US 64, near Ducktown. The Tellico River (Class III-IV) is about a fifty minute drive to the north. To reach the Tellico, cross to river right of the Hiwassee River at Reliance and keep on trucking. Drive into and through Tellico Plains, bearing left at the only downtown intersection. At the Tellico River turn right and drive upstream.

All streams in the following table are within two hours driving distance of the Hiwassee.

Alternate Trip	Rapids Difficulty	TRIP Points
Conasauga	II	72
Upper Little River	III(IV)	95
Lower Little River	III(IV)	103
Nantahala	II(III)	77
Ocoee	III-IV	104
Upper Tellico	III-IV	110
Lower Tellico	III	96

Hopeville Canyon

North Fork of the South Branch of the Potomac
(West Virginia)

TRIP Profile			
Scale Midpoint = 100			
Overall Difficulty	73	Rapids Difficulty	72
Volume x Gradient	68	Continuous Rapids	63
Average Gradient	86	Entrapments	72
Maximum Gradient	74	Inaccessibility	74
Total Gradient	69	Reputation	60

Actual Stream Data			
Max Rapids	II(III)	Stream Size	Small
Average Gradient	33	Length (in miles)	4
Maximum Gradient	40	Morphology Type	2

Overview

Hopeville Canyon is in the northeast sector of West Virginia in the Monongahela National Forest, a region known for its fine scenery. It's a region of majestic rocky upthrusts, thick forests, and rugged mountains. The highest point in the state is only a few miles away (Spruce Knob, Elevation 4,861 feet).

This area is part of the Potomac River headwaters, with so many forks and branches that it's hard to keep them straight. For the record, Hopeville Canyon is on the North Fork of the South Branch of the Potomac.

From the confluence of Seneca Creek and the North Fork of the South Branch, Seneca Rocks (one of the most impressive rock

254

formations in the region) is clearly visible. On the far side of that towering rock formation, the South Branch of the Potomac winds its way through Smoke Hole National Recreation Area.

Description

Scenery is the best part of Hopeville Canyon, whitewater second, and access a close third. Although the run is through farm country, the entire river right vista consists of distant views of outcroppings similar to Seneca Rocks.

The run begins where WV 28 first leaves the river, several miles downstream of Seneca Rocks. The preferred putin can be spotted from the road by a cave-like indentation in the cliffside across the river. As the run continues into the canyon, the highway conveniently disappears, only to reappear at the Assembly of God church near the end of the canyon. Continue past the church for a quarter mile and take out in the vicinity of the small tributary which enters from river left.

Summary

This run is good for training clinics, for novice and intermediate paddlers, and for anyone who appreciates beautiful surroundings. Because of the added volume from Seneca Creek, which flows into it only a few miles upstream of the putin, it's runnable through the spring and some of the summer, presenting mild, mostly straightforward Class II(III) rapids.

Water Levels

Petersburg is an indirect reading because it also reflects flow received from the South Branch out of Smokehole. Phone (703) 260-0305.

Hopeville Canyon
Gauge Location
Petersburg
Low: 2.3
Medium: 4.0
High: 5.0

Access

The main access route into the area is US 33, connecting I-81 in Virginia and I-79 in central West Virginia. However, both the putin and the takeout are located alongside Route 28, which parallels the river from Seneca Rocks downstream to the putin, and thereafter pulls

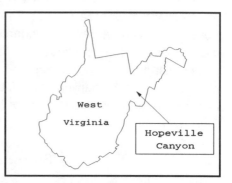

away from it as the stream finds its way into Hopeville Canyon. When the stream again emerges from the canyon, the road is waiting to escort it most of the way to Petersburg.

Miles From Hopeville Canyon	
Washington, DC 140	Pittsburgh, PA 225
Roanoke, VA 180	Columbus, OH 275

Other Information

Area Attractions

Look closely at the craggy spires of the Seneca Rocks formation. Oftentimes climbers can be spotted from the parking area at the juncture of US 33 and WV 28.

Spruce Knob, the highest mountain in West Virginia, is only a few miles away. A Forest Service road leads to its summit. Aptly

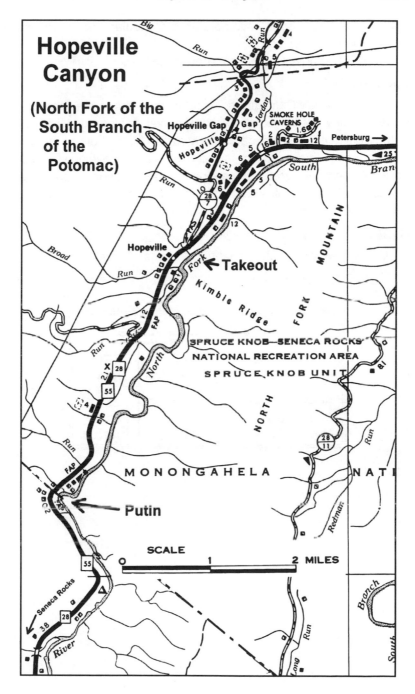

Hopeville Canyon

(North Fork of the South Branch of the Potomac)

Takeout

Putin

SCALE

0   1   2 MILES

named, the knob top is covered with a Canadian forest consisting predominantly of spruce.

The Smokehole Recreation Area is nearby.

Camping

Seneca Creek Campground was washed out in the flood of '85. It may or may not be rebuilt. A commercial campground is located at the confluence of Seneca Creek and the North Fork of the South Branch, near Seneca Rocks. Island Creek, an undeveloped National Forest campground (refer to the Monongahela National Forest Map), is located about 30 miles south on WV 28 on the bank of the Greenbrier River.

Maps

Get a copy of the Monongahela National Forest map.

Suitability for Rafting (On a 1 to 7 Scale): 6

Nearby Alternate Trips		
Alternate Trip	Rapids Difficulty	TRIP Points
Seneca Creek	II-III	89
Smokehole	II-III	na
Moorefield Gorge	III	na

Island Creek

(Tennessee)

TRIP Profile			
Scale Midpoint = 100			
Overall Difficulty	108	Rapids Difficulty	90
Volume x Gradient	73	Continuous Rapids	123
Average Gradient	158	Entrapments	117
Maximum Gradient	124	Inaccessibility	119
Total Gradient	92	Reputation	117

Actual Stream Data			
Max Rapids	III-IV	Stream Size	Micro
Average Gradient	110	Length (in miles)	2.5
Maximum Gradient	110	Morphology Types	3&4

Overview

Island Creek, part of the Obed/Emory watershed on Tennessee's Cumberland Plateau, charges down a narrow, steep and obstructed micro gorge that in its own intimate way is the most beguiling in the Southeast. It serves as a standard of comparison for Cumberland Plateau riparian scenery as it moves with sometimes startling velocity through long, continuous rapids that are difficult to scout, festooned with boulders, and largely devoid of eddies. Due to the structure of the streambed, its rapids are laced with surprisingly strong diagonal holes. In several places the stream rushes down solid slanted slabs of stone, picking up even more speed. For the size of the stream, the cross currents are both complex and powerful, and eddies -- what few there are -- are tempestuous, with

259

strong eddy lines.   Several rapids require considerable time and exertion to scout and are so long that

Mile(s)	Island Creek Top-To-Bottom Itinerary
0.0	Put in at the bridge near Catoosa checking station.
0.0 to 0.5	The first half mile is uninspiring brush dodging.
0.6	Slip-n'-Slide (Class III).
0.9	Write Yo' Mama (Class IV).
1.3	Compound Fracture (Class IV).
1.7	Rockhouse (Class IV).
2.0	Maelstrom (Class IV).
2.3	Islands.
2.5	Emory River confluence.
2.7	Nemo Bridge alternate takeout (upstream from the Island Creek/Emory River confluence).
8.2	Camp Austin on the Emory River.

the bottom cannot be seen from the top, leaving no room for paddlers without the ability to confidently eddy-hop down the stream's narrow corridor.

With high water, Island Creek rates Class IV+ because it becomes an unrelenting flush. Because of its difficulty, inaccessibility, and scarcity of high water, few have made the plunge down its bony corridor and most who did ran it with insufficient water and were disappointed.   The run tends to evoke startlingly disparate reactions, either awe bordering on reverence or an attitude of, "Is that all there is?" The explanation for such diametrically opposite reactions is as simple as fluctuating water levels. With enough water it's intense. With low water it's a bumpy Class II-III that doesn't live up to its reputation.

The scenery, however, is constant at all levels.   Constantly breathtaking, that is. Island Creek is a young stream (a drainage ditch, some contend) impetuously plummeting from the Cumberland Plateau to the Tennessee Valley, with frequent points of radical erosion where it's in the process of carving rock houses.   At one place it sluices through a jumble of boulders and breakdown detritus from a waterfall and flushes into a rockhouse in the canyon wall, a truly unique configuration. Ever paddled a cave? It's possible to eddy out inside the rock house!

Similar To. Bill Brown once wrote that this little creek was as beautiful as the Doe River Gorge, as technical as the Middle Prong of the Little Pigeon, and as mean as Crooked Fork Creek (also in the Obed system). Bill was right.

Description

Thick overgrowth clogs the stream for the first half mile. The first major rapid appears when the stream widens and obstructing bushes disappear. Slip-n'Slide (Class III), which has a couple of small drops at the top and then a long curving course over tilted solid rock with diagonal souse holes, ends by splitting around a midstream rock. Scout from river right, and run the rapid far right if you blunder into it without getting a look/see first.

A long obstacle course of technical Class II-III water follows Slip-n'Slide. (There's a tight squeeze about two-thirds through.) Look next for an undercut canyon wall on river left, where the stream veers right and drops out of sight. This is the second major rapid, Write Yo' Mama (Class IV), gatekeeper to an intense section of water. About a hundred yards long, Yo' Mama gets wild at higher flows, with surprisingly aggressive holes and dynamic eddy lines. Mama's bottom is not visible from her top because of stream curvature and boulder obstructions.

After a short respite comes a complex 70 yard rock garden. Look closely for a gravel beach on river left. Stop here and scout Compound Fracture (Class IV), a rapid with unnaturally jagged rocks. As with most Cumberland Plateau streams, loggers snaked a narrow gauge railroad up this narrow defile back around the turn of the century, long before highways penetrated this region. Close inspection of Island Creek's streamsides will reveal the remnants of the railbed. At one time or other these narrow gauge railroads snaked up every significant stream on the Cumberland escarpment, expediting the removal of virgin timber.

As the builders audaciously ascended these small canyons they would of necessity switch back and forth across the stream to avoid rock outcroppings and to utilize the best road surface. These artful, serpentine tactics are nowhere better demonstrated than on Island Creek. Because of its micro size, it must surely represent the apotheosis of the narrow gauge railroad building art. (Also note the same tactics on Laurel Fork in West Virginia, the Piney River in Tennessee, and Big Laurel Creek in North Carolina, among others.)

At one point along Island Creek the builders encountered a place with sheer rock walls on both sides of the stream. End of the line? Hardly. There was virgin timber upstream. The builders placed dynamite along river right and blasted, producing a stable rock-solid base for the railroad and bad news for paddlers a hundred years later, as the detritus fell into Island Creek only to be swept at high water to the small rubblefall that forms the final, ragged drop in Compound Fracture. If you flip here, be sure to have your plastic surgeon on standby.

At the bottom of Compound Fracture the stream first flushes into a sheer river left cliff and then, forty yards downstream, side-swipes a huge slab of dislodged rock that has fractured from the cliff and dropped into the stream.

More rock gardens and rock houses appear and then comes Rockhouse Rapid (Class IV), which begins with a steep slide into a pool. (Avoid river left above the slide.) The pool washes out through a boulder field with the left course going into a rock house. The rock house provides a convenient eddy at high water, and weird currents. A short calm ensues below the rock house, but ends in Maelstrom (Class IV), a rapid of significant intensity and technicality.

From the bottom of Maelstrom looking back upstream is one of the most remarkable sights in southeastern whitewater. The stream appears to spring forth from a cave in the wall of the cliff (the aforementioned rock house), then rush over a rubble heap and gather force for the plummet into Maelstrom, all in the context of an immense overhanging undercut cliff on river left.

Another short calm ends when the stream fans out to strain through several small islands. Similar to the beginning of the trip, these islands are shrouded in annoying overgrowth. Left is best. Below the islands, rapids moderate to Class II and soon the creek runs into the Emory River, about a quarter mile downstream of Nemo Bridge. From this confluence to the first downstream road access, Camp Austin, the Emory is predominantly flat.

Summary

Don't be misled by conflicting information about Island Creek. Run it at low water and you'll be disappointed, but with the right water level it is a genuine firecracker. The run is prime only when the Obed system is flush with water.

This creek (along with the upper Citico and the first miles of Tennessee's Piney River) are working definitions of the limits of navigability on the small end of the scale. Along with its small size and congestion (including undercut hazards and "unnatural" rock detritus), it is continuously steep. This combination produces a technical stream where precise and instantaneous maneuvering is the order of the day.

Although the entire run is only 2.5 miles and the first half mile is unpleasant bushwhacking, don't be surprised if a first descent requires four hours or more. Frequent scouting may be necessary at higher flows, and is recommended in any event in order to appreciate the unusual beauty of this miniature Cumberland treasure.

Water Levels

Volume in the Obed/Emory watershed is gauged at Oakdale on the Emory River. Readings are available from the Tennessee Valley Authority (TVA) by calling (800) 238-2264 and pressing code "3" following the recorded message.

The Oakdale gauge, although only a few miles downstream of Island Creek's confluence, is at the bottom of the Obed/Emory watershed and reflects drainage not only from Island Creek but also from the Emory and Obed Rivers and from Daddys Creek, White Creek, Clear Creek, Crook-

Island Creek **Gauge Location** TVA Emory at Oakdale
Low: 10,000 cfs Medium: 15,000 cfs High: 20,000 cfs

ed Fork Creek, and Crab Orchard Creek. In other words, Oakdale readings are, at best, a crude indicator of Island Creek volume. On one occasion the Oakdale gauge will read 20,000 cfs and Island Creek will be dry. On another occasion Island Creek will be flush with water when the Oakdale gauge reads only 7,000 cfs. The only way to know for sure is to drive to the Island Creek putin and look at the stream.

On the bridge gauge, 0.4 is paddling zero. When the flow looks like too much, it probably is, and going elsewhere may be prudent. Island Creek at high water can be brutal.

Access

Access to the putin is problematic much of the year because it's located within the Catoosa Wildlife Management Area (CWMA). Roads within the CWMA are closed from January to April and on selected other weekends for managed hunts.

If the Catoosa is open, the easiest way to Island Creek is from Wartburg, which is about twenty miles north of I-40 on US 27. Take the Catoosa Road out of Wartburg. Cross Nemo Bridge and continue on the serpentine Catoosa Road as it ascends the Emory River gorge wall. A mile and a half past Nemo Bridge the road forks at the Catoosa checking station. Bear left and within a few yards the road parallels Island Creek and then crosses a wood bridge. This bridge is the putin. The road which

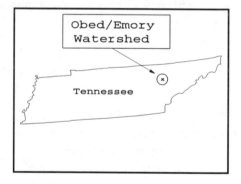

crosses Island Creek continues through the CWMA to the Crab Orchard Creek putin. The Island Creek putin also can be reached from Crab Orchard, Crossville, and Genesis Road by taking other roads which wind through the CWMA.

For takeout you have three alternatives. To go with the flow, paddle downstream for 5.5 miles on the Emory River to Camp Austin, reachable by driving back across Nemo Bridge through

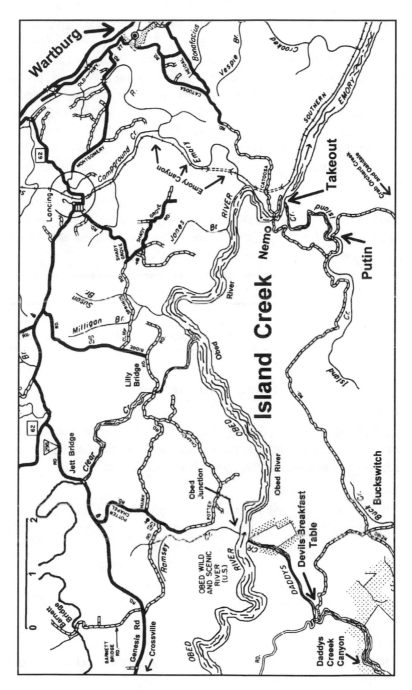

Wartburg and south on US 27/TN 29A to Oakdale, and up the county road which parallels the Emory River; or, in the opposite direction through the CWMA, across Crab Orchard Creek, into Oakdale, across the Emory River Bridge and the rail tracks, and up the same county road on the Emory River; or, through Catoosa backroads to the Camp Austin access on river right of the Emory.

Now for two preferred alternatives. The first is to paddle upstream on the Emory River about a quarter mile from the Island Creek confluence to Nemo Bridge. The current is not inordinately swift except for Nemo Rapid which can be skirted on river right.

The other alternative is to carry up to the Catoosa Road at Nemo Bridge from the Island Creek/Emory River confluence. The distance is less than half a mile. Either of the preferred takeout alternatives reduces the shuttle drive to about ten minutes.

Miles From Island Creek	
Knoxville, TN 57	Atlanta, GA 245
Nashville, TN 148	Cincinnati, OH 300

Other Information

Camping

Developed camping is available at Cumberland Mountain State Park, off US 127, about five miles south of Crossville, and at Frozen Head State Park, off TN 62, five miles east of Wartburg.

Hiking

By following the old narrow gauge railroad bed it's possible to bushwhack Island Creek on river right starting at the putin. The going is not easy as there is no established trail. Near the Emory River confluence, hikers can either cross the stream to river left and head up to Nemo Bridge, or stay on the same side and backtrack to the putin. Hiking is not possible on river left, due to sheer cliffs that front the stream.

Maps

Running shuttles in this watershed is frustrating without a good map. (It's often frustrating *with* a good map!) Check with the TVA,

1101 Market Street, 101 Haney Bldg, Chattanooga, TN 37402, or phone (615) 632-6082.

Nearby Alternate Trips

The Obed/Emory watershed contains 18 whitewater trips. The closest one to Island Creek is Crab Orchard Creek. Whenever Island Creek is runnable, Crab Orchard Creek probably is also. The Obed system is described in detail in *A Paddler's Guide to the Obed/Emory Watershed* by Monte Smith.

Alternate Trip	Rapids Difficulty	TRIP Points
Clear Creek	III+	97
Crab Orchard Creek	III+	98
Daddys Creek Canyon	III-IV	109
Obed River: Goulds Bend	III(V)	95
Obed River: DBT to Nemo	III(IV)	101

James River

Balcony Falls Section
(Virginia)

TRIP Profile			
Scale Midpoint = 100			
Overall Difficulty	73	Rapids Difficulty	72
Volume x Gradient	82	Continuous Rapids	75
Average Gradient	65	Entrapments	72
Maximum Gradient	58	Inaccessibility	110
Total Gradient	55	Reputation	60

Actual Stream Data			
Max Rapids	II(III)	Stream Size	Large
Average Gradient	11	Length (in miles)	5
Maximum Gradient	18	Morphology Types	1&2

Overview

Save this trip for late summer when all else is too low to run. Because of the large drainage area, there's nearly always enough water to run through this gigantic gorge which has both a parallel railroad and highway (although the latter is way up on the mountainside out of sight and sound of the river). Avoid this run when high winds are present. This section of the James may be the only river worse than the French Broad with respect to wind. On a bad day the wind can literally blow you over. The run is through a deep gorge, reminiscent in some minor respects of the Nolichucky, but with less intense whitewater. This is a popular fall colors trip

268

because the gorge walls are filled with mixed hardwoods. It also serves as a good training river, with quite a lot of Class II water.

Similar To. The Hiwassee in Tennessee, but with more and better rapids.

Mile(s)	Balcony Falls Top-To-Bottom Itinerary
0.0	Put in 50 yards upstream of the James and Maury confluence.
0.1	Confluence Rapid (Class III-).
0.5 to 2.5	Class II ledge rapids, with pools in between.
2.7	Balcony Falls (Class III-)
3.1	Current ends.
5.0	Trip ends with a mile-and-a-half flatwater paddle.

Description

The putin is actually on the Maury River (of Goshen Pass renown) but the Maury runs into the James only a few yards downstream of the putin. At the confluence watch for a rapid of the same name, Confluence (Class III-), which can require semi-intricate maneuvering at some water levels.

Once past Confluence the trip is a short three miles and all the rest of the rapids are Class II except for the last big one, Balcony Falls, which can be Class III at some water levels. "Falls" is a misnomer, as there is really no falls here. There is, however, a river-wide row of large boulders, with numerous routes through/between/among them. Origin of the name "Balcony Falls" is a mystery to this writer unless it's because the largest rock of all, a gymnasium-sized monstrosity on river right, can accommodate a "balcony" full of observers as other paddlers attempt the most challenging rapid of the run.

Summary

The run is short, scenic, and moderate in difficulty. It ends on slackwater. There is no good takeout without paddling about two miles of flatwater after the current ends.

Water Levels

Runnable except during the most severe drought conditions because of the size of the James River watershed and the contributory volume of the Maury. Call the James River Basin Canoe Livery if in doubt. (703) 261-7334

Access

To reach the Balcony Falls run from I-81, take US 60 into Buena Vista. Turn right in Buena Vista onto US 501 and head south toward Glasgow. At the split, bear right on VA 130, cross the Maury and head into Glasgow. Take the first left and drive a half mile to the putin, Locker Landing, which is on the Maury a few yards upstream of its confluence with the James, on the outskirts of Glasgow.

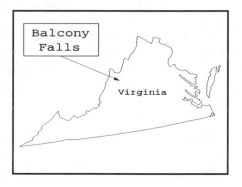

To shuttle, backtrack to US 501 and turn right (south). The highway twists into the mountains, overlooking the river for some distance. After about four curvy miles in the highlands, the road descends back to water level.

The traditional takeout, which entailed hauling up the bank and across the railroad tracks to US 501, was on river left, in the vicinity of where current ends and flatwater begins. However, railway moguls look dimly on trespassers. So do the courts. Crossing the tracks is a misdemeanor punishable by up to a $250 fine. As of when this book went to press, railroad enforcers were eagerly handing out tickets to trespassers. If caught, it'll cost you at least a

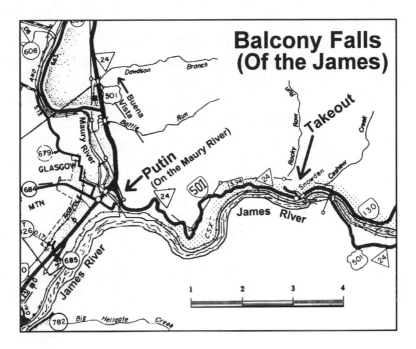

day in court, and possibly a fine on top of that. The prudent course is to paddle down the lake to the public boat ramp at Snowden.

Miles From Balcony Falls on the James River	
Lynchburg, VA 35	Charleston, WV 175
Roanoke, VA 60	Washington, DC 200

Other Information

Camping

A campground is available in Buena Vista near US 501.

Suitability for Rafting (On a 1 to 7 Scale): 7

The James River Basin Canoe Livery, located on US 60 a couple of miles north of Buena Vista and south of I-81, rents rafts and canoes for several James River floats, including the Balcony Falls section. Phone: (703) 261-7334.

TRIP Data

Average gradient numbers and TRIP profile data contained in the boxes at the beginning of this trip description do not include the flatwater mileage after the current ends.

Nearby Alternate Trips

Goshen Pass (Maury River), described elsewhere in this volume, is about one hour away, with outstanding Class III(IV) whitewater.

Johns Creek

(Virginia)

TRIP Profile			
Scale Midpoint = 100			
Overall Difficulty	112	Rapids Difficulty	117
Volume x Gradient	90	Continuous Rapids	123
Average Gradient	111	Entrapments	128
Maximum Gradient	124	Inaccessibility	110
Total Gradient	95	Reputation	139

Actual Stream Data			
Max Rapids	IV+	Stream Size	Micro
Average Gradient	50	Length (in miles)	5
Maximum Gradient	110	Morphology Type	3

Overview

Johns Creek is an anomaly. Even its location, near New Castle, is out of context. Whereas it would fit in with similar streams in West Virginia or on Tennessee's Cumberland Plateau, there's nothing similar to it nearby.

Even more anomalous is the contrast between its middle miles and those at the beginning and end of the trip. At the putin, Johns Creek looks like a lowlands drainage ditch. From its dismal appearance at the putin, it's hard to imagine there's any whitewater downstream. And at the takeout, it's a frisky Class II that just doesn't look big enough to be menacing. But don't let it fool you! In between the deceptive water at the top and bottom of this run is one of the most spirited small canyons in the Southeast, remarkably

273

similar to some of the Cumberland Plateau gorges in Tennessee. For two and a half exciting miles in the middle of the run, this little ripsnorter pulls out all the stops and blasts into the hydro hall of fame.

In many ways it's surreal. The putin is on a flat drainage ditch. The takeout is in a sleepy little Virginia hamlet. Yet in between all hell breaks loose. It's like pitching a game in the bush leagues. You're out there on the mound, feeling great, striking out batters left and right. Then you discover in the middle innings that the wimps you've been mowing down one-two-three have turned into Babe Ruth, Lou Gehrig, Ty Cobb, Rogers Hornsby, and Shoeless Joe Jackson. And, at the end of the game, after these guys have battered you all over the mound and the press corps is assembled to hear your feeble explanation, you point to the culprits on murderers' row and they're gone, replaced by the original cast, a ragtag unimpressive crew of Class II bush leaguers. That's kind of what it's like standing at the takeout, earnestly trying to make somebody understand that this mild mannered little creek really did just kick hell out of you only a couple of miles upstream!

Without question, tiny Johns Creek is a thriller in Virginia, an unmitigated screamer. Pour some water down it, and mile-for-mile its short gorge section is outdone in difficulty by very few streams in the Southeast. Because the watershed is so small, the creek must be run following locally heavy rains. Be advised that it can jump from low to high almost as fast as Superman can leap a tall building. Significant changes in volume can easily be camouflaged by the creek's mild-mannered appearance at the putin and takeout. Always check the gauge, and if at all possible, check with local paddlers who know the stream well.

Also, Johns Creek can harbor log jams. Although it's a tiny creek, it's a capital idea, on your first trip, to closely follow someone who knows it well.

Similar To. The canyon section of Johns Creek combines the best elements of two creeks on Tennessee's Cumberland Plateau: the steepness of Piney River and the big rapid proclivity of Daddys Creek Canyon.

Mile(s)	Johns Creek Top-To-Bottom Itinerary
0.0	Put in at the VA 311 bridge five miles north of New Castle.
0.0 to 2.0	Flat water.
2.0 to 2.5	Entry to the gorge.
2.5 to 5.0	Gorge with continuous Class III-IV rapids.
5.0	Fools Falls, or Exit Ledge (Class III+).
6.0	Take out on the outskirts of New Castle at the Rescue Squad building, or at the Route 615 bridge in town.

Description

For a mile below the putin it's nothing but moving flat water with cows on the banks and faint traffic sounds from VA 311 on river right. Gradually the traffic sounds diminish, then disappear. The pastoral landscape changes to a mixed forest of hemlocks and gigantic sycamores. The current slackens and the little stream looks terminally flat.

Then, just about the time you're convinced you've put in on the wrong drainage ditch, it begins. A most welcome one-foot stream-wide ledge breaks the monotony of flatwater paddling, followed by a fun Class III- rock garden. Suddenly you're on top of a double-drop Class III(IV) that sometimes harbors logs. Scout from the right if there's any question of how to run it. Look around, take a deep breath, cinch down your helmet, because for the next 2.5 miles there's not much opportunity for rest. Downstream of this introductory double-drop are thirteen major rapids/cataracts of Class III-IV(V) consequence, any one of which may be Class VI because of the unfortunate propensity of this small stream to harbor log jams.

A half mile below the introductory double-drop, the stream blows through successive rapids sandwiched between house-sized boulders that conceal excruciatingly blind screaming drops and turns through a canyon of awesome beauty and obstruction. If you can remember to count rapids from the top of the gorge, the sixth one is

As he rounded the bend and looked downstream, Bob Short suddenly realized how Bambi Meets Godzilla got its name. Johns Creek. Don Ellis photo.

unusually consequential. Three hundred yards of twisting, screaming, blind drops end in a row of boulders. Be cautious through here
because it's the single most likely candidate for a log jam. This
rapid, and the junk below it, is especially problematic because there
is no easy way to scout, portage or cheat it.

And the rapids just keep on coming, with each one seemingly
vying with its peers to embody even more turbulence and obstruction. The ninth or tenth major cataract denotes the deepest and
steepest part of this intimate Virginia canyon. Take a moment to
stop and look around. It's a canyon that could have been lifted
directly from Tennessee's Cumberland Plateau, with towering cliffs
alongside and huge boulders in the streambed.

When you're convinced that the canyon has already run for at
least eight or ten miles and the water intensity has to moderate any
minute, it doesn't. It just keeps coming at you.

Even as the gorge walls recede and the water finally moderates,
the little screamer slips in the largest sheer drop of all, Fools Falls
(Class III+). From upstream it looks like a fifteen foot sheer drop.
Although it's only six or seven feet, it's still a consequential descent
because it lands in a rock garden and the washout is swift enough
to produce a long swim in case of mishap. Scout from the left and
run angled right. Have your best brace ready and waiting at the
bottom.

After Fools Falls, mild whitewater of Class II(III) caliber characterizes the next mile. Road access (Route 311) is available on river
right before reaching the Route 615 bridge in town.

Summary

The canyon section of Johns Creek is not quite long enough to
put it into the Watauga Gorge class of difficulty. Nor is the stream
morphology as dangerously complex as that of the Watauga. But
the 2.5 mile canyon contains ample excitement nevertheless, with a
flushing intensity and healthy gradient reminiscent of the Piney River
in Tennessee, and a blind-drop, obstructed character similar to
Daddys Creek Canyon.

Water Levels

Johns Creek is gauged on the VA Route 615 bridge on the back side of New Castle. Zero on the gauge is a minimum run, and about 2.0 feet is a flushing experience.

Johns Creek Gauge Location New Castle
Low: 0.0 Medium: 1.0 High: 2.0

Access

New Castle, the takeout, is about 35 miles north of Roanoke on VA 311. To reach the putin, continue north on 311 for approximately five miles. The road climbs for most of the distance. When it levels out, stay vigilant. The little creek, which looks for all the world like some farmer's irrigation ditch, is all too easy to miss.

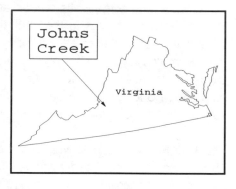

Miles From Johns Creek	
Roanoke, VA 35	Charlottesville, VA 155
Greensboro, NC 120	Bristol, TN 170

Lynn Aycock-Spangler on Johns Creek. Don Ellis photo.

John Van Luik on Coke Island. Johns Creek. Mayo Gravatt photo.

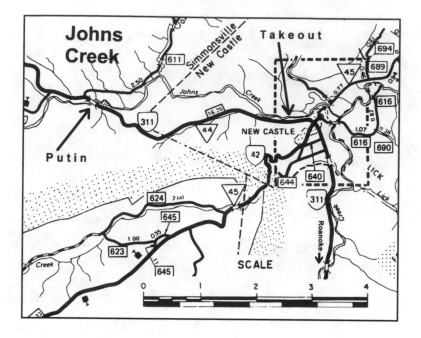

Nearby Alternate Trips

Balcony Falls on the James River is about 1.5 hours northeast, and Goshen Pass on the Maury River is about two hours north. Both streams are described elsewhere in this volume.

Laurel Fork
of the Cheat River
US 33 to the Dry Fork
(West Virginia)

TRIP Profile			
Scale Midpoint = 100			
Overall Difficulty	104	Rapids Difficulty	98
Volume x Gradient	97	Continuous Rapids	111
Average Gradient	104	Entrapments	94
Maximum Gradient	105	Inaccessibility	110
Total Gradient	165	Reputation	83

Actual Stream Data			
Max Rapids	III+	Stream Size	Small
Average Gradient	53	Length (in miles)	14
Maximum Gradient	84	Morphology Types	1&2

Overview

For those with time on their hands and both hands on the steering wheel, West Virginia highways can be highly rewarding. This is nowhere better illustrated than in the northeast sector of the mountain state. Heading west from Seneca Rocks on US 33 the highway parallels Seneca Creek, a small tributary of the Potomac, before winding skyward into the Spruce Knob highlands, crossing the ridge, and descending into yet another northern West Virginia watershed, that of the Cheat River. Continuing west, US 33 crosses four streams in quick succession, all coursing due north to join the

281

Blackwater in forming the Cheat River at Parsons. In order of east-to-west appearance these streams are: Dry Fork, Laurel Fork, Glady Fork, and Shavers Fork.

Many West Virginia paddlers consider Laurel Fork the best run in the Cheat watershed, but this is disputed by fans of Shavers Fork, the Blackwater, the Big Sandy, and even the Cheat Canyon. Nonetheless, Laurel Fork is indisputably outstanding in both scenery and whitewater. At higher flows the bottom nine miles are a non-stop adrenalin rush, at least on a par with Tennessee's Ocoee River.

Similar To. Crab Orchard Creek in Tennessee's Obed system in that it starts out twisting and turning with considerable maneuvering required, then becomes wide open and progressively bigger toward the bottom of the run. Laurel Fork, however, is perhaps twice the size of Crab Orchard. In its bottom miles, Laurel Fork with a good flow looks a lot like the Ocoee.

Mile(s)	Laurel Fork Top-To-Bottom Itinerary
0.0	Put in at the US 33 Bridge.
0.0 to 5.0	Fast water with a few minor ledges.
5.0	Eight-foot waterfall. Portage river left.
5.0 to 13.0	Gradual transformation into an open course with big waves and holes.
14.0	Takeout on the Dry Fork at Jenningston.

Description

The first three miles are mostly flat, but with good current and small waves in a generally unobstructed streambed. Occasional ledges occur until about five miles into the run where a gnarly eight foot drop appears. Eddy out and scout on river left.

This waterfall announces a radical change in tilt of the streambed. Down to this point the river bops along at 28 feet/mile. Downstream of the waterfall, the gradient increases by 139% for the rest of the trip! The last nine miles drop at an average rate of 67 feet/mile. Altogether, Laurel Fork drops 745 feet. Of all the trips reviewed in this book, Laurel Fork is second only to Tennessee's Piney River in total drop.

Below the eight-foot waterfall several ledges appear along with hydraulics that run diagonally across the stream. Toward the bottom of the run the tempo builds steadily as the streambed opens up into a course of constant waves and hydraulics. Some of these holes get downright nasty-tempered at high water, and could be keepers. Generally, the bawdiest ones can be anticipated and skirted, but paddlers unsure of their ability to deal with such hazards should go elsewhere when the bridge gauge reads 1.5 or higher.

A few yards before the takeout the Laurel Fork confluences with the Dry Fork. Takeout is on river left on the Dry Fork at Jenningston.

Laurel Fork Gradient	
Mile	Gradient
1	15
2	20
3	20
4	40
5	45
6	80
7	55
8	70
9	75
10	70
11	70
12	65
13	65
14	55

Summary

Laurel Fork is one of the real jewels of West Virginia whitewater. With the same overall gradient as Tennessee's Ocoee River, Laurel Fork is considerably steeper toward its bottom and with a good flow it's more exciting and more demanding than the Ocoee.

Water Levels

The Parsons gauge, minimum reading of five feet, can be used as a general indication: (412) 644-2890. At higher flows the last several miles of Laurel Fork can be dangerous because of the strong hydraulics.

Laurel Fork Gauge Locations	
Putin Bridge	Cheat River at Parsons
Low: 0.3 Medium: 1.3 High: 1.7	Low: 5.0 Medium: 6.5 High: 8.0

Access

The Cheat headwaters are in northeast West Virginia just over the ridge from Seneca Rocks. The nearest sizeable town is Elkins. The main access routes are US 33 east-to-west and either US 220 or US 219 north-to-south. Put in at the US 33 bridge between Harman and Wymer. Take out on the Dry Fork at Jenningston. From the US 33 putin, the shuttle is run either by driving west to Alpena and turning right on Route 12 through Sully, then right on Route 45; or driving east to Harman, left on WV 32, left on WV 72 to/through Red Creek, and left on Route 35 or Route 45 to Jenningston.

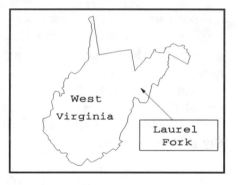

Miles From the Laurel Fork of the Cheat River	
Washington, DC 165	Pittsburgh, PA 205
Roanoke, VA 205	Columbus, OH 250

Other Information

Camping

Bear Heaven, one of the finest National Forest Service campgrounds in West Virginia, is located about eight miles from the putin, near Alpena.

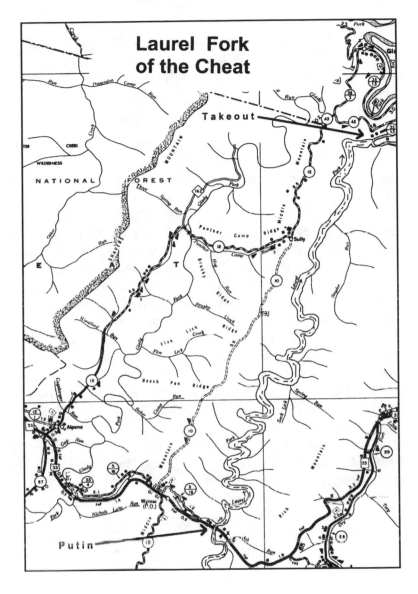

Laurel Fork
of the Cheat

Maps

The Monongahela National Forest map is an invaluable asset for finding such places as Bear Heaven. Available from The US Forest Service, US Department of Agriculture, Elkins, West Virginia.

Nearby Alternate Trips

Not only bears and John Denver, but also whitewater paddlers are almost in heaven while in this part of West Virginia. Laurel Fork of the Cheat is within easy driving distance of a bewildering array of whitewater. Runs on the other Cheat headwater streams (ranging from easy to difficult) are nearby. The Cheat Canyon and its tributary, Big Sandy, are to the northwest. The Potomac watershed is east (Smoke Hole, Seneca Creek, Hopeville Canyon, Moorefield Gorge) and north (the Kitzmiller runs on the North Branch and its tributary, the Big Stony). The Tygart Gorge and Middle Fork of the Tygart are northwest. The Cranberry and Williams to the south can be reached in under three hours, and the melange of streams around the Gauley/New River Gorge/Meadow area is less than half a day's drive to the south.

No wonder John Denver thought it was almost heaven.

Gauge readings on all the aforementioned streams are available from two recorded messages: (703) 260-0305 and (304) 529-5127.

Of the above streams, the following are described elsewhere in this volume: Big Sandy, Cranberry, Cheat Canyon, Hopeville Canyon, Middle Fork of the Tygart, New River Gorge, Seneca Creek, Tygart Gorge, and the Williams River.

Little River Canyon

Chairlift to Canyon Mouth Park
(Alabama)

TRIP Profile			
Scale Midpoint = 100			
Overall Difficulty	88	Rapids Difficulty	87
Volume x Gradient	82	Continuous Rapids	75
Average Gradient	82	Entrapments	106
Maximum Gradient	81	Inaccessibility	128
Total Gradient	78	Reputation	105

Actual Stream Data			
Max Rapids	III(IV)	Stream Size	Small
Average Gradient	29	Length (in miles)	6.5
Maximum Gradient	50	Morphology Type	2

Overview

When Peter Jenkins wrote his fascinating book about walking across America, he developed his own shorthand system for recording observations and impressions of places and people he encountered. When he reached Alabama his entries consisted repeatedly of "TAA," shorthand for "Totally Amazing Alabama." Peter was right. Alabama is full of pleasant surprises, and nothing in the state is more amazing or seemingly out of context than the Little River Canyon. The longest and deepest canyon in eastern America? You've got to be kidding? Located in Alabama? With the canyon running its entire length atop a mountain? Is that even possible?

Yes, it's possible, and it's all part of Alabama's charming penchant for gently disabusing visitors of their preconceptions. Northern Alabama in the vicinity of Fort Payne (home of the singing group "Alabama") exemplifies the many surprises that Peter Jenkins experienced as he walked across the state. Deep in the heart of Dixie it indubitably lies but northern Alabama is rough, mountainous terrain (a bona fide part of Appalachia), with a canyon that's one of the wildest, wooliest, and most inaccessible crevices in eastern America. How can this be?

The key to understanding Little River Canyon is Lookout Mountain, sprawling fifty miles southwest from Chattanooga, Tennessee, into northern Alabama. Not only is the mountain unusually long, it's also flat on top. Little River, the watershed for Lookout Mountain, begins and runs its entire length atop this flat, plateau-like mountain.

Unlike river canyons to the north, such as those in the Obed and Big South Fork of the Cumberland watersheds in Tennessee, which gradually flow into ever-deepening gorges, the Little River Canyon begins suddenly, with a bang, just downstream of the AL 35 bridge where the stream tears over forty-foot DeSoto Falls and begins its rampage. Parts of the canyon can be glimpsed from the myriad convolutions of the Canyon Rim Road which serves as the shuttle run. The upper six miles of this canyon, from AL 35 to the chairlift, were long considered unrunnable because of steep, near-totally obstructed drops liberally sprinkled with entrapments. Those upper miles are being run more frequently nowadays, and paddlers seem to be switching this section's name from "Suicide Run" to the "Avalanche Section."

The standard run (and the one described herein) is the lower part of the canyon, downstream of the Avalanche section, beginning at the old chairlift about midway down the canyon. The canyon walls in the lower section are not nearly so imposing as in the upper miles, but at least the paddler has a few moments between rapids to look at the surroundings and appreciate the context in which nature stages this deep south TAA whitewater drama.

Similar To. The upper canyon is unique. No one should visit this area without driving the rim road along the upper canyon and taking time to stop at some of the overlooks. The lower canyon, both in morphological configuration and whitewater, resembles the Obed/Emory watershed in Tennessee.

Mile(s)	Little River Canyon Top-To-Bottom Itinerary
0.0	Put in at the chairlift on the river right rim.
0.2	Circle Back (Class III-).
0.6	Eddy Hop (Class III+). Watch for undercuts.
1.0	Blue Hole Memorial (Class III+). Undercuts.
1.5	Bottleneck (Class IV).
3.2	Grabber (Class III).
5.3	Johnnies Creek Rapid (Class III).
6.4	Takeout at Canyon Mouth Park.

Description

This trip kicks off with an invigorating quarter-mile hike to the river, beginning at the old chairlift. Two trails are available. The obvious one (under the chairlift) is more difficult. Upstream about 100 yards is a better alternate.

Technical rapids begin forthwith downstream of the putin. Circle Back (Class III-) is the first of consequence, requiring a semi-circular 180-degree maneuver on the left side of the stream, around a large rock.

Eddy Hop (Class III+) is next on the agenda and merits a cautious approach because of its undercuts and the hole that forms at its second drop at higher flows. The rapid is a congested spot with a fast approach and a swift wash-out. Rocks in this one are undercut, especially river left, and that's where the current pushes you. For safety, consider positioning at least one throw rope in the vicinity of the worst undercut.

Blue Hole Memorial (Class III+) requires intricate maneuvering among large boulders which completely obstruct downstream vision. Turn left. Turn right. Left again. Then it erupts on you. It's a technical rapid, reminiscent of the Obed system.

Next up is the piece de resistance of the lower canyon, Bottleneck (Class IV), a rapid that resembles Bull Sluice on the Chattooga,

Gwen Drescher lines up for the last drop in Bottleneck. Little River Canyon in Alabama. Don Ellis photo.

except the approach on Bottleneck is obstructed. It requires successive 90-degree turns in turbulence before reaching the tough part, the diagonal ledge. Some paddlers use two eddies in order to ease the sharp turns. Others use only one of the eddies. And a few slip through without bothering with an eddy, although an eddy-less run requires finesse. The bottom diagonal ledge is reminiscent of the main drop in Bull Sluice. The trick on Bottleneck is to catch the tongue of water on far river right of the drop and ride it back diagonally to river left. Catch the tongue just so and the ride is velvet-soft, a regular boulevard, but the margin for error is thin.

A Class III appears shortly after Bottleneck, but it seems anticlimactic. Shortly after the unnamed Class III, stream morphology becomes less obstructed. By the time Grabber (Class III) and Johnnies Creek (Class III) appear, stream character has changed fundamentally from the initial two miles. Grabber and Johnnies are big, bouncy, jumbled-up rapids on the order of those found on West Virginia's Cheat Canyon.

Although minor rapids and fast water continue to the takeout at Canyon Mouth Park, the best action is unquestionably in the first one and a half miles, ending with Bottleneck.

Summary

This run has beautiful, crystal-clear water in a fantastic setting. Although the trip is more than six miles, it always slips by too quickly. The only real drawbacks are the putin, which really isn't all that bad because it's a downhill haul, and water availability. In total, expect nine rapids of Class III or higher difficulty, most of them bunched into the first mile and a half, with one of these a solid Class IV. Two other rapids, Eddy Hop and Blue Hole Memorial, are Class III+ or even low IVs at high water.

Water Levels

The Canyon Mouth Park gauge is on river right at the downstream edge of the campground. Fun minimum is 3.7 (270 cfs). Maximum prudent level (and Bottleneck isn't so prudent at this level) is 5.5 (1,850 cfs).

If Canyon Mouth Park gauge readings are not available, Little River Canyon is usually runnable if the Emory at Oakdale is over 2,000 cfs and Town Creek is over 300 cfs. Call TVA at (800) 238-2264 and press code "3" after the recorded message.

Little River Canyon Gauge Location Canyon Mouth Park
Low: 3.7 Medium: 4.5 High: 5.4

Canyon Mouth Park Gauge Conversion			
Feet	Cfs	Feet	Cfs
3.5	200	4.8	820
3.6	235	4.9	920
3.7	270	5.0	1025
3.8	300	5.2	1315
3.9	330	5.4	1670
4.0	360	5.6	2030
4.1	400	5.8	2370
4.2	450	6.0	2750
4.3	500	7.0	5200
4.4	550	8.0	7500
4.5	610	10.0	14400
4.6	670	12.0	22000
4.7	745	14.0	37000

An alternate gauge is on an east-side abutment at the AL 35 bridge crossing, where bare-bones is somewhere between 0.0 and 0.5, and 1.5 is getting high.

Access

Located atop Lookout Mountain in northeast Alabama, Little River Canyon is most easily reached from the north, south, and west via

I-59. Take the AL 35 (Ft. Payne) exit. Continue on AL 35 to AL 273 at Blanche. Turn south (right, coming from Ft. Payne) and drive about eight miles to the Little River. A right turn leads to Canyon Mouth Park. If the park isn't open, take out at AL 273. (Parking is limited at the AL 273 takeout.)

To reach the Little River from the east, take GA 20 into Alabama to AL Route 35. Turn left on AL 273 at Blanche and continue to the takeout.

To reach the putin from the takeout, turn right when leaving the park and drive up the side of the mountain to Canyon Rim Road, a crooked, roller-coaster of a road which, with a little luck, leads to the chairlift. The putin is at the base of the old chairlift.

Don't make the mistake of putting in at AL 35 (at the base of DeSoto Falls). A putin at AL 35 leads into the Avalanche section, not the run described above.

Miles From Little River Canyon in Alabama	
Chattanooga, TN 70	Birmingham, AL 100
Huntsville, AL 85	Atlanta, GA 105

Other Information

Camping

The most convenient location is Canyon Mouth Park at the takeout. It has hot showers. Also, DeSoto State Park is located nearby.

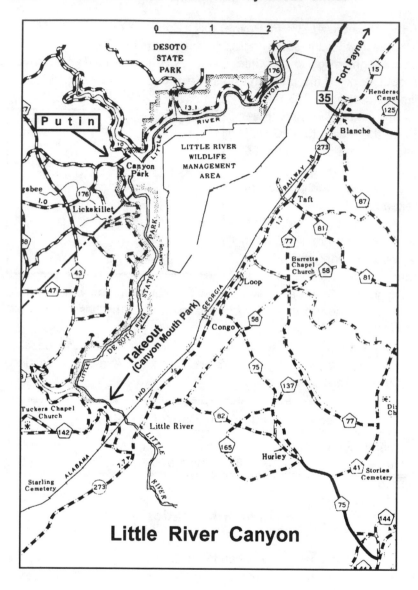

Little River Canyon

Little River in the Smokies

Upper Section:
Elkmont to the "Sinks"
(Tennessee)

TRIP Profile			
Scale Midpoint = 100			
Overall Difficulty	95	Rapids Difficulty	89
Volume x Gradient	83	Continuous Rapids	111
Average Gradient	116	Entrapments	72
Maximum Gradient	110	Inaccessibility	65
Total Gradient	135	Reputation	94

Actual Stream Data			
Max Rapids	III(IV)	Stream Size	Micro
Average Gradient	65	Length (in miles)	8.5
Maximum Gradient	90	Morphology Type	4

Overview

Which National Park is the most heavily visited? Yellowstone? Yosemite? Grand Canyon? Mickeymouseville in Orlando? No, America's most heavily visited National Park is the Great Smoky Mountains in Tennessee and North Carolina.

Is that possible? Yes, and most of the explanation can be summed up in three words: population and proximity. Well over half the population of the United States live less than a day's drive from the Smokies. And what the millions of annual visitors come to see is a natural wonderland, an upland rain forest with a profusion of flora and fauna. In the United States, only a few localities in the

295

Pacific Northwest receive more rainfall than the Great Smokies. Some form of precipitation falls somewhere in the Smokies every day of the year. Coupled with the dramatic contrasts in elevation between its peaks and surrounding valleys (Clingmans Dome is the second highest peak in eastern America), all this precipitation produces a spate of exciting whitewater.

The best run in the Smokies is the Little River which flows from the north slopes of Clingmans Dome through Elkmont Campground and alongside TN 73 until it exits the park near Townsend. In the 14.5 miles from Elkmont to Townsend it drops a total of one thousand feet, reaching a maximum rush of 130 ft/mi in the area around the Sinks. The Little River is a "busy" stream, requiring constant attention because of its scrambled streambed and steep gradient.

Mile(s)	Upper Little River Top-To-Bottom Itinerary
0.0	Put in at Elkmont Campground in the Smokies.
0.0 to 1.5	Busy Class II water.
1.5	Juncture of Elkmont Road and TN 73. Alternate putin.
1.5 to 3.0	Busier Class II water.
3.0 to 4.0	Class II+ technical water in a small trout stream.
3.5	Little Sycamore Rapid (Class II+/III).
4.0 to 6.0	85 ft/mi gradient.
4.0	TN 73 bridge.
4.2	Bridge Rapid (Class III+).
4.4	Scarface (Class III+), aka Slingshot.
4.5 to 5.9	One-and-one-half miles of non-stop Class II(III).
5.9 to 6.7	Metcalf Bottoms doldrums.
6.5	Metcalf Bottoms picnic and day use area.
6.7 to 8.2	Gradually increasing intensity, becoming Class III about a half mile above the Sinks.
8.2 to 8.5	Class III+ with successive drops, culminating in the . . .
8.5	. . . Sinks (Class IV+), a ten foot falls with vertical pinning possibilities.

This description focuses on the upper 8.5 miles from Elkmont Campground to the Sinks. The lower six miles are covered in the next description. Both sections of the Little River fall continuously through scrambled streambeds. The lower run is even more technical than the upper section. TN 73 parallels both runs closely. Both runs are entirely within the Great Smoky Mountains National Park and the scenery is outstanding.

Similar To. Similar to the Cranberry in West Virginia, except smaller.

Description

With a putin at Elkmont, the Little River offers fast Class II water for over a mile. As if to show off for the tourists, it picks up speed where Elkmont Road intersects with TN 73, the main road through the southwest sector of the park. Then it cinches its belt, takes a deep breath, and gets semi-serious, tilting at a steeper angle, where the difficulty shifts toward Class III.

Four miles below Elkmont, TN 73 and the Little switch sides. The stream swerves out of sight of the road and like a mischievous child away from parental supervision, quickly throws two fits. The first is a standard Class III+ technical fit (Bridge Rapid), but the second fit is something special where the stream blasts through a ten-foot-wide sluice with a jagged left-side ridge of rock. This is Class III+ Scarface. (A lot of paddlers are calling this rapid Slingshot, which is a good name too, but Scarface seems so apt because that's what you'll be if you sideswipe its jagged left side.) Coming out of these two Class IIIs the velocity continues even faster than upstream of the bridge for about a mile-and-a-half of non-stop Class II-III rapids.

Approaching Metcalf Bottoms, the gradient eases and a rather blah section ensues for half a mile. Once past this brief intermission, however, the stream revives with a vengeance, building intensity steadily for two miles. Slightly over eight miles downstream of Elkmont the stream bends sharply left into a strong Class III with an undercut ledge on river right. Below this ledge commences a quarter mile of continuous Class III drops that culminate in the Sinks, a ten foot plummet. The quarter mile of Class III immediately above the Sinks is premier Appalachian steep creek whitewater. Visible from the parallel TN 73 roadway, this water provides an excellent setting for photographers, especially the last two drops above the Sinks, waterfalls of about five feet, with unpredictable crosscurrents.

Use caution in running the biggest Sinks drop; vertical pins have occurred here.

Summary

For a story about treachery among jewelry thieves on and around the Little River in the Smokies, read The Great Swami Akalananda, in *River Stories: Tales From Bo Rockerville,* by Monte Smith, available from Pahsimeroi Press.

Water Levels

The stream rises and falls rapidly, but also frequently. Because of the unusually high annual precipitation in the Smokies, it will briefly pump up unexpectedly year-around. Call TVA at (800) 238-2264 and press "3" after the recorded message begins.

Little River Gauge Location TVA Little River at Townsend
Low: 275 cfs Medium: 500 cfs High: 800 cfs

Access

Little River flows off the west side of the Smokies in the vicinity of Townsend. From the west, US 321 leads to Townsend. From the east the access route is US 441 which runs north-south from Gatlinburg, Tennessee to Cherokee, North Carolina. It's the only (vehicular) tra-

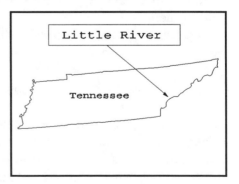

verse of the Smokies. Two miles south of Gatlinburg, Route 73 intersects with US 441, which leads to the Little River.

Put in at Elkmont Campground or any pullover alongside the road. Take out at the Sinks, either before or after running the big drop. The shuttle is along TN 73 (the Little River Road) and the Elkmont Campground access road, a spur off TN 73.

Miles From Elkmont Campground in the Smokies	
Knoxville, TN 45	Charlotte, NC 175
Chattanooga, TN 135	Atlanta, GA 250

Other Information

Area Attractions

Cades Cove is worth a visit. Ditto Clingmans Dome, which is accessible by highway. But the greatest treat in the Smokies, time permitting, is a hike to Mt LeConte (via Alum Cave Bluff Trail from US 441 on the Gatlinburg side, or the Appalachian and Boulevard Trails from Newfound Gap on US 441). See details under Hiking.

Camping

Elkmont at the putin is the tactical choice.

Hiking

One of the most unforgettable walks in the Smokies is Alum Cave trail, in spots as steep and scenic as Kaibab on the south wall of the Grand Canyon. The trailhead is on US 441 between Gatlinburg and Newfound Gap, about six miles south of Gatlinburg. The trail leads up to Alum Cave Bluff and from thence to the summit of Mt LeConte, second highest peak in the Smokies. From the bluff upward this trail is a high country classic, in places consisting of only a narrow pathway chiseled from solid mountainside with a steel hand cable bolted into the cliff for safety. Remarkably, a rustic lodge perches near the summit of Mt LeConte. The lodge is only four miles from the trailhead, though it may seem farther because of the steep climb.

Mt LeConte Lodge is accessible only via foot or helicopter. Although lacking electricity, in-room running water, central heat, etc.,

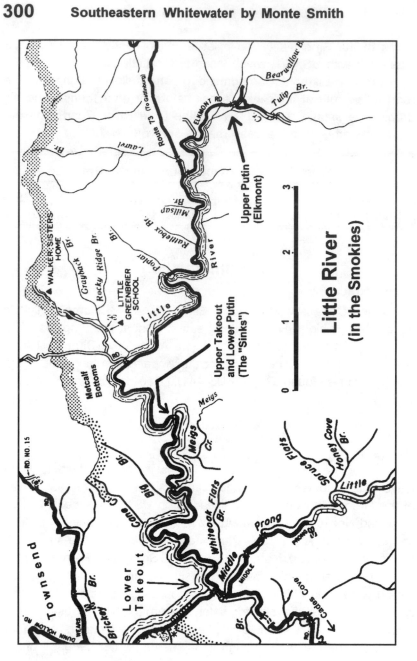

Little River
(in the Smokies)

the authentically rustic cabins provide adequate shelter, clean beds, and an atmosphere, at over 6,000 feet elevation, that is invigorating to say the least. Weather permitting, guests can sit on their cabin porches after dark and look down into the spangle of lights called Gatlinburg.

Dining at Mt LeConte Lodge is family style around long tables in the mess hall. The food is the essence of simplicity -- stuff you might not deign to eat in the lowlands. But on LeConte at this heady elevation after a four or five hour hike to reach the summit, in the thin mountain air and amidst the palpable camaraderie provided by other equally famished guests, ensconced in a dining hall that has steel bars over the windows to repel marauding bears, the simple fare tastes like nectar and ambrosia. For reservations, contact the LeConte Lodge office in Gatlinburg.

Another nice hike is up to the Chimneys, with a trailhead on US 441 about a mile south of the Alum Cave Bluff trailhead. There's no quaint lodge on top of the Chimneys (elevation 4,700 feet), but there's a view that's second to none in the Smokies. The National Park Service classifies this short hike (four mile round trip) as "very strenuous." Actually, its pretty easy walking, but admittedly the last quarter mile isn't suitable for the clumsy.

An excellent guidebook to Smokies trails is *Hiker's Guide to the Smokies* by Dick Muriless and Constance Stallings.

Rafting Suitability (On a 1 to 7 Scale): 0

Too small, too technical.

Recent Flooding

In 1994 the Little River experienced massive flooding. After the flood, the National Park Service closed access to the river. When this book went to press, it was not possible to determine the extent of streambed alteration.

Nearby Alternate Trips

Six runnable streams (see table below) tumble from the highlands of the Great Smoky Mountains National Park. Smokies streams are small, steep, technical, and runnable only after locally heavy rainfall. Moreover, special access problems are associated with several of them. The two streams with the best access (the Little River and the Middle Prong of the Little Pigeon) are described in this volume.

Whitewater Streams of the Great Smoky Mountains	
Stream	**Access or Other Problem**
Abrams Creek	Long shuttle.
Little River	Good access. Good whitewater.
Middle Prong	Good access. Good whitewater.
Oconoluftee	Access restricted by Cherokee Nation.
Raven Fork	Access restricted by Cherokee Nation.
West Prong	Runnable only after local deluge.

Little River in the Smokies

Lower Section:
The "Sinks" to the "Y"
(Tennessee)

TRIP Profile			
Scale Midpoint = 100			
Overall Difficulty	103	Rapids Difficulty	90
Volume x Gradient	89	Continuous Rapids	111
Average Gradient	124	Entrapments	117
Maximum Gradient	131	Inaccessibility	65
Total Gradient	118	Reputation	94

Actual Stream Data			
Max Rapids	III(IV)	Stream Size	Micro
Average Gradient	74	Length (in miles)	6
Maximum Gradient	120	Morphology Type	4

Overview

With a putin below the Sinks, this run contains some of the steepest gradient in the Great Smoky Mountains, and for added spice some paddlers put in two miles upstream at Metcalf Bottoms in order to run the screaming meanies in the quarter mile above the Sinks. An alternate putin at Metcalf Bottoms yields an eight mile adrenalin-pumping trip, with the pace significantly quickening in the quarter mile approaching the Sinks and continuing unabated for some distance downstream of the big drop.

The first mile below the Sinks exemplifies scrambled streambed morphology. Peering downstream, it looks like somebody stirred up

303

the streambed with a giant egg beater. Rocks everywhere. No clear path. In many instances, no discernible path. Things ease off considerably after a few miles and the parallel road (TN 73) permits takeout short of the usual "Y" to avoid some of the flatter water toward the bottom of the run.

Similar To. This section of the Little River is a miniature version of West Virginia's Cranberry River.

Mile(s)	Lower Little River Top-To-Bottom Itinerary
0.0	Put in at the Sinks, or go two miles upstream to the Metcalf Bottoms picnic area.
0.2 to 1.0	The steepest, most jumbled section.
0.6	Silver Diner (Class III+).
0.9	Unnamed Class III+.
1.6	Meigs Creek (river left). Rock wall on river right.
2.3	TN 73 Bridge.
3.2	The Tunnel (Class III).
3.4	The Elbow (Class IV+).
3.5 to 6.0	Easy Class II water.
6.0	Take out at the "Y" near the park boundary upstream of Townsend.

Description

Before running the big drop at the Sinks, remember that it has produced vertical pins. It's a tricky drop, especially on river left, because the landing is in a pigpen of rocks. More water makes for a smoother run, up to a point. At higher water levels an easier slot opens on river right over the highest point of the drop.

The most intense water begins within half a mile below the Sinks. The action here is steep and technical through a scrambled streambed with crystal clear water. The best rapid in this steep section is known as the Silver Diner (Class III+), a long, technical rapid with big drops and fast-moving water. About 500 yards downstream of the Diner is an equally difficult rapid. Somewhat shorter, but more intense because it's more obstructed. Scout from river right. Below this dynamic duo things moderate somewhat, but not at the expense of good Class II and III technical rock jumbles.

At mile 2.3 the stream crosses under TN 73 and enters the last section of difficult water. A short distance below the bridge two rapids occur in succession. The first is the Tunnel (Class III), where the streambed tilts to river right, pouring its current into the wall. After a short pool, an undercut bottleneck called the Elbow (Class IV+) appears. At low to medium water the Elbow is an entrapment hotel. At low water the entrapment potential can be appreciated only by scouting from river right. Run the Elbow only after careful scouting and with strong rescue support.

Below the Elbow the Little River switches to Class II, but its gradient never abates. The usual takeout is at the Y near the park boundary where TN 73 intersects with the road to Cades Cove.

Access

Little River flows off the west side of the Smokies in the vicinity of Townsend. From the west, US 321 leads to Townsend. From the east the access route is US 441 which runs north-south from Gatlinburg, Tennessee to Cherokee, North Carolina. It's the only (vehicular) tra-

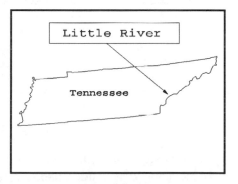

verse of the Smokies. Two miles south of Gatlinburg, Route 73 intersects with US 441, which leads to the Little River.

Put in at the Sinks alongside TN 73 in the Great Smoky Mountains National Park, or two miles upstream at Metcalf Bottoms. Parking space is limited at the Sinks putin. Shuttle all cars, if possible, to the takeout at the "Y", just inside the park boundary near Townsend.

For a local map, and information on Water Levels, Camping, Hiking and Nearby Alternate Trips, refer to the Upper Little River (Elkmont to the Sinks) description.

Upper Meadow River

Rainelle to Russelville
(West Virginia)

TRIP Profile			
Scale Midpoint = 100			
Overall Difficulty	102	Rapids Difficulty	107
Volume x Gradient	111	Continuous Rapids	135
Average Gradient	81	Entrapments	72
Maximum Gradient	103	Inaccessibility	119
Total Gradient	114	Reputation	105

Actual Stream Data			
Max Rapids	III(IV)	Stream Size	Medium
Average Gradient	28	Length (in miles)	15
Maximum Gradient	80	Morphology Type	2

Overview

For most paddlers, the mention of West Virginia instantly evokes two indelible whitewater images: the Gauley River and the New River Gorge. These two big brawlers are quintessentially West Virginia whitewater, with large volume and rapids galore. Admittedly, no other streams quite compare in size and notoriety.

Nonetheless, the Mountain State contains many other outstanding paddling opportunities. One of its eminently noteworthy yet relatively neglected streams is the Meadow River, a tributary of the Gauley. The Meadow's very location, sandwiched as it is between the New and the Gauley, contributes to its relative neglect. With the thundering spectacle of Summersville Dam to the north and the

306

awesome chasm of the New River Gorge on the south, few paddlers even notice the stream they cross as they barrel along US 19 between Question Mark and Summersville. That stream, which looks so inconsequential from US 19, contains two premier whitewater runs upstream of the bridge.

The uppermost run, subject of this description, contains "The Rapids," a four-mile stretch of uninterrupted Class III whitewater, basically a single rapid four miles long. The middle Meadow, which ends at the US 19 bridge, has its own description following this one. It's a Class II-III run strikingly similar to the Obed River and its tributaries in Tennessee.

The thing *not* to do with the Meadow River is get confused and put in at the wrong place. Because there's a third run on the Meadow, *beginning* at the US 19 bridge, that's one of the most dangerous in the East. It's a place that's best left to the likes of Bo Rocker and Swami Akalananda. (Those about to run the lower Meadow may need a book, but it's not a whitewater guidebook.)

Mile(s)	Upper Meadow River Itinerary
0.0	Put in at the garbage dump by the railroad tracks in East Rainelle.
0.0 to 8.0	Flat, but with current.
8.0	Alternate putin, if you can find it.
8.1	Railroad trestle, signaling the beginning of "The Rapids."
8.0 to 12.0	Four miles of non-stop Class III(IV) water.
12.0 to 15.0	Three-mile flat water paddle out, but with current.

Description

The flat paddle-in is the price of admission to a unique stretch of water: four miles of continuous Class III. Although the flat paddle-in is a long eight miles, there is moving current most of the way, with a 15 ft/mi average gradient. After eight miles a most welcome sight appears, a railroad trestle. This trestle signals that "The Rapids" are imminent.

And when the action begins, it is constant. To be sure, there are eddies galore, but there's really no demarcation into distinct rapids. They just sort of blend together into a seemingly endless whiteness. The gradient averages 65 ft/mi over these four nonstop miles and one mile drops 80 feet. It's not a good idea to start messing up at the top of The Rapids. Not only is it four miles long and nonstop, it's also progressively tilted. It gets better and better as it churns along. At low and medium water levels, this stretch is almost all Class III, with possibly a few short bursts of Class IV intensity. Moreover, as water rises above 6.0 feet on the Lookout gauge, the whole four mile section changes from Class III to solid Class IV. The upper Meadow at high water has motivated strong paddlers to kiss the ground with gratitude upon arriving at the takeout.

The biggest drop is near the end of The Rapids. It's not nearly so difficult as it first appears, except at higher flows when it forms a river-wide hydraulic.

When The Rapids peter out, flat water fills the last three miles to the takeout. Fortunately, as with the flatwater paddle-in, the flat paddle-out also features a welcome current to assist pooped paddlers.

Summary

Although it's a long trip with most of the miles consisting of flatwater, that's not what you'll remembered about this run. The part you'll remember is the four-mile-long The Rapids.

There are two keys to enjoying the upper Meadow. The first is to take it easy in the first eight flat miles and accept them for what they are, an admission tariff for a one-of-a-kind four-mile-long rapid. The ride is well worth the price of admission. The second key to enjoying the run is to watch the water volume. Because The Rapids are literally non-stop, increases in volume quickly boost this stream's difficulty level toward the stratosphere. Putting on at over 2,000 cfs is recommended only for advanced paddlers. At over 2,000 cfs it becomes one of the toughest runs in this book.

Water Levels

For gauge information, call (304) 529-5127 and listen for the Mount Lookout gauge reading. Five feet on the gauge is low; medium is about 5.8. At levels above 6.0 feet the upper Meadow is a tiger and above 6.5 feet the tiger gets hungry.

Mount Lookout Gauge Conversion			
Feet	Cfs	Feet	Cfs
4.2	320	6.2	1700
4.6	500	6.4	1900
5.0	720	6.6	2120
5.2	840	6.8	2360
5.4	980	7.0	2620
5.6	1140	8.0	4100
5.8	1310	9.0	5900
6.0	1500	10.0	8000

Access

On US 60 heading east, turn left in the middle of downtown Rainelle onto Snake Island Road and drive about four miles to the putin. If you get lost, ask directions to the garbage dump. That's where the putin is located. There's an alternate putin near the top of The Rapids,

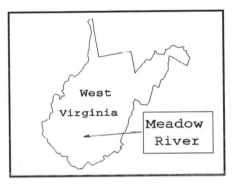

somewhere near Corliss. This writer, however, has not been able to locate it. The takeout is at Russellville, the first highway bridge downstream of Rainelle, accessed via a spur off WV 41.

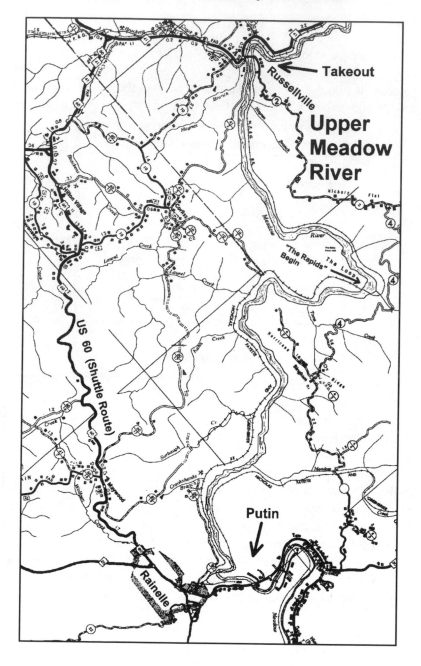

Takeout

Russellville

**Upper
Meadow
River**

"The Rapids"
Begin

US 60 (Shuttle Route)

Putin

Rainelle

Miles From the Upper Meadow River	
Roanoke, VA 134	Greensboro, NC 265
Pittsburgh, PA 210	Washington, DC 280
Cincinnati, OH 255	Cleveland, OH 320

Other Information

Camping

The Garvey Hilton, an abandoned park and ball field located about five miles from the takeout, near Lookout, is used by a lot of paddlers as a makeshift campground. Otherwise, there are Corps of Engineers campgrounds near the Gauley and commercial campgrounds near the New River Gorge.

Nearby Alternate Trips		
Alternate Trip	Rapids Difficulty	TRIP Points
Cranberry	III-IV	103
Upper Gauley	V+	138
Lower Gauley	IV+	109
Middle Meadow	II-III	93
Lower Meadow	VI	na
New River Gorge	IV+	106
Williams	III+	104

Middle Meadow River

Nallen to US 19
(West Virginia)

TRIP Profile			
Scale Midpoint = 100			
Overall Difficulty	93	Rapids Difficulty	91
Volume x Gradient	97	Continuous Rapids	99
Average Gradient	97	Entrapments	94
Maximum Gradient	85	Inaccessibility	110
Total Gradient	80	Reputation	72

Actual Stream Data			
Max Rapids	III	Stream Size	Medium
Average Gradient	45	Length (in miles)	4.5
Maximum Gradient	55	Morphology Types	2&3

Overview

Except for its difficult takeout, the middle Meadow is an ideal intermediate whitewater trip with moderate-difficulty rapids and outstanding scenery. Unless a vehicle can be driven to the river beneath the US 19 bridge, however, the thrill of the river can quickly fade into the agony of the takeout. The struggle up the (deceptively) steep slopes at the US 19 bridge can be an ordeal.

Similar To. Both the river corridor and the onerous takeout are remarkably similar to the rugged terrain of the Obed and its tributaries on the Cumberland Plateau in Tennessee.

312

Description

When WV 41 crosses the Meadow River at Nallen all is flat, as smooth as a mirror. And it remains that way for about a mile downstream as route 41 parallels the Meadow on river right. A pullover is located about two miles outside town where the current first is evident. Put in here.

Soon after the putin, highway 41 veers away from the river. From this point to the US 19 bridge four and a half miles downstream, the Meadow seemingly enters a look-alike contest with the Obed River in Tennessee, with big boulders in the stream, hemlock-clad rocky banks, and sandstone cliffs looming in the distance, as the river flows into an ever-deepening canyon.

Class II and Class III rapids begin soon after the putin and continue to the takeout. Nothing especially difficult, but plenty of opportunity to ferry and eddy and play, with three solid boulder-strewn Class III rapids and numerous others of technical Class II+ difficulty. There are multiple routes through all the rapids, with some possibility of cul-de-sacs at low water because of all the boulders. The many large boulders in the streambed necessitate considerable maneuvering, creating very pleasant paddling conditions for advanced intermediates. In fact, this section would receive every accolade in the book as an exemplary intermediate run were it not for the (ugh!) takeout.

Summary

Intermediate paddlers often end up in this part of West Virginia with wild-eyed advanced paddlers who disappear into the bowels of the New River Gorge or Gauley Canyon and aren't seen again until after dark. If it's possible to get a takeout vehicle to the river at the US 19 bridge, the middle Meadow is a handy-dandy, fast, short and scenic run that's one heck of a lot more fun than waiting around a takeout parking lot or sitting in camp all day.

Water Levels

Phone (304) 529-5127 for Mount Lookout gauge readings. A low run is 4.6 feet (500 cfs). About 5.4 (980 cfs) is medium, and it's getting high above 6.4 (1,900 cfs). Refer to the upper Meadow description for a Mount Lookout gauge conversion table.

Access

The putin is about two miles downstream of Nallen alongside WV 41. The take-out is at US 19. The shuttle is a breeze. From the putin, drive two miles north (away from Nallen) on WV 41 to the Mount Lookout road. Left for another two miles to US 19. Left on US 19 to the bridge. At least two roads lead down to the river, but they may be impassable. By all means, check to see. If so, drive a vehicle to the bottom and avoid the ordeal of emulating a grand canyon pack mule.

Miles From the Middle Meadow River	
Roanoke, VA 134	Greensboro, NC 265
Pittsburgh, PA 210	Washington, DC 280
Cincinnati, OH 255	Cleveland, OH 320

Other Information

For Other Information and Nearby Alternate Trips, refer to the upper Meadow description.

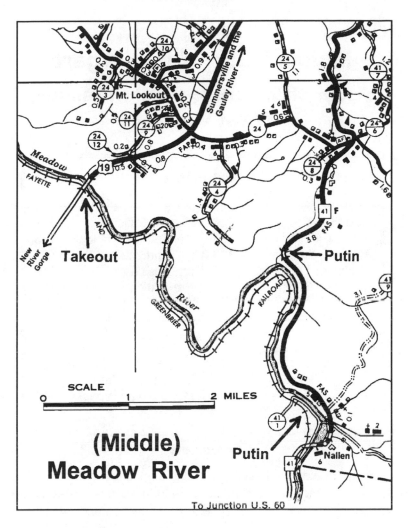

(Middle) Meadow River

Middle Fork of the Tygart

Audra State Park to the Buckhannon
(West Virginia)

TRIP Profile			
Scale Midpoint = 100			
Overall Difficulty	118	Rapids Difficulty	117
Volume x Gradient	133	Continuous Rapids	123
Average Gradient	123	Entrapments	94
Maximum Gradient	117	Inaccessibility	119
Total Gradient	107	Reputation	105

Actual Stream Data			
Max Rapids	IV	Stream Size	Small/Large
Average Gradient	50	Length (in miles)	7.5
Maximum Gradient	100	Morphology Types	4&3

Overview

Several of the trips described in this book begin on small, steep, technical streams only to confluence with larger rivers that contrast dramatically in volume, morphology, scenery, and whitewater. Juxtapositions like this underscore the diversity of rapids that are found on different streams and instill appreciation of the multiplicity of skills required to navigate varied whitewater conditions.

The Middle Fork trip is a prime example. This humdinger of a West Virginia technical run starts small, steep, and rocky. Along its rush to the Tygart it gets steeper, more obstructed and faster. Then it hits the big Tygart and the technicality element eases off a bit. But with all the added volume, the power of its rapids takes a quantum

316

Fritz Drescher at Thread the Needle. Middle Fork of the Tygart.
Don Ellis photo.

Fritz and Gwen Drescher on Middle Fork of the Tygart. Don Ellis photo.

jump (the gradient x volume interaction effect). It's a splendid combination, going from tight, steep, and rocky to big and powerful. Although most Middle Fork rapids fall into the technical Class III or III+ difficulty range, the big water on the Tygart (approaching Class V at higher levels) must be factored into the overall difficulty picture. For that reason, the run should be considered solid Class IV.

Mile(s)	Middle Fork of the Tygart Itinerary
0.0	Putin at Audra State Park.
0.1	Slide Rapid (Class III-) at the putin bridge.
0.1 to 1.5	Continuous rocky Class II-III rapids.
1.5	Island Creek Rapid (Class III).
1.6 to 2.2	Continuous rocky Class III-III+ rapids.
2.3 to 2.8	Continuous steep, congested Class III+ or IV- rapids.
2.4	Long, congested approach with sizeable drop at bottom (Class III+ or IV-).
2.5	Thread the Needle (Class IV).
2.6	Rock Dodge (Class III+).
2.8	Confluence with the Tygart.
4.6	S Turn (Class IV+).
4.9	Shoulder Snapper (Class IV).
5.0 to 6.4	Class III to III+ rapids.
6.0	Hook (Class III+).
6.6	Buckhannon confluence. Possible takeout.
7.7	Alternate takeouts, river left and right.
13.0	Philippi.

Description

With a putin at Audra State Park, action begins almost immediately with an easy Class III under the bridge. If in doubt, scout from the bridge or from either bank. Run it at low water along the river right bank, down a zig zag route, or with more water down the center.

Below the putin rapid the pace eases off somewhat into rocky Class II-III rapids, but the intensity builds steadily, including one S-turn with double drops at about mile 1. Island Creek (Class III) is the first rapid that everybody is sure to remember, named for the small island by which this rapid can be recognized. A long, sloping approach (a flume/slide) over solid bedrock ends in a large curler/hole which is much less consequential than it looks initially. Scout from the smooth rock surface along river right.

Below Island Creek Rapid, the pace quickens. The drops are bigger, the congestion worse, and the gradient semi-serious. At approximately two and a half miles a long approach leads to a sizeable drop over a ragged boulder ledge (Class III+ or IV-). This formidable rapid is hard to eddy scout.

Probably the most impressive rapid on the run is Thread the Needle (Class IV). Scout from river left. First inspection suggests it is unrunnable. Then, a route on river left suggests itself. But the best course is a bob-and-weave route right of center. Thread the Needle is the most obstructed and possibly the most difficult rapid on the Middle Fork, but the most surprising one is just downstream. Rock Dodge (Class III+) is a spot on river left where the flow rolls into a large boulder and bounces off, straight into a pinning rock.

Below the Tygart Confluence

If there's enough water to run the Middle Fork, there'll be a ton of it in the main Tygart, which makes for an equally exciting (but very different) run from the Middle Fork and Tygart confluence to the takeout. Details on this section of the river can be found in the Tygart Gorge description.

Summary

The first half of the trip on the Middle Fork is highly technical with much twisting and turning required in order to negotiate many irregular ledges through cluttered chutes. It constitutes some of the very best technical water in West Virginia. Perhaps not as good as the Cranberry, but getting close. The second half of the run is on the much larger Tygart River through a gorge renowned for its powerful rapids.

Water Levels

Although correlation between the Belington gauge and Middle Fork water is far from perfect, the gauge at Belington on the Tygart provides a useful reference point.

Middle Fork Gauge Location Tygart at Belington
Low: 4.5 Medium: 5.5 High: 6.5

Access

The putin is at Audra State Park, about eight miles from Belington on WV 11. Belington is in north-central West Virginia, about 55 miles south of Morgantown. Four takeouts are possible. The first is at the mouth of the Buckhannon, reducing the total trip to six and a half miles. From Audra State Park cross the Middle Fork and continue about half a mile to Carrollton Road. Turn right onto Carrollton Road and continue to the Buckhannon. At the Buckhannon crossing, take the small road downstream as long as it parallels the river. This takeout entails a boat carry from near the mouth of the Buckhannon. Takeouts two and three are on 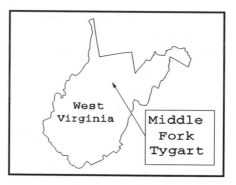 opposite sides of the river about one mile downstream of the Buckhannon. To reach the river left alternate takeout from Audra State Park, cross the Middle Fork and continue on WV 11 across the Buckhannon to US 119. Turn right and head toward Philippi. Take the last right turn before intersection with WV 57. A small black metal sign with white "water gauge" letters identifies the inconspicuous turn. This road looks like a private drive as it winds through farms to a reclaimed strip mine bench overlooking the Tygart. (Hint: park a shuttle vehicle, preferably a high-profile and bright-colored one, so it will be clearly visible from the river.)

Getting to the third takeout, on river right, is a long shuttle. Take WV 11 to Belington, and then US 250 north toward Philippi to the WV 250/10 intersection. Turn left and continue to juncture with WV 30. Bear right and continue through Mount Liberty to the fork with WV 30/6. Bear left and continue to where the road closely parallels the railroad tracks.

The fourth takeout is in Philippi. From Belington take US 250. This takeout entails about four additional miles of flatwater paddling.

Miles From the Middle Fork of the Tygart	
Morgantown, WV 50	Pittsburgh, PA 135
Columbus, OH 240	Washington, DC 275

Other Information

Camping

The campground at Audra State Park is one of the best state park campgrounds in the Southeast, with many sites located alongside the Middle Fork, yielding convenient river access from the park.

Miscellaneous

The Middle Fork seems longer than it is, a phenomenon common to high intensity runs with densely congested streambeds (consider also Wilson Creek Gorge, Island Creek, the upper Tellico, and Johns Creek). The distance from Audra State Park to the Tygart Confluence is described as six miles in one guidebook. Topographic maps, however, peg the distance at slightly under three miles. Of course, the author of the other book has a point. Counting all the twists, turns, and ferries back and forth across the stream searching for exit chutes from all the myriad intricate rock gardens, the distance from Audra to the Tygart is at least six miles. Probably more like twelve!

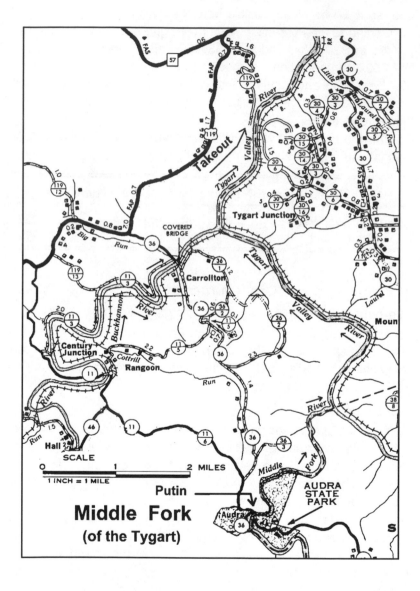

Middle Fork
(of the Tygart)

Nearby Alternate Trips

The Tygart Gorge can be run with a putin at Belington even if the Middle Fork is low. Cheat River headwater tributaries are nearby: Shavers Fork, Laurel Fork, and the Blackwater. Of these alternates, the Tygart Gorge and Laurel Fork of the Cheat are described elsewhere in this volume.

Middle Prong of the Little Pigeon

Great Smoky Mountains National Park
(Tennessee)

TRIP Profile			
Scale Midpoint = 100			
Overall Difficulty	99	Rapids Difficulty	85
Volume x Gradient	80	Continuous Rapids	111
Average Gradient	134	Entrapments	106
Maximum Gradient	131	Inaccessibility	74
Total Gradient	102	Reputation	72

Actual Stream Data			
Max Rapids	III	Stream Size	Micro
Average Gradient	85	Length (in miles)	4
Maximum Gradient	120	Morphology Types	3&4

Overview

The Middle Prong of the Little Pigeon tumbles out of the northeast sector of the Great Smoky Mountains National Park approximately six miles east of Gatlinburg. This sector of the park is known as the Greenbrier District and forms the watershed for the north slopes of the loftiest peaks in the main Smoky spine, including Mt. LeConte, Mt. Guyot, Mt. Kephart, Mt. Sequoyah, and Mt. Chapman. Although a small stream, the run is exciting because of its healthy gradient, rocky streambed, and magnificent Smokies scenery.

Similar To. One of the smallest streams in this volume, the Middle Prong is reminiscent of the Citico.

324

Mile(s)	Middle Prong of the Little Pigeon Itinerary
0.0	Put in at the bridge two road miles upstream of the ranger station.
0.3	Picnic area.
0.2 to 1.5	Fast water. Tight, technical, rocky.
1.2	Elbow Turn (Class III).
3.0	Ranger Rapid (Class III+).
3.3	TN 73.
3.7	Takeout on loop road off TN 73.

Description

Runnable only after locally heavy rains (which occur frequently in the Smokies), this tiny, technical little jewel is lightning fast and as rugged as the bears that wade in its shoals. The putin is at the bridge two road miles upstream of the Greenbrier Ranger Station, alongside the road that continues up to Ramsey Cascade.

At the putin the stream is frisky, and it soon becomes fast and technical. Several Class III rapids occur in the miles to the TN 73 bridge, but even the sections without major rapids are technically challenging because of the rocky streambed.

The biggest rapid is in the vicinity of the ranger station (Ranger Rapid, Class III+) and consists of a series of offset multi-channel ledges which can be run zig-zag fashion. Scout from river left.

Shortly downstream of Ranger Rapid the stream passes under TN 73 and exits the park. The section downstream of the TN 73 bridge is milder than the upstream stretch. Take out half a mile below the bridge where a side road provides easy access.

Summary

Although a road parallels the run, it's usually offset about fifty yards and hence rarely visible from the river through the dense Smokies vegetation. The perspective from the stream is of an isolated mountain rain forest. This little stream is rarely paddled, but it is a real treat when enough water is available.

Water Levels

The TVA gauge on the Little Pigeon at Sevierville provides an approximate indication of stream conditions. Call (800) 238-2264 and press code "3" after the recorded message. A reading of 1,000 cfs is usually needed for a zero level run. Sixteen hundred puts some spirit in the little stream, and when the gauge reads 2,500 cfs its likely to be running high.

Access

The access road is US 321/TN 73 between Cosby and Gatlinburg on the north side of the Great Smoky Mountains National Park. To reach the putin, look for signs to the Greenbrier District Ranger Station. After turning off TN 73/US 321, the ranger station is on the right and the putin is found by continuing upstream to the bridge crossing. The takeout is half a mile outside the park on a loop road.

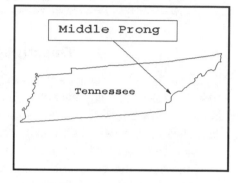

Miles From the Middle Prong of the Little Pigeon	
Gatlinburg, TN 10	Bristol, TN 115
Knoxville, TN 50	Atlanta, GA 170

Other Information

Camping

Cosby Campground, in the park, is 10 miles east.

Hiking

A trail begins a short distance above the putin, winds up to Trillum Gap, and continues to the top of Mt. LeConte. *Hiker's Guide*

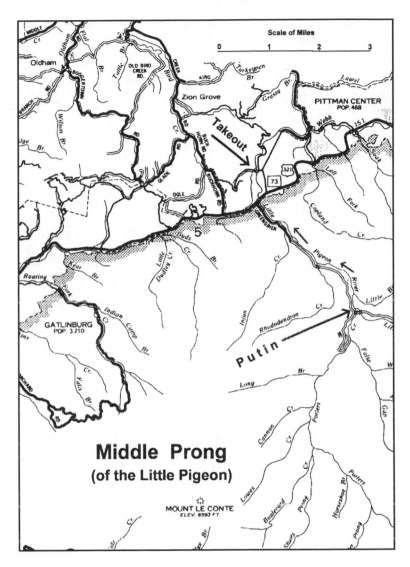

Middle Prong
(of the Little Pigeon)

to the Smokies (a Sierra Club Totebook) by Dick Muriless and Constance Stallings) is a helpful reference work.

Nearby Alternate Trips

Little River in the Smokies (described elsewhere in this volume) is the nearest alternate run.

Nantahala River

Powerhouse to Wesser
(North Carolina)

TRIP Profile			
Scale Midpoint = 100			
Overall Difficulty	77	Rapids Difficulty	72
Volume x Gradient	72	Continuous Rapids	87
Average Gradient	90	Entrapments	60
Maximum Gradient	81	Inaccessibility	65
Total Gradient	96	Reputation	72

Actual Stream Data			
Max Rapids	II(III)	Stream Size	Small
Average Gradient	38	Length (in miles)	8
Maximum Gradient	49	Morphology Type	1

Overview

Nantahala is a Cherokee word meaning "Land of the Noonday Sun," a reference to the deep, verdant gorge through which the river flows. Although the name may reflect a small amount of Cherokee exaggeration, the stream is definitely ensconced in a deep gorge, and the valley floor *is* so narrow in places that the river, US 19, and the railroad have to vie aggressively for scant available space.

The Nantahala is immensely popular, and its location, twenty-five miles south of the Great Smoky Mountains National Park -- the most visited national park in the country -- is in no small part responsible. Surrounding terrain -- some of the most rugged in the Southeast --

is nothing short of majestic. In fact, the Appalachian Trail crosses the river at Wesser, which is the takeout.

Wesser is also site of the Nantahala Outdoor Center (NOC), renowned for its whitewater and other outdoor instructional programs, as well as for its outfitter shops and restaurants.

And on top of everything else, there's the river itself, unquestionably one of the most attractive in the Southeast, sparkling and glistening with an enthralling magic charm as it winds its way through this historical stronghold of the venerable Cherokee. On or off the river, it's a treat just to spend time in the vicinity.

And more and more people are electing to spend at least some of their time on the river, which is just about perfect for novice and intermediate paddlers alike. It has eight miles of Class II water consisting mostly of standing waves and easy river bends, but there's also an exciting Class II+ rapid (Pattons Run) located 200 yards below the putin, and one challenging Class III rapid (Nantahala Falls) near the takeout. Due to its gradient, the trip is fairly swift. Two runs in a day are feasible and, thanks to a parallel road and numerous access points, partial runs of any length are possible. Novice paddlers, who may be intimidated by Pattons Run and the fast current in the first two miles, can put in at Ferabee Park, two and a half miles downstream of the standard access.

Take all the positive attributes above, and add to them the fact that the river enjoys dam released water all summer long, and you have an explanation for why the Nantahala can be so crowded during summer months. On late summer weekends, the downriver procession approximates a flotilla, with rafters numbering in the thousands and private boaters in the hundreds.

Description

US 19E closely parallels the river until near the top of the gorge. Look for the putin about eight miles upstream of Wesser, where US 19E leaves the river and heads up the gorge wall toward Topton. The putin is a short distance downstream of a generating station where the Nantahala's water is returned to its natural streambed after a diversionary trip (through a huge pipe) from a reservoir high

Mile(s)	Nantahala River Top-To-Bottom Itinerary
0.0	Putin: Expect a lot of company on the Nantahala, especially in mid-to-late summer. The congestion is eased somewhat by a large, paved parking lot and a specially constructed putin area.
0.1	Once into the main flow, the water sweeps downstream fast into Pattons Run, a bouncy, splashy Class II+ that terrifies novice paddlers who are running the river for the first time.
0.2 to 4.0	Gradient of 45 ft/mi in this section generates fast current over gravel bars and around minor obstructions, producing near-continuous Class II water conditions.
0.2 to 0.5	Virtually nonstop standing waves. Great for tandem canoes. Wave train mania.
1.0	First bridge, a secondary road.
2.2	Gauge on river left, on the edge of the clearing.
2.5	Second bridge. This is the shuttle road (US 19). Ferabee Park access is on river right just past the bridge, and serves as an alternate putin.
4.0	Rock Quarry, river left. Fast current, stay right.
4.0 to 7.5	The gradient eases considerably until near the end of the run.
7.7	Nantahala Falls (aka Lesser Wesser), a Class III rapid. Its complex currents have humbled many good paddlers.
7.9	Takeout.
8.1	Class VI Worser Wesser, just downstream of the NOC.

in the mountains. Because the water is diverted from near the bottom of the reservoir, it's temperature will be cold (about 45 to 50 degrees), even during July and August. In summer months the cold water often produces a mist, or fog, that hugs the water, sometimes limiting visibility to only a few feet.

The Upper Miles

Once out of the specially-constructed launching pool and into the main current, it's a swift 150 yards to where the river hooks sharply right and pours into an exciting Class II+ rapid called Pattons Run. Enter this rapid just right of center. Although it's not a difficult rapid, the current *is* swift, and the rapid does spring up surprisingly soon after launch. Hence, Pattons Run tends to cause a lot of excitement and plenty of swims. Nervous novices may want to scout Pattons from the convenient highway pullover prior to putting on the river. To heighten enjoyment of Pattons, catch the river left eddy and then play back and forth across the main current, timing your moves so as to dodge river traffic.

A series of standing waves, downstream of Pattons Run, delights novice paddlers (and jaded old experts, too, for that matter). The water is always sparkling and cold, and the river gives good views of the Nantahala Gorge walls. As a general rule, stay to the right of all islands, beware occasional bridge abutments, avoid a few trees that seem to grow in the watercourse (especially 50 yards downstream of Pattons Run), and a pleasant float should ensue until the vicinity of Nantahala Falls (Class III), which paddlers new to the river will want to scout.

Nantahala Falls

Take out on river right well above Nantahala Falls and walk down for a look/see. It's a short, abrupt drop (but not really a waterfall) with complex cross currents and a long, curvy, bouncy approach. Smack in the middle of the rapid is an hydraulic that occasionally grabs and holds small rafts. The hole (generally) spits out people or other objects that thrash around a bit, but it can definitely hold small rafts and inner tubes and other such bulbous objects, like overweight tourists.

Conventional wisdom says that Nantahala Falls must be run on the tongue of water jetting from left-to-right. That's because far left hosts a small drop with some turbulence and threat of foot entrapment. Far right is a rockstand. And then there's the hydraulic right of middle. That leaves (or so the story goes) an entry left of center to avoid the hole, but quickly moving laterally to exit river right. After watching a typical weekend procession of canoes, kayaks, tubes, rafts, people, dogs, and miscellaneous multi-colored unclassifiable objects flush through the rapid, however, the inevitable conclusion is that Nantahala Falls can be run every-which-a-way: down the left side, left-to-right, right-to-left (though it requires some effort), threading through the far right rocks, even straight over the hydraulic. The key is not to get caught in the hydraulic. With a few paddle strokes for added propulsion, virtually any hard boat will easily slice through the hole. Trouble develops occasionally, however, when boats turn in the waves upstream and drop into it sideways.

Admittedly, watching others flush through Nantahala Falls is often as much fun as running it. On pleasant weekend afternoons scores of onlookers gather at the rapid to celebrate the spectacle. These "spectators" quickly become expert judges of skill and style, applauding particularly good (and bad) runs. It's quite a road show, alongside US 19 in the fabled Land of the Noonday Sun.

Amidst all the gaiety, it's easy to forget that moving water -- even water as seemingly benign as the Nantahala -- embodies tremendous force, and hence potential danger. Two fatalities have occurred on the river left side of the rapid, both caused by foot entrapments as swimmers flushed over the drop after coming out of their boats upstream. In an effort to preclude such tragedies, responsible agencies in the Nantahala Gorge plugged the underwater crack that caught the swimmers' feet.

The takeout, courtesy of the NOC and/or other outfitters, is 150 yards below Nantahala Falls. Don't forget to take out. A Class VI cascade lurks around the next downstream bend.

Summary

The Nantahala River is a good Class II+ float, a good beginning raft trip, a good summer float when everything else is dry, and a good place to make new paddling friends or rendezvous with old river buddies. For experienced paddlers, the Nantahala is a helpful reintroduction to whitewater after being away for a while. After a couple of trips down the "Nanny" to work out the kinks, it's only an hour's drive to the Ocoee, or an hour and a half to either the Tellico or Chattooga.

Water Levels

The Nantahala is usually runnable only when the power plant above the putin is generating. Volume does fluctuate, however. When a lot of volume is flowing down the natural streambed (joining that released from the power plant), the Nantahala can be a different experience. Not a few paddlers have put on the river thinking that the volume is invariant, only to discover a pushy Class III where mild mannered Class II+ Pattons Run usually resides. If in doubt, inquire at the NOC.

Access

The Nantahala is in western-most North Carolina south of the Great Smoky Mountains National Park on US 19 between Bryson City and Andrews. Put in at the Nantahala access alongside US 19, about three miles east of Topton, North Carolina. Topton is at the intersection

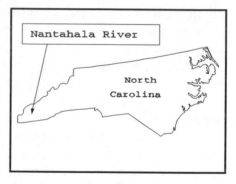

of US 19 and US 129, about midway between Chattanooga, Tennessee and Asheville, North Carolina and almost due south of Knoxville, Tennessee. US 19 parallels the river for the entire run. Take out at the NOC, 150 yards downstream of Nantahala Falls. Takeout is possible on either river right or left, but look for signs, as the rules governing which side is appropriate seem to change from time to time.

Miles From the Nantahala River	
Asheville, NC 86	Chattanooga, TN 128
Knoxville, TN 90	Atlanta, GA 132

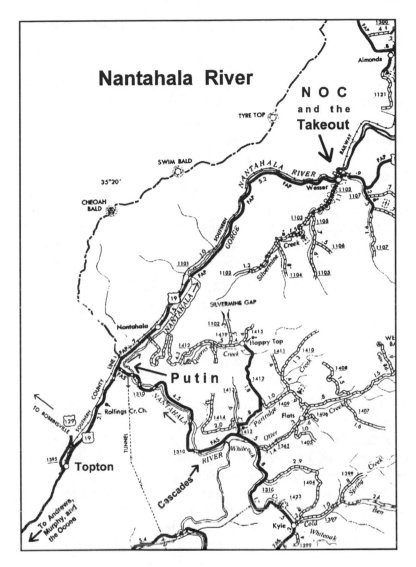

Other Information

Camping

As with most heavily used rivers, nearby camping space is always at a premium. A good bet is usually Lost Mine Campground, but it fills fast.   Call for reservations.   Other campgrounds are available along the river.

Nantahala Outdoor Center (NOC)

At the takeout, the NOC runs a large multi-service operation including restaurants, instructional programs, rental cabins, motel, and outfitter shops.   Their restaurants offer reasonable prices, wholesome food, generally good service and an ambiance consistent with the beautiful Nantahala River, alongside which their entire complex is situated.   The NOC offers a year-round instructional program in a variety of outdoor activities, as well as international adventure travel opportunities.   Their whitewater instruction program is state of the art, and they stand behind all equipment sales.   The same dependable service is available both in the stores at Wesser (the takeout) and in their mail order sales operation (800) 367-3521.

Suitability for Rafting (On a 1 to 7 Scale): 7

Watch the hole at Nantahala Falls.   Otherwise, it's well suited for beginning and novice rafters.   Canoes, kayaks, rafts, guides, and all the associated paraphernalia are available from several outfitters located alongside US 19 through the gorge.

TRIP Profile

The TRIP profile describes a stream of modest difficulty, with scores mostly in the seventies and eighties.   The highest score is Total Gradient (96), reflecting the substantial total drop (over 300 feet) from putin to takeout.   The lowest score, Entrapments (60), deserves comment.   Although relatively free of dangerous entrapments, fatalities due to foot entrapment have occurred on the Nantahala, reflecting the fact that risk is an inevitable companion on all whitewater rivers, however benign they may seem.   The next lowest score, Inaccessibility (65), reflects presence of the parallel road.

Nearby Alternate Trips

The closest alternate trip is the upper Nantahala above the powerhouse, runnable whenever locally heavy rains pump up the water level in the natural streambed.   The road past the powerhouse parallels the stream to the top of the mountain, providing convenient access for scouting. And scouting is what you'll want to do before running the collection of Class V cascades near the top of the run. Below the cascades is a fast-moving stretch of Class III(IV) water that's a real hoot on those rare occasions when there is sufficient water.

The trips listed in the following table are no more than a two-hour drive from the Nantahala, and are described elsewhere in this volume. For reference, the Nantahala has 77 TRIP points, and rapids of Class II(III) difficulty.

Nearby Alternate Trips		
Alternate Trip	Rapids Difficulty	TRIP Points
Chattooga Section III	III(IV)	86
Chattooga Section IV	IV(V)	116
Hiwassee River	II	70
Upper Little River	III(IV)	95
Lower Little River	III(IV)	103
Ocoee River	III-IV	104
Upper Tellico River	III-IV	110
Lower Tellico River	III	96

New River Gorge

Cunard to Fayette Station
(West Virginia)

TRIP Profile			
Scale Midpoint = 100			
Overall Difficulty	106	Rapids Difficulty	117
Volume x Gradient	140	Continuous Rapids	99
Average Gradient	73	Entrapments	117
Maximum Gradient	65	Inaccessibility	110
Total Gradient	68	Reputation	128

Actual Stream Data			
Max Rapids	IV+	Stream Size	Large
Average Gradient	20	Length (in miles)	6.5
Maximum Gradient	27	Morphology Type	2

Overview

West Virginia whitewater is almost on a different scale than elsewhere in Appalachia, and its power and size is nowhere better showcased than in the New River Gorge, perhaps the state's most paddled stream. In a state that's justifiably renowned for colossal rapids, the New River Gorge has some of the biggest of the big. Volume is at the core of the gorge's excitement. At medium levels the big river will carry 4,000 to 6,000 cfs. High water on the New Gorge begins somewhere around 6,000 cfs (about 3 feet on the Fayette Station gauge). Most paddlers will agree that 7,500 cfs is getting pretty rambunctious, but as always, defining "high" is a personal and subjective matter. Experienced decked boaters run the gorge at practically all levels. Open boaters with bullet-proof rolls routinely make the run at 12,000 cfs, and it's been run in canoes at 30,000 cfs. Needless to say, an unfailing roll is mandatory at these levels. A touch of madness helps also. (As a point of reference, commercial rafters cease operations at approximately 20,000 cfs.)

Regardless of the water level on any given day, the New River Gorge clearly is no place for those averse to large volume. Not only are the rapids big and forceful, many of them are obstructed by large boulders which necessitate maneuvering in very powerful currents, cross-currents, and hydraulics. Some rapids are fraught with undercut hazards. Although the gradient is a modest 20 ft/mi, the rapids are of the full-grown West Virginia variety: big, brawny and bodacious.

The rapids aren't the only thing that's big. The river twists through an awesome chasm. At the takeout, the New River Gorge Bridge towers 876 feet above Fayette Station Rapid. The longest single arch bridge in the world, it's also the second highest bridge in the United States. (Royal Gorge Bridge in Colorado is higher.) The gorge is so deep that once a year in October one side of the bridge is closed to traffic and the nearby community of Fayetteville sponsors "Bridge Day," an all-afternoon celebration that attracts, among others, BASE jumpers from all over eastern America. (BASE is an acronym derived from the objects from which they jump: Buildings, Antennae, Structures, and Earth [i.e., cliffs].) Illegal for the rest of the year, on Bridge Day parachuting from the bridge is declared legal and jump junkies strap on parachutes and hurtle themselves into the unpredictable cross winds of the gorge, trying to land safely 876 feet below on a small gravel bar at the bottom of Fayette Station Rapid.

Similar To. A mixture of the Cheat Canyon and Lower Gauley.

Description

Before the Cunard access road was improved, most paddlers put in upstream at Thurmond and suffered through six miles of flatwater before reaching the fun stuff. The alternative, which took about as long as paddling the flatwater, was to pay a local resident by the name of "Sleepy" to load boats on his flatbed truck and haul them down a rutted trail to the river. Naturally, this adventure was known as "Sleepy's shuttle." Now, with the improved Cunard access, you can drive the family sedan to the very spot that once only Sleepy's rugged old rig could reach, enabling you to miss a lot of flatwater and thereby make up enough time to run the gorge twice in the same day.

Mile(s)	New River Gorge Top-To-Bottom Itinerary
0.0	Cunard putin.
0.5	Upper Railroad (Class III).
0.7	Middle Railroad (Class III).
1.0	Lower Railroad (III+). Entrapment peril at low water (under 2,000 cfs).
1.0 to 3.0	Six or seven Class III rapids that are good to "loosen up" the muscles and work out the kinks before hitting the Keeney Brothers.
3.0	Upper Keeney (Class III).
3.1	Middle Keeney (Class IV).
3.3	Lower Keeney (Class IV+).
3.7	Lollygag (Class III).
4.3	Dudleys Dip (Class III+).
4.5	Double Z (Class IV+).
5.0	Turtle Rock (Class III+).
5.1	GreyHound Bus Stopper (Class III+).
5.3	Upper Tipple (Class III).
5.4	Lower Tipple (Class III).
6.0	Undercut Rock (Class IV).
6.5	Fayette Station Rapid (Class IV) and the take-out.

If for some reason you do put in at Thurmond, you'll find only one rapid, Surprise (Class III), before the Cunard putin. Surprise is a good introduction to the massive wave trains downstream. It's a big, open rapid, full of waves and holes.

The Railroad Trilogy

Using the Cunard access, the rapids begin soon after putin and continue unabated for six and a half miles to the New River Bridge. The first series of rapids is the Railroad trilogy, recognizable from upstream by the railroad trestle. Upper Railroad is a huge hole created as large volume rumbles over a riverwide ledge, with a steeper drop on river right. A center rock marks the path of least turbulence. Run just right of the center rock for the easiest slot. The biggest hole, and possible enders, are found on river right. Middle Railroad (Class III) is a continuance of Upper. The best tactic is to get left into the main wave train and have fun.

Lower Railroad (Class III+) is another matter altogether. An undercut rock in midstream poses grave danger at low water. It's situated about 50 feet from the river left bank and is not obvious, even when scouted from river left. The rock faces upstream, like an open clam. At levels of 3,000 cfs or higher, the danger is reduced because the rock is well-covered. Between 2,000 and 3,000 cfs, water hits the top of the shell, pillows up and flows around the hazard. Below 2,000 cfs (0.0 at Fayette Station) the undercut becomes partially exposed. The lower the water, the more the exposure and the greater the danger. At levels below 2,000 cfs, consider skirting lower Railroad on river right (even though it will be bony) or running it over the steepest drop on far left.

One canoeist flushed under the rock at low water. After a tense moment he bobbed to the surface forty yards downstream, having somehow managed to exit his boat and flush underneath the undercut rock. He was physically unharmed but his canoe was unretrievable. A week later it broke up, ripping in half. A year after the canoe paddler's close call, a kayak paddler flushed under the rock. Unlike the open boater, he was unable to escape his craft. Trapped in his boat, he died. A plaque in his memory was affixed to a rock on river left.

The Keeney Clan

Several small (by New River standards) rapids appear in the next two miles. Then the Keeney clan congregates. Upper Keeney, recognizable from upstream by "Whale Rock" on river left, is a minor

*Bill Hay toys with Greyhound Bus Stopper on New River Gorge.
Don Ellis photo.*

Lower Keeney on the New River Gorge. Mayo Gravatt photo.

constriction (Class III) at low and medium levels, when the best course is to run through the main wave train and eddy left behind Whale Rock. At higher levels upper Keeney takes on added significance because it merges with middle Keeney. Starting at about 6,000 cfs, upper Keeney is merely the entrance to middle Keeney. In order to catch the river left eddy behind Whale Rock at higher levels one must run a few feet right of Whale Rock and, once past the rock, paddle hard to break out of the wave train and cross the eddy line. Otherwise, the wave train continues nonstop into middle Keeney.

Middle Keeney (Class IV) is non-trivial. The volume constricts and blasts through a boulder field, producing a crazy-quilt pattern of waves and holes. Look it over and pick your path, it's runnable just about anywhere. At higher flows left of center is generally preferable, if for no other reason than that the right side of the rapid never stops, melding into lower Keeney. At 6,000 cfs and higher, middle Keeney is one powerful critter, kicking up toward a Class V rating, with progressively larger waves until the biggest of all is encountered near the bottom.

Lower Keeney (Class IV+) is a rapid of Gauleyesque proportions which sweeps from right to left. When entering this big West Virginia bundle of energy, start right center and paddle like hell toward the right because the rapid definitely blasts floating objects toward river left, which harbors "Wash Up Rock" near the bottom. Far right is too rocky at low and medium levels, but at high water it's better padded and about the only sane way through this big bully. Lower Keeney is the most difficult rapid on the river at lower levels. As the water rises it actually gets easier, and several other rapids (including middle Keeney) eventually surpass it in difficulty. However, for the added enjoyment of big water fiends everywhere, beginning somewhere around 7,500 cfs the three Keeney brothers join hands to form a single long megarapid of Class V+ caliber.

Double Z and Its Ilk

Lollygag and Dudleys Dip are Class III(III+) rapids that serve as transition from lower Keeney's big-water madness to the more maneuver-intensive water downstream, epitomized by Double Z (Class IV+), a long, violent rapid that should not be run without some idea of what's in store. The rapid is about 100 yards long and harbors an undercut rock in midstream about 40% of the way through the craziness. The main objectives are to avoid this undercut rock and generally run down the right side, dodging holes. To make things interesting, a row of rocks block river right entry, requiring entry near the center of the river. The usual tactic is to enter center and immediately dive into one of the eddies downstream of the row of rocks. Then comes an eddy-ferry toward river right in order to peel out into heavy current and head downstream through bodacious waves and holes. At levels over 6,000 cfs, Double Z becomes a hornet's nest of explosive energy.

Turtle Rock (Class III+) and Greyhound Bus Stopper (Class III+) are so close they're practically the same rapid. Turtle Rock is usually run with an entry from river right, then working consistently to the left in order to miss Greyhound Bus Stopper. At high water, however, the Bus Stopper gets really nasty and can be run tight against river right (over the low water ender spot). Even hardcore surf fiends avoid the Greyhound hydraulic.

Three other powerful rapids remain before the grand finale at Fayette Station, including Undercut Rock, nominally a Class III+ or IV which becomes one of, if not *the* wildest ride on the river at high water. Basically a scaled-down Double Z, at high water Undercut Rock really escalates in difficulty, rivalling the Z in craziness and garnering a Class IV+ rating. The undercut is near the top of the rapid on river right, after which some wild whitewater occurs until the final four foot ledge which harbors Invisible Rock. Invisible Rock (aptly named) is hard to spot from upstream. At certain levels, it harbors a pretty good pourover hole. (The New River Gorge Bridge is first visible from the approach to Undercut Rock Rapid.)

The Bridge Jumper

The Fayette Station takeout is in the shadow of the awesome New River Gorge Bridge. Paddlers have a choice. They can run Class IV Fayette Station Rapid and then take out, or take out above the rapid. Those running through Fayette Station Rapid in October should watch the sky for parachutists. This writer once completed a run through the gorge, unaware of what Bridge Day was all about. A parachutist dressed in a clown suit (red nose and all!) was blown off course and landed on the gravel bar within a few yards of his boat. The clown ran over and asked, excitedly, "How'd you get that boat in here?"

"I put in at Thurmond and floated down the river," I replied.

"You floated through those rapids up there?" the clown asked, pointing upstream toward the rapids that are visible from the bridge 876 feet above.

"That's right. And some even nicer ones farther upstream."

"Man, you're crazy," he concluded. "You could get killed doing a fool stunt like that!"

Sermon delivered, he quickly gathered his parachute and scrambled aboard his shuttle vehicle, a flatbed trailer hitched behind a large farm tractor. As the tractor driver negotiated the serpentine road to the top of the gorge, the clown busily packed his chute so he'd be ready to jump again the minute he arrived back atop the bridge.

Summary

Those who profess to know about such things (professors, naturally) claim that the New is the second oldest river in the world, behind only the Nile River of Africa. Old it may be, but feeble it ain't. In the heart of the gorge, both rapids and scenery reach awesome proportions. At low to medium levels the run is exciting, and at high water it's a real bull, a convincing lesson in volume x gradient interaction. With a (comparatively) meager average gradient of 20 ft/mi, the big river generates enormous rapids, three of which may be Class V at high water (middle Keeney, Double Z, and Undercut Rock). Above 7,500 cfs, the Keeneys blend together, forming a megarapid of Class V+ difficulty. Also, at high water Greyhound Bus Stopper might be terminal. The river's not inconsequential at low flows either, when it still has ten or twelve significant rapids, including at least two low Class IVs. Moreover, low water makes its undercuts more pernicious, especially the one at lower Railroad Rapid.

The redeeming feature of the New is that it's runnable during summer, when all else may be desiccated. But remember, the lower the flow, the greater the hazard at lower Railroad.

Water Levels

Volume at Thurmond, six miles upstream of the putin, is available from (304) 529-5127.

New River Gorge Gauge Location Thurmond
Low: 2,100 cfs Medium: 4,000 cfs High: 6,000 cfs

A gauge is also located at Fayette Station, the takeout. The following table translates Fayette gauge readings into cfs.

Fayette Station Conversion	
Feet	**Cfs**
-2	1,072
-1	1,704
0	2,440
1	3,352
2	4,436
3	5,820
4	7,550
5	9,550
6	11,400
7	14,100
8	17,200
9	20,200
10	23,800
11	25,800
12	30,000

The New is paddler salvation during parched summer months, when the river is rarely too low to paddle. In drier summers, it will occasionally drop to the 1,000 to 1,400 cfs range. Even at this level all rapids are runnable, with the possible exception of lower Railroad.

Most gorge veterans, however, consider anything below 3,000 cfs to be low, 6,000 cfs to be a healthy reading, and 7,500 cfs suitable only for advanced paddlers.   Preference for water level, however, is subjective.   Only a few years ago levels of 6,000 cfs were considered unthinkable by most paddlers.   But standards and abilities progress continually, and the New River Gorge seems to be one of those places where the outer limits of volume manageability are constantly redefined.

This big stream is sometimes under-rated because of its proximity to the upper Gauley, only thirty minutes away on US 19. However, this stalwart of southern whitewater rivers provides over six demanding miles of near-continuous high caliber Class III/IV/V challenge.   If you've run it in the past and were disappointed, odds are you merely ran it at too low a level.   In recent years the trend has been to run it at higher and higher flows.

A proviso may be in order, nonetheless, because for southeastern paddlers, rapids of the New River Gorge are often a first introduction to West Virginia whitewater.   First-trip paddlers on the New are always surprised, and sometimes overwhelmed, by the power of its rapids.   Paddling skills required for the gorge are different than those needed on steeper, more technical streams. Paddlers on the river for the first time may want to avoid high levels. A recommended first trip level, for advanced intermediate paddlers, is 2,000 to 3,000 cfs.

Access

Put in at Cunard and take out beneath the gigantic New River Bridge, underneath US 19, between Beckley and Summersville.   The shuttle isn't bad, considering the terrain. To reach the putin from the US 19 bridge, drive south (toward Beckley).   Turn left at the light and drive through Fayetteville.   Turn left onto Gatewood Road on the out-

skirts of town. In four to five miles, look for the sign to the Cunard putin.

Miles From the New River Gorge	
Pittsburgh, PA 219	Washington, DC 320
Cincinnati, OH 225	Cleveland, OH 280
Greensboro, NC 245	Atlanta, GA 540

Other Information

Camping

Several commercial campgrounds are located in the vicinity of the New Gorge. Inquire locally. Some paddlers stay at the Garvey Hilton near Lookout, an abandoned park and ball field. A large Corps of Engineers campground is located near Summersville Dam.

Suitability for Rafting (On a 1 to 7 Scale): 7

Oar rafting heaven. The gorge is immensely popular with rafters, and many commercial outfitters are congregated in the Thurmond, Fayetteville, and Summersville environs. (The Chamber of Commerce in Fayetteville will give you the latest phone numbers.)

TRIP Profile

The Volume x Gradient Interaction score (140) is the fifth highest of any trip in the book. Drop into Greyhound Bus Stopper and you'll know why.

The high Reputation score (128) is largely deserved. Rapids Difficulty and Entrapment scores, both at 117, indicate that the New Gorge is almost twice as difficult on these dimensions as the average trip described in this book. Notice that these robust scores occur notwithstanding puny gradient figures.

Nearby Alternate Trips

The Gauley River is only a few miles north on US 19. The Meadow River also is nearby. Both these streams are described elsewhere in this volume.

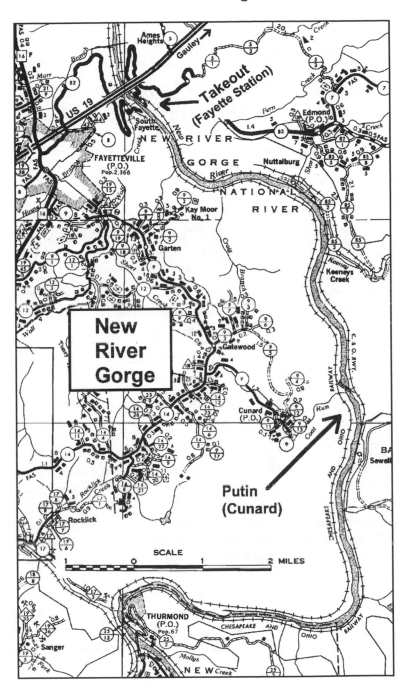

New River Gorge

Takeout (Fayette Station)

Putin (Cunard)

SCALE

1   0   1   2 MILES

Nolichucky Gorge

Poplar to Erwin
(North Carolina)

TRIP Profile			
Scale Midpoint = 100			
Overall Difficulty	101	Rapids Difficulty	92
Volume x Gradient	126	Continuous Rapids	99
Average Gradient	89	Entrapments	94
Maximum Gradient	88	Inaccessibility	110
Total Gradient	101	Reputation	117

Actual Stream Data			
Max Rapids	III(IV)	Stream Size	Large
Average Gradient	37	Length (in miles)	9
Maximum Gradient	60	Morphology Type	2

Overview

The Nolichucky is one of the South's premier big mountain rivers, springing forth full grown when the Toe and Cane Rivers confluence a short distance upstream of the putin near Poplar, North Carolina. The biggest and best rapids appear in the first mile, but what the rest of the run lacks in whitewater, it more than compensates for in outstanding scenery. The Nolichucky gorge is awesome, one of the most impressive in the Southeast. To convey proper perspective of the Nolichucky country, consider that the putin is some fifteen miles (as the crow flies) from Roan Mountain and a mere twenty miles from the highest peak in eastern America, Mount Mitchell. The surrounding terrain is large scale (by eastern standards), and the

350

Nolichucky itself is a sizeable stream, cutting an imposing swath through the heart of the Unaka Mountains.

The Nolichucky is not an overly difficult river except at higher water when the first two miles turn into a nonstop flush because of the large volume, considerable gradient, and constricted streambed. Rapids near the top of the gorge begin to exhibit Gauleyesque characteristics starting at about 2,000 cfs.

Mile(s)	Nolichucky Gorge Top-To-Bottom Itinerary
0.0	Put in downstream of Poplar, NC.
0.3	Railroad trestle.
0.4	Railroad Trestle Rapid (Class III+).
0.5	On the Rocks (Class III+).
0.7	Jaws!
1.0	Quarter Mile intro (Class III).
1.3	Quarter Mile Rapid (Class IV).
2.0	Roostertail (Class III+).
4.0	Rock Twist (Class III).
5.0	Sycamore Shoals (Class III).
5.4	Sousehole (Class III).
5.9	Tennessee state line. Devils Creek on river left.
8.8	Takeout near Erwin, Tennessee.

Description

A short distance downstream of the putin, the stream passes underneath a railroad trestle and rushes into the gorge with a roar and a hard left turn through Railroad Trestle Rapid (Class III+). Enter this Railroad Trestle Rapid in river center or to the right of center and then pick the best route, depending on water level, through the ensuing waves and holes.

On the Rocks (Class III+) is the next rapid of significance. The first chute is usually run from right to left and then veering sharply either right or left for the rest of the rapid. Scout on the left.

On the Rocks is followed by Jaws!, a big hole at higher levels (skirt on river left), and two smaller rock garden rapids.

The next big rapid is Quarter Mile (Class IV). There are many routes through this long, technical maze of rocks and old railroad scrap metal. None of the drops are really big, but there are a lot of them. Depending on flow, it can range in difficulty from Class III+ to Class V. It can be run straight through by staying right of center, but it's more fun to zigzag back and forth via eddies and ferries around and through its myriad obstructions. The last drop in Quarter Mile is a riverwide ledge that can be run in several places at low or medium levels, but which is best skirted down the chute on river left at higher flows.

Roostertail (Class III+) appears about two miles into the run. It's a double drop with eddies on both sides after the first drop. At one time this rapid had a large rock in its middle over which water spewed at high velocity, forming an impressive "roostertail." A flood, however, rolled the rooster rock on downstream and today the only tail in the rapid belongs to the hapless paddler who happens to swim it. At most flow levels Roostertail is more than a Class III but not quite a Class IV, hence its listing herein as a Class III+. Somewhere around 2,000 cfs, however, this rapid attains legitimate Class IV power and difficulty. Looking at it from downstream, it forms an impressive cascade of white foaming beauty.

Roostertail is the last really big rapid on the river, although there are smaller rapids throughout the gorge and several grabby holes at higher flows. The quality of the whitewater experience downstream of Roostertail is highly dependent on flow. At lower flows these miles are pretty much a drag. With more water they become eminently more interesting, with about a half dozen Class III and Class III+ rock gardens.

About five miles into the run the Nolichucky hooks sharply right, throwing the river against a river left retainer wall. On the right is a beach (Sycamore Shoals) and downstream is a long curving rapid ending in a row of rocks across the river that constrict the flow into a narrow slot, forming a curious hydraulic (Sousehole, Class III). Downstream of Sousehole, as the size and power of the rapids diminish, the size and majesty of the mountains on both sides of the stream increase.

At mile 5.9 the river flows from North Carolina into Tennessee and Devils Creek enters on the left. A trail leads up the creek a short distance to a series of slides and waterfalls.

Downstream, Tennessee's part of the gorge is less technical and less difficult than upstream miles, giving the paddler more time to soak in the surroundings, which are nothing short of spectacular. The lower part of the Nolichucky Gorge is one of the most awesome mountain spectacles in the East.

Two significant drops appear in the last couple of miles, the last one marked by an odd rock formation on river left. The rock has a volcanic appearance.

Summary

Often runnable into the summer because of its sizeable watershed, the Nolichucky Gorge has recently become popular with commercial outfitters who offer raft trips in spring and early summer.

The first two miles of the gorge are always interesting. At low water they consist of technical rock dodging. At high water the first two miles are big, in-motion, and -- for unfortunate swimmers -- brutally unforgiving.

After the second mile, flow level greatly influences the quality of the whitewater experience. At low water these miles are less than impressive. With plenty of water, the Class II-III action continues nonstop almost to the takeout.

Regardless of water level, however, its scenery justifies the trip.

Water Levels

Gaining an accurate impression of gorge water conditions is not easy. TVA's gauge is downstream at Embreeville and its readings never seem to correspond closely to actual gorge conditions. A direct reading is available from the gauge near the putin at Poplar. Outfitters in the area monitor this gauge. For Embreeville gauge readings, call TVA at (800) 238-2264 and press code "3" after the recorded message.

Nolichucky Gorge Gauge Location Nolichucky Putin	Nolichucky Gorge Gauge Location TVA at Embreeville
Low: 1.7 Medium: 2.4 High: 3.0	Low: 1,000 cfs Medium: 1,750 cfs High: 2,500 cfs

About 1,000 cfs on the TVA Embreeville gauge is enough to run all the major rock jumbles. About 1,600 cfs to 1,800 cfs make the first two miles pretty exciting, and they really start cooking over 2,000 cfs. For the first two miles, it can be a thin dividing line between optimally high and just plain too high. As a point of reference, commercial rafting companies cease operations at 5.0 on the putin gauge.

Access

Erwin, Tennessee, the fulcrum for the Nolichucky shuttle, is located on US 23/19W in far-east Tennessee midway between Kingsport, Tennessee and Asheville, North Carolina. To reach the putin at Poplar, North Carolina, take TN Route 30 (Tenth Street in

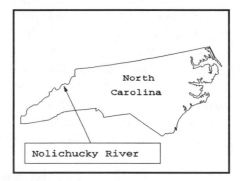

Erwin) east into the Cherokee National Forest past Rock Creek Campground, into the Unaka Mountains, across the Appalachian Trail at Indian Grave Gap, and down into North Carolina. The takeout is south of Erwin near Unaka Springs. The easiest takeout is near Nolichucky Expeditions.

Miles From the Nolichucky Gorge	
Asheville, NC 60	Roanoke, VA 205
Knoxville, TN 125	Atlanta, GA 270

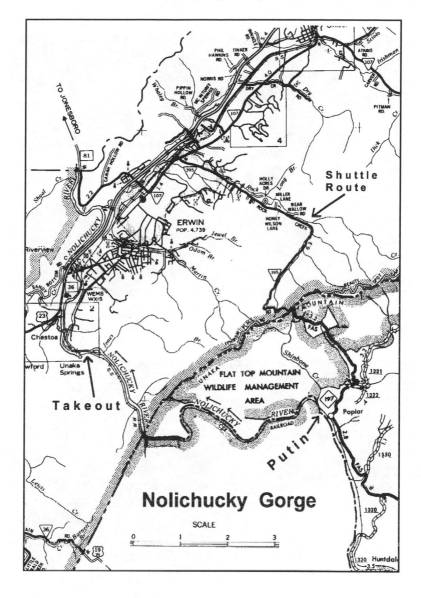

Nolichucky Gorge

Frank (the Flying Ace) Billue goes airborne. Lower Keeney. New River Gorge. Don Ellis photo.

Bill Hay at the top of On the Rocks. Nolichucky Gorge. Mayo Grovatt photo.

Other Information

Camping

The easiest solution is to camp at Nolichucky Expeditions near Erwin and use the camp as a takeout. Otherwise, consider Rock Creek Campground on the shuttle road (TN 30) between Erwin and Poplar.

Hiking

The Appalachian Trail practically runs through the campground at Nolichucky Expeditions.

Hikers occasionally walk along the Clinchfield Railroad, which parallels the Nolichucky through its gorge. However, at the top of the gorge, just below Poplar and upstream of the first rapid, hikers must make a dangerous trestle crossing. Approaching trains from Erwin cannot be seen because of the curvature of the tracks and they cannot be heard because of the roar of the rapid immediately downstream. The trestle is so narrow that when a train roars across, it overhangs considerably on both sides. Locals say that numerous fatalities have occurred here.

Suitability for Rafting (On a 1 to 7 Scale): 7

Water permitting, several outfitters offer Nolichucky Gorge raft trips. Check with the Erwin Chamber of Commerce for current phone numbers.

TRIP Profile

Notice that the most extreme score is on volume x gradient interaction (126). This robust score means that the Nolichucky is about twice as difficult (on this dimension) as the average trip described in this book. This relatively high score comes not from high average gradient, but from a combination of modest gradient and substantial volume. Not surprisingly, this combination produces a number of memorably grabby holes.

The TRIP profile was calculated at 1,750 cfs. As volume climbs above this level, the volume x gradient interaction score escalates radically, especially in the first two miles.

If the relatively modest inaccessibility score (110) is surprising, remember that a railroad parallels the river through the gorge. Otherwise this score would be much higher.

Nearby Alternate Trips

The French Broad [Class III(IV)] is near Hot Springs, North Carolina. It's described elsewhere in this volume.

Obed River

Goulds Bend
(Tennessee)

TRIP Profile			
Scale Midpoint = 100			
Overall Difficulty	95	Rapids Difficulty	95
Volume x Gradient	85	Continuous Rapids	87
Average Gradient	83	Entrapments	117
Maximum Gradient	103	Inaccessibility	110
Total Gradient	95	Reputation	117

Actual Stream Data			
Max Rapids	III(V)	Stream Size	Small
Average Gradient	30	Length (in miles)	10
Maximum Gradient	80	Morphology Types	2&3

Overview

The Obed watershed, located near Knoxville, Tennessee, corrals some of the most exciting paddling in the Southeast into a remarkably circumscribed geographic area. If we use the Devils Breakfast Table on Daddys Creek (an Obed tributary) as the epicenter of an imaginary circle with a radius of twenty miles, the circle encompasses 142 miles of runnable whitewater! Few other localities can support such a claim. Not only is the whitewater abundant, but the watershed also contains several spectacular canyons. As a whole, the Obed/Emory system is perhaps the most beautiful watershed in the Southeast.

359

To understand the Obed system, one must visualize the Cumberland Plateau, from which the watershed pours. According to geologists, this plateau is an uplift that was formed when continents collided. Although this explanation of the plateau's origin sounds more like one of Sylvester Stallone's movie scripts than a scientific theory, the indubitable result is indeed an uplift, a plateau, that rises hundreds of feet above surrounding valleys and basins. The uplift is only some twenty-five to fifty miles wide east-to-west, but it extends from northern Alabama through Tennessee into the Cumberland Mountain stubble of eastern Kentucky, and continues northward under other names through Pennsylvania and into New England.

Naturally, rain that falls on a plateau drains over the edge into the valleys below. After the continental collision, rainfall undoubtedly trickled over the edges in many small rivulets, much as water poured onto a table top runs off in many directions. Gradually, the water formed shallow troughs and meandered to the edges, to drop straight down hundreds of feet to the valley floor, forming what must have been visually stunning waterfalls. As the streams deepened their troughs, the waterfalls progressively migrated upstream, diminishing in height. Today, incessant erosion has created canyons with hundreds of diminutive "waterfalls" instead of a single big drop at the edge of the plateau.

The stark beauty of the Obed canyons contrasts with the austere surroundings of the plateau, where topsoil is thin, farming is of the subsistence, dirt-scrabble variety, industry is virtually nonexistent, and the once-magnificent forests are only a dim memory. This is coal country, with most of it extracted via environmentally devastating strip mines. Harry Caudill captured the ethos of the region in his evocative work *Night Comes to the Cumberlands*. Caudill wrote about the part of the Cumberlands he knew best, eastern Kentucky, but the issues he confronted apply to the Tennessee Obed region as well.

Little has changed since Caudill published his landmark volume. The region remains isolated and little known to outsiders. Yet it hosts an extraordinary watershed with superb wilderness characteristics. So superb, in fact, that fifty miles of the Obed and its two major tributaries (Clear Creek and Daddys Creek) were added to the National Wild and Scenic Rivers System in 1976. Actually, the federal study team recommended 100 miles for inclusion in the system, with 82 of the 100 miles qualifying for "wild" designation, indicating that the stream corridors were substantially free of human infringement and existed predominantly in a pristine condition. No wonder that the late Harry Roberts once characterized this area as ". . . possibly the last great wilderness recreation area in the eastern United States."

Mile(s)	Goulds Bend Top-To-Bottom Itinerary
0.0	Put in at the US 127 bridge (Bishop Bridge) three miles north of Crossville about 200 yards from I-40, near Shoney's.
0.0 to 2.0	Mild gradient and Class I-II water.
2.1 to 4.0	60 ft/mi gradient.
4.1 to 4.7	Steepest gradient, with one mile at 80 ft. Contains, in order of appearance: the Esses (Class V), Ender Falls (Class III-), and Knuckle Buster (Class IV-).
7.1 to 10.0	Mostly flat.
10.0	Take out at Adams Bridge on Genesis Road, about eight miles north of I-40.

Description

Goulds Bend is the uppermost run on the Obed River, beginning at the US 127 bridge just as the river ends its plateau-top meanderings and heads downhill toward the Tennessee Valley. Most of the trip is through a deep, isolated gorge. The average gradient over the ten mile course is 30 feet/mile, but its 300 feet of total drop are not evenly distributed. It has three miles of flatwater, but it also has one Class V rapid, one that's often rated Class IV, and a lot of others of the Class II-III variety, creating tight and technical conditions with abundant boulders and an occasional tree obstructing the course.

The first two miles are Class I-II in difficulty. It gains momentum over this course, however, with increasing gradient and added volume from small tributaries. A gradually deepening gorge begins one mile after the putin. The next two miles drop at 60 feet/mile, and the mile after that has a gradient of 80 feet/mile, the steepest of the Obed River.

In the heart of the gorge you'll find the toughest rapid in the Obed/Emory watershed, a Class V zig zag course through a narrow channel called the Esses, with turns so tight that it's exceedingly difficult to bend a boat through them. Failure to make the turns can easily result in a pinned or lost boat, for the rocks on either side are radically undercut. (Hint: If you portage, use river right and avoid a back-breaking haul over the river left boulders.)

Next on the agenda is a place called Ender Falls, a series of small drops. With enough water, the last of these drops produces forceful enders, sometimes propelling boats completely out of the river, landing them on surrounding rocks.

The other well known rapid on Goulds Bend is Knucklebuster (aka Knuckle Falls), which most people regard as a low Class IV. To be sure, Knucklebuster is difficult to run, but more because of its congested approach than anything else. This rapid is really a Class III waterfall of about five feet that would be a lot simpler with a clear approach. However, it has a small island which clogs the top of the waterfall. It can be approached from either right or left of the island, but there's not enough distance between the island and the waterfall to permit proper alignment for the forthcoming descent. The tendency of the rapid is to push boats into the deepest slot on river right. Stay left on the drop.

The rock outcropping on river left downstream of Knucklebuster is undercut. This is not obvious from upstream, but it's a hazard for swimmers.

Knucklebuster heralds the beginning of the end for the best Goulds Bend whitewater. Below this spot the gradient moderates considerably and the last two miles to the takeout at Adams Bridge are flat.

Summary

You have to admit, Goulds Bend is a great name! (Maybe Sylvester Stallone could use as the title of his next film.) The whitewater's pretty good, too, with a Class V rapid that most paddlers portage and a Class IV that bangs up a lot of people. Otherwise, rapids are Class II-III.

The story of a flash flood on this section of the Obed appears in *River Stories: Tales From Bo Rockerville,* by Monte Smith, available from Pahsimeroi Press. (Sorry, Sylvester, but Oliver Stone's already bought the story rights!)

Water Levels

The Obed/Emory gauge is located at Oakdale on the Emory River, many miles downstream of Goulds Bend. Because the gauge is so far downstream, the correlation between Oakdale readings and Goulds Bend water conditions is far from perfect. To obtain gauge readings, call TVA at (800) 238-2264 and press code "3" after the recorded message. Low, medium, and high readings are 3,500 cfs, 5,500 cfs, and 7,500 cfs, respectively.

Access

The Obed system is located near Crossville on the Cumberland Plateau in Tennessee, between Knoxville and Nashville. Crossville is accessible from east and west via I-40 and from north and south via US 127. Put in at the US 127 bridge (Bishop Bridge) three miles north of Crossville and 200 yards off I-40. (When exiting from the Interstate, use the US 127 Crossville exit and look for Shoney's.)

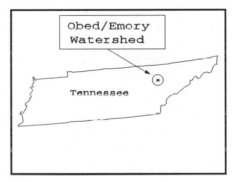

Take out at Adams Bridge on Genesis Road. To run the shuttle from the putin, take I-40 east about a mile and a half to the Genesis Road exit. Turn left onto Genesis Road and drive north for about eight miles to Adams Bridge.

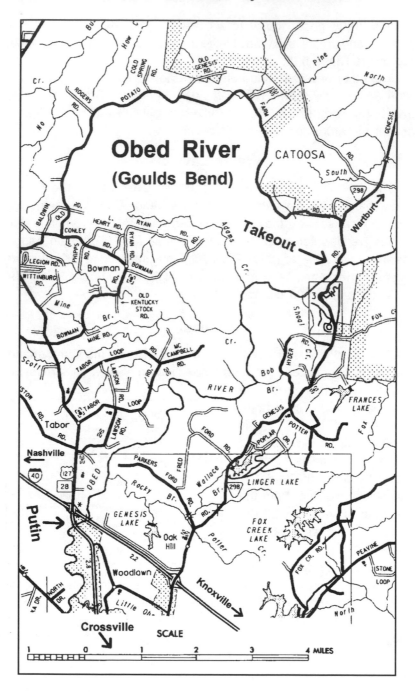

Obed River
(Goulds Bend)

Miles From the Obed River	
Knoxville, TN 55	Atlanta, GA 215
Nashville, TN 110	Cincinnati, OH 280

Other Information

Camping

Developed camping is available at Cumberland Mountain State Park, off US 127 about six miles south of Crossville. Frozen Head State Park, off TN 62 five miles east of Wartburg, is on the other side of the watershed.

Hiking

Check with the rangers at Frozen Head State Park.

Maps

Check with the TVA, 1101 Market Street, 101 Haney Bldg, Chattanooga, TN 37402, or phone (615) 632-6082. Ask for the Obed/Emory watershed map.

Suitability for Rafting (On a 1 to 7 Scale): 0

Nearby Alternate Trips

The Obed/Emory watershed contains 18 whitewater trips, several of which (listed in the table below) are described elsewhere in this volume. For complete details on the system, including summaries of twenty years of streamflow data and a photograph of Eugene (Bo) Rocker, refer to *A Paddler's Guide to the Obed/Emory Watershed,* by Monte Smith.

Alternate Trip	Rapids Difficulty	TRIP Points
Clear Creek	III+	97
Crab Orchard Creek	III+	98
Daddys Creek Canyon	III-IV	109
Island Creek	III-IV	108
Obed River: DBT to Nemo	III(IV)	101

Obed River

Devils Breakfast Table to Nemo
(Tennessee)

TRIP Profile			
Scale Midpoint = 100			
Overall Difficulty	101	Rapids Difficulty	96
Volume x Gradient	110	Continuous Rapids	99
Average Gradient	79	Entrapments	128
Maximum Gradient	74	Inaccessibility	128
Total Gradient	97	Reputation	117

Actual Stream Data			
Max Rapids	III(IV)	Stream Size	Medium
Average Gradient	26	Length (in miles)	12
Maximum Gradient	40	Morphology Type	2

Overview

This trip is through the Obed National Wild and Scenic River's most majestic canyon, complete with place names to evoke vivid images. If you've never seen it, try to imagine how Devils Breakfast Table looks. It's not a rapid, you know, but a stone monolith. How did it get its name, Devils Breakfast Table? And Nemo? Who came up with that name? And what does it mean? The motto of Scotland is Nemomeimnelacessit, which means "No one attacks me with impunity." Is that what Nemo on the Emory River originally meant? And then there's OmyGod! Rapid, one of the most graphic names east of Body Snatcher and south of Mind Bender. And of all the rock gardens on all the rocky rivers in all of Appalachia, did you ever stop to wonder why there's only one *Rockgarden?*

This trip provides exposure to three different streams. The usual putin is at the Devils Breakfast Table on Daddys Creek, which provides a two mile technical creek prelude to the Obed River. After nine miles on the Obed, the last mile is on the Emory River.

At lower flows, the first two miles on Daddys Creek are rocky, but relief occurs once the main stem of the Obed doubles the volume. Volume is again boosted substantially when Clear Creek joins the Obed shortly downstream of Rockgarden, and a minor boost occurs when the Emory confluences with the Obed less than a mile above the takeout at Nemo. The last miles on the Obed and Emory Rivers bear little resemblance to the first two miles on diminutive Daddys Creek.

Although the average gradient for this trip is a moderate 26 feet/mile, this figure is potentially misleading because the Obed is a ledge/pool river, and its drops are often through eroded ledges which have formed rock gardens peppered with undercuts.

Description

Daddys Creek from the Devils
Breakfast Table to Obed Junction

From the eerily beautiful setting of the Devils Breakfast Table, Daddys Creek frolics through two miles of Class II creek rapids to Obed Junction. The course is moderately technical at lower flows with a gradient of 32 feet/mile.

Obed Junction to
Clear Creek Confluence

At Obed Junction the stream changes from a creek to a river, and flows into the Obed's rugged and inaccessible canyon. It's ten miles downstream to the first bridge crossing and over five miles to the first 4WD exit (Canoe Hole).

The first three miles below Obed Junction feature a gradient of 20 feet/mile and Class II and Class II+ rapids, some of which become Class III at higher flows. Most of these rapids are short, twisting drops. Over these miles the river flows into an ever-deepening canyon. As the canyon walls increase in height, they crowd closer to the riverbed. When the sheer sandstone canyon walls reach a height of about 300 feet, the paddler enters the Obed River's most magnificent mile. The gradient increases to 40 feet/mile and produces three named rapids and half a dozen unnamed Class II-III declivities. In order of appearance, the named rapids are: Ninety Right-Ninety Left, OmyGod!, and Rockgarden.

Mile(s)	DBT to Nemo Top-To-Bottom Itinerary
0.0	Put in at the Devils Breakfast Table on Daddys Creek inside the Catoosa Wildlife Management Area.
0.0 to 2.2	Daddys Creek at 32 feet/mile.
2.2 to 6.4	The most scenic part of the main Obed. Deep canyon with 27 feet/mile gradient.
2.2 to 5.0	Moderate difficulty Class II-III rock gardens into an ever-deepening canyon with 20 feet/mile gradient.
5.0 to 6.0	The Obed River's finest mile, deepest canyon, best whitewater. Forty feet per mile gradient.
5.0	Ninety Right-Ninety Left (Class III-).
5.3	OmyGod! (Class III+).
5.7	Rockgarden (Class IV).
6.0	Submarine Falls (Class II+).
6.4	Clear Creek confluence (river left). Hike to the top for a splendid view.
7.0	Canoe Hole, long pool. Emergency 4WD access on river left.
8.7	Keep Right (Class III).
9.0	Widow Maker (Class III).
11.0	Emory River confluence.
12.0	Nemo Bridge takeout (river left, upstream of the bridge).

Ninety Right-Ninety Left is formed by a jumble of boulders through which the river threads, narrows, and drops. There are multiple routes, but the most fun entails entering from the left and executing successive 90 degree turns, the second of which is on the lip of the main drop.

OmyGod! is the next named rapid. With Oakdale gauge readings between 2,000 and 3,000 cfs, it has a rocky approach with standing waves toward the bottom as the Obed is constricted to a few feet, pitched over a ledge, and propelled into OmyGod! rock abutment. The rock abutment on bottom right is allegedly undercut. With more than 3,000 cfs, OmyGod! widens out, forming additional eddies, holes, and wave trains.

It's prudent to scout the next rapid, Rockgarden, from river right. It's trickier than it looks. From its upstream approach, it looks like nothing at all, just another rocky Obed declivity. Even from the perspective provided by scouting, it doesn't look like all that much. It's not visually impressive at lower flows. But it's deceptive, with a complex arrangement of boulders and bizarre, boiling, cross currents. Some of its rocks are undercut, including one spot on river right toward the bottom of the rapid called Marys Crotch (which, incidentally is where the current takes boats at lower flows). At 3,000 cfs and higher, the undercuts are better covered, and the rapid is probably safer, but the whole thing comes alive with exploding energy.

Clear Creek Confluence
to the Emory River

At the point where the Obed meets Clear Creek, less than a mile below Rockgarden, a trail leads upward to an overlook providing an eagle's eye view into both canyons. It's a short hike and well worth the required time and energy.

With the addition of Clear Creek's volume the streambed widens. Gradient diminishes to 20 feet/mile over the next four and a half miles to confluence with the Emory. As the gradient eases, the canyon walls recede. Below the Clear Creek confluence, a rapid with standing waves and holes leads to a long pool known as Canoe Hole. On the left bank a 4WD access road leads to the top of the canyon near Lilly Bridge on Clear Creek.

Below Canoe Hole, two rapids appear that at low water are Class II+. In the magical range of about 2,000 to 2,500 cfs, however, they sparkle to life as Class III rapids.

Three-quarters of a mile below Canoe Hole the canyon walls crowd the river for the last time, forcing the streamflow sharply right and into a long Class III called Keep Right. Enter center or left of center and quickly work to the right for the second drop, then through fifty yards of splashing fun. After another long pool, Widow Maker (Class III) appears. A huge flat-topped rock on the left forces the river around in a semi-circle and provides the best standing waves on the Obed. The water here is powerful, but benign. Run straight into the wave train for the most fun or skirt down the left side near the flat top rock for a smoother ride.

Widow Maker is the Obed's last Class III rapid. There are several enjoyable Class II rapids in the remaining miles to the Emory River, but they are separated by long pools.

Emory River

At the Emory River confluence a railroad tunnel is visible on river left. The little creek that flows into the Obed just upstream of the tunnel entrance is the Emory River! When the two streams merge, the Obed usually carries about twenty times the volume of the Emory. The remaining mile to Nemo Bridge is moderate in gradient (15 feet/mile), but a definite improvement over the long pools just upstream. There are two Class II rapids, the second of which is formed by a streamwide ledge. The ledge can be run anywhere, but more water, turbulence, and a stronger hole are on far left. At Nemo Bridge, paddlers have the option of floating 200 yards downstream and running Nemo Rapid, a Class III that at higher flows develops sizeable hydraulics.

Summary

Devils Breakfast Table to Nemo is one of the Southeast's finest paddling trips. This is the Obed system's premier canyon.

The trip begins at the Devils Breakfast Table on Daddys Creek with two miles of small, technical rapids. It then graduates to the Obed River and its finest canyon scenery and whitewater, with vertical cliffs up to 400 feet and whitewater to Class IV.

With added volume from Clear Creek, rapids become less technical but more powerful. Finally, the Obed emerges from its isolated canyon and joins the Emory River.

Although all but one or two rapids are Class II-III, this run is ill-suited for anyone lacking good boat control in turbulent, technical water. The trip has numerous spots where radically undercut rocks must be avoided.

Water Levels

Volume in the Obed system is gauged at Oakdale on the Emory River. Readings are available from the Tennessee Valley Authority (TVA) at (800) 238-2264. Press code "3" after the recorded message and listen for "Emory at Oakdale."

A putin at DBT requires approximately 1,200 cfs. (However, 700 cfs is enough for an Obed Junction alternate putin, and 300 cfs will support a trip downstream from Canoe Hole.) A medium level is about 2,500 cfs, and high begins at about 3,500 cfs. In fact, above 3,000 cfs a lot of small technical rapids wash out and the Obed begins to resemble just another big volume river. Above 5,000 cfs, other trips in the system are more fun. Like every other river, this one has been run at outrageous levels. A group of open canoeists once tried it at 24,000 cfs and the turkeys did pretty well until they hit the mile of the Obed that contains Rockgarden.

Access

The Obed/Emory watershed is in Tennessee, about fifty miles west of Knoxville. Access to the usual putin, Devils Breakfast Table (DBT) on Daddys Creek, is problematic much of the year because it's located within the Catoosa Wildlife Management Area (CWMA). Roads within the CWMA are closed from January to April and on selected other weekends during managed hunts.

DBT -- assuming it's accessible -- is at the heart of the Catoosa Wildlife Management Area. Roads from Crab Orchard and from the Peavine exit off I-40 lead to Devils Breakfast Table, or it can

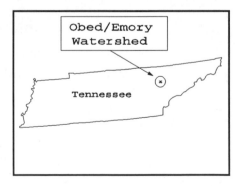

be reached from Wartburg via the Nemo Bridge road. Another approach is from Genesis Road via the Obed at Potters Ford and through the CWMA. Regardless of the route, it's hard to locate. If you don't feel completely lost and disoriented as you're searching for it, chances are you're on the wrong road.

The shuttle from DBT to Nemo is on river right of Daddys Creek through the CWMA. From the Devils Breakfast Table putin, go to Buck Switch, the first intersection, and turn left. Turn left again at the Catoosa Checking Station (Island Creek will be on your right), go over the ridge and down to Nemo Bridge on the Emory. Allow about forty minutes, one-way, for the shuttle. If DBT is closed, several alternatives are available.

Antioch Bridge, outside the Catoosa Wildlife Management Area, can serve as an alternate putin, but this adds 6.5 miles of Class III-IV whitewater to an already long twelve mile trip. But, if you can get a takeout vehicle into Canoe Hole and use it as a takeout, Antioch as a putin becomes highly feasible, shortening the trip to about 14 miles of technical whitewater and combining two of the best runs in the southeast (Daddys Creek Canyon and DBT to Nemo).

Obed Junction, also outside the CWMA, can serve as another alternate putin when the CWMA is closed or when Daddys Creek is too low to run. However, the road into Obed Junction is rough, possibly impassable by motor vehicle, and carrying boats the half mile to the river may be necessary.

To locate the Obed Junction access, take Genesis Road north from I-40 near Crossville. Cross over the Obed River (Adams Bridge), pass Genesis Checking Station and drive for what will seem like an eternity. About three quarters of a mile before Jett Bridge (over Clear Creek) turn right onto Plateau School Road. In about 2.5 miles look for a thicket of evergreens on road right. This is the "road" into Obed Junction.

To run the shuttle to Nemo from the alternate Obed Junction putin, drive back to Genesis Road and turn right (east). Jett Bridge is at the bottom of the hill. Continue across Jett Bridge to the TN 62 intersection. Turn right. Continue through Lancing, across the rail tracks, and up the hill. At the top of the hill (about a quarter mile past the rail crossing) take the fork to the right. It crosses the Emory River. One mile past the Emory, turn right onto old US 27 and drive

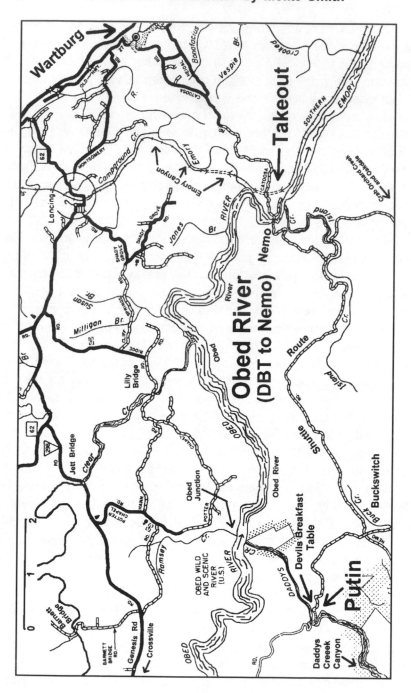

Barbara Littlefield on the Rockgarden. Obed National Wild and Scenic River. Julie Keller photo.

Julie Keller and Francis Cheung, at Diamond Splitter on the Ocoee. Jeff Peters photo.

up the mountain toward Wartburg. On the edge of Wartburg look carefully on road right for a faded sign pointing the way to "Catoosa." Turn right onto this road. Bear right after one block and then persevere. With a little luck the paved road will turn to a gravel surface and thereafter to dirt and/or mud, and then plunge downward. At the bottom of the abyss, ancient Nemo Bridge spans the Emory River. (Perhaps it has lasted so long because no one attacks it with impunity!) Access is on river left upstream of the bridge. Take care not to block other cars parked at the access. Round trip shuttle from Obed Junction to Nemo is one and one-half to two hours, depending on driving style and number of wrong turns.

Vehicles parked at Nemo Bridge and Obed Junction have been vandalized in the past. It's advisable to post sentries at both localities.

Miles From the Obed River	
Knoxville, TN 55	Atlanta, GA 215
Nashville, TN 110	Cincinnati, OH 280

Other Information

Camping

Developed campsites are available at Cumberland Mountain State Park, off US 127 about six miles south of Crossville, and at Frozen Head State Park, off TN 62 five miles east of Wartburg.

Hiking

Check with the rangers at Frozen Head State Park or at the Obed National Wild and Scenic Rivers headquarters in Wartburg.

Maps

The Obed system is compact geographically, but complex nonetheless, due to its myriad interlaced canyons. When paddling the system, a good map is a valuable asset, and they're available from the Tennessee Valley Authority (TVA) at 1101 Market Street, 101 Haney Bldg, Chattanooga, TN 37402, or phone (615) 632-6082.

Suitability for Rafting (On a 1 to 7 Scale): 6

Water availability is the biggest problem.

Wild and Scenic River Status

The Obed was one of America's first National Wild and Scenic Rivers, and is administered by the National Park Service, with an office in Wartburg.

Nearby Alternate Trips

The Obed/Emory watershed contains 18 whitewater trips. The system is described in detail in *A Paddler's Guide to the Obed/Emory Watershed,* by Monte Smith. Other Obed/Emory trips described elsewhere in the present volume are listed in the table below.

Alternate Trip	Rapids Difficulty	TRIP Points
Clear Creek	III+	97
Crab Orchard Creek	III+	98
Daddys Creek Canyon	III-IV	109
Island Creek	III-IV	108
Obed River: Goulds Bend	III(V)	95

Ocoee River

(Tennessee)

TRIP Profile			
Scale Midpoint = 100			
Overall Difficulty	104	Rapids Difficulty	110
Volume x Gradient	123	Continuous Rapids	123
Average Gradient	105	Entrapments	72
Maximum Gradient	93	Inaccessibility	65
Total Gradient	91	Reputation	117

Actual Stream Data			
Max Rapids	III+(IV)	Stream Size	Large
Average Gradient	54	Length (in miles)	5
Maximum Gradient	67	Morphology Type	2

Overview

A hundred miles due north of Atlanta, the Toccoa River creeps silently across the Tennessee state line into Polk County, where it changes its name to the Ocoee and magically slips into the skin of a cat.

A cat? The Ocoee becomes a cat?

Indeed, the Ocoee *must* be part cat. After all, only a cat has nine lives. What else can explain the fact that this river has already died twice, yet it's still alive and kicking?

The First Fatal Assault ...

... was chemical. The Ocoee flows through the copper basin, an area intensively mined for its copper ore since way back in the nineteenth century. (US 64 from Ducktown to Cleveland is still known locally as the Old Copper Road.)

In the early days, those immense copper smelters were fired with wood fuel. Over the years, their voracious appetites stripped the watershed of its trees, literally sucking up entire forests of virgin timber and belching out megatons of filth and poison in return.

As timber barons were systematically denuding the watershed of its timber, airborne sulfur dioxide, a byproduct of copper smelting, entered the atmosphere and combined with water molecules to form sulfuric acid, which then condensed every evening and early morning in the form of dew -- acid dew, that is -- poisoning and denuding the remaining undergrowth in the area and producing an environment where nothing would grow.

For years plant life was alien to the copper basin. It's red clay soil was as barren as the Sahara. Environmental degradation was so severe that the region showed blightly on satellite photographs.

With no plant life to anchor the soil, every rainstorm produced progressive soil erosion. Eventually, all topsoil washed away. The Ocoee River was laden with chemical poisons. The stream was so polluted that nothing could live in it.

That was the its first death.

The Second Assault

But some people weren't convinced that chemically dead was dead enough. After all, the river was still flowing, wasn't it? No use taking unnecessary chances. They decided to really hammer it. They dammed the river and diverted every drop of its waters into a flume that ran along the side of the gorge, up on the side of the mountain, high above the desiccated streambed.

There, that should do it! First poison it into submission. Then dam it. Then divert it. And finally, hide its carcass in a flume. Out of sight, out of mind.

And that's pretty much the way it was. For many, many years. Until . . .

. . . That Fateful Day in 1976 . . .

. . . when TVA management, which had lulled itself into a false sense of complacency, discovered that the diversion flume had

Guy and Pam Wyche ripping up Tablesaw Rapid on the Ocoee.
Don Ellis photo.

deteriorated so badly that the river had to be returned to its natural bed while they rebuilt the flume.

What they didn't anticipate at the time -- indeed what they had no way of even comprehending at the time -- was that when they let the river down off the mountain to make those flume repairs, it was tantamount to letting the proverbial cat out of the proverbial bag. The return of the natural river, notwithstanding its pitiable water quality, created seventh heaven for whitewater paddlers.

Within weeks of its return to the natural streambed, the five mile section of river below the TVA dam was attracting paddlers from all over the East. With its constant flow rate, relatively large volume, healthy gradient, and continuous waves and holes, it became practically every paddler's favorite run. It attracted a lot of attention. It was described (erroneously) as the toughest water in Tennessee. Paddlers came to the river in droves. Several rafting businesses sprang up. River use grew steadily.

All the while, however, TVA worked feverishly to restore the flume. When they finished, they diverted the river back up onto the mountainside. After protracted negotiations, an act of Congress was needed (literally) to recompense TVA for spilling water back into the natural streambed for recreational purposes. Today, an agreement is in effect that TVA will spill recreational levels of water back into the streambed on weekends, selected holidays, and other negotiated days from April to October.

The Voodoo Cadre

In the meantime, scientists were trying everything they could think of to restore plant life to the decimated copper basin: new fertilizers, specially developed plants and grasses, innovative soil treatments, imported sod, witch doctors. And at last the concerted effort began to pay dividends. (Had to have been the voodoo!) Stands of trees actually began to take root, and new grasses began to thrive.

The effect of stemming the incessant erosion was highly beneficial to Ocoee water quality. And it needed to be, for when the stream was first returned to its bed in 1976, its water quality was atrocious; it was little more than a liquified toxic waste site.

One fellow from nearby Tellico Plains who paddled the Ocoee regularly when it was first returned to its streambed kept having an earache.   When he reluctantly went in for an exam, his doctor discovered a hole in his eardrum. Acidic water from the Ocoee had literally eaten a cavity through his tympanic membrane!

Happily, water quality has improved substantially today.   The stream is often sparkling clear, although still biologically questionable.

Mile(s)	Ocoee River Top-To-Bottom Itinerary
0.0	Put in at the bottom of the ramp beside the dam alongside US 64, at the top of a Class III+ rapid called Snow White.
0.4	Gonzo Shoals (Class III).
0.8	Broken Nose (Class III+).
0.9	Second Helping (Class III).
1.4	Double Suck (Class III)
1.7	Double Trouble (Class III+).
1.9 to 2.6	Continuous Class II+ and Class III rapids.
2.6	Flipper (Class III).
3.0 to 3.4	The Doldrums.
3.9	Tablesaw (Class IV).
4.2	Diamond Splitter (Class III).
4.5	Torpedo (Class III).
4.8	Cats Pajamas (Class III).
5.0	Powerhouse (Class III+).
5.2	Take out on river right.

And now, having survived lethal chemical and mechanical assaults, the Ocoee River faces perhaps its biggest challenge: the danger of being loved to death.   As host of the 1996 Olympic whitewater events, the Ocoee will feel unprecedented pressures from its hundreds of thousands of adoring visitors, not only during the Olympics, but in succeeding years as its popularity mushrooms.

If it's past history is any indication, however, the river will come through this latest challenge roaring like the cat that it is: a big mountain lion.

Similar To. The West River in Vermont, except wider, more powerful, and (believe it or not) not quite as crowded. Not yet, anyway.

Description

The view at the putin is enough to intimidate anyone paddling the river for the first time. The water spills over the top of a high diversion dam, enters the old streambed, and blows through a rubble field of debris. It's solid white for as far downstream as you can see. Hence the name: Snow White (Class III+).

As for running the snow baby, just about any line is possible, but on your first trip, scout the rapid from the parallel highway and plan your route carefully. The general recommendation is to go with the flow and don't swim. People who swim this rapid, especially if it's their first trip on the river, have a hard time ever forgetting it.

Broken Nose (Class III+) is the next big rapid, and like so many big rapids on rivers with a parallel road, it appears where the road pulls away from the stream. Hence scouting is not convenient from the road, and is difficult from the river as well. This rapid is located on river right, separated from the rest of the stream by a demi-island. It is formed as the streamflow is constricted by the small island and dropped over two ledges. Currents here are fast and not easy to read, as they first converge and swerve forcefully toward the river right bank and then fan out and veer left over the second drop. Look for two small eddies on river right after the first drop. Catch one and catch your breath and the rest of the rapid will be a lot easier.

Double Suck is a Class III ledge with weird water and a surprisingly strong hole at the base of the drop. The rapid is clearly visible from US 64 and is a good place to hot dog for tourists. It's scoutable from the chunk of rock in midstream.

Double Trouble (Class III+) is a couple of powerful wave/holes that appear in quick succession, and was for many years a favorite play spot. Many paddlers would spend an hour or longer playing the holes and dodging river traffic. A recent flood, however, robbed the spot of some of its appeal. Double Trouble appears at the bottom of a long stretch of Class II-III water, as the river bends right. A half mile of continuous Class II-III water, ending in Flipper (Class III), follows Double Trouble.

After the Doldrums, get ready for Tablesaw (Class IV), where the stream is channeled to a narrow chute, creating the most turbulent water on the river. When the Ocoee was first returned to its natural streambed, a rock at the bottom of this chute created a dynamic "roostertail" of spray. (Hence its name, Tablesaw.) Several years later the rock shifted and the waterspout diminished substantially. The spring 1990 floods rolled the boulder farther downstream. (Although its namesake feature is now missing, the Tablesaw name seems to have survived.) To compensate for its missing "saw blade," the rapid deepened its entry hole and extended it almost across the river. Below the entry hole the rapid has two diagonal roiling waves, followed by slingshot velocity, crazy cross currents, and wave action that blasts boats toward Plymouth Rock at the bottom right.

Next, and close enough to swim through if you screw up at Tablesaw, is Diamond Splitter (Class III), where some paddlers spend half the day playing the hole on river left. The conventional run is river right of Diamond Splitter rock. Catch the eddy on the right at the top of the rock, and then run from right to left through the biggest waves. For added excitement, try catching the eddy at the base of Diamond Splitter Rock.

Torpedo (Class III) is the next major rapid. It's a sling-shot kind of affair with a micro eddy on the left midway through. This short rapid is actually more difficult at lower flows.

Just upstream of Powerhouse Pool is a Class III boulder jumble known as Cats Pajamas. Left of center is an open course with holes at the bottom, but hot doggers often head straight into the two rocks at the bottom middle of the rapid. A narrow "slot" runs diagonally between these rocks. Darting through the slot is a move called "skinning the cat." Cats Pajamas runs into a pool, the only one on the river. (The Doldrums consist of moving flat water).

Powerhouse Rapid (Class III+) is below the pool, where a bridge spans the river. Powerhouse is host to Hell Hole, another feature that has changed substantially over the years. Hell Hole ain't so hellish any more. Nonetheless, if it still looks a little like purgatory to you, skirt it by jumping into the big eddy on river left midway down the rapid.

When you leave this eddy, however, you'll want to run the last half of Powerhouse rapid on far river right. River left and river center downstream of Hell Hole is occupied by a broken ledge that creates many good spots to get trashed. If you're in the eddy on river left, the trick is to work across to river right through a strong current and catch the main tongue of water for the final drop. Regardless of how you flush through the last part of Powerhouse, there'll be plenty of agitated water, replete with waves and holes, a fitting finale for a fine river trip. The takeout is a short distance downstream on river right.

Summary

The Ocoee has a lot of whitewater action because of its healthy gradient, busy streambed, and substantial volume. Not much technical skill is required to run the river, but the waves and holes and cross currents provide plenty of excitement and can cause swims. Because of the river's size and power, and the length of some of its rapids, swims can be memorable, producing scrapes and bruises galore. Accordingly, the river lives up to much of its reputation.

If you've never ventured upon the Ocoee, here's a listing of twelve prominent features that you can expect:

1. Expect to see hordes of people at the putin. As many as 5,000 river users on a peak holiday.
2. Expect to see rafts, rafts, and more rafts.
3. And then, around the first bend . . . expect to see even more rafts!
4. Expect fast water, good gradient (54 feet/mile), constant waves and holes, turbulent rapids, and tricky crosscurrents.
5. Expect boiling, cauldron-like drops.
6. Expect a wide river bed, with several possible routes on most of the rapids. The few exceptions, like Table Saw, make for forceful chutes.

7. Except through the Doldrums, expect continuous Class II, Class III, and Class III+ rapids, with from one to three (depending on who's doing the rating) Class IVs.

8. Expect to find a parallel (and busy) US highway. (US 64, the Old Copper Road)

9. Expect absolutely no opportunity for warmup. The putin is at the top of a long, turbulent Class III+ rapid (Snow White).

10. If you swim any of the major rapids, expect to get scratched up pretty good.

11. Expect at least one nitwit tourist to yell at you from a commercial raft, "Hey! Are you Burt Reynolds?"

12. Expect lots of turkey gobble at the takeout, sometimes reaching ear-damaging decibel levels. Believe it or not, these loud squabbles are often about bragging rights to the longest swim in Ocoee history!

Water Levels

It's dam controlled, runnable only when TVA closes the diversion flume and spills water into the natural streambed. Release schedules are negotiated annually, but ordinarily include weekends and holidays from April to October. Otherwise, the stream is occasionally runnable following monsoons or whenever TVA is forced to close the flume for maintenance or repair work. Standard release is 1,250 cfs, but varies. Above 2,000 cfs it gets more interesting. During the 1990 flood the author can attest that it was run at 6,000 cfs -- and possibly at higher levels.

Access

The Ocoee headwaters are in north Georgia, where it is known as the Toccoa River. From its origin near the southern terminus of the Appalachian Trail it flows northward, crossing into Tennessee in the southeastern corner of the state (Polk County). The popular whitewater section of the Ocoee is closely paralleled by US 64, between Ducktown and Cleveland. Access points are obvious. In fact, the main challenge in getting to and from the river is beating a path through the throngs.

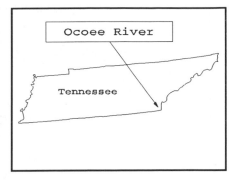

Miles From the Ocoee River	
Chattanooga, TN 54	Atlanta, GA 128
Knoxville, TN 80	Nashville, TN 187

Other Information

Camping

Thunder Rock, located behind the powerhouse upstream of the putin, is a paddler favorite. The Ocoee Wildlife Management Area is south of the Ocoee, with many roadside campsites. The Cherokee National Forest is north of the river, with several developed campgrounds, including Chilhowee. (See the map recommendation below.)

Hiking

The Cherokee National Forest is interlaced with trails. The Cohutta Wilderness is only a few miles to the south. Trails also will be found in the Ocoee Wildlife Management Area.

Maps

The best map for campground location and forest service road cruising is that of the Cherokee National Forest, published by the US Department of Agriculture. Write: Cherokee National Forest, Forest Supervisor, US Forest Service, P.O. Box 400, Cleveland, TN 37311.

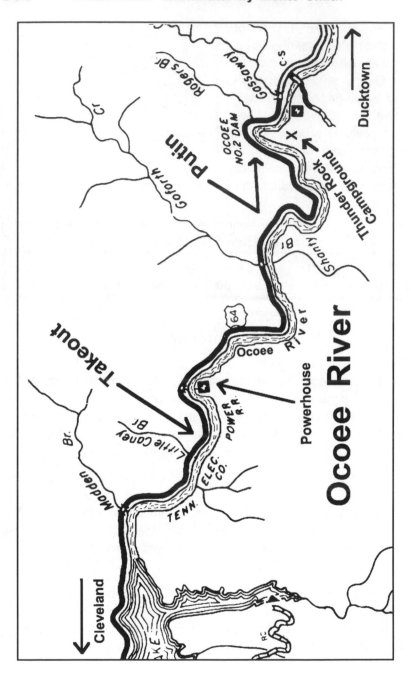

Carole Kierce and Jane Moses on the Ocoee River. What better way to celebrate a birthday? Don Ellis photo.

The Ocoee Surge

The Ocoee "surge" is experienced by positioning one's boat on the dry rocks downstream of the dam shortly before TVA turns on the water. At first, you'll feel like an absolute idiot sitting there in your boat amid the rocks, in the middle of a bone-dry river bed, trying hard to ignore the tourists who're pulling over on US 64, pointing and gawking at you, blowing their horns and laughing derisively.

But when that engineer in the powerhouse closes the flume and twelve hundred cubic feet of water every second surges over the top of the dam, the laugh's on them. The trick is to catch the crest of the first wave and ride it hell for leather as it advances down the dry streambed. This requires something akin to prescience because, perched on the downstream face of the forward-advancing wave, with tons of water bearing down from upstream, you'll be staring into a dry, rock-strewn streambed and trying to guess which of a dozen corridors the forward wave will take. A right guess keeps you on the downstream face of the advancing wave. A wrong guess can result in a lot of water crashing down on top of you.

Reading the dry streambed is kind of a knack. Some paddlers have it; others don't. And it doesn't take long to figure out which group you're in. Those without the knack seldom try this stunt a second time.

Suitability for Rafting (On a 1 to 7 Scale): 7

Rafting Nirvana. Numerous commercial outfitters are located along US 64. Contact the Cleveland or Ducktown Chamber of Commerce for the latest phone numbers and other information.

Nearby Alternate Trips

Alternate Trip	Rapids Difficulty	TRIP Points
Chattooga Section III	III(IV)	86
Chattooga Section IV	IV(V)	116
Conasauga	II	72
Hiwassee	II	70
Upper Tellico	III-IV	110
Lower Tellico	III	96

Piney River

(Tennessee)

TRIP Profile			
Scale Midpoint = 100			
Overall Difficulty	131	Rapids Difficulty	133
Volume x Gradient	111	Continuous Rapids	135
Average Gradient	123	Entrapments	151
Maximum Gradient	131	Inaccessibility	137
Total Gradient	174	Reputation	117

Actual Stream Data			
Max Rapids	III-IV	Stream Size	Micro-Small
Average Gradient	73	Length (in miles)	11
Maximum Gradient	120	Morphology Type	3

Overview

Piney River is born atop the Cumberland Plateau. When it pours over the edge, it drops 800 feet in eleven river miles, splashing down near Spring City, Tennessee. It runs through terrain so rough and remote that trying to bushwhack through it is a lesson in humility. This little wildcat of a river screams down these eleven miles and is still kicking when it reaches the takeout at Shut-in Gap Road.

The Piney is tiny at the putin, but two miles downstream it merges with Moccasin Creek and commences an act of dazzling whitewater legerdemain. From Moccasin Creek it's practically a single rapid over eight miles long. Admittedly, some sections are more precipitous than others, but the entire distance is rapid. Sometimes very rapid. Expect three waterfalls (from six to eight feet high), one Class IV+ rapid, a number of IV- rapids if the bridge gauge is reading over

3.0 feet, and innumerable Class IIIs. Undercut rocks abound, and hence the Class IIIs are not ordinary rapids in any sense of the word. They often harbor potential undercut entrapments. In case of mishap, access points are few and hard to locate. The canyon is 600 feet deep in places.

Similar To. The Piney is a blend of the Chauga Gorge, Crooked Fork Creek, and Daddys Creek Canyon. Its falls aren't as high as on Crooked Fork or the Chauga, but the gradient is unremitting with four continuous miles at 100 feet/mile or better.

Mile(s)	Piney River Top-To-Bottom Itinerary
0.0	Put in atop the Cumberland Plateau.
0.0 to 0.7	Mostly flat.
0.8 to 2.3	Snappish micro creek, with gradient steadily increasing until it is 100 feet/mile at the juncture with . . .
2.3	Moccasin Creek, where snappish creek becomes wildcat micro river and tumbles into Piney Gorge.
2.4	Guardian Falls (Class III-), a seven foot sheer drop.
2.4 to 6.4	Four miles of pure screaming hair. The gradient never ebbs below 100 feet/mile. Continuous Class III(IV) rapids.
4.5	Signal Falls (Class III). Riverwide falls in the middle of the steepest gradient.
4.7	NoMistake (Class IV+). Aka Rocker Knocker.
5.8	Hungry Jack (Class III+)
6.5	Emergency access, river right. Not well marked.
6.5 to 11.0	Class III(III+) rapids.
7.5	Duskin Creek. River left.
8.5	Suspension footbridge over river.
11.0	Take out at or below the bridge on river right.

Description

Don't make the serious mistake of judging the Piney by its appearance at the putin, where it's so narrow you can spit across it. Literally. Despite its scrawny appearance, this river contains a lot of whitewater. It also has plenty of undercuts, and the most total drop of any run described in this book.

The first mile is mostly flat, but the gradient builds steadily until it's dropping at the rate of 100 feet/mile when Moccasin Creek contributes its volume and the combined flow pitches into a gorge with a decided tilt. The bottom seems to drop out, starting with Guardian Falls (Class III-), a seven foot drop around a boulder positioned in midstream. Run left, and get ready for four miles of nonstop Class III(IV) intensity. At moderate flows everything is manageable. But as the water rises, get ready for a nonstop adrenalin rush. These miles don't wait downstream for you to arrive, they come screaming upstream to greet you. Watch for logjams as you negotiate drop after undercut drop through a narrow, steep corridor with pell mell rush and few eddies. At higher water, these miles are intensely pushy.

In the first four miles below Guardian Falls, expect two more waterfalls of the five to eight foot variety, two or more Class IV congested rapids if the flow is over 3.0 feet, one Class IV+ rock jumble, and continuous technical Class IIIs. These rapids are manageable individually, but the Piney doesn't serve them individually. They come tightly bunched in two's, and three's, and six-packs. Be prepared to run quarter mile bursts of continuous blind screaming Class III drops without eddies. Be prepared to run these tight, twisting, serpentine concourses with flawless execution. Give this small wildcat of a river its due respect and you'll be a happier camper at day's end.

Signal Falls (Class III+), the most visually impressive waterfall on the run, appears in the midst of the hoariest section of whitewater, where a big rock demi-island forces most water river right into a sloping, curving sluice reminiscent of Island Creek or Crooked Fork Creek morphology. Thirty feet upstream of the drop an angled curler slings boats hard to the right side of this riverwide drop of about six to eight vertical feet. The drop's real significance is neither its difficulty nor its beauty, both of which are substantial, but rather its role as landmark. (Hence its name, Signal Falls.) It signals that the next rapid downstream is NoMistake (aka Rocker Knocker), the toughest rapid on the run. Class IV at lower water, NoMistake becomes a real problem when the takeout bridge gauge reads over 3.0 feet. From upstream it appears to be just another blind drop around a boulder obstruction, but it's that and something more. Scout from river left.

(For the story of how this rapid was named, see Rocker Knocker Rapid in *River Stories: Tales From Bo Rockerville,* by Monte Smith, available from Pahsimeroi Press.)

The other well known rapid is Hungry Jack, which marks the beginning of the end of the pure screaming hair section. Just downstream of Hungry Jack is a rapid with an undercut rock wall on the right. Below here the intensity moderates substantially, but five miles of Class II-III water remain with a gradient always in excess of 50 feet/mile and with brief spurts back into the range of 80 feet/mile. Rapids in the last five miles are still technical, but they're boulevards compared with the four miles below Guardian Falls. Undercut rocks are, however, still in abundance.

About 4.5 miles above the takeout a 4WD access can be located on river right, providing an emergency egress. From this trailhead, which is not easy to spot from the river, it's about a mile to the top of the gorge, fifty feet across the ridge top, and then two miles down the side of the Cumberland escarpment to Ideal Valley Road.

Downstream of the emergency egress, it's another mile to Duskin Creek, on river left. Past Duskin, a maintained trail runs along river left about a half mile to a footbridge where the trail crosses over to river right and ascends the ridge. The trail doesn't return to the river until downstream of the takeout parking lot. In its last mile or two, the Piney calms down to a relatively unassuming Class II pace.

Summary

Few rivers have such intensity. It's a hair run above 3.0 feet on the takeout gauge. If you have trouble, don't expect anybody to march to the rescue. The surrounding terrain isn't conducive to rescue marches. In the pure screaming hair section, there are no established trails in or out of the gorge, and bushwhacking is a nightmare.

Water Levels

The nearest telemetric gauge is the Emory at Oakdale, which needs to read at least 3,000 cfs before the Piney is likely to have enough water for a trip. (Call (800) 238-2264 and press code "3" after the recorded message.) This is a crude predictor, however, and local rainfall patterns can be deceptive. A gauge is painted on a pylon at the Shut-in-Gap Road Bridge (river left).

Piney River Gauge Location Shut-in-Gap Road
Low: 2.0 Medium: 2.5 High: 3.0

(Eugene (Bo) Rocker once developed a prediction equation for estimating Piney River volume. Bo originally published his findings, entitled Predicting Water Volume from Afar, in the prestigious *Behavior Homoautomobilus Journal*. Highlights of his research, and of the controversy it generated in the scientific community, especially those with direct implications for Piney paddlers, can be found in *River Stories: Tales From Bo Rockerville*, by Monte Smith, available from Pahsimeroi Press.)

Access

The takeout is at the Shut-in Gap Road bridge near Spring City, on the way to Stinging Fork Pocket Wilderness. To reach the takeout from Spring City, take TN 68 north toward Crossville and Cumberland Mountain State Park. On the northern outskirts of town, about a block south of the Piney River bridge, turn left onto Shut-in Gap Road and drive to the first and only bridge.

The putin is reached via the community of "Old" Evensville, located 9.9 miles south

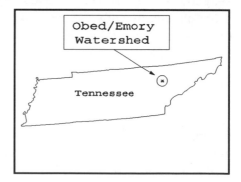

of the center of Spring City, or 7.2 miles south of the US 27/TN 68 intersection, or about one mile south of the "New" Evensville Post Office. Turn right onto the "loop" at old Evensville, cross the railroad tracks, go through the community and in one mile locate a four-way intersection. Continue through the intersection, which is tantamount to continuing straight up the side of the Cumberland escarpment. In 2.7 miles, at the crest of the escarpment, bear right at the fork and continue four miles to the first bridge. Believe it or not, this small rivulet is the Piney River. A one way shuttle is twenty miles and takes about forty minutes.

Miles From Piney Tavern	
Chattanooga, TN 55	Nashville, TN 145
Knoxville, TN 65	Atlanta, GA 6180

Other Information

Bridges

Bridges, like everything else, are replaceable. The present takeout bridge on Shut-in-Gap Road replaced one that had served for nearly forty years. The new bridge works well, facilitating transportation. But progress has its price. The sad thing about the new bridge is that it destroyed an irreplaceable wildlife habitat.

For many years the old bridge served as the sole domicile for a local wild man. He ate dogs and road kill and whatever else he could scavenge (and maybe an occasional kayaker too, judging from his breath), and he used to get mad as hell whenever the water would come up and excited paddlers would scramble down the bank, peer intently in the direction of his lair (in order to check the gauge), and then break into hoots of uncontrolled merriment. It got to where the poor man dreaded to see rain clouds approaching -- for he knew a slew of paddlers couldn't be far behind. He never figured out that the paddlers clambered down the bank to look at the gauge, not to spy on him and his inimitable lifestyle. The wild man thought they came around after every heavy rain specifically to hoot at him and make his life a little more miserable.

Admittedly, that wild man -- after years of abuse from the likes of Eugene (Bo) Rocker and the Dickson Decked Boaters -- was capable of some hootin' of his own. (When the bridge demolition crew arrived, he was convinced they worked for Bo Rocker! But that's another story.)

Unfortunately, the new bridge that they constructed on the same site never lived up to the wild man's expectations. (There was something about the smell of fresh concrete that he didn't like.) A significant element of local color was lost when the wild man took up residence elsewhere.

(Fortunately, he didn't move far. According to Bo Rocker -- who somehow always knows about things like this -- the wild man moved into the attic at Piney Tavern, at which venerable establishment he also works as bouncer. And yes, you guessed it. Further details are available in *River Stories: Tales From Bo Rockerville,* by Monte Smith, available from Pahsimeroi Press.)

Camping

Newby Branch Forest Camp can be reached by continuing across the bridge at the takeout and up the escarpment. Turn left in 6.3 miles and go another 0.7 miles to the camp. Primitive camping, but an okay place. Fifteen minutes from the takeout.

Hot showers are available at Cumberland Mountain State Park, located five miles south of Crossville on US 127. Take TN 68 north out of Spring City. Drive about twenty miles to the southern outskirts of Crossville and turn left onto US 127. The park is one quarter mile on the right, about thirty minutes from the Piney River takeout.

Hiking

Both day hiking and overnight backpacking trails are nearby.

Twin Rocks Overlook. An easy 2.5 mile hike from the takeout picnic area to Twin Rocks, an overlook providing panoramic vistas of both the Piney gorge and the Great Valley of the Tennessee.

Stinging Fork Pocket Wilderness. A moderate three mile hike. The trailhead is reached by continuing five miles across the Piney River on Shut-in-Gap Road to a parking area on the right.

Piney River Trail. This trail begins at the takeout picnic area and heads upstream, paralleling the river (on river right) for three miles to a suspension bridge. After crossing the river it parallels the Piney on the other side (river left) until Duskin Creek. It then follows Duskin Creek to the Newby Branch Forest Camp, for a total length of ten miles. A good weekend backpacking trail, with attractive campsites along Piney River and Duskin Creek.

Maps

USGS: Pennine 118 NW, Evensville 118 SW. The Pennine USGS quad is a recommended companion for a trip down the Piney. Use the Evensville quad to help locate the putin.

Nearby Alternate Trips

When the Piney River is running, the rest of the lower Tennessee Cumberland Plateau is likely to be overflowing with paddling opportunities. For hair crazies, the Caney Fork Gorge (Class IV-V) is less than an hour from the Piney and almost surely has water if the Piney is runnable. The entire Obed/Emory system, with over a dozen trips, is less than an hour's drive north on TN 68, and the Tellico is about an hour's drive south on TN 68. If the Piney is running real high, nearby Whites Creek, a premier Cumberland Plateau Class II-III trip, is probably also runnable.

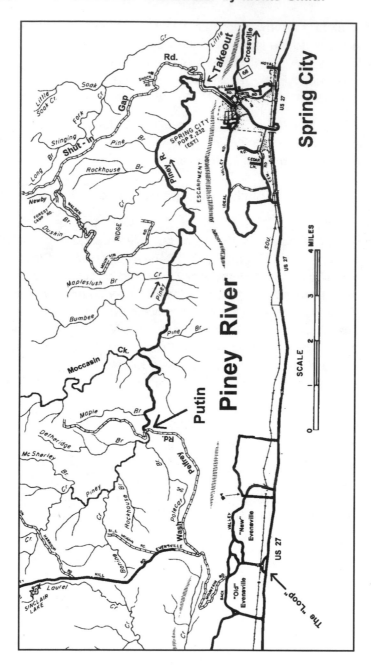

Seneca Creek

(West Virginia)

TRIP Profile			
Scale Midpoint = 100			
Overall Difficulty	89	Rapids Difficulty	76
Volume x Gradient	79	Continuous Rapids	99
Average Gradient	117	Entrapments	72
Maximum Gradient	106	Inaccessibility	74
Total Gradient	116	Reputation	72

Actual Stream Data			
Max Rapids	II(III)	Stream Size	Micro
Average Gradient	67	Length (in miles)	6
Maximum Gradient	85	Morphology Type	1

Overview

Seneca Creek is a tiny, fast-flowing stream that cascades from the highlands around Spruce Knob (highest point in West Virginia), flows through farmland, and empties into the North Fork of the South Branch of the Potomac River in the shadows of Seneca Rocks, near the intersection of US 33 and WV 28 southwest of Petersburg, West Virginia. Because the shuttle road is parallel and stream velocity is fast, Seneca Creek can be run two or three times in the same day, or it and another local stream, such as Hopeville Canyon or Moorefield Gorge, can be run in the same day. Unfortunately, this run is possible only after heavy rains on Spruce Knob.

Similar To. Seneca Creek is similar to the Farmington River in Connecticut, although only about one-third the size. On both

401

streams an overall healthy gradient is distributed evenly over the course of a mostly open streambed, producing continuous high velocity conditions but few big rapids.

Mile(s)	Seneca Creek Top-To-Bottom Itinerary
0.0	Put in at the washed-out National Forest Campground on Route 7.
3.0	Onego
3.1	Farmers Bridge Rapid (Class III).
6.0	Takeout near confluence with North Fork of the South Branch.

Description

The distinguishing characteristic of Seneca Creek is its constant velocity. It moves along, with the first four miles clocking in at 74 feet/mile. Because the gradient is so evenly distributed and the streambed morphology is for the most part Type 1 (predominantly clear of obstructions), there are few major rapids. There are, however, miles of waves and holes. As the water rises, moreover, the little stream becomes a real flush and the hole at Farmers Bridge deserves inspection. (This drop can be scouted from the side of US 33.) Farmers Rapid is not much at low to medium flows but at flush it forms a recirculating hydraulic because of its U-shaped ledge. Prior to the flood of '85 the highlight of a Seneca Creek run was Junkyard (Class III), but the flood moved the Junkyard somewhere downstream.

The gradient moderates toward the bottom of the run, slowing to a mere 47 feet/mile in the last three miles. The run ends with an unforgettable view of Seneca Rocks. Look closely and you may spot climbers on the massive rock face.

Summary

It's hard to plan a trip on Seneca Creek. But if you're in the Potomac headwaters and there's plenty of water, give Seneca Creek a try. Although tiny, there's never a dull moment.

Water Levels

The Petersburg gauge is a rough indicator. Seneca Creek is only a fraction of the flow as measured at Petersburg and hence discrepancies often exist between gauge readings and actual stream conditions. Generally, about 3.5 on the Petersburg gauge indicates that Seneca may be runnable, and 6.0 feet suggests that it definitely is. Phone (703) 260-0305.

Access

To reach the putin from Seneca Rocks (the intersection of US 33 and WV 28), take US 33 six miles east and turn left on Route 7. Put in at Seneca Campground. The shuttle is along Route 7 and US 33, both of which parallel the creek, although sometimes at a distance.

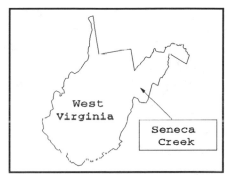

Take out at the confluence with the North Fork of the South Branch near Seneca Rocks.

Miles From Seneca Creek	
Washington, DC 140	Pittsburgh, PA 225
Roanoke, VA 180	Columbus, OH 275

Other Information

Camping

Seneca Creek Campground is at the putin. A commercial campground is available at the takeout near the confluence of Seneca Creek and the North Fork of the South Branch of the Potomac. Smoke Hole and Big Bend campgrounds are located in the Smoke Hole area of Seneca Rocks National Recreation Area. Dolly Sods campground is about fifteen miles north. Judy Springs and Spruce Knob Lake campgrounds are in the Spruce Knob National Recreation Area about twenty-five miles southwest. Island Creek, an undeveloped National Forest Service campground, is located about thirty miles south on WV 28 on the Greenbrier River.

Maps

Get a copy of The Monongahela National Forest map, available from: The US Forest Service, US Department of Agriculture, Elkins, West Virginia. Phone: (304) 636-1800. The aforementioned campgrounds, as well as other area attractions, can be located with this map.

Nearby Alternate Trips

North Fork of the South Branch of the Potomac from Seneca Creek to Hopeville Canyon (Class I-II).

Hopeville Canyon on the North Fork of the South Branch (Class II-III).

South Branch of the Potomac, known as the Smoke Hole run (Class II-III).

Moorefield Gorge on the South Fork of the South Branch of the Potomac (Class III).

The Cheat Watershed begins on the west side of Spruce Knob.

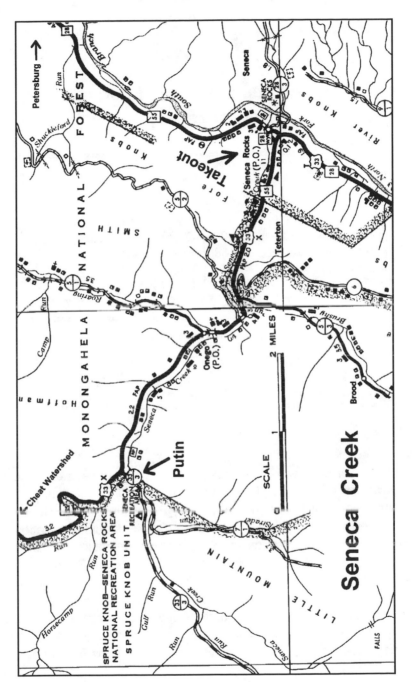

Tellico River

Upper Section: The "Ledges"
(Tennessee)

TRIP Profile			
Scale Midpoint = 100			
Overall Difficulty	110	Rapids Difficulty	97
Volume x Gradient	88	Continuous Rapids	123
Average Gradient	158	Entrapments	117
Maximum Gradient	138	Inaccessibility	65
Total Gradient	85	Reputation	117

Actual Stream Data			
Max Rapids	IV(V)	Stream Size	Small
Average Gradient	110	Length (in miles)	2
Maximum Gradient	130	Morphology Types	2&3

Overview

Scenic crown jewel of Tennessee mountain streams, the Tellico's headwaters are near the Tennessee-North Carolina state line on the western edge of the highest, most rugged section of the Unakas, only a few miles southwest of the Great Smoky Mountains National Park. From these lofty origins the small stream plummets to the Great Valley of the Tennessee, with Tellico River Road closely paralleling the stream from its inception until it reaches the valley, twenty-five scenic miles downstream, on the outskirts of Tellico Plains. Were it not for this parallel road, the Tellico would be a whispered legend among paddlers, something on the order of the Caney Fork Gorge. Few other rivers crowd so many fine runnable

406

ledges and exciting rapids into so few miles, as found on its upper section. If this stream ran through an isolated gorge, it would be attempted by very few paddlers and its reputation for difficult whitewater would equal or surpass that of the Watauga Gorge.

The most popular paddling section of the Tellico begins about half way down the mountainside at the first bridge upstream of Bald River Falls and continues seven miles to the juncture of Tellico River Road and the Tellico-Robbinsville transmountain highway. Although "only" seven miles in length, this section is usually broken into two runs, the first consisting of only two miles. Local paddlers refer to the top two miles as the "upper" or "ledges" run, and the bottom five miles as the "lower" or "Ranger Station" run, because its takeout is near the Cherokee National Forest Ranger Station. The upper and lower sections are described separately herein because that is how most paddlers experience them, at least initially.

With "only" seven miles of river, why are the two sections usually run separately? Because . . .

1. The upper section is steep and chock-full of major rapids and waterfalls. Most paddlers require several hours to scout and paddle these two miles. For many paddlers, the first two miles are a full day's enjoyment.

2. The lower section also is chock-full of good rapids, challenging in their own right but decidedly milder in character than those upstream. The lower five miles is a favorite of many paddlers who would never consider running the upper section.

Some paddlers, however, combine the two sections into one run, and for this reason all rating scales in Chapter Three contain three Tellico entries: one for the upper Tellico, one for the lower Tellico, and a third rating for the two sections combined.

Similar To. The series of ledges on the upper two miles are rather unique in the Southeast. Otherwise, the Tellico is an equal-parts admixture of two of West Virginia's finest: the Cranberry and the Laurel Fork of the Cheat. It has the gradient of either West Virginia stream, and a level of technicality about mid-way between them. For scenery, however, the Tellico is peerless.

Mile(s)	Upper Tellico Top-To-Bottom Itinerary
0.0	Put in at the first bridge upstream of Bald River Falls.
0.1	Top Ledge, a six foot river-wide Class III+ waterfall with an obstructed Class III approach.
0.3	Dirty S, a twisting S-shaped Class III+ drop over a jagged ledge.
0.5	Middle Ledge, a slanting eight foot Class III+ waterfall.
0.6	Cry!Baby, a Class III+ with pinning potential.
0.7	Baby Falls, a 14 foot Class V waterfall which, at higher flow levels, will recycle and thrash boaters caught in its backwash. It has a difficult approach and an inhospitable washout.
0.8	Diaper Wiper (Class IV), the washout for Baby Falls, replete with pinning opportunities.
1.0	Bald River Falls, an 80 foot plummet on river left.
1.0	Bald River Rapid, a Class III- just below Bald River confluence.
1.6	Approach to Jerrods Knee, Class III+, consisting of three Class III rapids jammed together into a series of twisting, churning troughs through strange, diagonal rock formations.
1.8	Jerrods Knee, a fast-moving double-drop Class IV. Becomes Class V at high levels. Undercut rock on river left of last big drop.
2.0	Takeout bridge for the upper (ledges) run, and putin for the lower run.

Description

The utility of a parallel scouting road is nowhere better demonstrated than on the upper Tellico. Without the easy reconnoitering afforded by the parallel road, the two mile ledges run would take the better part of a day, much of it expended in bank-scouting rapids that from upstream look as if they drop into a bottomless abyss. With the road, however, all major drops can be scouted during the drive upstream to the putin.

Put in above the first bridge upstream of Bald River Falls. Line up right of the midstream pylon and get ready. From this point, the next pool of substantial length is two miles downstream, at the bottom of Jerrods Knee. Immediately past the bridge is a rocky Class III with no good route through it. Pick the best route depending on water level. It's runnable either left or right, but it's bumpy and fast-moving either way, ending at the brink of Top Ledge (Class III+), a six foot sheer, river-wide waterfall with a short recovery pool. At high flows Top Ledge forms a hazardous, river-wide hydraulic. At lower levels it's a piece of cake. The best point to run is usually just about midstream, for optimal use of the short recovery pool.

Fast-moving Class II water leads to Dirty S, an uneven ledge that requires an "S" shaped maneuver. (It's runnable straight over the left side at 700+ cfs). Dirty S is generally less difficult and more forgiving than it appears, but the right side is occasionally clogged with logs. Scout from the left bank.

One half mile below the putin the Tellico offers a second waterfall, Middle Ledge (Class III+), an eight foot drop. Best scouted from the rock outcropping at the base of the falls on river left, where the best route (a diagonal tongue running from left to right) can be seen clearly. From upstream, look for a small curler that marks the edge of the diagonal tongue. This drop is a little unnerving because to run it correctly, you want to let the water pivot your boat on the lip of the falls, from straight downstream into a 45 degree angle toward the river right bank. The pitfall is the ease with which the pivot can continue too far, pitching boats under the waterfall. Rescues are most easily accomplished from river right at the base of the falls.

Cry!Baby (Class III+) appears at the end of a long bend in the river. On the left (but barely discernable from river level) is a vehicular pullover beside Tellico River Road. It's possible to take out here and portage and/or scout Baby Falls, which is 75 yards downstream. Cry!Baby is a congestion of rocks, with pinning possibilities on river right. With adequate water, the best route consists of threading through the rock jumble on river left. Special caution is appropriate because Class V Baby Falls is only a short distance downstream. At high water the distance is short indeed!

Once through Cry!Baby, Truth or Consequences eddy on river left permits scouting of Baby Falls. This micro eddy is at the top of a jumble of rocks that form the entry to the falls. Miss Truth or Consequences eddy, and Baby Falls and Diaper Wiper are imminent stops on the itinerary.

Scout the Baby from river left. Throw ropes are best positioned, however, at the base of the falls on river right. Baby Falls changes character significantly at high water. With increased flows an hydraulic develops which can thrash boaters. (It's possibly a double hydraulic, with the second one forming underneath the cap rock at the base of the falls.) The best place to run the falls is right of center. The drop is clean on that side and wet exits/upsets tend to wash into the river right eddy at the base of the falls.

Portages are possible from Truth or Consequences eddy above the falls on river left by lowering boats with rope into the pool below the big drop. Many people, however, take out above upstream Cry!Baby and use Tellico River Road to portage around Baby Falls. The problem with this longer portage is how to get back to the river. And where? Above or below Diaper Wiper (Class IV), the washout to Baby Falls?

(An account of the only known successful tandem canoe run of Baby Falls appears in *River Stories: Tales From Bo Rockerville,* by Monte Smith, available from Pahsimeroi Press.)

As if the Baby itself weren't enough excitement, the Class IV washout at the base of the falls is brimming with boat pinning opportunities. Diaper Wiper is a wide (by Tellico standards) river-wide slide that drops the river some 20 feet. There is no good way to run Diaper Wiper. Because of obstacles in the middle and on the right side of the slide, the lesser evil is tight left, down a shallow slide into a sluice which turns 90 degrees right and drops through a rock garden.

From downstream, the combined 35 foot drop of Baby Falls and Diaper Wiper form an impressive vista. Interestingly, some paddlers run the fourteen foot Baby Falls drop and then portage around Diaper Wiper. Others portage the falls and run the Wiper! Different strokes for different folks.

After Diaper Wiper, five hundred yards of non-stop technical Class II water brings the bridge over Bald River into view on river left. Behind the bridge is Bald River Falls, an 80 foot plummet. The Bald River confluence serves as an alternate putin for those who enjoy high gradient technical rapids but wish to avoid waterfalls. Just below the confluence, a Class III- appears. The next half mile is continuous technical Class II.

When the river makes a sharp left turn around a roadside parking area, its character changes. This is a good place to stop and scout Jerrods Knee, and its approach, which consists of three closely spaced rapids. The first rapid is easy, with a small eddy on river right. It will seem distinct, however, because it's definitely bigger than anything in the preceding half mile. Entry rapid #2 consists of a series of complex, technical troughs through strange, diagonal rock formations. Entry rapid #3, the toughest of the trio, is an obstructed chute requiring a ninety degree right turn at the bottom. Be sure to catch the eddy on river right at the bottom of entry rapid #3, because Jerrods Knee is the next stop on this downhill tour and it makes the entry trio look like child's play. At lower water the three entry rapids can be negotiated, more or less, individually. Somewhere around 600 cfs they blend together, forming one long, bony "entry."

Below the entry trio a change in river tenor occurs. The stream-bed funnels all water into a turbulent, multiple-drop, fast-moving, zig-zag courseway called Jerrods Knee, a Class IV that becomes outrageous at high water. At levels above 700 cfs it's a moot point trying to separate the approach from the main rapid, and this whole frothing mess, from the bend at the top to below Jerrods Knee, becomes a quarter mile of high difficulty intensity. At 700 cfs it's still high-level Class IV, but the transformation to Class V occurs somewhere in the 700 to 1100 cfs range. The left side of the last big drop harbors an undercut, made all the worse because it seems innocuous on first inspection. A short pool below Jerrods Knee leads to the takeout bridge for the upper run and the putin for the lower.

Summary

The upper two miles on the Tellico River is a non-stop adrenalin rush, with outstanding ledges (one of them fourteen feet), technical rapids, and an abundance of scenic beauty. At least three rapids deserve careful scouting: Baby Falls, Diaper Wiper, and Jerrods Knee (including its approach).

Water Levels

Zero level is around 200 cfs, and about 400 to 600 cfs is a good range for either section of the Tellico. Over 700 cfs is appropriate only for advanced paddlers, and when the gauge reaches 1,250 cfs it's time to check out nearby Citico Creek. The gauge, located on river right a few miles downstream of the whitewater section on the outskirts of Tellico Plains, can be accessed via TVA's recording: (800) 238-2264. Press code "3" during or after the initial message.

Access

The Tellico River is located near Tellico Plains in east Tennessee, northeast of Chattanooga and southeast of Knoxville. It's not easy to find, but it's worth the effort. The easiest route is to locate TN 68 (it intersects I-75 and US 411) which runs near Tellico Plains. Exit TN 68 and drive into Tellico Plains. Once downtown, take the left fork (TN 165) and follow it a quarter mile to the Tellico River. At the bridge, take the right fork (continuing on TN 165) and head upstream on river left. In four miles look for the Oosterneck parking area on the right. This is the takeout for the lower run. At Oosterneck the road forks again. The left fork becomes

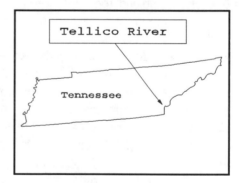

the Tellico/Robbinsville trans-mountain highway heading to Indian Boundary and points east. The right fork is Tellico River Road and closely parallels the river to its origin near the Tennessee-North Carolina border high in the mountains. Drive up the river road to scout rapids. Put in anywhere alongside the road, wherever stream conditions look most inviting. For the upper run, put in at the first

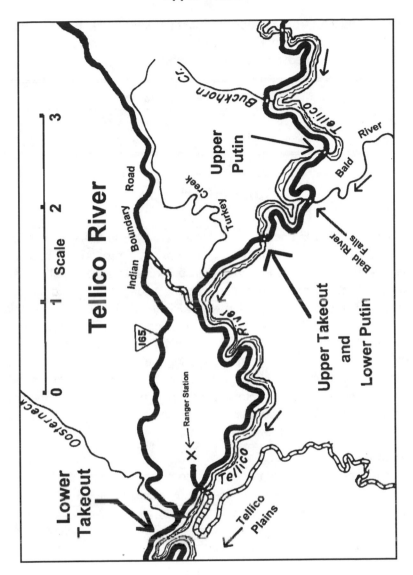

bridge upstream of Bald River Falls (seven miles from Oosterneck) in order to catch all the action, and take out whenever the fun isdone. Some people use the bridge at Bald River Falls as an alternate putin to avoid the upstream waterfalls. The most common starting points for the lower section are at the bridge 200 yards below Jerrods Knee or at Turkey Creek (one mile below Jerrods

Knee). Take out at the aforementioned Oosterneck parking area. Shuttles are on Tellico River Road. Shuttles can be walked, in a pinch, or hitch-hiked by the adventurous.

Miles From Tellico Plains			
Knoxville, TN	 70	Asheville, NC	 125
Chattanooga, TN	 78	Nashville, TN	 201

Other Information

Camping

Car camping is unsurpassed. Nowhere else in eastern America can one enjoy such outstanding campsites from an automobile. Stop at the ranger station near Tellico Plains and buy a Cherokee National Forest map. Any campground along the Tellico is gorgeous. The same goes for the North River. Or Holly Flats on Bald River way up near Wacheesie. Or Doublecamp Creek Campground on Citico Creek. Or the Indian Boundary overflow. And a lot of others. The area is becoming more popular, not only with river lovers but also with day hikers, picnickers, backpackers, hunters, off-road vehicle drivers, mountain bikers, and equestrians. Generally speaking, however, good campsites will be available except on July Fourth and Labor Day weekends.

Fishing

This area offers some of the best trout fishing east of the Rockies. In addition to the Tellico, three other premier trout streams are nearby: Bald River, Citico Creek, and North River. Bald River and North River are Tellico tributaries. A trout hatchery is located on the upper, upper Tellico and used to stock the Tellico, Citico, and North River.

High Country Car Tours

For those who enjoy exploring mountain back roads, the Tellico region is a veritable mecca, the best southeastern America has to offer. Be sure to drive up Wacheesie Mountain (if the road is passable; otherwise hike it), and don't miss the Tellico-Robbinsville trans-mountain highway. Then there's the road over Indian Boundary to the Citico country. Wherever you go, take binoculars, a compass and every available map. From the heights of the trans-mountain highway (TN 165), depending on weather conditions, one can often see clear across the Great Valley of the Tennessee, north to Harriman at the bottom of the Obed/Emory watershed, and at night across the spangle of valley communities. Time permitting, check out Coker Creek, scene of one of America's first gold rushes; Joyce Kilmer, with perhaps the most easily accessible first growth forest remaining in the Southeast; and the Great Smoky Mountains, only a few miles northeast.

Hiking

For an outstanding day hike, walk up the Bald River Trail, beginning at the falls; or run a shuttle and walk downstream on the same trail from Holly Flats to Bald River Falls. Or walk to the Bobs Bald-Naked Ground high country from near Beech Gap on the Tellico-Robbinsville trans-mountain highway. Or up to Hangover Lead from Big Fat Gap (both of which were named for Bo Rocker!). Joyce Kilmer and Slickrock wildernesses, both adjacent to the Tellico high country, contain backpacking trails. The terrain is similar to the Great Smoky Mountains National Park, but with only a fraction of the trail usage.

History

The spiritual homeland of the Cherokee Nation was along the Tellico River, in a section of the Great Valley which the Indians called Tanasi, near the confluence of the Tellico and the Little Tennessee. The site is under water now, thanks to avaricious Tennessee politicians and their beloved Tellico Dam.

Lodging

Rental cabins are available on the outskirts of Tellico Plains and possibly at Green Cove, near the Tellico headwaters.

Maps

The National Forest Service publishes an excellent map of the Cherokee National Forest.

Suitability for Rafting (On a 1 to 7 Scale): 0

    Baby Falls would not be fun in a raft. Generally, the stream is too technical for rafts. The Nantahala Outdoor Center occasionally holds kayak and canoe clinics on the Tellico, but otherwise, commercial activity is rare. Traipse to the Ocoee, about 20 miles southwest for commercial raft trips.

Nearby Alternate Trips		
Alternate Trip	Rapids Difficulty	TRIP Points
Citico Creek	III(IV)	101
Hiwassee River	II	70
Upper Little River	III(IV)	95
Lower Little River	III(IV)	103
Obed (Goulds Bend)	III(V)	95
Ocoee River	III-IV	104
Piney River	III-IV	131

Tellico River

Lower Section: The Ranger Station Run (Tennessee)

TRIP Profile			
Scale Midpoint = 100			
Overall Difficulty	96	Rapids Difficulty	88
Volume x Gradient	91	Continuous Rapids	111
Average Gradient	101	Entrapments	117
Maximum Gradient	103	Inaccessibility	65
Total Gradient	88	Reputation	105

Actual Stream Data			
Max Rapids	III	Stream Size	Small
Average Gradient	50	Length (in miles)	5
Maximum Gradient	80	Morphology Type	2

Overview

Gradient in excess of 100 feet/mile spells hair water, and that's what to expect on the upper Tellico. Gradient of 50 feet/mile spells controlled excitement, and that's exactly what to expect on the lower Tellico.

Significantly less difficult than the two mile upper section, the lower Tellico is an ideal Class II-III technical whitewater stream. Its overall gradient of 50 feet/mile produces continuous rapids amidst outstanding scenery, with a parallel road. And it's predictable: drive upstream on the parallel road and the gradient increases; drive downstream and it decreases. The procedure is simple: drive along

Tellico River Road, select a stretch that looks most appealing, put your boat in the water, put yourself in your boat, and take off.

The mile-by-mile gradient story looks like this:

Upper Tellico Gradient	Lower Tellico Gradient
Mile 1: 120 Mile 2: 100	Mile 3: 80 Mile 4: 53 Mile 5: 45 Mile 6: 40 Mile 7: 32

The average gradient on the lower section, 50 feet/mile, is almost equal to that of the Ocoee, but unlike its big cousin a few miles to the south, gradient on the Tellico is not distributed uniformly. The first mile drops at the healthy rate of 80 feet, producing some fast-moving, challenging whitewater. Some paddlers elect to skip most of the first mile and put in at Turkey Creek, for a four mile run with an average gradient of 43 feet/mile.

Mile(s)	Lower Tellico Top-To-Bottom Itinerary
0.0	Put in at the bridge 200 yards downstream of Jerrods Knee.
0.0	Putin Rapid, a rocky, technical Class III.
0.1	Ledges (Class III).
0.4	Judging Rock (Class III). Aka Bounce-off-Boulder or Keyhole.
0.8	Turkey Creek, alternate putin.
1.7	Crack-in-the-Rock, technical Class III.
2.5	Gregs Nose (Class III).
3.2	Submarine (Class III-).
3.4	Pylon Rapid (Class III-).
3.7	Reeders Rock. Class II rapid with a Class VI entrapment danger.
4.7	Ranger Road, old takeout.
5.2	New takeout.

Similar To. The Tellico is an equal-parts admixture of two of West Virginia's finest, the Cranberry River and Laurel Fork of the Cheat, with a level of technicality about mid-way between the two.

Description

The lower Tellico begins with a bang, with a putin at the top of a rocky Class III rapid that runs underneath the bridge. Then, a mere 150 yards downstream, the river fans out across a series of irregular ledges, creating a rapid of the same name, Ledges (Class III). Scout from the road on river right. The usual route is down the left side.

At 0.4 mile Judging Rock (Class III) appears, preceded by a 40-yard long rock garden. Some paddlers call this Bounce-off-the-Boulder (BOB) or Keyhole, and consider it the toughest rapid on the lower Tellico.

Turkey Creek, at mile 0.8, serves as an alternate putin. As such, it affords almost a mile of continuous Class II+ water before serving up the first Class III, Crack-in-the-Rock, a technical rapid that requires successive ninety degree turns to run through its namesake crack. With enough water a straighter route is possible on river right, but check for obstructions first. Scout from the parallel road. Crack actually gets easier with more water -- up to a point, anyway -- because it's so technical at low water. Until the water gets really high, its maximum difficulty is reached at about 250-300 cfs.

Gregs Nose is an irregular ledge with a rock in the center. It can be run either side of the center rock. From upstream this drop looks insignificant. Perhaps that's why more swims occur here than anywhere else on the lower Tellico. From upstream the right chute appears the clear choice. It's neither clear nor the better choice. River right (for years the only route because of a logjam on the other side of the rock) is difficult at any water level. River left is preferable if it's clear of obstructions, but the approach is blind. It's hard to tell if anything's blocking the river left drop until you're practically going over it.

Submarine (Class III-) appears where the river flows very close to the parallel road. This rapid is runnable either down a converging chute on river right or over the middle. The latter course is more fun with lots of water. Pylon Rapid (Class III-) is a series of drops, the first of which is most turbulent, and separates not a few paddlers from their boats. Following drops are minor, but fun to play. Toward the bottom, an old bridge pylon occupies midstream.

The lower Tellico is a relatively forgiving river, except for one spot that is insidious at low water. This spot, located 3.7 miles below the putin, is recognizable from upstream by a lone sycamore tree clinging tenaciously to an outcropping of rock on river right. The place is called Reeders Rock and, like Woodall Shoals, it looks harmless. But it isn't.

The hazard is formed as the river flows over a small ledge, only a two foot drop. But the ledge and its approach are tilted left, into an inconspicuous undercut rock which captures 70% of streamflow at 200 cfs. Not only is the undercut rock inconspicuous, the tilt of the riverbed is not noticeable until too late. At low water the decided streambed tilt combines with a smooth stone streambed bottom to sweep the shallow water and anything in or on it into the undercut. On low water runs the best route is to portage across the rocks on river right. At higher water the undercut is less of a problem, but river left should be avoided nonetheless. When running this drop, get right and stay right. Except for the undercut rock hazard, Reeders Rock is an easy Class II rapid, which makes it all the more insidious.

(The story of how Reeders Rock got its name, entitled The Way We Were, is included in *River Stories: Tales From Bo Rockerville,* by Monte Smith, available from Pahsimeroi Press.)

Several other Class II and Class II+ rapids appear below Reeders Rock but they seem anticlimactic after the upstream excitement. A bridge spans the river 4.7 miles below the putin where Ranger Station Road intersects with Tellico River Road. The takeout is half a mile downstream.

Summary

Few streams equal the Tellico in whitewater action per mile, and no stream surpasses it in beauty of surroundings. Combining the upper and lower trips produces seven river miles and 470 feet of vertical drop, one Class V waterfall, two Class III+ waterfalls, two Class IV rapids, several technical Class III+ rapids, seven named

Class III rapids, numerous unnamed Class II-III rapids, a Class II with a Class VI danger element, and inspiring scenery. Moreover, with a little stamina and an early start it can be run twice in the same day.

It has all the trimmings. What more could you ask? Even its name has a magic sparkle: Tellico!

Access

The Tellico River is located near Tellico Plains in east Tennessee, northeast of Chattanooga and southeast of Knoxville. It's not easy to find, but it's worth the effort. The easiest route is to locate TN 68 (it intersects I-75 and US 411) which runs near Tellico Plains. Exit TN 68 and drive into Tellico Plains. Once downtown, take the left fork (TN 165) and follow it a quarter mile to the Tellico River. At the bridge, take the right fork (continuing on TN 165) and head upstream on river left. In four miles look for the Oosterneck parking area on the right. This is the takeout for the lower run. At Oosterneck the road forks again. The left fork becomes

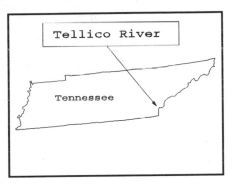

the Tellico/Robbinsville trans-mountain highway heading to Indian Boundary and points east. The right fork is Tellico River Road and closely parallels the river to its origin near the Tennessee-North Carolina border high in the mountains. Drive up the river road to scout rapids. Put in anywhere alongside the road, wherever stream conditions look most inviting. For the upper run, put in at the first bridge upstream of Bald River Falls (seven miles from Oosterneck) in order to catch all the action, and take out whenever the fun is done. Some people use the bridge at Bald River Falls as an alternate putin to avoid the upstream waterfalls. The most common starting points for the lower section are the bridge 200 yards below Jerrods Knee and Turkey Creek (one mile below Jerrods Knee). Take out at the aforementioned Oosterneck parking area. Shuttles

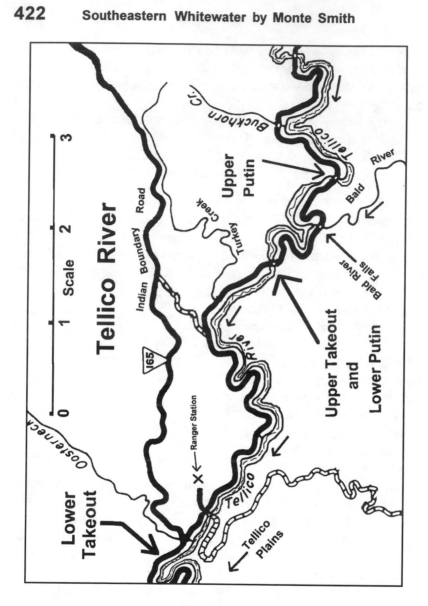

are on Tellico River Road. Shuttles can be walked, in a pinch, or hitch-hiked by the adventurous.

Miles From Tellico Plains	
Knoxville, TN 70	Asheville, NC 125
Chattanooga, TN 78	Nashville, TN 201

Other Information

Refer to the upper Tellico description for information on Water Levels, Camping, Fishing, Hiking, History, Maps, Rafting, and Nearby Alternate Trips.

Tygart Gorge

Belington to the Buckhannon
(West Virginia)

TRIP Profile			
Scale Midpoint = 100			
Overall Difficulty	112	Rapids Difficulty	108
Volume x Gradient	144	Continuous Rapids	99
Average Gradient	93	Entrapments	106
Maximum Gradient	95	Inaccessibility	110
Total Gradient	109	Reputation	117

Actual Stream Data			
Max Rapids	IV+	Stream Size	Large
Average Gradient	31	Length (in miles)	13
Maximum Gradient	70	Morphology Type	2

Overview

In a state with an abundance of big mountain rivers, it's all too easy to overlook the Tygart. Which would be a shame because it has a lot of good whitewater. Moreover, one of its tributaries (the Middle Fork, described elsewhere in this volume) features some of West Virginia's best technical steep creekin'.

The Tygart throws in several "Gauleyesque" size rapids just to let paddlers know they're really in West Virginia. To make things more interesting, it has two kinds of rapids. The first kind drops over well-defined ledges with constricted chutes. One of these, Hard Tongue, is visually impressive and difficult to run (upright). Its other kind of

Don Bowman on Hard Tongue. Tygart Gorge. Don Ellis photo.

rapids are big-volume boulder gardens. One of these, S Turn, can border on Class V at higher flow levels.

The overall gradient figure of 31 feet/mile for the Tygart Gorge is potentially misleading because it begins with over three miles of flat water and ends with a mile of the same. Excluding the flat water sections, the middle 7.5 miles drop at an average of 47 feet/mile -- and that's truckin' for a big river in an obstructed streambed. In fact, one section of the Tygart Gorge (below Middle Fork confluence) drops at the rate of 70 feet/mile and several other miles accelerate to almost this gradient. When 2,000+ cfs drop 70 feet/mile, there's ample opportunity to rediscover the volume x gradient interaction effect.

A railroad parallels the river through the gorge, but mars the scenery negligibly. Most paddlers never notice it unless a locomotive chugs along.

Similar To. Blend together equal parts of the New River Gorge, Upper Gauley, Nolichucky Gorge, and the Big South Fork of the Cumberland Gorge -- and the Tygart Gorge results. It's not strictly like any of these other runs, but it has characteristics of each and a difficulty level just about the average of the other four.

Mile(s)	Tygart Gorge Top-To-Bottom Itinerary
0.0	Put in at Belington on river left downstream of the WV 11 bridge.
0.0 to 3.5	Mostly flat water, but with current.
3.7	Keyhole (Class III+).
4.5	Hard Tongue (Class IV).
4.5 to 7.0	Class III water.
8.0	Confluence with the Middle Fork.
9.8	S Turn (Class IV+).
10.1	Shoulder Snapper (Class IV).
10.2 to 11.6	Class III-III+ rapids.
11.2	Hook (Class III+).
11.8	Buckhannon confluence, possible takeout.
13.0	Alternate takeouts, river left and right.
17.0	Philippi.

Description

For about three and a half miles below Belington the big stream is flat, but with a good current at medium to high flows. The first big rapids are ledges where the flow is constricted to one or two channels, forming powerful chutes. The first of these is known as Keyhole. Scout from river right to determine if either of the two routes beckons. Both are fast and powerful with some associated pinning hazard. Other ledges follow, the most memorable of which is Hard Tongue where the river focuses to a single channel, blows into the left wall of the canyon, rolls back on itself, and drops six feet into a cauldron. Hard Tongue is a weird rapid. Attempts to run it often end in tragi-comedy, with boats and bodies hurtled into the cauldron in an amazing variety of postures.

From Hard Tongue to near the Middle Fork confluence, the gradient stabilizes at around 45 feet/mile, producing fairly continuous Class III water including the Gates, where a row of large boulders form three slots. Run the middle slot.

Eight miles below Belington the Middle Fork contributes its volume. Below the Middle Fork confluence the river rests for a short while, but then it revs up again, pulls out all the stops, and plummets at the rate of 70 feet/mile for over a mile. Watch for S Turn (Class IV+), a long curving rapid (hence the name) full of holes, waves, rocks, and high intensity turbulence. S Turn is recognizable by a row of boulders which obstruct downstream vision. Perfunctory scouting can be accomplished from atop these boulders. For more thorough reconnoitering, try river right. Enter from the right or (at higher flows) from river left and head into a veritable maelstrom of holes, waves, and rocks. S Turn builds in intensity toward the bottom. With equal volume, some paddlers think S Turn rivals Pillow Rapid on the upper Gauley in both size and explosive power.

The next rapid is Shoulder Snapper (Class IV), a sloping drop of about ten feet into a boulder garden. Vertical pins have occurred here at low water. With more flow it becomes safer, but the holes and cross currents at the bottom become wild. The secret to a successful run is in hitting the "slot." The slot, always on river right, changes location somewhat with flow. Scout this big bruiser carefully from river right and set up safety ropes in case of mishap.

Without benefit of a rope, swims below the Snapper usually continue into the next rapid.

Several Class III rapids occur in quick succession below the Snapper until, a little more than a mile later, another bruiser appears. The bruiser is Hook, a Class III+ where the stream slams into a stack of river right boulders and rolls back suddenly, producing big holes and waves. It's not nearly as bad as it looks over there on river right, but many paddlers sweep around the bend and into the rapid before they realize where they are, then take one frantic look at the mayhem on river right and panic while trying to work back left through big waves and holes.

Hook is the last of the big bruisers, but not the last rapid. Several smaller rapids occur before the railroad trestle (dreaded omen of impending flatwater) looms across the river at the point where the Buckhannon enters the Tygart on river left. Some groups take out here (after paddling 100 yards up the Buckhannon) and walk up the railroad tracks three quarters of a mile to Carrollton Road. Alternate downstream takeouts are described in the Access section. From the Buckhannon confluence, the Tygart changes to a flat water configuration for the next mile to the alternate takeouts, and continues flat thereafter all the way to Philippi.

Summary

A big river with plenty of action. Its only problems are its takeouts.

Water Levels

Minimum on the Belington gauge is about 3.5 feet. The river is pushy at 6.0 feet. Seven feet is a prudent maximum. Phone: (703) 260-0305.

Tygart at Belington Gauge Conversion			
Feet	Cfs	Feet	Cfs
3.5	410	6.0	1910
3.6	460	6.2	2050
3.8	565	6.4	2190
4.0	675	6.6	2330
4.2	785	6.8	2470
4.4	895	7.0	2610
4.6	1010	7.5	3000
4.8	1130	8.0	3400
5.0	1250	8.5	3820
5.2	1370	9.0	4270
5.4	1490	9.5	4770
5.6	1630	10.0	5270
5.8	1770	11.0	5880

Access

The putin is at Belington in north-central West Virginia, about 55 miles south of Morgantown. Four takeouts are possible. The first is at the mouth of the Buckhannon, reducing the total trip to under ten miles. From Belington, take WV 11 about eight miles to Audra State Park. Cross the Middle Fork of the Tygart and continue about half a mile to Carrollton Road. Turn right onto Carrollton Road and continue to the Buckhannon. At the Buckhannon crossing, take the small road downstream as long as it

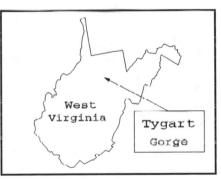

parallels the river. This takeout requires a boat carry from near the mouth of the Buckhannon.

Takeouts two and three are on opposite sides of the river about one mile downstream of the Buckhannon. To reach the river left alternate takeout from Belington, take WV 11 to Audra State Park,

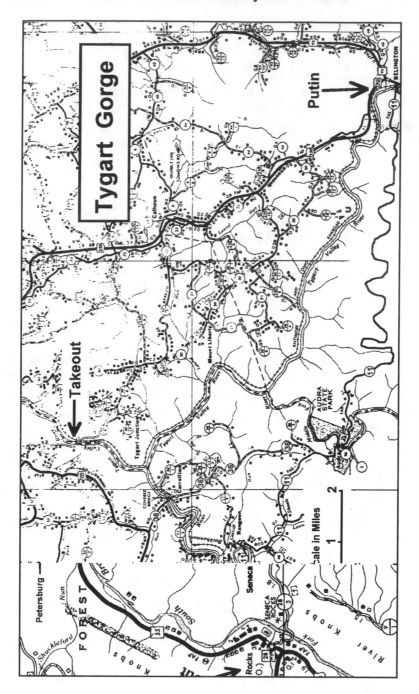

cross the Middle Fork and continue on WV 11 across the Buckhan-non to US 119. Turn right and head toward Philippi. Take the last right turn before intersection with WV 57. There is a small black metal sign with white "water gauge" letters marking the inconspicu-ous turn. This road looks like a private drive. Drive through farms to a reclaimed strip mine bench overlooking the Tygart. Hint: park a shuttle vehicle so it will be clearly visible from the river. Takeout here entails carrying boats a short distance up the side of the strip mine bench.

The third takeout is on river right about a mile below the Buckhannon confluence. From Belington, take US 250 north toward Philippi to the WV 250/10 intersection. Turn left and continue to juncture with WV 30. Bear right and continue through Mount Liberty to the fork with WV 30/6. Bear left and continue to where the road closely parallels the railroad tracks.

The fourth takeout is in Philippi. From Belington take US 250. This takeout adds about four miles of flatwater paddling.

Miles From the Tygart Gorge	
Morgantown, WV 55	Pittsburgh, PA 140
Columbus, OH 230	Roanoke, VA 200

Other Information

Camping

Audra State Park is the best bet. Turn onto WV 11 at the light in downtown Belington, cross the Tygart, and continue about eight narrow, winding miles. Its attractive campsites are nestled alongside the Middle Fork of the Tygart River.

Suitability for Rafting (On a 1 to 7 Scale): 5

The Tygart is not an ideal rafting river because of the large ledge drops with constricted sluiceways. Rumor is, however, that commer-cial outfitters offer guided trips at optimal flows. Inquire locally.

Nearby Alternate Trips

When the Belington gauge is 5.0 or higher, consider an alternate putin on the Middle Fork at Audra State Park. This provides for a combination of steep and technical whitewater on the Middle Fork and big and powerful rapids on the Tygart.

At high water, the Buckhannon has a superb Class III-IV section. The Potomac and Cheat headwaters are an hour to the east of the Tygart Gorge, and the Cheat Canyon and lower Cheat tributaries are an hour to the north. The Cranberry/Williams/Gauley/Meadow/New complex is two hours to the south.

Watauga Gorge

Guys Ford to Lake Watauga
(North Carolina)

TRIP Profile			
Scale Midpoint = 100			
Overall Difficulty	142	Rapids Difficulty	178
Volume x Gradient	97	Continuous Rapids	135
Average Gradient	148	Entrapments	151
Maximum Gradient	152	Inaccessibility	128
Total Gradient	126	Reputation	139

Actual Stream Data			
Max Rapids	V(VI)	Stream Size	Small
Average Gradient	100	Length (in miles)	5
Maximum Gradient	150	Morphology Type	5

Overview

The Watauga flows down a streambed of almost unbelievable congestion, tilted at an average angle of 100 feet/mile, but with two half-mile stretches that drop at 200 feet/mile, producing an unremittingly technical run where blind chutes are the norm and cul-de-sacs are commonplace, as the stream sluices through sieve after sieve of dense boulder obstructions. Without a leader who knows the stream well, first trips unfold as a seemingly interminable succession of blind drops through corridors of undercut boulders into misanthropic hydraulics. Much of the trip is through massive, complex rock jumbles where the typical downstream view consists of four or five cracks, one of which must be selected, often with no more than the

433

cursory examination provided by a few precious seconds of frantic back paddling. The strain of constant, critical decision-making can build to ordeal proportions. Needless to say, as the water rises, the stream gets pushy. An apt two word description of the Watauga Gorge is "maximum intensity."

Nestled among the boulder jumbles are such notable rapids as Hydro, Meat Grinder, and the El Horrendo of the South (Big Splat of the southern latitudes), Stateline Falls. Most rapids are Class III or Class IV, but they are classified as Class III or IV because they have recognized chutes or "lines" of that difficulty. These same rapids, however, sometimes harbor Class VI traps only a few feet across the streambed from the "approved" chutes. Moreover, there is no surcease. From the first Class III about half a mile below the putin to Sycamore Falls four miles farther downstream, the river is essentially a technical, twisting, undercut-infested rapid. Accordingly, this run is appropriate only for advanced paddlers in good physical condition willing to acknowledge that mistakes almost invariably will entail serious consequences.

The Watauga's streambed complexity would produce an exciting run with half the gradient, but due to the average gradient of 100 feet/mile, "exciting" is a mild euphemism. Frenetic might be a better adjective, and even this term is appropriate only at moderate flows. As volume increases, push quickly comes to shove and the paddler finds him or herself weaving through complex rock jumbles at a too-fast pace. At only 300 cfs it's a challenging run. At 500 cfs it's a vigorous workout. Seven hundred cfs produces a metaphysical experience, and above that . . . well, good luck!

Not only does Watauga Gorge have a triple-digit average gradient, a recirculating hydraulic that rivals Woodall Shoals on Section IV of the Chattooga, dozens of undercut rock formations, and countless technical rapids, but it's also home to Stateline Falls, a 16 foot drop which in itself makes the run unforgettable. What happens at Stateline Falls is that the river drops through several slots. One of its center slots is runnable, but that slot is flanked by drops too horrendous to send your mother-in-law down. In the runnable slot, water drops 16 feet and explodes into rocks with an intensity that makes Sweets Falls on the Gauley look like a municipal water fountain.

Mile(s)	Watauga Gorge Top-To-Bottom Itinerary
0.0	Put in at Guys Ford Bridge, a quarter mile off US 321 between Boone, NC and Hampton, TN.
0.0 to 0.5	Mild Class II rapids.
0.5	Initiation (Class III).
0.6	Toothpick (Class III+).
0.7	Jumble One (Class IV).
0.9	Hydro (Class V), aka Exterminator.
1.1	Jumble Two (Class IV).
1.2	Pretender (Class III).
1.3	Pivot Rock (Class IV).
1.5	Escape Hatch (Class III+).
1.6	UAWMF (Class IV+).
1.7	Twister (Class III).
1.8	Little Cousin (Class III)
1.9	Little Brother (Class III+).
2.1	Sieve City (Class IV).
2.4	Congesterol (Class IV).
2.6	Screaming Undercut (Class III).
2.9	Focus Left (Class III).
3.1 to 3.4	The Calm (Class II-III).
3.5	Zorro (Class IV+).
3.7	Meat Grinder (Class IV).
3.8	Dancer, aka Dianas Ledge (Class III).
4.0	Stateline Falls (Class VI).
4.2	Cubic Rock Drop (Class III).
4.3	Browns Ferry (Class IV).
4.4	Sycamore Falls (Class III).
4.5	Watson Island (Alternate takeout on river left).
4.5 to 5.0	Anticlimactic Class II(III) rapids.
5.0 to 5.5	Lake paddle to campground takeout (lake left).

To make matters worse, Stateline's location is extremely difficult to anticipate from upstream. Even from the last possible eddy, there's nothing in the downstream view that says a 16 foot plummet is lurking just around the next bend. From this last eddy, there's no horizon line. The rest of the approach looks absolutely innocuous. For this reason, a number of paddlers have inadvertently blundered into the falls.

Like a number of other "rapids," Stateline was once considered unrunnable. When Bo Rocker and his derelict gang first started paddling this gorge in the 1970's, they never considered running Stateline Falls. Even to them, running the falls seemed insane. Then one day one of his group got too far ahead, didn't realize where he was, blundered into the drop -- and came out alive. In succeeding years, other paddlers inadvertently flushed over the falls, and although in some respects they were never the same again, they all survived. And of course, the mere fact of their survival was more than sufficient inducement for others to intentionally run the big drop. Nowadays, with continually advancing technique and equipment, hotdogs are deliberately running Stateline Falls, and undoubtedly the practice will become more commonplace. Nevertheless, it's not a drop to take lightly.

Similar To. This writer has never run the upper Yough, but several paddlers have advised him that it's probably the closest parallel to the Watauga. As for Stateline Falls, the Watauga's most memorable drop, it's in some ways a mirror image of Big Splat on West Virginia's lower Big Sandy, but otherwise the two rivers aren't very similar.

Description

At the Guys Ford Bridge putin it gives no clue of the mayhem that it harbors downstream. It looks like any other innocuous little Class II mountain creek. Downstream of the putin the deception continues for half a mile, with nothing more than Class II rapids until a small tributary enters on river left, identifying the first rocky Class III, Initiation, a twisting drop over a broken ledge. Toothpick (Class III+) is next, normally one of the more fun-filled rapids on the stream. Like other Watauga rapids, however, it's subject to blockage by logs.

Jumble #1 (Class IV) is the real initiation to the Watauga, recognizable from upstream by a clump of sycamores on river right. In 25 yards, the stream drops 10 to 12 vertical feet through a

If it looks congested, that's because it is. Bob Whaley's inaugural trip down the Watauga Gorge. UAWMF rapid. Monte Smith photo.

Any (upright) line on Stateline is a good line. Monte Smith is the paddler. Watauga is the river. Don Ellis photo.

trashpile of boulders. Enter the jumble left of center and pick the best route depending on water level.

Hydro (Class V) is approximately one mile below the putin, and signals that the real fun is about to begin. Merely scouting this rapid can induce vertigo. It begins with a quick right turn and drop into a U-shaped obstructed trough that at some levels (around 300 cfs) forms a tunnel of water. The water tunnel pounds into a river right cliff, rolls back to flush through a small rock garden, gathers momentum, and funnels down to about 10 feet in width before dropping another seven feet into an hydraulic that rivals Woodall in recirculating propensity. The only way to miss the hydraulic is to portage. The only way through it is to punch it. Start paddling hard on river right and take the drop angled left with as much speed as possible. Consider posting safety ropes on the rocks along river left. At some water levels Hydro may merit a Class VI rating because of its weird tunnel of water at the top and serious hydraulic at the bottom.

Savor the short pool below Hydro because immediately downstream of it the river catapults into a veritable labyrinth of technical rock mazes, some of which are so tortuous that from the bottom looking back upstream you may be unable to determine how you came through. For the next two miles the Watauga broadens into a sizeable streambed that is clogged with boulders, some of which are undercut. Interspersed among the boulder mazes are formidable rapids, several to Class IV difficulty.

This two mile section begins with 350 yards of continuous, high difficulty Class II-III rapids that give way to Jumble #2, another Class IV rock pile. Either of the two left chutes is preferable. Next is Pretender (Class III), which bends left, rolls right, forms a hydraulic and ends by hammering into a river right undercut rock. Pivot Rock (Class IV) deserves a look-see prior to running. There are two ways to enter. The main flow swirls in from river left forming some funky water as a hydraulic forms below a submerged ledge. A left-entrance run necessitates a surf/ferry across the face of the hydraulic in order to pitch into a major wave/hole concatenation while making a 90 degree left turn and avoiding namesake Pivot Rock (on the left). An alternate entry can be accomplished through the small rock jumble at the top river right of the rapid, with a small drop and splat down at the top of the lively washout, thereby avoiding all the fuss of ferrying through the funky water.

A brief respite (relatively speaking) below Pivot is interrupted by another bizarre river-wide jumble of rocks. Paths can be found on river left, but the scenic route through Escape Hatch (Class III+) is a double drop on river right through a narrow, rocky corridor that provides an outstanding photographic backdrop.

UAWMF! (Class IV+), one of the toughest rapids on the river, starts with a 7 or 8 foot drop through a jagged boulder field. At low water the challenge is to find a way through the drop. High water slingshots the paddler into a gymnasium-sized wall of rock on river right (and hence its name, UAWMF!). The bottom of UAWMF! is a river-wide ledge of three to four feet. Run left to avoid a Section IV Crack-in-the-Rock formation on river right. An interesting exercise at the bottom of UAWMF! is to pull over to the rocky river left bank and look back upstream. It's a potentially unnerving realization to think that you just paddled through that labyrinth of rock and spurting water.

Immediately downstream of UAWMF! is Twister (Class III+) where the river swirls left to go around a raised ledge, then swings sharply back right, completing a 180 degree turn while dropping numerous feet. Twister is all the more exciting because of the velocity attained and the rocks toward the bottom. Two Class IIIs follow, either or both of which will be Class IV at higher flows. The first, Little Cousin, is nothing special, just another Watauga treat with multiple blind drops into funky hydraulics down a rock corridor with undercuts on both sides. Little Brother, however, is more memorable. It's a twisting, crashing, blind crazyquilt of misplaced boulders set amidst a region of extremely technical and continuous water.

Downstream, the most severe blockage yet appears, Sieve City (Class IV), with a couple of sycamores growing out in the middle of the rock jumble and the river threading through in a dozen fragmented ribbons. Most of the volume snakes over to river left. Don't go with the flow. Run the right side if water permits; otherwise enter center and work right. The undercuts in the center and left are lethal traps. Congesterol (Class IV) is next. Look for a narrow corridor on river right with a sudden left turn near the bottom. The left/middle of this rapid consists of a maze of switchbacks.

After another screaming Class III drop into another undercut, look for Focus Left (Class III), which is exactly where the paddler should go because river right features a major infestation of undercut rocks. On the left side, run the seven foot drop right of center because the left side boils into a boulder, forming a strange hydraulic.

After this drop the river inexplicably transforms from a state of extreme congestion to a more open concourse of Class II-III water with clean drops. For the first time in over two miles, downstream visibility exceeds 100 yards. Looking farther downstream, the canyon walls reveal that the stream executes a major turn to the left, and drops appreciably. This sudden transformation of streambed from complexly scrambled to merely obstructed is known as the Calm, and it can lull paddlers who are on the river for the first time into a false sense of security. The common perception of first-time paddlers when they reach this point in the Watauga Gorge is that the worst part is over, that from here on out it's Bubba home free. Practically Miller Time. But it ain't so.

Zorro (Class IV+) interrupts the Calm. From upstream a major blockage is visible (especially a barn-sized chunk of rock on river right), but an unobstructed path of Class III water appears to wind its way through the mess. Catching the left eddy at the top of the rapid is a capital idea because it's the last possible haven from which to observe the stream begin its imitation of the letter Z, forming in the process some Gauley-sized waves and diagonal holes, any of which will gleefully demonstrate the phenomenon of windowshading.

After passing the major blockage that creates Zorro, the streambed opens up again. In this section of the river, it's a good idea to look around for landmarks. From this point onward, confusion about relative location can produce trauma, literally. Looking downstream, a prominent mountain (actually part of the gorge wall) is visible in the distance. The mountain is a failsafe indication that el horribilus aquatarius lurks not far downstream.

Meat Grinder (Class IV) is next on the agenda. The name is apt, as 80% of the streamflow rolls over a hump, encounters a jagged impediment, and mangles anything that drops into this trough. To avoid this fate, catch the tongue of water on river left that shoots by the hazard. This unusual rapid actually gets more difficult at lower water because the chute on the left is harder to hit.

The last warning that el dreadnaughticus declivitus is imminent is Dancer, aka Dianas Ledge, a Class III drop of about five feet that kicks hard right at the bottom. Although one can proceed for some distance past Dancer, for safety reasons it's kosher to pull out on river left at any time and commence scouting for Stateline Falls (Class VI). Another clue that the falls is near can be found on river right. In the quarter mile above the big drop, river right gradually changes from a boulder field into a solid wall of noticeably dark rock.

Why all the cues as to the location of Stateline Falls? Why so much circumspection? For two simple reasons:

> Of all the major drops described in this book, Stateline Falls is *the* one you don't want to run unintentionally.

> Of all the major drops described in this book, Stateline Falls is perhaps *the* easiest one to flush into unintentionally.

The final approach to the falls is 100 yards of Class II-III water that look innocuous. The last practicable eddy is on the left immediately following a drop of about four feet. Passing this eddy, the Class II+ course curves to the left and enters the Sluice of No Return before hooking sharply back right and . . . dropping. Once into this sluice, going over the waterfall is a certainty without having scouted first. Only one lonely micro eddy exits, and anyone flushing inadvertently into the sluice is not likely to see it in time. Even from the safety of the last practicable eddy, one cannot tell that the waterfall is almost within a stone's throw. That's because there's no horizon line from upstream. As the stream curves left in the approach, it is heading toward the rocks on river left. The rocks form a seemingly benign backdrop. Only yards before the brink of the falls, the stream suddenly swerves right and drops 16 feet through four cracks (slots? crevices? crannies?). River left crack is a no-no region of mini crevices and pinning opportunities. The right slot is a nightmare. These drops (and the approach) should be examined in minute detail by anyone considering a run. As unpleasant as it looks, successful runs have been made (at carefully selected water levels) through the right side of one of the middle slots, angled right to avoid the boulder at bottom left onto which most of the water crashes. However, even at optimal flow levels this rapid/waterfall is a Class VI drop, and the near-universal choice is to portage along the river left trail.

The waterfall appears at mile four, almost astraddle the North Carolina-Tennessee state line. Shortly downstream, the Watauga attains its maximum width, fanning out across a stone surface with most of the water gradually pulling to river left of a gigantic cubic boulder in midstream. Do not go with the flow, as river left drops into a Class VI entrapment. Instead, work to river right through a series of shallow channels to arrive at the river right side of Cubic Rock (Class III) and enjoy a fourteen foot slide/plummet into a small pool. Two hundred yards later the last Class IV (Browns Ferry) appears as the Watauga defines a powerful curve into the river right cliff and around another (but smaller) cubic boulder.

Sycamore Falls (Class III) is the last significant drop, a six foot descent that's always a humdinger, regardless of water level. Downstream, but within sight of Sycamore Falls, is the upstream tip of Watson Island, which should be run on the right unless the alternate takeout at the island is used. Another half mile of anticlimactic river paddling produces Watauga Lake, and a half-mile lake paddle reveals a commercial campground (lake left) which can be used as takeout, with permission. When the reservoir is drawn down, the river continues half a mile past the campground to the vicinity of Pioneer Landing.

Summary

The Watauga is incredible. It's a steep creek freak's wet dream come true. Anybody who flushes out the bottom of this gorge still craving excitement probably has a chemical imbalance.

Because of its hazards, it's not suitable for every paddler. But for those with the requisite skill, attitude and stamina, it's a technical playground with few equals.

Water Levels

TVA maintains a telemetric gauge at Sugar Grove, several miles upstream of the putin. (Phone (800) 238-2264 and press code "3" after the recorded message.) Paddling zero is about 200 cfs. An enjoyable low level is 300 cfs. Above 300 cfs, it gets pushy fast, as stream conditions change significantly with added water. Five hundred cfs is a medium-high level. Above 700 cfs, it's Katie bar the door.

Access

Located between Boone, North Carolina and Hampton, Tennessee, the putin is at Guys Ford Bridge, a quarter mile off US 321. The turnoff to the putin is 3.2 miles east of the Tennessee-North Carolina state line. Takeout is either at Watson Island or Lake Watauga. The turnoff to Watson Island is 5.3 miles west of the turnoff to the putin, but the road down to the river is rough and may be impassible. To reach the Lake Watauga takeout from the putin, drive west 5.9 miles on US 321 to the first paved right turn, a shortcut to

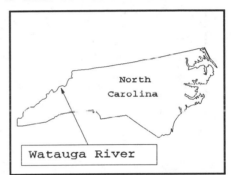

Pioneer Landing. Turn right at the only intersection. Pioneer Landing can serve as a take out, or continue another mile up the lake to a commercial campground operation (located on river left). Total length of the shuttle run is nine miles, one way.

Although it's hundreds of feet above the river, US 321 parallels the Watauga on river left. If it's necessary to walk out of the gorge, left is generally preferable. A trail begins just upstream of Stateline Falls and leads to US 321 at the Tennessee-North Carolina state line.

Miles From the Watauga Gorge	
Johnson City, TN 44	Charlotte, NC 117
Winston-Salem, NC 102	Roanoke, VA 201

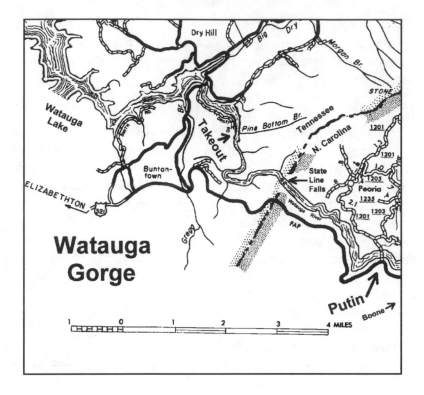

Other Information

Area Attractions

The top of Roan Mountain is an expansive rhododendron garden. Peak blossom, usually during the latter half of June, produces a stunning spectacle.

Camping

Limited camping space is available at the putin, downstream of Guys Ford Bridge on river left. A small commercial campground (oriented to camping trailers) is located at the takeout. Primitive camping is available at Rat Branch on Lake Watauga. Roan Mountain State Park is about 45 minutes from the takeout.

Hiking

A trail leads into the gorge just upstream of Stateline Falls, on river left. The trailhead is on private property off US 321 at the state line sign.

Suitability for Rafting (On a 1 to 7 Scale): 0

Not suitable for rafts of any type at any water level.

Nearby Alternate Trips

The Doe River Gorge (Class III-IV) is thirty minutes from the takeout, and the Elk River (Class II) is about twenty minutes from the takeout. The Doe is described elsewhere in this volume.

Williams River

Tea Creek to Three Forks
(West Virginia)

TRIP Profile			
Scale Midpoint = 100			
Overall Difficulty	104	Rapids Difficulty	102
Volume x Gradient	95	Continuous Rapids	123
Average Gradient	106	Entrapments	117
Maximum Gradient	103	Inaccessibility	65
Total Gradient	139	Reputation	83

Actual Stream Data			
Max Rapids	III(IV)	Stream Size	Small
Average Gradient	55	Length (in miles)	10.5
Maximum Gradient	80	Morphology Type	2

Overview

Located in the Monongahela National Forest in southeastern West Virginia, the Williams is only three miles (as the crow flies) from the Cranberry River. Although those three aerial miles translate into a shuttle drive of about 45 minutes, runs on both streams are possible in the same day, water permitting. Generally when one stream is running the other one is too, although the Cranberry seems to come up a little more frequently. A dusty road parallels the Williams from the putin at Tea Creek Campground until all whitewater plays out, permitting road scouting of most rapids and trips of any desired length. In season, the Williams is a popular trout fishing stream. On days following a restocking release, anglers can be thick as flies along its banks, and at least as irksome.

Although it's just over the ridge from the Cranberry, the Williams is a very different river. Whereas the Cranberry is the apotheosis of West Virginia technicality, the Williams is basically a get on board and truck downstream fast river. With lots of water, it's a taste of Idaho in southeast West Virginia. Its gradient is a healthy 55 feet/mi over the 10.5 mile whitewater run, and three of these miles clock in at 80 feet/mile. On a stream with no major waterfalls to eat up chunks of the gradient, this produces high-velocity non-stop Class II-III conditions and short stretches of Class IV difficulty, earning an overall rating of Class III+.

As we all know, stream conditions change as volume fluctuates. The Williams River, however, changes more than most. At low flow levels around 400 cfs, it's a Class II-III romp. Following heavy rains, however, when the volume temporarily rises up into the vicinity of 800 to 1,000 cfs, the Williams River changes into a Class IV extravaganza of waves, tenacious hydraulics of every description, and recurrent pourovers.

Increased volume on most rivers has the effect of exacerbating the difficulty of major rapids, pushing Class IIIs up to Class IVs, for example. This occurs on the Williams too, but something else happens. Virtual non-rapids (minor Class II play spots) transmogrify into significant rapids, so that with added volume the Williams seems to actually manufacture new rapids. This phenomenon doesn't happen on many rivers, but it definitely happens on the Williams (also on Daddys Creek Canyon in Tennessee). A high water run on the Williams consists of continuous Class III-IV action, gnarly hydraulics, one Class IV+ rapid and a potential trap. A high water run on the Williams River is one of the most thrilling experiences in southeastern whitewater. For an unforgettable treat (and possibly tendonitis of both elbows), run both the Williams and the Cranberry at high water on the same day.

Similar To. At higher water, it's similar to a lot of western rivers of similar size and volume: fairly uniform gradient, mostly open streambed, plenty of big holes, some pourovers to dodge, and high velocity. At lower flows, it's basically a high-velocity Nantahala.

Mile(s)	Williams River Top-To-Bottom Itinerary
0.0	Put in at Tea Creek campground.
0.0 to 1.1	Fast-moving Class II whitewater.
1.1	Tempo increases to Class II+. (Class III at high water.)
1.4	First major rapid. Watch the hydraulics at high water.
1.5	Temporary respite.
1.7	Island with fast water at the bottom of left chute.
2.3	River-wide obstruction, followed by waves and holes.
2.4 to 4.6	Uninterrupted whitewater.
2.6	Class III rock garden that culminates in . . .
2.7	. . . a potential entrapment hazard on river left (at high water).
2.8	Bannock Shoals (Class III).
3.8	Hells Portal (Class III to Class IV+, depending on level).
3.9	Major rapid.
4.1	Broken ledge. Class III+.
4.6 to 5.5	Respite.
4.6	Small islands.
5.9 to 7.4	High intensity resumes.
7.4	Brief respite.
7.7	Crescent-shaped ledge.
8.0	Small island.
8.6	Booger Hole forms at high water.
10.5	Three Forks Bridge.

Description

By all means, use the parallel road to scout the major rapids and hazards before starting a trip, especially if the water is high. At high water, scouting is worthwhile not only because of stream velocity and a scarcity of eddies, but also because of a potential trap and a rapid (Hells Portal) that may border on Class V. Both the trap and Hells Portal are difficult to anticipate from river level and it helps a great deal to have some idea of where they're located and what maneuvers they require.

From the putin at Tea Creek this little hotdog races along, producing fast moving Class II water for the first mile. At mile 1.1, a midstream boulder identifies the first spot that will be Class III at high water, with a large hole on river right and a wave train to river left of the boulder. At mile 1.4 the first Class III+ (Class IV at high water) appears, consisting of a rock jumble with most of the water flowing right into a diagonal hydraulic that at some levels may feed back into an undercut rock. The preferred route is a chute on river left. After this dose of excitement the stream reverts to high velocity Class II for about a mile.

After a small tributary on river left and a small island with most of the volume going left, the tempo picks up again and continues to build steadily through a series of obstructions that form progressively bigger hydraulics. Another river-wide broken obstruction is followed by major hydraulics and a long Class III rock-strewn rapid that ends in a potential cul de sac. From upstream, vision is blocked by a large boulder on river right that constricts the flow and forces the water toward the left embankment and into a trap formed by two offset rocks, the second of which is undercut and prone to attract logs and tree limbs. This trap is inconsequential at low to medium flows, as the force of the water is greatly mitigated and the trap can be spotted in plenty of time to avoid it. At high water, however, much of the volume is forced into the trap and a paddler must move quickly to cut across the flow to the safety of river right. The best way to avoid a problem here is to anticipate its location and run much farther right (kissing the right-side boulder) than appears necessary from upstream. As measured from the parallel road, the trap is at mile 2.7. From the river, look for the aforementioned boulder on river right and a culvert that protrudes from under the road on river left. If the water is high enough to activate the danger of the trap, the culvert probably will be spewing water into the stream, from a height of about ten feet.

Bannock Shoals, a long sweeping Class III rapid, introduces two miles of high intensity whitewater. At low to medium levels these two miles consist of continuous Class II-III conditions. At high water, stream conditions change to continuous Class III-IV (with one Class IV+), with high velocity, constant waves and holes, and several problematic pourovers.

At mile 3.8 the stream bends away from the road and as it sweeps back left constricts to a mere fifteen feet as it blows through Hells Portal, a rapid that varies from Class III to Class IV+, depending on water level. This rapid commands attention at any level because of the undercut rock hazard on river right of the final drop, but it has to be seen at a thousand cfs to be fully appreciated. With ample volume, just getting through the approach is an accomplishment, as a river-wide hole develops upstream of the main drop. The center of this hole forms a recirculating hydraulic. Fortunately, there's usually a tongue of transit left of center. Once past the approach hole, look for the tip of a triangle-shaped rock downstream on the first drop.

At high water the idea is to run as closely as possible to the right of this rock in order to enter the biggest drop as far left as possible. At lower levels the line is less critical and one can even catch a river left eddy below the triangular rock. The final drop in Hells Portal is something else. The river is squeezed down to about fifteen feet between two enormous boulders. The boulder on the right is undercut and sometimes jammed with logs. In the middle of the drop a hydraulic forms on the upstream face of a large wave. The hydraulic covers about 60% of the fifteen foot portal and at some levels will surf objects laterally into the river right undercut. This hydraulic is hard to punch at high flow levels, but can be avoided altogether by running tight against river left (hence the admonition above about kissing the right side of the triangular rock, which is situated on river left just upstream of the wave/hole). This rapid could pose serious problems for rafts. An even bigger hole awaits at the bottom of the drop. At lower flows the hydraulic phenomena are weakened and Hells Portal logs in at Class III or III+. The undercut hazard is still there, nevertheless, and for this reason the prudent paddler will take a long hard look at this rapid before running it.

At high water, the next mile features an incredible display of hydraulic phenomena. Only a hundred yards downstream of Hells

Portal is another rapid, Class III or IV, depending on water level. Then, in a quarter mile, a broken ledge can be recognized from upstream by two large rocks, between which most of the volume swerves. Strong holes develop on either side of the center chute at high water. Below this center-chute-rapid the stream really revs up until two small islands with trees growing in the current signal a brief respite at mile 4.8. After a half mile of Class II respite, the stream again gains velocity and features more wave/hole/obstruction action for another mile. At high water some of the holes and pourovers are tenacious. At mile 6.4 the first pool appears, followed by another island and a mile of relative quietude.

But, it ain't over until it's over, and the Williams has more to offer. After growing flatter and wider and seemingly meeker and milder, the mountain stream cinches its belt and throws one last fit. And what a fit! Beginning with a massive shoals filled with holes and obstructions (like something off the lower Big Sandy) the river roars over a crescent-shaped ledge with a total sloping drop of about five or six feet and continues with Class III action for about a mile to the biggest hydraulic of all, Booger Hole at mile 8.6. Barely noticeable at lower water, this spot becomes a real monstrosity (Class IV+) at high water.

Milder action continues all the way to Three Forks Bridge at mile 10.5, but everything in the last mile and a half is anticlimactic. At low water, everything below the crescent-shaped ledge at mile 7.7 is anticlimactic. Because of the parallel road, take out is possible anywhere along the run.

Summary

If you're lucky enough to catch the Williams with water, by all means take the time to run it and become one of the few paddlers who have. This is one of the Southeast's least paddled premium whitewater trips. It's an exciting stream that blasts along at surprising velocities. This is one stream that definitely takes a quantum jump in excitement when available water rises past "sufficient" and into the neighborhood of "abundant." Most trips ever taken on the Williams were at "sufficient" levels. If at all possible, coincide your visit with an occasion of ample water. High water on the Williams is an exhilarating, unforgettable experience.

Water Levels

The Craigsville gauge on the Gauley and the Cranberry River gauge provide rough indications of water availability on the Williams. A minimum of 12.0 at Craigsville and 4.0 on the Cranberry are needed for a paddling zero run. However (as with all indirect gauges), these are approximations. Daily readings from both the Craigsville and Cranberry gauges are available from (304) 529-5127.

Access

Access is easy once you reach the stream, because of the parallel road. Getting to this neck of the woods, however, can really eat up the clock. (Which partly explains why relatively few paddlers have run it. Water unavailability is the rest of the explanation.) It's in south central West Virginia, and if you're at the nearby Gauley/Meadow/New area and suddenly have the bright idea of spending an hour driving over to the Williams --

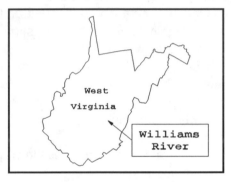

forget it! Although it looks that close on the map, we're talking West Virginia backroads convolutions at their best. It's a two-to-three hour drive from the Gauley, and that presumes you know the roads.

Once on the scene, however, access is simple. Because of the parallel road, putins and takeouts are unlimited. Usual putin is at Tea Creek, two miles off scenic WV 150. Take out is anywhere along the parallel shuttle road.

Miles From the Williams River	
Charleston, SC 110	Richmond, VA 240
Roanoke, VA 155	Washington, DC 285

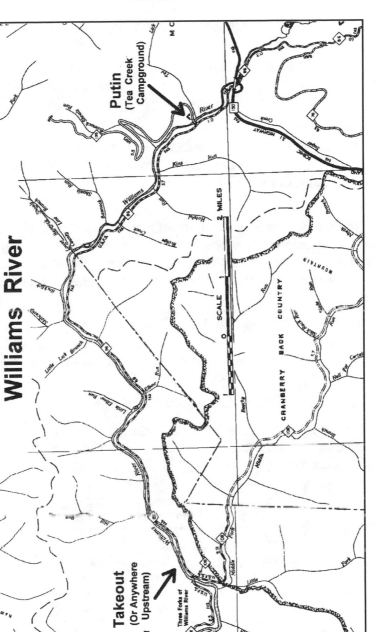

Other Information

Area Attractions

Cranberry Glades Botanical Area is located on the Cranberry River headwaters, on WV 39 between Marlinton and Richwood. Snow Shoe ski resort is nearby.

Camping

Tea Creek campground (National Forest Service) is located at the putin. Several other campgrounds are in the area, including two on the nearby Cranberry River.

Maps

The Monongahela National Forest map, available from the Forest Service, is useful in locating the Williams and in negotiating the backroads between it and the Cranberry. This map can be obtained from the Cranberry ranger station on WV 39 two miles outside Richwood.

Suitability for Rafting (On a 1 to 7 Scale): 5

Somewhat small for rafting, but it's possible at higher flows. Rafters should scout Hells Portal and the potential trap at mile 2.7 before putting on.

Nearby Alternate Trips

Driving times from the Williams to the alternate streams in the table below vary from forty-five minutes for the Cranberry to two and a half hours for the Gauley.

Alternate Trip	Rapids Difficulty	TRIP Points
Cherry River	III	na
Cranberry	IV	103
Upper Gauley	V+	138
Lower Gauley	IV	109
Laurel Creek	III	na

Wilson Creek Gorge

(North Carolina)

TRIP Profile			
Scale Midpoint = 100			
Overall Difficulty	108	Rapids Difficulty	117
Volume x Gradient	72	Continuous Rapids	135
Average Gradient	145	Entrapments	106
Maximum Gradient	117	Inaccessibility	74
Total Gradient	86	Reputation	117

Actual Stream Data			
Max Rapids	IV(V)	Stream Size	Micro
Average Gradient	96	Length (in miles)	2.5
Maximum Gradient	100	Morphology Type	4

Overview

Wilson Creek, the spunky little rascal, heads up atop Grandfather Mountain. Rolling off the back of the craggy promontory (Elevation 5,837 feet), it flows under the Blue Ridge Parkway while still a freshet. As Wilson rolls south out of the Blue Ridge Mountains it passes within ten miles of Linville Gorge and a scant forty miles from Mount Mitchell, highest peak in eastern America (Elevation 6,684 feet). No wonder it's such a scrapper, springing as it does from some of the roughest terrain in the southern Appalachians.

Although diminutive in size and length, the gorge run on Wilson Creek is a non-stop, no-holds-barred adrenalin rush containing two of the most eventful miles described in this book. It's heavy-duty whitewater, a scaled-down Watauga. It's small, steep, and technical, a creek paddler's delight, adorned with four uncharacteristically (for

455

a micro stream) powerful rapids of Class IV or V difficulty. The big rapids are mixed with a dozen or more Class III-III+ ledges and boulder jams, and several holes (two in particular) that are unusually sticky at higher flows. Practically the entire two mile run is a rapid, consisting alternately of sheer drops and blind bursts through scrambled boulder fields. Several of the unnamed rapids are ledges of five or more feet that would be big deals on most other runs.

Mile(s)	Wilson Ck Gorge Top-To-Bottom Itinerary
0.0	Put in at the top of the gorge. Ledges begin immediately.
0.1	Tricky Class III ledge system, followed by severe congestion.
0.2	Large slide on river left that forms a strong hydraulic at high flows.
0.3	Approach to Bigg Drop (Class III+).
0.4	Major rapid #1: Bigg Drop (Class IV+).
0.5	Major rapid #2: Stonehenge, aka Boatbuster (Class IV), followed by a narrow corridor, ledges, and holes.
0.6	Strong hydraulics at high water.
0.7	U Turn (Class III+).
0.8	Major rapid #3: Stairsteps (Class IV).
0.9	"Unrunnable" jumble.
1.0	Approach to Razorback (Class III+).
1.1	Major rapid #4: Razorback (Class V).
1.2	Rock and Roll (Class III+).
1.3 to 1.4	Sticky (and possibly dangerous) hydraulics.
1.7	CF Junior (Class III).
2.0	Broken diversion dam. Run on river left, through the breech.
2.1	Take out (with permission) at Brown Mountain Beach. Otherwise continue downstream a half mile to . . .
2.6	. . . the alternate takeout at Adako Road Bridge.

The stream pours through a micro gorge north of Morganton, North Carolina, that's popular with the general public. On summer weekends hundreds of people will be in the gorge -- swimming, fishing, soaking photons, imbibing spirits . . . whatever. A forest service road parallels the run on river left, though it's rarely visible from the river as it hugs the cliffsides a hundred feet or more above the stream.

Description

A putin at the top of the gorge delivers the paddler immediately into maneuver-intensive ledges, holes, and boulder gardens. Look for double slides, followed by a larger slide which is pinched tight against the stream's left side. At high flows, the hole at the bottom of this slide is sticky.

Below this river-left slide, the stream bends right into a dense, seemingly impenetrable jumble of rocks. This is an opportune place to stop and reconnoiter -- from river left -- because this technical Class III+ rockgarden culminates in the first of Wilson Creek's four major rapids, Bigg Drop (Class IV+), a sloping descent of about 10 vertical feet. Coming out of Bigg's entrance rock garden, all you'll be able to see downstream is horizon line. Aim for left center of that horizon line and get ready for an exhilarating sling-shot hurtle into the foaming hydraulic vortex at the bottom. The hole at the bottom isn't sticky at most levels, but it sure looks sinister. Once out of the hole, Bigg is followed by a recovery pool, the longest one on the run.

To add a little excitement to the standard run over Bigg Drop, try catching the river right micro eddy on the brink of the falls. Then ferry across toward river left for the drop. This little maneuver provides a dynamic eddy turn and gives downstream photographers a chance to anticipate your approach. But if you go for the eddy, don't miss it!

After Bigg Drop, Wilson wastes no time in heading toward Stonehenge (aka Boatbuster), its second major (pick one: rapid, cascade, cataract, waterfall). It's recognizable from upstream by a cube of granite at the top of the drop. Stonehenge is a short, furious, bad-tempered, rocks-at-the-bottom Class IV or V combination waterfall and crevice-kind-of-rapid that is best anticipated because once you

Monte Smith takes the plunge on Bigg Drop. Wilson Creek Gorge.
Don Ellis photo.

Fritz Drescher on Wilson Creek Gorge. Don Ellis photo.

come blasting 'round the left-hooking bend, it's hard to find a parking place. The first drop is sizeable. The landing is hard. At low water the rocks crunch boats. At high water the hole eats boats. Quickly eddy right or left if needed and then prepare for another forty yards of hurtling over successive ledges as you flush through a narrow sluice with weird diagonal holes. The narrow outflush to Stonehenge is not recommended for swimming, as its dynamic hydraulics have been known to bash objects repeatedly against the sides of the narrow rock corridor. Up-close and personal action photographs or video footage can be captured in this area of the gorge.

Next is U-Turn (Class III+), an exercise in boat control through a screaming 180 degree hair-pin turn. It begins with a diagonal technical slot running from right to left. (Alternatively, run the first part straight down the middle for a five foot vertical drop.) Then the fun begins as the flow heads for the river left cliff, drops to the right and veers around a megarock as it completes a 180 degree turn with a tight radius.

The third major rapid is marked by yet another seemingly impenetrable rock jumble. Run Stairsteps (Class IV) down the river left corridor over successive drops spaced about two boat lengths apart. The total drop in Stairsteps is 10 to 12 feet. As the water accelerates through the drops it gains torque and becomes quite violent. The washout is not clean. Swims here invariably are rough. Trying to roll near the bottom of Stairsteps is an invitation to decapitation.

The next rapid (Unrunnable Jumble) was pretty much a mandatory portage at low-to-moderate water levels until a flood partially opened a right-side chute. Pull out and take a look at it first, however, because the total vertical drop is at least twenty feet through a twisting, careening, makeshift route.

Swirling, twisting, and crashing, Wilson rushes toward its fourth (and biggest) major rapid with wild abandon. From upstream, the big drop at Razorback can be recognized by a sheer vertical cliff on river right and a pronounced tilt of the streambed. The creek seems to flow into a humongous crevice. And does.

The 200 yards above Razorback are as good as technical Class III+ paddling gets. The approach consists of closely spaced drops that continue until the brink of Razor. (The first drop in the approach has an undercut rock on river left.)

Treat yourself to a look/see prior to running the Razor, if you can stop in time. The drop of about 10 or 12 feet is transected by a jagged razorback-like ridge of rock. The right chute tumbles into a pit of rock and hydraulic, reverses, and flows out at an acute angle. Over on the left side, just for variety, is one of the surer pinning opportunities on planet Earth.

With a healthy flow, the steep approach is pushy to the extreme and tends to shove paddlers into the big drop before they realize it. Scout it for sure, and pick the route that looks best. (Which, to many paddlers, is the portage on river left.) Some run it river right, but don't attempt it over there if the water is low. Beware river left, a serious pin is possible. At selected water levels some paddlers run over the middle, veering just to the left of the razor's blade and landing right of the big rock at bottom left. But the consequences of misplaying the middle route are tumbling into either right or left chasms, perhaps upside-down or sideways, or backwards, or all three. Rate the Razor Class IV+ or V.

At the bottom of Razorback, someone in your group's bound to exclaim, "This is the longest two miles I've ever paddled! Where's the takeout?" And yet Razorback is less than a mile and a quarter downstream of the putin!

Below Razorback, there's more to come, including another rapid of Class III+ difficulty (Rock and Roll). When Rock and Roll ends, the creek pitches into successive hydraulics. With higher flows these holes become potentially terminal keepers.

Next comes another ledge that can be run straight over the middle for a sheer five foot drop, or diagonally from right to left to smooth out the descent. More swirling ledges and drops follow, and then CF Junior (Class III) makes its appearance, a rapid with a slide that creates a strong diagonal wave at the bottom.

Finally, Brown Mountain Beach comes into view. (Remember the old song, *Brown Mountain Light?* It was written about a mysterious light on Brown Mountain, a guardian peak of Wilson Creek.)

Brown Mountain Beach is a popular swimming and sunning location for locals. In warm months, don't get too distracted by the hordes downstream and ignore the old diversion dam that snakes across a broad shoals and forms the last rapid of the gorge. Run through the breech on river left. The river right side of this old dam has partially eroded near the base, but the top portion of the structure remains intact, creating a hole that's big enough for a paddler-less kayak to squirt through, but small enough to jamb a boat that has a paddler in it.

On summer weekends Brown Mountain Beach is not unlike a scene from Francis Ford Coppola's movie *Apocalypse Now,* with scads of people cavorting amidst deafening sounds amplified to unintelligible screeching static. As paddlers float by, wondering why in the world these people drive all the way to the edge of the wilderness just to blare their cheap sound systems to the outdoors, the Brown Mountain Beach bunch, in true uncomprehending reciprocal cultural pluralism, are asking one another why anybody in their right mind would be so tastelessly intrusive as to disturb their session of rapt music appreciation by floating tacky-colored plastic boats through their compound.

The clash-of-cultures surrealism of a summer weekend at Brown Mountain Beach is augmented by the sudden transmogrification of river morphology. The gorge abruptly ends here and the creek degrades immediately to a brush-congested, unattractive courseway. Arrange takeout at Brown Mountain Beach if possible. (A token fee may be involved and your tympanic membranes may never stop vibrating, but it's still worth it.) The alternative is to fight the brush half a mile to the first convenient roadside access.

Summary

As intense as a teenage love affair, Wilson Creek Gorge is premier southeastern creek paddling. Although steep, continuous, and unremittingly technical, Wilson is relatively forgiving. It has a small pool after all its bigger rapids except Stonehenge and a parallel road to expedite rescues. Notwithstanding the complexity of its streambed morphology, its TRIP entrapment score (106) is only slightly above average. Wilson's biggest hazard is probably its numerous ledge-formed hydraulics. At high water these holes are tenacious, and can form terminal recirculating hydraulics.

If you're into hardcore technical whitewater, put this one on your "must do" list. If you aren't into paddling hardcore technical rivers but nevertheless would like to see individual rapids that make anything on the Ocoee look anemic, here's your opportunity. Because of the parallel road a grandstand view of most of the big rapids is available with only a short scramble along the cliffs.

Water Levels

Wilson Creek is small, but it drains a part of the Black Mountains that receive a lot of rain. The rainfall is not uniform, however, so the creek pumps up often but unpredictably. Even during summer months, mountaintop cloud bursts occasionally open brief windows of opportunity for paddling this little jewel.

A gauge is affixed to the river left upstream pylon of the Adako Road bridge, near the alternate (downstream from Brown Mountain Beach) takeout. The numbers on this gauge are about six inches high, with six inches between each number and hash marks every three inches. Thus, 0.0 is the middle of the zero that's painted on the bridge. The bottom of the zero is -3 inches and the top of the zero is +3 inches. Three inches below the bottom of zero (-6 inches) is considered paddling zero, a level that may require one or two portages. A low run is the bottom of zero (-3 inches). As the level rises up into the zero the creek provides a livelier trip, and when it reaches the top of zero (+3 inches)

Wilson Creek Gauge Location Adako Road Bridge
Low: Minus 3 inches Medium: Plus 3 inches High: Plus 9 inches

it becomes positively animated. At only three inches above the top of 0 (+6 inches) it's Katie bar the door and avoid the holes below Rock and Roll. At 1.0 foot it becomes an expedition and several holes become potentially terminal, possibly including the one on river left upstream of Bigg Drop. Local paddlers report running parts of the gorge at 3.0 feet, but it's an all-out flush at anything above one foot.

From these comments it should be obvious that small fluctuations in water level on the Wilson Creek bridge gauge produce large changes in conditions upstream in the canyon. This is because the creek at the bridge gauge is about 175 feet wide, which is many times its width through most of the gorge. Some passages in the gorge, such as those following Stonehenge, are only a few feet wide. Hence a change of an inch on the takeout bridge gauge can translate to feet in the narrow passages upstream. When in doubt, scout from the parallel Forest Service road and keep one thought foremost in mind: there's always more water down in that tiny gorge than road scouting suggests. Even when it looks too low, there's usually enough water for technically skilled paddlers to make the descent.

Access

Morganton, which abuts I-40 about sixty miles east of Asheville, is the gateway city. Take the NC Route 18 exit from I-40 and drive two miles into Morganton. Switch to NC 181 in downtown Morgan-

ton and drive north thirteen miles. Turn right at Smyrna Baptist Church onto Route 1337 (Adako Road or Brown Mountain Beach Road) and drive 4.5 miles to Wilson Creek. Turn left and drive up Wilson Creek (on river left) to Brown Mountain Beach, the most convenient takeout.

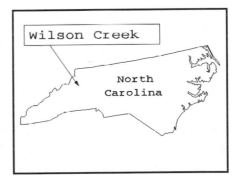

To reach the putin, contin-ue upstream past Brown Mountain Beach where tarmac turns to a dusty Forest Service road that's clogged with vehicles in summer. Wilson Creek is in the micro gorge that's on the left, driving upstream. Most of the gorge rapids can be scouted from this road, with some exertion, by scrambling repeatedly up and down the gorge walls whenever something looks interesting.

Stairsteps, one of the creek's four biggest rapids, is hard to locate from the Forest Service road. But once located, the over-hanging cliff provides a splendid bird's eye perspective.

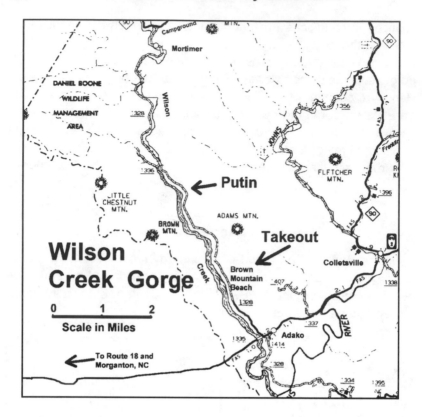

Put in at the top of the gorge, about two road miles above Brown Mountain Beach, at the point where the road first returns to stream level. An alternate putin is available 0.75 miles upstream at a bridge for those desiring to warm up before pitching pell mell into the gorge.

Miles From Wilson Creek Gorge	
Boone, NC 37	Charlotte, NC 88
Asheville, NC 77	Winston-Salem, NC 110

Other Information

Wilson is not well known, except locally. Bob Benner mentions the gorge in *Carolina Whitewater,* but excludes the Bigg Drop section because of its high difficulty and ten foot falls. Nealy's description in *Whitewater Home Companion Volume II* is accurate, entertaining, and informatively illustrated. It's perhaps his best stream description.

Area Attractions

The area around Wilson Creek, especially northward, abounds with scenic attractions. To mention but a few . . .

The Black Mountains are forty miles to the west, capped by Mount Mitchell, highest point east of the Dakota Black Hills. An outstanding trail, one of the most scenic in North Carolina, winds from the summit down the side of the mountain.

Grandfather Mountain, only a few miles north of Wilson Creek, is site of the annual Scottish Highland Games festival. Although now prohibited, hang-gliders once soared from its rugged promontories when wind conditions were favorable. (The mountain is privately owned and operated and there is an admission fee.)

Roan Mountain, which towers over both the Doe and Watauga River gorges, is an hour's drive away. The mountain top is covered with rhododendron gardens. When they bloom in June, the heights are glorious.

Mountains are everywhere. Blue Ridge, Unaka, Iron, Black, Smoky. Call them what you will, they're all part of the southern Appalachians and they're here in profusion. One way to enjoy them is to drive along the . . .

Blue Ridge Parkway. It starts at Smokemont in the Great Smoky Mountains National Park and winds along the mountain heights for hundreds of miles, into Virginia and north, without a single billboard or traffic light.

And there's Linville Gorge, with some of the most rugged terrain in the East. Numerous day hikes are available. Permits are required for overnight backpacking.

Camping

Mortimer, a National Forest campground, is nine miles upstream of the putin. From the putin at the head of the gorge, drive upstream a short distance to a bridge, cross it and bear right alongside Wilson Creek. Continue 8.2 miles to Whaleys Store at the intersection of

Wilson Creek Road and NC 90. Turn left. Mortimer is on the right within 200 yards.

Hiking

The Ladders Trail at Grandfather Mountain is a standout. So are the trails at Linville Gorge.

Suitability for Rafting (On a 1 to 7 Scale): 0

TRIP Profile

Don't be misled by the relatively mild overall TRIP score of 108. This score is depressed by the short length of the trip. Mile-for-mile, Wilson Creek is right up there with the toughest runs described in this volume. It's certainly one of the most continuous (TRIP score for continuous rapids = 135).

Nearby Alternate Trips

The nearest alternate run is the section of Wilson Creek above the gorge, which provides a mild Class II trip. This section runs through private property, however, and access may be a hassle.

When Wilson is runnable, the Doe (Class III-IV) and Watauga (Class IV-V) sometimes are. Both streams are located north of Wilson Creek. The Doe is within an hour's drive and the Watauga is within an hour and a half's drive of Wilson Creek. North Fork of the Catawba (Class II-III), near Marion, is also within an hour's drive. Both the Nolichucky Gorge, Class III(IV), and the French Broad, Class III(IV), are two hours distant.

All these alternate trips are described elsewhere in this volume.

Pahsimeroi Press Order Form

Mail orders to:
Pahsimeroi Press
PO Box 190442
Boise, ID 83709

Ship To: _____

_____

_____

Phone (Optional): _____

Title	Author	Qty	List Price	Total
Southeastern Whitewater	Monte Smith	__	$22.00	$_____
A Paddler's Guide to the Obed/Emory Watershed	Monte Smith	__	$11.95	$_____
Rating Rapids and Rivers	Monte Smith	__	$9.95	$_____
River Stories	Monte Smith	__	$13.95	$_____
Smokescreen (a novel)	Monte Smith	__	$13.95	$_____

Subtotal $_____

Idaho residents add 5% state sales tax $_____

Shipping: Add $3.00 for single book orders...................... $_____
(Orders for two or more books are shipped free)

Total Enclosed $_____

Quantity discounts available. Please inquire.